Product Cost Estimating and Pricing:
A Computerized Approach

Also by the Author

Computerized Accounting Methods and Controls
Computerized Financial Controls
Computerized Financial Forecasting and Performance Reporting
Computerized Financial System Standardization

Product Cost Estimating and Pricing:
A Computerized Approach

Michael R. Tyran

Prentice-Hall, Inc.
Englewood Cliffs, N.J.

Prentice-Hall International, Inc., *London*
Prentice-Hall of Australia, Pty. Ltd., *Sydney*
Prentice-Hall Canada, Inc., *Toronto*
Prentice-Hall of India Private Ltd., *New Delhi*
Prentice-Hall of Japan, Inc., *Tokyo*
Prentice-Hall of Southeast Asia Pte. Ltd., *Singapore*
Whitehall Books, Ltd., Wellington, *New Zealand*

© 1982 by

Prentice-Hall, Inc.

Englewood Cliffs, N.J.

*All rights reserved. No part of this
book may be reproduced in any form
or by any means without permission in
writing from the publisher.*

This publication is designed to provide accurate and authoritative information in regard to the subject matter covered. It is sold with the understanding that the publisher is not engaged in rendering legal, accounting or other professional service. If legal advice or other expert assistance is required, the services of a competent professional person should be sought.

—*From the Declaration of Principles jointly
adopted by a Committee of the American
Bar Association and a Committee of Publishers
and Associations.*

Library of Congress Cataloging in Publication Data
Tyran, Michael R.
  Product cost estimating and pricing.

  Includes index.
  1. Cost accounting—Data processing. 2. Price
policy—Data processing. I. Title.
HF5686.C8T94   658.8'16'02854   82-3753
                                      AACR2

ISBN 0-13-724039-2

Printed in the United States of America

To my family plus new in-laws:
Jamie Benad (Tim's wife) and Scott Dunn (Linda's husband)

Michael R. Tyran, for more than a quarter of a century, has designed, developed, implemented, and supervised a wide variety of computerized financial information systems relative to management accounting and planning.

Now the president of Tyran Associates Limited, the author has held key financial posts with General Dynamics, Pomona Division, as assistant to the controller and chief of Computerized Financial System Planning. His background also includes positions as manager of Computerized Financial Systems and Procedures and manager of Management Budgets and Forecasts at the Lockheed Missile Systems Division. His other credentials include services as corporate director of Management Budgets and Planning at Collins Radio Company and Assistant Budget Director for Ramo-Woolridge (now TRW).

He is the author of four books published by Prentice-Hall: *Computerized Accounting Methods and Controls* (two editions), *Computerized Financial Controls, Computerized Financial System Standardization,* and *Computerized Financial Forecasting and Performance Reporting.* Mr. Tyran is a frequent contributor to national financial journals, for which he has twice been awarded the National Association of Accountants' Lybrand Gold Medal. He is a fellow in the Planning Executive Institute, and his name appears in *Who's Who in America* and *Who's Who in the West.*

What This Book Will Do for You and Your Company

This book is a practical guide on the subject of computerized cost estimating procedures and related material as it applies to product pricing. Various techniques and cost projection approaches are discussed in depth to provide the reader with rewarding ideas for cost savings and innovative methods for enhancing the cost estimating and pricing objectives.

The book will assist you in avoiding costly mistakes in the cost estimating function which can have an unfavorable impact on customer cost proposals, profit goals, and return on invested resources. The techniques and related material discussed are realistic and conducive to mechanization; they will definitely improve your estimating activities in achieving sound product pricing objectives.

Highlights of the contents that are of particular interest and value to anyone responsible for setting realistic and profit oriented pricing are as follows:

- The *principles involved* in sound estimating practices are described and illustrated to provide a fundamental basis for developing and implementing reliable cost estimating techniques.

- *Key statistical tools*, so vital to expeditious and realistic cost estimate development, are presented in "how-to" terms.

- The *methods used* in satisfying the accounting requirements for cost estimate development and their practices are discussed and evaluated for maximum utilization.

- Computerized *time and dollar saving techniques*, discussed throughout the book, should culminate in clerical personnel displacement, accelerated estimate development, and flexibility in incorporating price changes when required.

- *Progress curve applications* are emphasized as well as their "how-to" use in developing manpower requirements, inventory evaluation and cost projections and in achieving sales price goals. Proper utilization of learning curve techniques described will aid an organization in negotiating more profitable contracts by appropriate recognition of the cost influences resulting from the employee learning process.

- *Basic criteria* used in the development of a profitable manufacturing proposal are presented in succinct terms for clarity in understanding.

- *Guidelines to sound product pricing* techniques in marketing a competitive and customer-receptive product are highlighted.

- *Requirements for manpower projections*, scheduling, and pricing, with their impact on the cost estimate, are discussed. The mechanical step-by-step forecasting procedure will save countless hours of effort.

- *Visual displays of estimating procedures* and requirements will provide the reader with a keen insight into the computerization processes which knowledge should preclude the expenditure of thousands of dollars for system design, development, and implementation.

- *Material and other direct costs* are a significant element in the product total costs. The planning procedures most commonly used in projecting these costs are fully defined.

- *Product price competitiveness* is of prime importance in the survival and growth of all progressive organizations; therefore, considerable emphasis has been placed on the development of sound manufacturing overhead estimates. The procedures presented will provide many time-saving ideas on "how-to" project overhead expenses and monitor and control these expenditures in order to preclude profit dilution.

- *Progressive trends* in cost estimating activities are concerned with computerized modules in order to facilitate historical data evaluation, develop mathematical application factors, provide time-saving flexibility in making changes to customer proposals, perform routine and detailed computations, and, most importantly, reduce the clerical work force. A successful mechanical model to achieve these capabilities and implement an "on-going" system with minimal development cost and effort is described in this book.

- After the cost estimate has been developed and customer sales materialized, *a means must exist to monitor and measure* the validity of cost projections in view of their influence on achieving profit objectives. Evaluation of cost performance is discussed in depth in this book because of its importance to successful future estimating endeavors. It further provides management with data necessary to make sound decisions when corrective action is required in cost control.

- There are literally *hundreds of manual effort saving ideas* throughout the book relative to cost estimating and pricing development which will serve the purposes of both the computer and manual oriented organizations.

What This Book Will Do for You 9

This book includes scores of varied flowcharts and illustrations to guide and provide the reader with concrete approaches to realistic cost estimating and pricing. The visual displays include the use of progress curve techniques in cost projections, influence of standards on labor, material and overhead, variance analyses, cost correlation to direct labor, cost estimating overview, accounting procedures relationship to cost estimating, job order versus process cost systems, computerized proposal status data flow system, manpower forecast by project display, manload versus units in process chart, production unit development schedule, mechanical cost data projection systems, cost performance report formats and many, many other pertinent exhibits in the estimating and pricing environment.

The data and ideas presented are practical and readily adaptable for most organizations' immediate use. The techniques described can produce tangible time and dollar savings with minimal time required in developing similar mechanical estimating capabilities. Significant dollar savings will materialize from a dramatic reduction in clerical manpower required to manually develop detailed cost estimates. Computerized modules will be substituted for manual task performance. The advanced techniques will sophisticate the estimating and pricing functions and will prove to be cost-effective and product pricing beneficial toward increased sales and profits.

M. R. Tyran

Contents

What This Book Will Do for You and Your Company   7

1. Critical Considerations in the Estimating Process   17

    Objectives of the Cost Estimate   18
    General Characteristics of the Estimate   19
    Cost Estimating Procedural Checklist   19
    Relevant Factors in Estimate Preparation   21
    Use of Previous Estimates   22
    Historical Cost Records   23
    Establishing Estimating Standards   23
    Relative Scope of Cost Estimate   24
    Cost Determination Considerations   24
    Determinants in Product Evaluation   27
    Computerized Cost Estimate Records   27
    Disposition of Variances   29
    New Product Estimate Development   29
    Role of the Estimating Organization   32
    Centralization Versus Decentralization   32
    Ideal Background of the Planning Estimator   36
    Management Decisions and the Cost Estimate   37
    Estimating Versus Standard Cost Systems   38
    Avoiding Errors in Estimating   39
    Shortcuts in Cost Estimate Development   41
    Advantages of an Estimating Cost System   42
    Disadvantages of an Estimating Cost System   42
    Estimating Pointers   43

2. Tested Statistical Techniques for Mechanical Cost Estimating   45

    Project Evaluation   46
    Cost Behavior   47
    Price Estimating Trends   47
    Cost Estimate Summary   49
    Statistical Formula Estimating   50
    Linear Correlation   55
    Breakeven Point Analysis   58
    Ratios and Proportions in Estimating   59
    Index Numbers for Price Correction   61

Weight Ratio Theorem   62
Developing a Machine Hour Rate   64
Special Tooling and Services   68
Estimating Special Tooling   68
Project Support (Test Equipment)   69
Rate Capability of Special Tooling   71
Effort Expended vs. Program Completion   73
Statistical Estimating Highlights   75

3. Standard Costing for Realistic Cost Performance   77

Standard Cost Definition   78
Types of Standard Costs   78
Current Versus Measurement Standard Costs   79
Misconceptions Relative to Standards   80
Characteristics of Standard Costing   81
Considerations in Setting Standards   82
Responsibility for Setting Standards   87
Comparative Effectiveness in Setting Standards   88
Revision of Standards   89
Use of Standard Costs in Accounting   90
Standard Cost Records   90
Advantages of Utilizing Standard Cost   91
Problems Associated with Actual Cost Systems   92
Estimating Versus Standards   93
Standard Versus Budgeted Costs   93
Aspect of Cost Reduction   93
Adopting Standard Costs for Small Organizations   95
Direct Labor Variance Development   99
Direct Material Variance Development   101
Advanced Concepts on Standards   103
Future Outlook of Standard Costing   104
Computerization and Standard Costing   104
Standard Costing Pointers   105

4. Procedural Cost Accounting: Prime Tool for Assessing the Cost Estimate   107

Cost Estimate System Overview   108
Estimate System Versus Standard Cost   110
Cost Estimate Accounting Process   110
Cost Determination Criteria   110
Procedural Accounting Systems   112
Continuous Process Accounting   112
Job Order Cost Accounting   115
Production Department Accounting   117

Contents

    Job Order Versus Process Cost Systems   117
    Alternate Accounting Method Considerations   120
    Direct Product Costing   121
    Cost Accumulation System   125
    Cost Collection Reporting   129
    Direct Versus Indirect Costs   131
    Master Audit File Process   132
    Cost Control Requirements   133
    Estimating Pointers   136

5. The Marketable Manufacturing Cost Proposal   **137**

    Request for Quotation   138
    Proposal Decision Criteria   138
    Types of RFQs   140
    Manufacturing Proposal Organization   141
    Responsibilities of the Manufacturing Estimating Group   141
    New Proposal Requirements   144
    Bid Proposal Overview   146
    Cost Proposal Development   148
    Computerized Bid Development   153
    Bid Presentation Expense   154
    Basis for Contract Awards   154
    Types of Government Contracts   155
    Work Scheduling   157
    Make-or-Buy Operational Considerations   157
    Make-or-Buy Data Flow   158
    Make-or-Buy (MOB) Plan   158
    Manufacturing MOB Responsibility   160
    MOB as Basis for RFQs   161
    Factors Other Than Costs in MOB Decisions   162
    Product Costing for MOB Decisions   163
    Proposal Status Reporting System   164
    Estimating Pointers   167

6. Computerized Product Pricing Techniques   **169**

    Pricing—Art or Science   170
    Considerations in the Pricing Process   171
    Pricing Economics for Achieving Profitability   173
    Cost Fundamentals as a Pricing Basis   174
    Impact of Costs on Pricing   176
    Direct Costing in Pricing Decisions   177
    Cost Absorprion Approach to Pricing   179
    Cost Aspects in Competitive Pricing   180
    Sales Price Determination Factors   181

Computerized Product Pricing 185
Profit Criteria in the Selling Price 188
Pricing Contract Change Orders 190
Pricing Inter-Divisional Transfers 192
Flexible Pricing for Commercial Products 193
Price Considerations on Defense Contracts 197
Product Pricing Highlights 199

7. Mechanical Manpower and Labor Cost Planning in Product Price Estimating   **201**

An Approach to Manpower Planning 202
A Manpower Planning Procedure 203
Computerized Labor Hour/Manpower Model 206
Direct Labor Dollar Projections 208
Direct Manpower Forecast Based on Hours 208
Indirect Labor Manning 211
Estimating Operating Labor Time 212
Direct Labor Time Standards 212
Labor Quality Standards 214
Labor Rate Standards 214
Labor Cost Estimates 215
Manpower Loading for RFQs 215
Operating Department Manpower Projections 217
Direct Manpower Forecast by Project 219
Special Tooling and Service Manpower 221
Production Planning Process 224
Manpower and Labor Cost Development for Sales Projections 226
Labor Cost Estimate Pointers 227

8. Computerized Planning for Projecting Material and Other Direct Costs   **229**

Direct Material and Other Direct Costs 230
Accounting for Material Costs 231
Methods Used in Pricing Requisitions 232
Analysis of Material Costs 234
Material Usage Variance 235
Material Price Variance 236
Projected Bill of Materials 237
R & D Material Forecast 238
Other Direct Cost Projections 238
Estimating Direct Material Costs 239
Material Price Trends 240
Material Usage Ratio 240
Shrinkage, Scrap, and Waste 241

Contents 15

    Material Price Standards 242
    Make-or-Buy Assessment 244
    Problems Associated with Material Projections 244
    Material Budgets 248
    Estimating Pointers 249

9. Manufacturing Overhead Accumulation, Distribution, and Application in Cost Estimating   **251**

    Manufacturing Expense Accumulation 252
    Expense Characteristics 253
    Transaction Records for Expense Collection 255
    Actual Versus Predetermined Overhead Rates 257
    Overhead Distribution Philosophies 259
    Primary Overhead Distribution 260
    Secondary Expense Distribution 262
    Resolving the Reciprocal Dilemma 265
    Methods for Overhead Application 266
    Disposition of Over- and Under-Absorbed Overhead 268
    Setup and Operating Rates 269
    Factory Overhead Under Government Contracts 269
    Distribution Costs Under Government Contracts 270
    Unallowable Costs Under Government Contracts 271
    Cost Considerations Under Government Contracts 271
    Developing Standard Overhead Estimates 273
    Machine Hour Rate for Overhead 274
    Manufacturing Expense Budgets 275
    Estimating Pointers 278

10. Progress Curve Utilization Techniques in Cost Estimating   **279**

    Cost Estimate Projections 280
    Progress Curve Fundamentals 282
    Logarithm Graph Plotting 285
    Progress Curve Formula 285
    Aspects of the Progress Curve Theory 286
    Progress Curve Time Allowances 288
    Practical Application of the Progress Curve 290
    Curve Use in Manpower Requirements 290
    Curve Use in Inventory Evaluation 293
    Curve Use for Sales Prices and Production Cost Goals 295
    Curve Applications Relative to Costs 298
    Basic Progress Curve 299
    Curve Based on First Unit Estimate 301
    Curve Effect from Effort Deletions 303
    Curve Effect from Added Effort 304

Curve Effect for "New" Added Effort 304
Curve Effect from Changed Effort 306
Curve Application Using Standard Hours 307
Progress Curve Computerization 308
Progress Curve Highlights 308

11. Computerized Cost and Schedule Surveillance for Performance Evaluation and Control 309

Past and Prevailing System Deficiencies 310
System Development Objectives 310
Cost Collection System 311
Work Package System 314
Work Authorization and Budget Control 315
Process Data Overview 316
Computerized Operating System Considerations 318
Cost Tracking and Performamce System 319
Cost/Schedule Reporting Requirements 323
Program Evaluation and Review Technique (PERT) 329
Variance Analysis and Reporting 331
Initiating Internal Cost Controls 332
Incentive Profit 333
Computerized System Capabilities 333
Cost and Schedule Tracking Highlights 334

12. The Computerized Estimating System in Action 335

An Approach to Prevailing Problems 336
System Objectives 336
Price Proposal and Cost Collection Interface 337
Estimating System Interface with Budget Development 339
Cost Estimating Process 342
Computerized Estimating Fundamentals 344
Program Control Requirements 349
Cost Estimate Processing Events 350
Curve Spread Technique 352
Aspects of Direct Labor Estimating 354
Direct Material Costing 356
Miscellaneous Direct Costs 357
Internal Evaluation of Direct Costs 357
Overhead Application 358
Planned Results from Computerization 359
Mechanical Estimating Highlights 360

Index **361**

1

Critical Considerations in the Estimating Process

All profit-oriented organizations, small or large and including the individual entrepreneur, are in the cost estimating business whether they produce a tangible sales product(s) or perform services. The difference in the physical pursuit and degree of this effort is relatively dependent upon the complexity of the product/service, unique customer specifications, repetitive occurrence of new product design/development and change requirements, specific organizational needs, and management established policies and procedures.

There is no escape from the estimating task if an organization is to survive in profitability and achieving continual progress in paralleling and/or surpassing its competitive posture, increasing sales, penetrating new markets and satisfactorily meeting customer demands within an acceptable price range.

Cost estimating must be a continuing process in order that the estimate(s) constantly reflect the changing environment in terms of labor, material, and overhead price trends as well as technological improvements in production equipment and processing methods.

OBJECTIVES OF THE COST ESTIMATE

There are a number of specific and generalized objectives associated with the estimating process which are highlighted as follows.

- Cost estimates should represent a projection of what costs will be rather than what they should be and also should reflect the best intelligence available which is obtained from reference to cost sheets, pricing files, judgmental experience of the marketing organization, and customer input.

- Before cost quotations and negotiations can be conducted with the present or potential customer, the organization must clearly define its product/service proposals, including detailed estimated costs.

- As new product development is undertaken, historical experience *may* be irrelevant to the specific product components, processing requirements, and type of equipment to be employed. In such a case, utmost

Critical Considerations in the Estimating Process

care must be exercised to investigate the specific needs and associated costs to be reflected in the estimate.

- From time to time, technological advances may dictate product changes or processing which must be assessed in detail and costed so that a determination can be made as to the economic feasibility of incorporating the proposed changes.

- Costs must be predetermined in order that an evaluation can be made as to whether product design, development, and manufacture of new products should be pursued in view of the cost aspects, competition problems, and customer market acceptability. A realistic analysis could indicate increased sales and profits or *losses* due to a decision based on an inappropriate or poorly developed cost estimate.

- The cost estimate is often used to resolve the decision to make or buy parts from outside vendors. The assessment could be highly relevant to product pricing on the basis of economic advantages.

GENERAL CHARACTERISTICS OF THE ESTIMATE

Cost estimates as opposed to formal job order and process cost accounting systems do not represent a complete cost system nor is that their objective and utilization. They are predetermined costs that are used to establish a selling price in advance of the actual product production. Cost estimate systems however should complement and correlate with the basic principles of a formal cost accumulation system in order to achieve data compatability for comparisons and evaluation.

Cost estimates are developed for each product by prime cost segregations such as direct labor, raw material, overhead, and other direct costs. The cost estimate elements should be identified to the product, component, operational process, and to the work performing organization.

As actuals become available, they are compared to the cost estimate in summary and detail. Detailed comparisons include cost elements, operational tasks, and pertinent department and/or cost center. The purpose for the data comparisons is to isolate specific variances for correction in the actual environment or reflect the differences, if valid and significant, in future cost estimate revisions or new estimate development.

COST ESTIMATING PROCEDURAL CHECKLIST

Exhibit 1-A provides an overview insight into the prime basics involved in the cost estimating process. A brief description of this overview follows.

20 · *Critical Considerations in the Estimating Process*

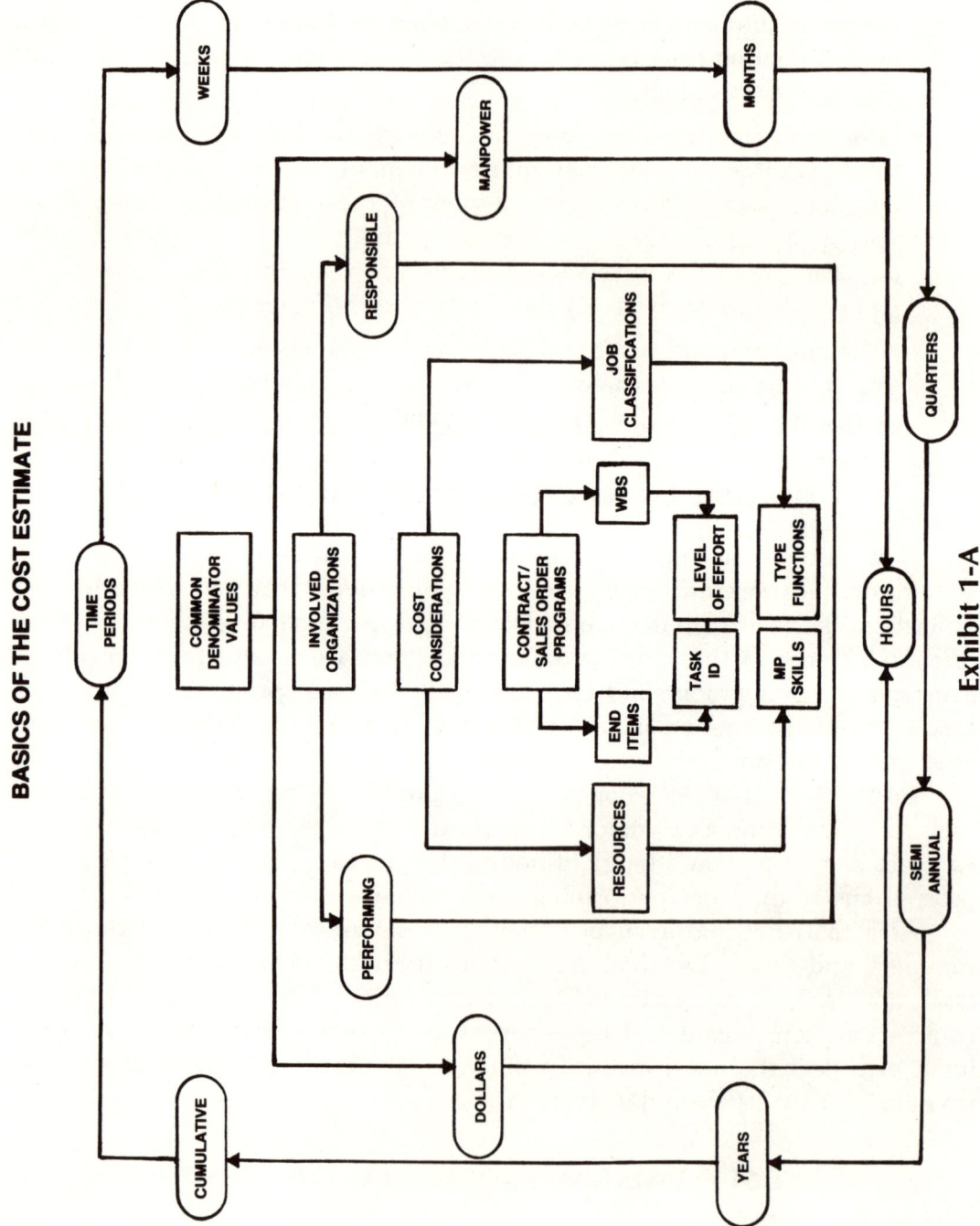

Exhibit 1-A

Critical Considerations in the Estimating Process 21

- The cost estimate is developed by specific time periods based on production processes, and comparable actuals are accumulated.
- The prime common denominator in most cost estimates involves manpower requirements and the translation of the effort into projected hours to be worked and their associated labor costs.
- The organizations participating in the estimating effort are segregated into two classifications: those that physically perform the work and those that have quality and quantity product completion responsibility.
- Cost considerations include the type of job classifications and manpower skills required to accomplish the tasks and their attendant wage rates; the type of functions to be performed in the operating climate; and the cost of resources to be used, such as plant facilities, equipment, and machinery.
- The pertinent contract, sales order, and/or projects must be identified so that the estimated and actual costs can be properly collected and charged. Costs are further identified to the work breakdown structure (WBS), associated level of effort in terms of hours and cost, and completed product items.

The above considerations are all-important in the cost estimating process and data segregations, and summations are readily achievable in the computerized program.

RELEVANT FACTORS IN ESTIMATE PREPARATION

Estimating is to project for each product, in terms of its components, what the actual costs will be based on history, if applicable, and on the most current intelligence relative to the future operations.

Cost estimates involve a number of factors which have a decided impact on the realism and adequacy of the estimating processes and its goals. The more common considerations are discussed below but not necessarily in the order of sequence and relevancy to all organizations. Their individual importance is predicated on the complexity of the organization, the degree of finiteness and detail to be reflected in the estimate, and management directives.

Product/project identification, utilization and capability objectives. This factor could include the type of market to be serviced and potential sales volume.

Pertinent design drawings and detailed specification requirements for new product development or prevailing product proposed changes. Specifications would include components, quantities, and type of raw material and parts. On product changes, detailed modifications must be defined.

Production volume magnitude must be delineated within the time-limitation scheduling. Production volume would be segregated into the initial and subsequent quantities which are associated to time periods of production and delivery to the customer(s).

Adequacy of facility and equipment availability must be assessed to determine if the production volume can be achieved. This evaluation may indicate the need for more space, lighting improvements, a different floor layout, and so on. Relative to equipment, technological advances may have outmoded current equipment capabilities.

Operational processing procedures may have to be revised as a result of new methods or internal recommendations for processing improvements.

New equipment would probably dictate changes in operating methods. Time and motion studies may be required. Learning curve trends may have to be revised. Anticipated increased product output could affect the cost estimate data and production scheduling.

Raw materials and parts must be defined as to type, quantity, and price per unit. Price is predicated on the prevailing market trends and vendor contact. Scheduled date of need and delivery must be negotiated with the vendor.

Availability of sufficient and skilled manpower must be assessed. Projected wage rates by job classification must be determined.

Projected overhead rates by organization must be computed or obtained from the involved financial organizations.

Adequacy of financial resources to accomplish the above objectives must be affirmed by the financial planners. Management must resolve and approve cost estimate and production plans before effort is initiated.

Pertinent historical records must be assessed as a guide to the cost estimate determination. Formal actual cost records must be collected and maintained for cost comparisons and reporting purposes.

USE OF PREVIOUS ESTIMATES

It is a generally accepted principle that no new product estimate is without precedent in some form or another from previous cost estimates. Some of the operational processing steps may be the same, or minor modifications may be required. The latter is a less difficult task than starting with a new specification would be. More or less labor time may be required due to process changes, but the previous estimate will be of considerable assistance in making this adjustment. When raw material type or quantity have to be revised, knowledge of basic requirements, based on previous estimates, can simplify this task significantly.

The planning estimators should analyze the detailed elements of cost ex-

Critical Considerations in the Estimating Process

perienced on products previously manufactured. They can then establish relationships between the old and new estimate proposal in developing new estimates. Relevant standards should be established as a guide to future projections. Previous estimates are also used for comparison to actual cost experience on completed products. Consideration must be given to such factors as change in labor rates, processing time spans, overhead rates and material type and quantity.

HISTORICAL COST RECORDS

Cost records represent the actual costs of products currently or previously manufactured. Frequently, the records reflect unit or component part costs that can be used in the current estimate process.

The planning estimator converts product design drawings and specifications into anticipated expenditures for the elements of cost. The planning data required are actual historical costs plus some adjustments that reflect wage, material price, and overhead rate changes. This approach, if applicable, would simplify the estimate development and assure greater accuracy.

Generally, cost sheets are maintained which delineate costs for specific operations and products. This type of record could serve as the starting point of reference in cost estimate development. Formal accounting records indicating product history costs are also very useful in the estimating environment.

ESTABLISHING ESTIMATING STANDARDS

Standards are established by reviewing each element of accumulated cost experienced on prior products, then developing valid relationships to the products to be estimated. New or changed processing methods or additions/substitutions of components must be separately assessed and judgmental allowances provided in the estimate proposals for the differences.

When valid operational processing relationships are developed, they become representative and characteristic of actual standards set by scientific techniques. Cost element values are influenced by certain product characteristics which are classified as *factor determinants*. Therefore, the cost factor application to the involved operations can result in a high degree of cost estimate competency.

Constant analysis and refinement of these standards can significantly improve accuracy, timeliness of estimate development, and valid utilization of the standards in estimating. In some cases, dependent upon organization complexity, these types of standards could supplant time and motion studies and other standard-setting methods.

Historical cost sheets provide the detail of previous cost estimates and actuals associated with specific jobs or operations, type of product, and process involved. They should be used as the initial reference point in the estimating task. On similar or compatible products, costs can often be readily estimated by only updating changes in time and price for labor and quantity and price for material.

RELATIVE SCOPE OF COST ESTIMATE

Before commencing the cost estimate, determine the purpose for which it is intended and the scope of effort to be involved. This is very important because of estimate output timeliness, relative cost of the task, and resource investment. The evaluation should be made and communicated to the planning estimators before they undertake data analysis and computations.

For example, on large and complicated sales orders that will require considerable organizational commitment in investment resources, the necessary time and effort must be given to the project estimate development. This will give a high degree of accuracy and realism to protect the investment resources and also to establish a profitable return on the product selling price. The estimate must be compiled in depth and supported by sound and logical assumptions and judgment. The content of this type estimate will naturally vary considerably from that of establishing a minimum sales price on unique or special customer orders.

On designated "one-shot" or special orders, estimate costs can be readily calculated by *scaling down or up* previous estimates that are compatible to the task(s) involved. Considerable support detail is generally unnecessary. Resource investment is relatively minor. Time consumption and effort is maintained at minimal levels. Major policy decisions are usually not involved. Estimate approvals are limited and the cost estimate development uncomplicated.

COST DETERMINATION CONSIDERATIONS

The most common methods used in estimating costs involve the continuous interpretation, analysis and use of (1) historical record files which are a part of the formal accounting system in most organizations and (2) previous cost estimate projections which are based on cost projections that are predicated on cost investigation of related products and their processing needs. Estimating costs for services to be rendered follow the same pattern of previous costs for similar services. These costs are anticipated labor rate changes and/or task modifications due to revisions in the magnitude of the work to be performed.

The major difference between certain informal procedures and formal records (cost accounting subsidiary ledgers) which represent repetitive cost collection effort and encompass certain informal procedures (spot checks, operating level cost accumulation) is the expense involved due to the additional clerical effort required. However, the formal record keeping approach undoubtedly yields more reliable data for cost estimate development.

Critical Considerations in the Estimating Process

Cost estimating is not an exact science; certain indeterminables result from the uniqueness of new product development and/or major modifications of a prevailing product. The prime objective of sound estimating is to project a realistic product price based on known historical experience and the judgmental evaluation of future operating costs.

Cost Classifications

There are various costs involved in producing a product or performing a service. The individual costs are defined and identified to specific account numbers as delineated in an organization's chart of accounts. Costs are basically segregated into two major categories—direct and indirect.

Direct costs represent those expenditures which are specifically identifiable to an organization's product, such as direct labor, material, manufacturing expense, computer usage, direct travel, and consultants.

Indirect expenses include support type costs which are not readily identifiable (or practical) to a specific product, such as indirect labor, supplies, business expense, and utilities.

Overhead or indirect expenses are further segregated into fixed, semi-variable, and variable. This subject is discussed in depth in Chapter 9.

Determining Line of Regression

In most organizations, expense segregation projections are achieved through the least squares approach; costs are plotted (scattergraph) against production volume or other determinant base (direct labor hours). A representative statistical line is drawn through the plot points to establish the correlation relationship. The extension of the line to the left vertical axis designates the fixed expense portion of the costs.

A scattergraph is shown in Exhibit 1-B. Supervision costs are plotted against the independent variable—direct labor hours. A simplified version was employed to obtain a total average variable rate of .1338 ($29,300 divided by 219,000 hours) in Exhibit 1-B. The usual statistical least squares approach was not used (based on the equation $Y = a + b$) because it is discussed in later chapters.

To obtain the related point values for drawing the regression line, the rate was applied to two volumes of activity (12,000 and 24,000 hours) and supervision costs resulted in values of $1,606 and $3,211 respectively. The two encircled points were located and the representative line drawn.

In some organizations, depending upon data relationships, the statistical approach (equation solving) is more accurate and provides both the fixed and variable dollar values. The average variable rate method is more expedient but may not truly represent unusual fluctuations between time periods.

26 — Critical Considerations in the Estimating Process

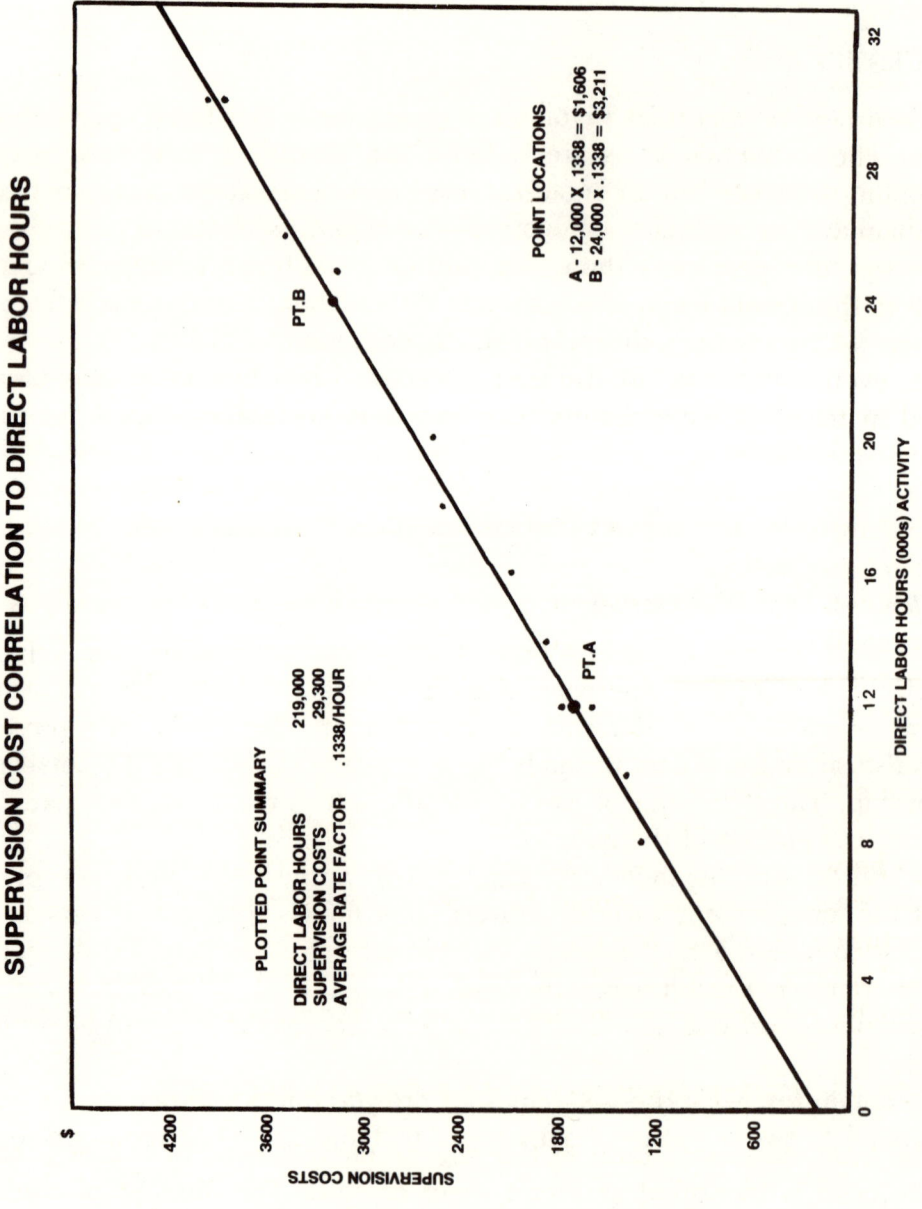

Exhibit 1-B

DETERMINANTS IN PRODUCT EVALUATION

A number of determinants are used in cost evaluation and estimating. Some are more suitable for one type of organization than another. In some instances, all of the determinant considerations may be applicable, required, and used in cost analysis. Costs are evaluated by their component parts, type of processing, elements of cost, and/or other special criteria.

In *component part analysis*, each specific part is identified and costed, and its relationship is established to the total product cost. This finite approach provides significant accuracy in the cost estimate. Further, it reflects a basis for determining whether the part can be more economically produced internally or purchased from outside sources. It may be that the purchased part is better constructed, cheaper, more advanced, and/or it will provide an improved capability to the overall product use.

Type of *processing operations* cost analysis and estimating can be very helpful, even invaluable, in the cost estimate. Each individual operation is assessed in terms of its necessity, function, time performance, and associated cost. This method of cost appraisal is a dependable tool for projecting future costs on similar or slightly modified operational tasks. Operation costing provides greater accuracy in the estimate since it reflects cost at the lowest level of product production.

Elements of cost assessment is a very common method of cost analysis and estimating. When the various operations involved in producing a product are known, it is a fairly simple task to cost the elements used such as direct labor and product material composition. Overhead expense is most generally estimated by applying a rate, based on past history, to direct labor hours or dollars or machine hours based on their applicability.

Other criteria in estimating would include the determination of the relationship between the present and previous product composition and production processes. Similarities would be isolated for appropriate costing. Certain manufacturing processes are quite common among products such as cutting, bending, drilling, moulding, casing and so on. Historical actual data and previous estimates can play an important role in developing realistic cost estimates.

COMPUTERIZED COST ESTIMATE RECORDS

The basic document used in the manual environment to collect product estimate costs is identified as a cost sheet or card. The number of cards or sheets used is generally dependent upon the extent of the operational processes involved. The estimate record would include the following:

- Date of estimate.
- Product and other pertinent identification.

- Work performing organization—department and/or cost center.
- Type of operation by organizational unit.
- Employee classification, time to be used, and wage rate per hour.
- Type of material, quantity, and price per unit.
- Number of hours involved and overhead rate by organization.

If more than one card is necessary to record the operations in completing a product, a summary master card would be required to combine the individual operation and assembly costs to obtain the total estimate.

The above type of record(s) are used in estimating the cost of the task in the production cycle, preparing price lists, and proposing bid prices to customers. As actuals become available, an additional record is required to compare the cost estimate to the actuals for variance determination.

Computerized Environment

The above manual process of record keeping is acceptable in organizations in which the products are few and the processing operations uncomplicated and limited in scope. The manual effort required to prepare and maintain the few records needed is not overly time-consuming nor costly. In larger organizations with multi-product production and advanced processing procedures and technology, the manual effort becomes prohibitive because of human resource utilization, timeliness, and cost.

The logical solution to this dilemma therefore is to use computer power. The process is as follows:

- Input the initial basic estimate data by organization, including organization and task operation identification.
- Enter labor classifications, wage rates, and time involved in each operation.
- Enter type, quantity, and unit cost of material to be used in product processing.
- Input labor effort time and overhead rates per hour by organization.
- The computer performs the calculations by individual record and summarizes the information to the individual product levels.
- Mechanization of the actual cost collection in compatible form to the estimate designations would provide file records which would be merged with the estimate cost files. Variances would be mechanically generated and an output report would be produced for analysis.
- The records could be readily and specifically extracted as required.

The computerized process would provide greater accuracy, flexibility in making additions, deletions or changes to the input data. Formal record keep-

Critical Considerations in the Estimating Process 29

ing would replace a multitude of singular cards and sheets which could be subject to loss or misplacement plus the filing effort. Computing timeliness and reporting would be achieved. Dependent on the relative size of the organization, considerable manpower effort would be avoided and greater effectiveness would be reflected in cost estimate processing and reporting.

Cost Estimate Adjustments

As indicated above, estimates are revised and updated as cost actuals become available. The comparison of estimates versus actuals results in variance computations which are investigated to determine whether the estimate requires adjustment. It is possible that actual costs were distorted and considered unreliable costing guidelines due to unusual operational problems, employee inefficiencies, excessive material usage or spoilage, or change in product components. Under these circumstances, the integrity of the original estimate would be maintained as a guide to future costing.

DISPOSITION OF VARIANCES

Various alternatives can be considered in the disposition of variances; prevailing organizational accounting procedures govern which method should be used. Some of the more common disposal procedures are as follows:

- Transfer over and under differences to a reserve account, and periodically close out the values to cost of sales.
- Reflect the variances over the quantity of products produced during the relevant period. This approach would affect the cost of sales and finished goods account values.
- Allocate the variances to the various products based on their values.

Generally, if variances are minor, the values are written off to cost of sales or directly to the profit and loss account.

Depending upon the degree of variance analysis required, the variance assessment can be by individual elements of cost, product cost, product line summary, and/or by organizational unit.

Computerized variance evaluation can significantly reduce the task effort, provide advanced timeliness in accomplishment, and ensure flexibility for in-depth analyses of the resultant differences between actuals and the cost estimate.

NEW PRODUCT ESTIMATE DEVELOPMENT

An overview of the processes involved in developing a new product cost estimate is displayed in Exhibit 1-C. In some organizations, more or less proce-

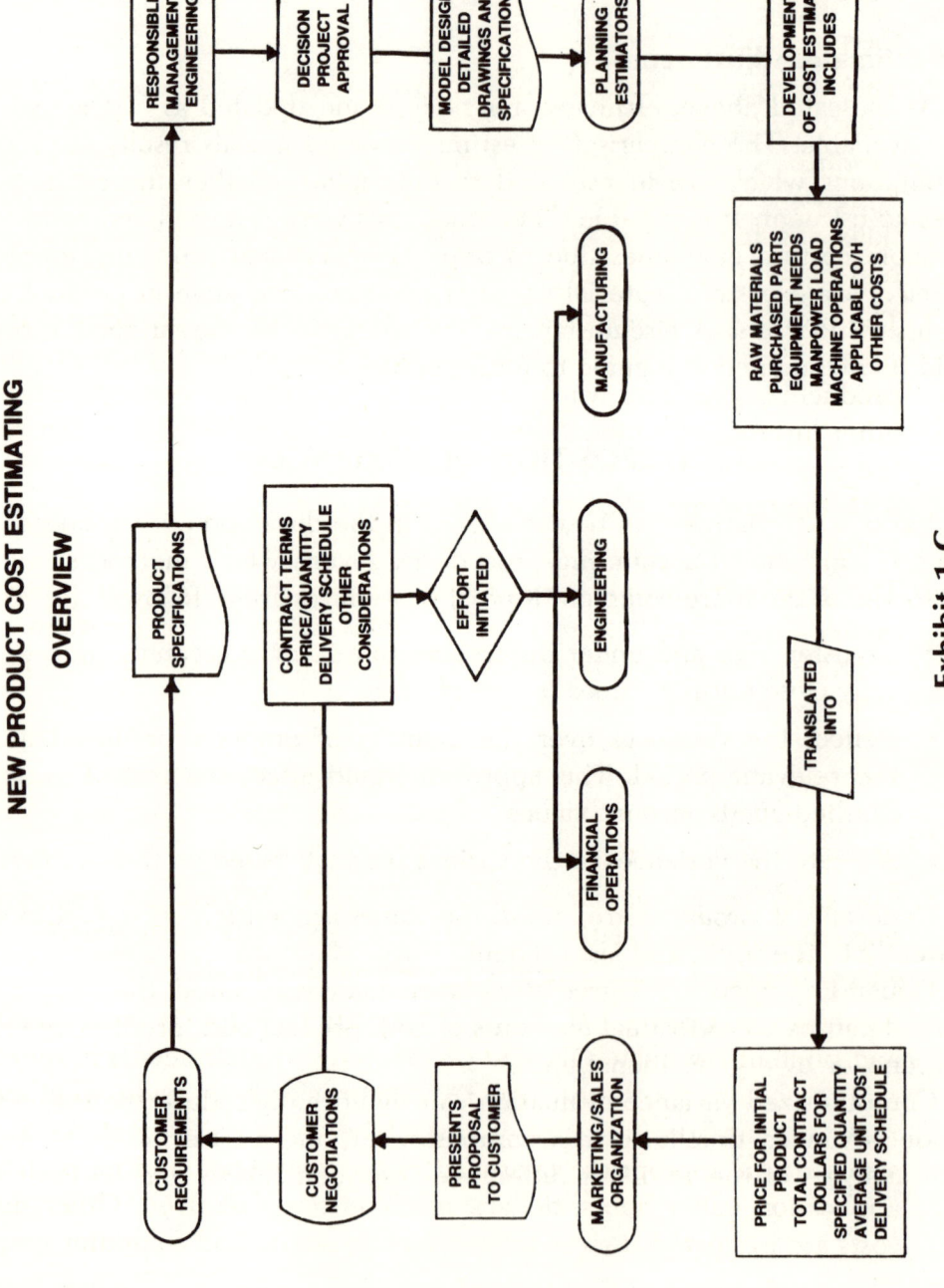

Exhibit 1-C

Critical Considerations in the Estimating Process

dural steps may be required and/or the sequencing of events can vary because of an organization's internal practices. A description of the process follows:

1. On customer new product proposals, *detailed specifications* are submitted indicating what the product is, its components, how it is to be used, and the capability characteristics and performance. The complexity of the product governs the amount of detail to be provided.

2. The responsible management and the engineering task force organizations (including production specialists) *review the proposal* to determine specifically what is required to meet the product's needs. This includes design and development goals; availability and suitability of manpower skills, machinery, tools and facilities; effect on other in-house production capacity; and length of time to the initial production cycle.

3. The *results of the investigative study* reveal whether the project is feasible and economically desirable to undertake in view of the prevailing production schedule, available resources, and project compatibility with other internal activities. A *decision* is made at this point to either reject the proposal or proceed with it. Often, the initial findings are discussed with the customer relative to possible project changes in specifications, components, processing, and/or other special considerations.

4. The *go-ahead decision* activates task initiation in terms of prototype model design and detailed product drawings and specifications that, upon completion, are provided to the planning cost estimators. Specifications include product components, quantities, type of operational processes with associated time spans and equipment utilization, plus other pertinent considerations required to perform the task. The results of this initial effort is communicated to the customer and any changes or conditions are negotiated.

5. The planning estimators *develop a cost estimate* based on past experience and records relative to similarities in product components, size, shape, intended utilization, and processing operations.

6. As shown in Exhibit 1-C, the *cost estimate includes* (1) type, quantity, and price of raw materials, and (2) manpower requirements in number, skills, time involved, and cost. A determination is made whether to *make or buy* specific parts or assemblies. New equipment needs are assessed. An appropriate overhead rate is developed and its particular application (labor hours, dollars, machine time) resolved. Other direct costs are evaluated such as subcontract assistance and computer usage.

7. The *development of the detailed cost data* results in a product cost to which is added G & A expense and profit margin to obtain a product selling price. Total costs for the specified quantity is determined. The proposal estimate includes scheduled delivery dates.

8. The completed proposal is *presented to the marketing/sales organization* and responsible management for review, change and/or approval prior to customer negotiations. The contract terms include quantity and price, delivery schedule, product description, and any other considerations necessary to effect contract understanding and resolution.

On follow-on contracts for similar products, the above procedure is greatly simplified since the product requirements are known and the prior cost estimate is revised only for changes in labor rates, material prices, overhead rates, scheduled dates for product delivery quantities, and possibly profit margin.

ROLE OF THE ESTIMATING ORGANIZATION

Although specific factors may vary among organizations depending on organizational structure, product complexity, and unique requirements, certain general objectives govern most estimating activities which are as follows:

- Responsibility for developing the detailed cost proposal.

- Preparation of estimates to establish realistic performance standards.

- Estimating costs as a basis for determining product price; although other factors become involved in the final price such as economic conditions, competition, sales aspects, and profit margin.

- Projecting costs as a determinant in evaluating and verifying the type of product to be produced from the standpoint of economic feasibility and customer acceptance and demand.

- Providing cost estimates as a control for monitoring cost performance.

- Cost estimates are involved in the evaluation of make or buy proposals, and the findings, along with recommendations, are presented to management for consideration and decision.

- Review and analyze any proposed changes to product's composition and/or improvement in view of basic cost and profit margin revisions, new facility or equipment requirements, and their probable effect on processing operations.

CENTRALIZATION VERSUS DECENTRALIZATION

Depending on the objectives and the type of organization involved, the estimating function can be centralized or decentralized, or a combination of both organizational forms can be used.

Centralized Estimating

Preliminary basic cost estimates are developed in concerned sub-organizational units (engineering, manufacturing, etc.), and the data is forwarded to a central estimating control group for review, coordination, and resolution. This refers to single unit organizations (one company).

In multi-tiered organizations that include more than one division and/or subsidiary, the operating cost estimate is developed in each individual organization and forwarded to the central estimating control group. The proposal estimate is reviewed and additional data is reflected that is not commonly available at sub-organizational levels such as the following:

- Scope of management's operating plan objectives and profit goals.

- Corporate expense allocations, G & A, and selling expense projections.

- Cost effect and associated allocation of corporate-wide research and development programs.

- Manpower and fund expenditure constraints relative to capital asset acquisitions.

- Effect of inter-organization work transfers and costs.

After resolution of the final details, reconciliation of functional organization differences, and appropriate management approvals, the cost proposal is forwarded to the corporate estimating control group.

At this estimating level and in conjunction with the responsible management, the cost proposal is thoroughly evaluated in terms of realistic projections, overall corporate objectives, availability of adequate financial resources, effect on cash flow, profit goals, comparison to other organizations' proposal submissions and priorities, and inter-organization coordination. Additions to and revisions of the proposal are communicated to the estimate-submitting organizations, and any problem areas are negotiated and resolved.

The final approval of the estimate composition is the responsibility of corporate management, particularly, on major proposals. Customer negotiation activities are undertaken by a participating team of corporate and concerned organizational representatives.

Because of the importance and effect of major cost proposals on overall corporate objectives, operating plans, and investment return, the centralized estimating has a number of *advantageous aspects* such as:

- Hierarchy approval of a profitable selling price.

- Inter-organization coordination and resolution of problem areas.

- Assurance of financial resource availability and project support.

- Alternate customer terms and conditions are resolved in pre-negotiation initiation and all concerned participants are knowledgeable of corporate intents and goals.

- Concerned organization assurance that proper responsibility has been specifically delineated for task accomplishment.

- The representative negotiating team would have decision-making prerogatives available to a specified degree in the customer negotiating process.
- After effort has been initiated on the negotiated proposal, progress and performance can be effectively monitored and reported to varying levels of concerned management who have actively participated in the detailed development and negotiation of the cost proposal.

Decentralized Estimating

In the decentralized climate, organizational units, such as department/division, develop and negotiate their own cost proposals. Cost estimate requirements and guidelines are directly initiated by management or a designated representative such as the controller and/or marketing organization. The organization may or not have a centralized estimating group of specialists, depending on organizational practices and needs. Skilled estimating technicians may not be required if the concerned supervision is experienced and familiar with the specific characteristics and costs of the product(s) being produced. Some type of central review and coordination group is desirable or even required, depending upon the scope of operations.

Cost estimates are developed in the functional units. Costs are based on historical experience with allowances provided for known or anticipated changes that will occur in the future. These include wage rate and material price increases, expanded or contracted volume production, and addition of new products.

If there is a central group of estimators, they actively participate in the detailed cost estimate preparation with the functional organizations. Possibly, these estimators would act as consultants and maintain close liaison with the estimate development organizations. The review and coordination of the estimate would be performed by the management-designated responsible organization. The final proposal would be submitted to management for further review and approval. Direct customer negotiations would be performed by the decentralized organization.

This type of cost estimating may be adequate in smaller, uncomplicated organizations with a few standard and repetitive products. However, before decentralized organizations are given the responsibility for their own cost development and negotiation, the upper echelon management should investigate to verify that the decentralized units have the competency to perform this important function. Senior management should place certain constraints on what type and dollar value of the cost proposal would be the responsibility of the decentralized units. Further, responsible management would want to have final approval authority before a proposal is actually presented and negotiated with the customer. These precautions are desirable for internal control and audit purposes.

Critical Considerations in the Estimating Process

The *disadvantages* of decentralized estimating include delays and information distortions that may occur as the data is processed through each department for coordination, concurrence, and resolution. The individual organizations may have their own interpretation of the responsibilities for specific task performance and pricing plus the intended objectives of the overall estimating requirements. Individual organization viewpoints are frequently biased. Estimating expertise may not be available in decentralized units, and it is usually more difficult to measure cost performance and identify the individual(s) responsible for cost deviations. Inadequate cost estimating could affect overall management objectives such as favorable operations, return on investment, cash flow, and profit goals.

Basic Criteria in Type of Estimating Organization

The size, structure, and complexity of an organization's operations plus management's mandate relative to estimating responsibilities govern the type of estimating organization required for maximum effectiveness. In either of the above approaches, a central control group is highly desirable for review, coordination, and resolution of sub-organizational levels of responsibility and contribution to the cost estimate process. A suitable combination of the applicable centralized and decentralized characteristics could be a reasonable, compatible solution in most organizations.

Control of the Estimating Function

Control responsibility of the estimating activity varies among organizations. In some instances, control is delegated to the Controller/VP of Finance, Marketing Executives, Production Executives, or the General Manager.

To be most effective, responsive, and unbiased, estimating should be under the direct surveillance and control of the General Manager or his designated representative to preclude influencing price setting by finance, marketing, or production organizations. This would prevent possible internal friction and misunderstandings. Duplicate effort and overlapping responsibilities would be minimized. Cost development coordination and internal problem resolution would be effected at the highest level of authority.

Since the estimating function is a concerted task involving all organizations to some extent, it should be a constructive and unbiased activity with the responsibility for final decision-making under the direct control of the General Manager.

Computerization Aspects

Mechanization of the estimating process lends itself effectively to processing data for either centralized or decentralized types of operations. Computers can be used for (1) accumulating historical data, (2) developing applicable factor correlations, (3) performing necessary detailed computations, (4) segregating and summarizing the information into selective and interpretive groupings for analytical review and estimate finalization.

Revisions can be readily effected. Management can put prerogatives, judgments and decisions into the computer system for timely report outputs. "What if" gaming to select and test alternate courses of action can produce the most representative and realistic cost proposals and sales prices.

IDEAL BACKGROUND OF THE PLANNING ESTIMATOR

The ideal estimator possesses experience and capabilities that reflect advantageously on the accuracy and realism of the cost estimate development. Some of the significant attributes, knowledge and experience are as follows.

Estimating techniques. The estimator should have appropriate knowledge and expertise in the techniques used in preparing the cost estimate. These include the use of statistical factoring, ratios, index numbers, data correlation assessments, machine hour rate calculations, product weight theorem, establishing standards and trends, plus familiarity with other type methods common in successful cost projections.

General engineering background. This capability is desirable due to the necessity for estimating costs on new product development or significant changes in prevailing products. The task entails understanding design drawings, blueprints, detailed product specifications, and processing.

The estimator may be requested to determine if further engineering will be required before he can complete the cost estimate. Most important, the estimator must be able to communicate effectively with engineering personnel and understand their operations, problems, and objectives.

Production considerations. The estimator should be familiar with the manufacturing: the various operations involved, the types and cost of labor for the individual tasks of product production, materials to be used, and types of machines and other tools required.

The estimator must have knowledge of available tools and equipment in order to preclude the possibility of including new requirements in his estimate if the existing resources are adequate to use. He should be aware of the plant production capacity, so that he can determine whether the time allowed for producing the product is sufficient to meet the scheduled delivery dates.

The estimator must be familiar with the prevailing production schedule to determine if it will accommodate new or additional products, or whether it will be necessary to install new machinery and/or extend work hours.

Close liaison and contact with appropriate production personnel should provide the answers to many of the questions and decisions posed above.

Plant layout. The estimator should know the physical layout of the plant facilities as they apply to the product production. Further, he or she must be cognizant of the sequential events that occur on the production line. This is necessary for relating the cost estimation process to the physical production of the product.

Accounting function exposure. The estimator should be familiar with common accounting principles and practices to readily analyze and interpret cost sheet data relative to their pertinence and use in his estimating activities. He or she should know the source and flow of cost data into accounting records and reports. The cost estimate composition should follow accounting practices and requirements in order to reconcile and measure cost performance results.

Further, the estimator should have first-hand experience with overhead rates: (1) their application to production activities and (2) causes for their fluctuations in changing operation environments. He or she should be able to communicate effectively with accounting personnel.

Economic background. The successful estimator will have an understanding of the effects resulting from changing economic conditions, which will aid him in projecting increases or decreases in labor costs and commodity prices as they apply to his estimates. He will be cognizant of supply and demand and their effect on future trends that would be reflected in the cost estimate.

Practical Pointers. Effective cost estimating is contingent on the capabilities discussed above. Usually, no one individual possesses all of the identified desirable attributes. However, in an organization that is staffed with a number of personnel, certain individuals would be specialists in the various qualifications required; their pooled knowledge would be reflected in cost estimating.

In smaller estimating groups where specialists are lacking, there must be communication with and dependence on personnel and task specialists outside of the estimating function for assistance in fulfilling cost development background requirements. Under these circumstances, the estimator must be an intelligent and effective communicator to gain the information required.

MANAGEMENT DECISIONS AND THE COST ESTIMATE

A realistic cost estimate provides the basis for a number of managerial decisions relative to organizational policies, practices, and conduct of its operational activities. It represents one approach to the collection of cost data and provides reasonable guidelines to cost surveillance and control. Examples of policy decisions that are often made possible through effective cost estimating practices include the following, although not necessarily restricted thereto.

- Is it economically feasible to produce and market a given product based on cost competitiveness, resource availability, additional investment requirements, profitability, and prospective customer acceptance?

- Should component parts be manufactured internally or purchased at a cost saving from outside vendors?
- Would an additional product mix be complementary or a dilution to profit objectives?
- Should alternative design and specifications be considered to reduce costs that at the same time preclude the possibility of reduced or loss of sales volume?
- Can material substitutes be used with no impairment on a quality product production?
- Will new processing methods and machinery improve the return on investment?
- Can the cost estimate serve as a reliable basis for measuring cost performance?
- Is it possible to establish a reliable and equitable product selling price based on the cost estimate?

Reference to historical experience on cost estimates will generally provide the answers as to whether developed cost estimates can be used for the pertinent managerial decisions to the specific points outlined above.

ESTIMATING VERSUS STANDARD COST SYSTEMS

An estimating cost system is recognized as a short-cut procedure of product costing that does not utilize formal detailed record keeping which are more costly to maintain. The prime differences between the estimating and standard cost systems are as follows:

- Standards are based on the use of more advanced or sophisticated techniques and engineering studies such as time and motion, standardized processing methods, and statistical models relative to material usage.
- Standard cost variances are reviewed and evaluated to ascertain the specific causes of the deviations; whereas cost estimating variances are generally used to adjust current and future cost estimate data.
- Standard costs are more comprehensive in scope and purpose and reflect the total gamut of operations; whereas estimated cost objectives are generally dedicated to a specific product(s) and/or product line.

The similarities between the two systems are (1) both have as their objective the projection of product/service costs and (2) pertinent records are maintained to measure cost performance results and provide a basis for cost control surveillance.

Critical Considerations in the Estimating Process

The objective of estimated costs is to provide cost data for each product process. This predetermination is accomplished in advance of product production. Further, the estimator's prime concern is not past history per se, although that is one criterion, but rather the estimating of costs for projected future periods. The more relevant philosophy is to project the true environment of what the costs should be based on past performance and anticipated changing conditions in terms of cost behavior.

A sophisticated approach to estimating involves a thorough review and understanding of the probable operating future climate in terms of production, processing improvements, learning curves, and cost trends. Formal budgeting can materially assist in the estimating process because it is a detailed, systematic approach in projecting future conditions, based on the latest economic and market intelligence. Management and operating executives judgmental premises and reasoning plus their experience have been incorporated in the budget plan. The developed information is provided in-depth and reflects the combined thinking of all concerned. Therefore, it is concluded that a well-defined and planned budget can be an effective reference point and tool to a successful cost estimating system.

AVOIDING ERRORS IN ESTIMATING

Major contributors to errors in the cost estimate are attributable to the personnel involved in the task. Problems can arise from (1) an error in judgment, (2) insufficient familiarity with the components/product and detailed operational processes involved, (3) inadequate advanced information on new product requirements, (4) unreliable historical records as a foundation for making the estimate, (5) inadequate dedication of time and effort to the project, and (6) poor or inexperienced analysis of the task to be accomplished.

Effective estimating is significantly based on the estimator's experience. He or she must be intensely oriented to the product requirements in terms of product components and labor functions to be performed. The estimator must possess mature judgment and be competent to interpret cost data systematically as it applies specifically to the product cost that is being estimated.

Uncontrollable Errors

Certain uncontrollable sources of errors are beyond the control of the estimator. Some of the more common problems are (1) changes in equipment or operational processes, (2) decline in efficiency, (3) greater than anticipated improvement in the learning curve which leads to accelerated production at lower cost, (4) unexpected occurrences such as storms which interfere with the use of facilities or needed utilities, (5) union-called strikes, (6) fire damage, (7) machine failures, or (8) material unavailability or rapid deterioration thereof. Any of the above situations could lead to an inaccurate estimate that cannot be attributed to an estimator's competency.

Controllable Errors

Other errors that can be minimized or avoided by the estimator include the following:

1. Using adequate time to analyze and develop a comprehensive estimate that is based on the most reliable facts and sound historical data references.
2. Using sufficient contact time and discussion with engineering and production specialists when in doubt about product components or specific operational processes that are involved.
3. Maintaining proper coordination with procurement personnel relative to future material price trends.

The estimator must thoroughly review his cost estimate for any omission or duplication. This task can best be performed by another individual (estimator) who is not as close to that particular estimate and therefore can more readily isolate and discover errors.

Employing too much data averaging tends to distort the data being developed. Sometimes it is difficult to preclude the use of averaging as it simplifies application factor development. This can lead to task oversimplification by assuming similarities and relationships that, in reality, may not exist.

Inadequate estimating knowledge or experience could result in errors. They can be avoided by sound personnel training and careful selection of qualified personnel who have compatible educational background and proven estimating qualifications.

Percentage of Error Calculations

When cost element variances are completed, they are divided by the combined total of the estimated completed production cost and the work in process ending inventory. An example of the process is illustrated below.

Cost Element	Variance	Work in Process Ending Inventory	Completed Production Cost
Labor	$200	$180	$18,000
Material	100	120	12,000
Overhead	300	90	9,000

VARIANCE CALCULATION

Labor	Material	Overhead
200 ÷ (180 + 18,000)	100 ÷ (120 + 12,000)	300 ÷ (90 + 9,000)
200 ÷ 18,180	100 ÷ 12,120	300 ÷ 9,090
1.1%	.825%	3.3%

The cost element process accounts in finished goods and cost of sales values are next adjusted by the variance percents to determine the amount of the adjustment to be made to the original balances and possibly to subsequent estimates.

SHORTCUTS IN COST ESTIMATE DEVELOPMENT

Various techniques can be employed to accelerate the development of cost estimates. The approach is contingent on the complexity of the estimate, the amount of detail and data verification required, management edict, and organization policy. If the magnitude of resource commitment and investment are large and critical to an organization's survival, do not use shortcut methods; also if an unreasonable or invalid estimate negotiated may result in dire consequences on the accomplishment of prevailing in-house projects.

Having determined through appropriate evaluation that the shortcut approach is feasible and acceptable, consider the following methods:

- Use of *mathematical statistical models* that have been developed based on historical data relationships which will permit factor applications for computing the estimate requirements. This would include the association of various processing operations to their compatible cost elements. Product component parts would be similar and the material type, content, and costs related directly.

- *Previous estimates* could be readily *modified* to reflect (1) increased or decreased work effort, (2) lower wage rates, and (3) changes in material quantity, price, operating functions, and time. Price adjustment factors would be applied to previous estimates to develop the new estimate data.

- *Segregation of the effort and material* required into major and minor segments of cost with the estimating concentration being directed to achieving a realistic estimate of the major costs. The minor costs would result from the application of established factor relationship to major costs.

- Cost estimate could be based on *previous product weight* and cost per unit, *relative size and shape* of product dimensions and/or *rate per direct labor hour* of production.
- The most versatile technique would be the *use of computer power* wherein a flexible designed system would be fed predetermined inputs and the processing steps would be accomplished mechanically to provide the output. The computerized system however would have to incorporate various processing modules which were adapted to varying data manipulations for achieving specific results.

Shortcut estimates can often lead to inaccuracies; the keys to their successful use are careful investigative effort and thorough testing before they are employed to develop realistic cost projections.

ADVANTAGES OF AN ESTIMATING COST SYSTEM

An estimating cost system is an abbreviated accounting system wherein formal records are kept to a minimum; therefore, this type of system is inexpensive to operate. When the estimating system is used, it can be assumed that the products are repetitively standard and involve relatively uncomplicated operations. Generally, the system satisfactorily provides the information required for developing quotes to the customer of price lists and policies and serves as a guide to production and manpower requirements. In many instances, the cost estimating system represents a preliminary approach to the development and implementation of formal procedures to the accounting control aspects of estimating.

DISADVANTAGES OF AN ESTIMATING COST SYSTEM

It is often difficult to estimate product costs to an extreme degree of accuracy, particularly if products are varied and operations are complex. This is true in those industries producing highly sophisticated equipment and parts such as aircraft, missiles, submarines, and space vehicles. The estimating cost system is not satisfactorily geared to these types of operations.

Cost estimates are periodically updated to reflect actual costs, but in the interim the sales price may have been established too low (resulting in the loss of operating revenue) or too high (which precludes its competitiveness in the market).

The operation of an estimating cost system may not adequately reveal soon enough some basic operating deficiencies such as poor labor performance, inefficient utilization of material, and excessive overhead expenditures. Cost variances may be inappropriately allocated. Each organization using a cost estimating system must carefully evaluate the pros and cons of its usage before total commitment is made to this type of costing and pricing.

ESTIMATING POINTERS

The critical considerations relative to a successful estimating system are reviewed in terms of objectives, problems, characteristics, tasks, and the development process. This information is vital in determining whether an organization should implement a full-scale estimating system. The aspects of computerization are described along with the benefits to be achieved in enhancing the accuracy, timeliness, and development of realistic projections with reduced effort and costs. Budgeting and standard costs are assessed in terms of their contribution to the estimating activity. Controllable and uncontrollable error sources are highlighted to alert estimators of potential problems.

The pros and cons of adopting an estimating function and to what degree to do so are discussed to provide an organization the facts and realities for making a judgment on the scope of its estimating endeavors.

2

Tested Statistical Techniques for Mechanical Cost Estimating

In most manufacturing activities, there exist a number of technical relationships between cost and other factors which are useful in developing cost estimate patterns. The relationship patterns can be scientifically computed in symbolic terms of specific formulas or reduced to a graph or table for use by the planning estimator. Estimating tables can be developed by analyzing the costs experienced on similar products previously manufactured to ascertain the cost influences of the various characteristics of the product. By comparing and plotting cost values against varying physical characteristics such as size and width, the correlation between these factors and their cost values can often be determined within practical limits. The common statistical techniques most often used in estimating are the subject matter of this chapter.

PROJECT EVALUATION

Costs may be estimated by analyzing the project relative to the separation by cost elements, operational tasks, component part segregations, or by various other special methods.

If the operations required to manufacture a certain item can be clearly identified, then generally there is little problem in determining the *direct labor and material* for each task and project. *Overhead* would be applied as a percent of direct labor dollars or a rate per direct labor hour based on historical experience. This method then reflects the *cost element segregation*.

When the *operational tasks* are known and defined, this approach can often be utilized as a basis for estimating time and material for a project or product. This method is used in conjunction with component part segregations discussed below. Involved in productional tasks are such operations as drilling, milling, grinding, cutting, polishing and so on.

Estimating production costs is made easier and more precise by evaluating the product in terms of its *component parts* before the estimating units are selected. By considering each part or combined selections separately, a comparison can be made to similar parts previously produced or differences noted. This permits a comprehensive, realistic estimate to be developed based on past experience records.

Special methods for estimating costs include the determination of unit costs based on the aggregate type of costs involved. For example, costs may be established by relating the proposed product or procedural task to a similar type of product produced in the past. Based on this approach, a rate per pound or unit can be readily ascertained and adjusted for anticipated future cost eventualities.

COST BEHAVIOR

Different costs react variably to changes in production volume. The planning estimator must be cognizant of the varying behavior of the element comprising the cost of the product to be estimated. There are very few expenses, for example, that can be truly classified as 100% variable or fixed.

Variable costs generally fluctuate in relatively the same proportion as production volume, whereas *fixed costs* may increase in incremental steps with increased volume, but they do not decrease as fast or significantly with decreased volume. *Semi-fixed* costs are characterized by a curve or simple linear patterns on a graph chart. They may remain fixed over narrow ranges of activity but can rise or fall rather rapidly to successively new levels over wider ranges of volume activity.

Seasonal costs are certain operating expenses that exhibit patterns in amounts because of differences in temperature, humidity, length of daylight available and so on over the year's cycle. For example, heating costs are heavy in the winter months as versus negligible in the summer. The same is relevant to other utilities such as building and ground maintenance.

These types of costs cannot always be anticipated with the appropriate charge to product costs. Some costs may be extremely variable and occur in infrequent time intervals. Examples of these types of costs can be caused by extraordinary machine breakdown and repairs, building and premise damage from fire or floods, unusual use of water due to heat or drouth. To anticipate these costs, some organizations set up a contingency reserve account based on past experience. An estimated monthly value is written off against the income statement with a credit to the reserve as is often the case with accounts receivable.

Knowing the various facets of cost behavior will lead to an increased effectiveness in cost analysis of historical experience and provide a sound basis for estimating reliable future costs.

PRICE ESTIMATING TRENDS

The planning estimator should maintain constant liaison with the sales, finance, and production organizations to be aware of current conditions and occurrences in those functional areas that may affect his estimating activities. This is very important, especially when the prospective sales business is to be of significant magnitude.

Cost estimating should provide prices for catalog sheets and quotations on special work which would be used by the sales organization in their customer contacts. The estimators should further peruse trade journals and pertinent periodicals for information that may have any influence on the product being produced or on market prices.

In turn, the sales organization should keep the estimator advised of any changes in sales policies and market conditions, as well as intelligence obtained relative to competitors' products and prices.

After product quantities have been determined, the next step is to apply the current price(s) or cost rates. Appropriate consideration should be given to reflecting *anticipated future costs* for labor, material, and overhead in order that realistic estimates are compiled. This is of prime importance during inflationary periods, when the labor markets are subject to unusual fluctuations and material prices are experiencing frequent changes. The overhead factor is subject to many adjustments due to changes in organizational structure, use of expense materials, and revised utilization of machinery and equipment.

Material Price Trends

Anticipated future prices or material cost trends are generally available to the estimator from the procurement organization, trade journals, other pertinent periodicals, and vendor intelligence. Prices should be based on the current prices for normal quantities rather than small or odd lots and should be specific relative to grades, quality, and brands.

In situations where cost data are based on predetermined estimating standards, it is necessary to estimate costs on a replacement cost basis. This is done by converting the standards to *anticipated* future prices for materials and wage levels. The standard price list should also reflect the anticipated prices, to preclude constant price list reissues and also to provide an on-going capability to readjust estimating cost standards to any desired market base.

Estimating Overhead

The procedure used in assigning overhead is often dependent on the degree of exactness required in the final cost figure. A given operation can be performed in more than one way by using alternative methods or equipment. For example, if other work is scheduled to encompass the entire available time of certain items of equipment, the costs must be reflected in terms of alternative processing methods or available equipment.

Predetermined Overhead Rates

Overhead rates used in estimating may be subject to future changes if the product to be estimated is projected to be produced in large quantities and in separate or isolated sections of the plant. Under these circumstances, this work displacement may require *more or less* lighting, heating, power expense, indirect labor, and machinery as compared to small lot production or if the work is performed in locations where other products are being produced. Generally, the same procedure of overhead application should be used in the cost estimate that prevails in the organization's cost system. Following this procedure provides the cost estimator and cost department with compatible estimates to compare with actual costs, and thereby relative standard costs can be established.

Most part standard overhead rates used to distribute overhead to the cost of a product include design, tools, and part drawing expense. In calculating the cost of special items, it is desirable to reduce the standard overhead rate by the cost which is represented by its total contribution to the expenses discussed above.

Setup and operating rates. If a high degree of accuracy is required in the cost estimate, it is common practice to establish separate setup and operating burden rates for overhead costs in a given production center. In addition to this segregation, it is sometimes advisable to break down the operating rate for machine overhead into two parts in recognition that some overhead items will not change much, if at all, as the rate of output or activity fluctuates. For example, segregation of fixed and variable costs may require the use of two rates or calculations for overhead costs. A *standing machine rate* is computed from the relationship of fixed overhead to nominally available operating time; a *running rate* is calculated from the relationship of the variable overhead to the machine time operation at normal speed.

In developing cost estimates as an aid in price or output decisions, it is important that some segregation of these dissimilar types of cost be made. The establishment of both standing and running machine rates provides the capability for more precise estimating in situations where differential rather than normal costs are required.

COST ESTIMATE SUMMARY

Specific calculations and extensions refer to only parts of the estimate and must be presented in summary form. In instances where the number of detailed estimating sheets are large, it is common to find a summary sheet in the estimate file. *Under the computerized process*, as the detailed estimate is being compiled, the data is inputted into the computer and summaries by estimate and part numbers are derived in the format displayed in Exhibit 2-A. Required calculations are accomplished mechanically. If it is necessary to calculate the estimated cost of several parts making up a complete unit or assembly, the detailed labor cost and material by specific part number within the assembly number are selected from the file and summarized into an Exhibit 2-A format.

The summarized total costs include quantities, the number of pieces estimated, cost of setup and operating labor (per piece or thousand pieces), material cost (each unit or thousand), and total material and labor costs as shown under the column captioned as "prime cost." Overhead cost is segregated to differentiate between setup and operation. The total of the above cost items then represents the estimated cost of the product.

Provision is also made on the summary sheet to include the estimated *tool cost*. These costs are shown separately in the summary, as it may be advantageous to set a price based not only on the cost of tools for the immediate requirements but also for estimated future needs as well.

STATISTICAL FORMULA ESTIMATING

Using a statistical approach to cost estimate development is not new to many organizations, but utilizing computer technology is yet to be totally explored. Many alternative approaches can be employed in providing the bases for determining the most appropriate direction to pursue in cost estimating.

As in most business information systems, the basics involve collecting pertinent and selective data, defining the processing steps to meet predetermined objectives, outlining the report requirements, testing the results to assure processing reliability, and continually upgrading the processing procedures to meet new requirements.

Defining Formula Estimating

Formula cost estimating is accomplished through the use of pertinent mathematical formulas which represent cause and effect relationships between cost and the specifications that define the function of the product being developed. Cost variations are excluded which are not pertinent to product specifications. Variations can be attributed to time and production quantity. The objective is to base the estimate on specific quantity and rate of production at a point in time. Time cost indices, cost analyses, and learning curve studies provide the basis for scheduling nonpertinent cost effects.

Formula Development

This task entails the following considerations in selecting the most appropriate cost estimating formula based on historical experience.

COST ESTIMATE SUMMARY

PART NO.	ESTIMATE NO.	DESCRIPTION	NO. OF PARTS	LABOR SETUP	LABOR OPERATION	MATERIAL	PRIME COST	OVERHEAD SETUP	OVERHEAD OPERATION	TOTAL COSTS

CUSTOMER _____ ASSEMBLY DRAWING NUMBER _____ DATE _____
ESTIMATE NO. _____ PART NO. _____ DESCRIPTION _____
COST PER _____ PARTS — ON BASIS OF _____ PARTS

COST OF PARTS
ASSEMBLY LABOR
TOOL COSTS
TOTAL COSTS

ESTIMATED BY _____

Exhibit 2-A

- Carefully analyze reliable historical data to determine what correlations, if any, exist among prevailing data elements.

- Select pertinent data for further investigation through the use of visual displays of relating costs to product/components, processing operations, weight, or other variables.

- Use the least squares approach and other statistical methods to derive the most compatible mathematical relationship and formula in the development of the cost estimate.

- Testing the selected formula method using historical data to determine results for comparison to actual past experience. More than one formula may be needed to meet varying needs.

To accomplish the above, it may be necessary to utilize the combined services of knowledgeable, experienced estimators, statisticians, and computer specialists if the processes are to be mechanized.

Computer Input

On new estimate development, the input consists of price factors that reflect a dependent variable and independent variables which are represented by product specifications, unit weights, operational requirements and so on. Any number of selected independent variables can be entered into the system.

System Overview

Exhibit 2-B displays the processing steps in developing a mathematical cost estimating formula. A brief description follows:

- The left side of the exhibit typifies the manual approach and the dash lines indicate its conversion to the mechanical process. The processing steps are the same except for human versus mechanical data processing.

- Historical experience is the source of the data relative to costs, product specifications, and the operations involved in developing and manufacturing the product.

- The input is provided or extracted by the estimator from the records for analysis and by establishing pertinent and valid relationships. Estimators' experience and judgment play a vital role in developing sound correlations.

- Using various statistical techniques, estimate formulas are constructed which reflect the relationship between independent/dependent variables. Pertinent raw data is inputted into the computer, the program is manipulated and converted into mathematical relationships.

Statistical Techniques for Mechanical Cost Estimating 53

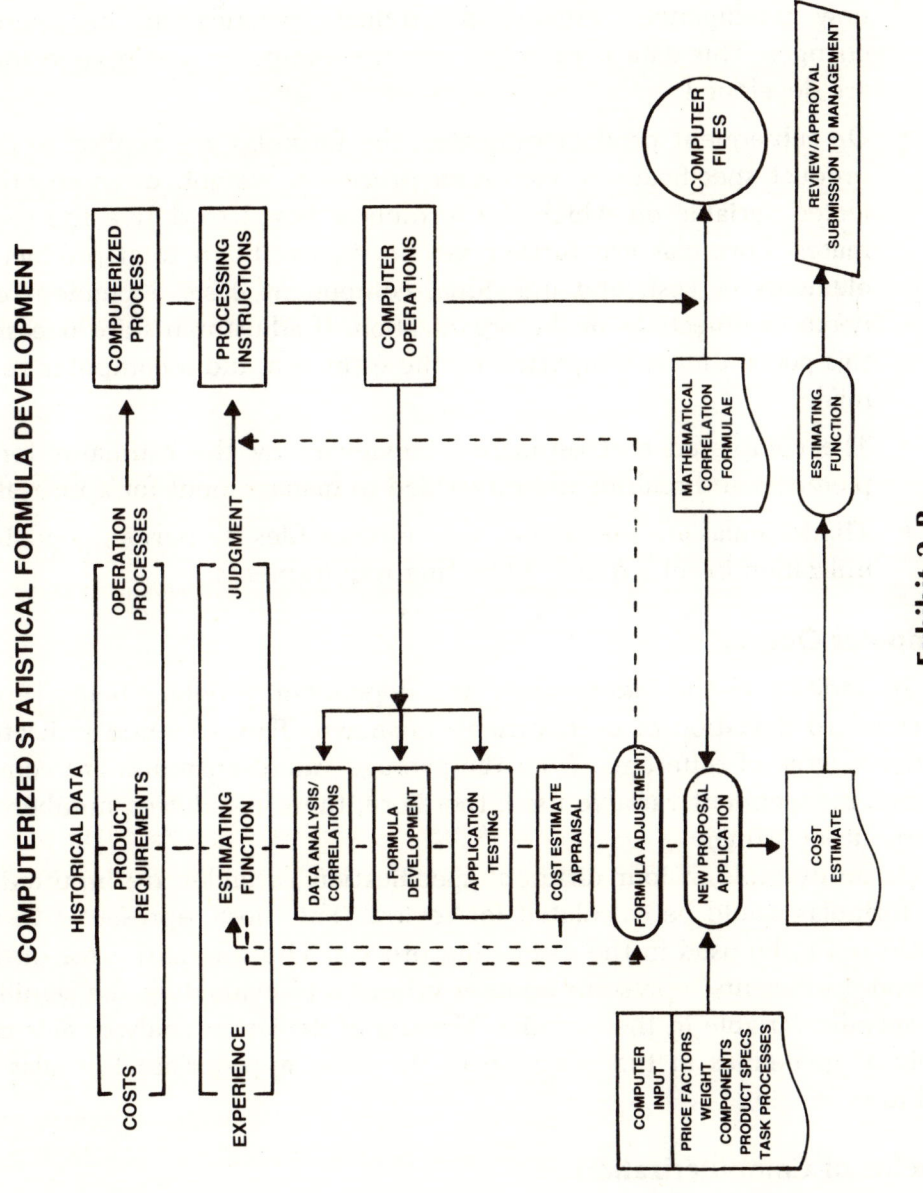

Exhibit 2-B

COMPUTERIZED STATISTICAL FORMULA DEVELOPMENT

- As a test to the validity of the selected formulas, they are applied to historical independent variables to re-affirm that the resultant dependent variables are comparably compatible with past actuals.

- The results from the above processing are carefully evaluated by the estimators; adjustments are made to the proposed formulas based on new intelligence, anticipated product specification, or operational changes. This data is then fed into the computer and revised formulas are developed.

- On subsequent product estimates, the formulas are applied to defined product specifications, operation processes, weight, or some other selected variable on which the formula is based to derive the cost estimates. Formulas are further developed to obtain total product costs, elements of cost, and individual component costs dependent on the needs or objectives of the organization. If adjustments are necessary at this point, they are inputted by the estimator and a computer re-run is made.

- The completed cost estimate is reviewed by the estimator for completeness and realism and forwarded to management for approval.

- The formulas are maintained in computer files for periodic updates and utilization in subsequent estimating requirements.

Computer Output

In addition to the independent and dependent variables being reported, the standard deviation of each variable is shown. The deviation indicates the relative degree of difference from the average value. Formulas are computed for each independent variable used; therefore, there could be a number of different output listings.

As an example, if four different specification variables are inputted, then four formulas would be calculated for review. The most representative would be selected to be used in the estimating process. The standard error of the regression coefficients represents another criterion of evaluating the significance of a specific variable in the formula. The use of deviation analyses aids considerably as guidelines in the selection of the most appropriate formulas to be used in estimating.

Benefits of Computerization

In the development of mathematical formulas for cost estimation, the computer system has proven to be an invaluable tool for the following reasons:

- Facilitates cost collection and organizes masses of data into logical, compatible patterns for effective storage, retrieval, and reporting.

- Develops relationships between two sets of data as a criterion for establishing cost estimate formulas and checks results with deviation analyses as a means to appropriate formula selection.

- Stores, segregates, and integrates pertinent product specifications, operational processes, and their associated costs.

- Performs a multitude of alternative mathematical computations based on program instructions, and outputs the data for review. Manual effort in terms of time and cost would make it prohibitive to achieve the ultimate desirable results.

- Calculates multiple regression and variable formulas, that would require considerable manual effort, and provides a basis for validating results through computing the degree of standard deviation and error of regression coefficients.

- Readily incorporates formula adjustments into the computer program.

- Applies factor tables and correlation formulas, so that new cost estimates become readily available for product costing and review.

- Incorporates cost analyses and indices as well as learning curve factors in cost estimate formula development.

LINEAR CORRELATION

In planning and estimating, it is often necessary to ascertain and measure the relationship between two or more statistical data series. This can often lead to a conclusion that, as one data series increases, another follows suit, but it may be not in the same proportion. For example, as direct labor hours increases, the variable overhead may follow the same trend line, whereas fixed expense will generally remain fairly static. As sales climb, costs generally also increase. Sales influence receivable balances, and payables follow costs. Increased productivity results in more labor hours and costs; also some of the effect could be reflected in greater expenditures for material and increased inventory balances. Another common correlation is the indirect to direct personnel ratio—as direct labor headcount increases, the indirect labor force becomes greater but not in the same relative proportion.

Scattergraph Concept

If two related data series were to be platted with an independent variable (direct labor hours for example) placed on the X axis and a dependent variable (pertinent overhead expenses) on the Y axis, the result in terms of point location plots reflect the scattergraph concept. If there is a definite relationship from plotting the related variables, the points will follow a definite trend line of movement.

If the relationship were perfect, then for every given value on the *X* axis, there would always be indicated a certain relative value on the *Y* axis. In this situation, all of the plotted points would coincide with the line instead of the points being scattered above and below the trend line.

When the data series are incorrectly associated, a definite value of *Y* will result when a given value of *X* is selected. With the more or less imperfect relationship, the variation will cause the points to depart from the indicated line or curve and create a scatter. If there is a high degree of association, the scatter will be confined to a narrow "path." An example of this association is shown in Exhibit 2-C which highlights the breakeven concept. The less perfect the relationship between two sets of data, the greater will be the departure (plot points) from the indicated trend line.

Line of Regression

The trend or direction of this movement may be defined by means of a "least squares" line or curve that is commonly identified as the *line of regression*. If the trend of the data is linear, the resulting equation will be Y = a + bX. The values of *a* and *b* are obtained from solving the normal equations of:

(1) $\Sigma(Y) = Na + b\Sigma(X)$
(2) $\Sigma(XY) = a\Sigma(X) + b\Sigma(X^2)$

Standard Error of Estimate

The representative equation is used to estimate a theoretical value of *Y* for a given value of *X*. If the relationship is not perfect, the actuals will not coincide with the theoretical value due to the variations about the line. If the scatter is definitely measured, the variation is then allowed for and a range established within which all values will fall. The measure used for this purpose is identified as the *standard error of estimate* which is similar to *standard deviation*. The standard deviation measures the scatter about the *arithmetic mean* while the standard error of estimate is a measure of the scatter about the *line of regression*. The equation used is:

$$Sy = \frac{d^2}{N}$$

Sy = standard error of estimate
d = deviation of actual values (Y) from the theoretical values (Yc)
N = number of observations or plot points.

The solution of the equation will indicate the validity of the correlation between two sets of data that may be used in the estimating process.

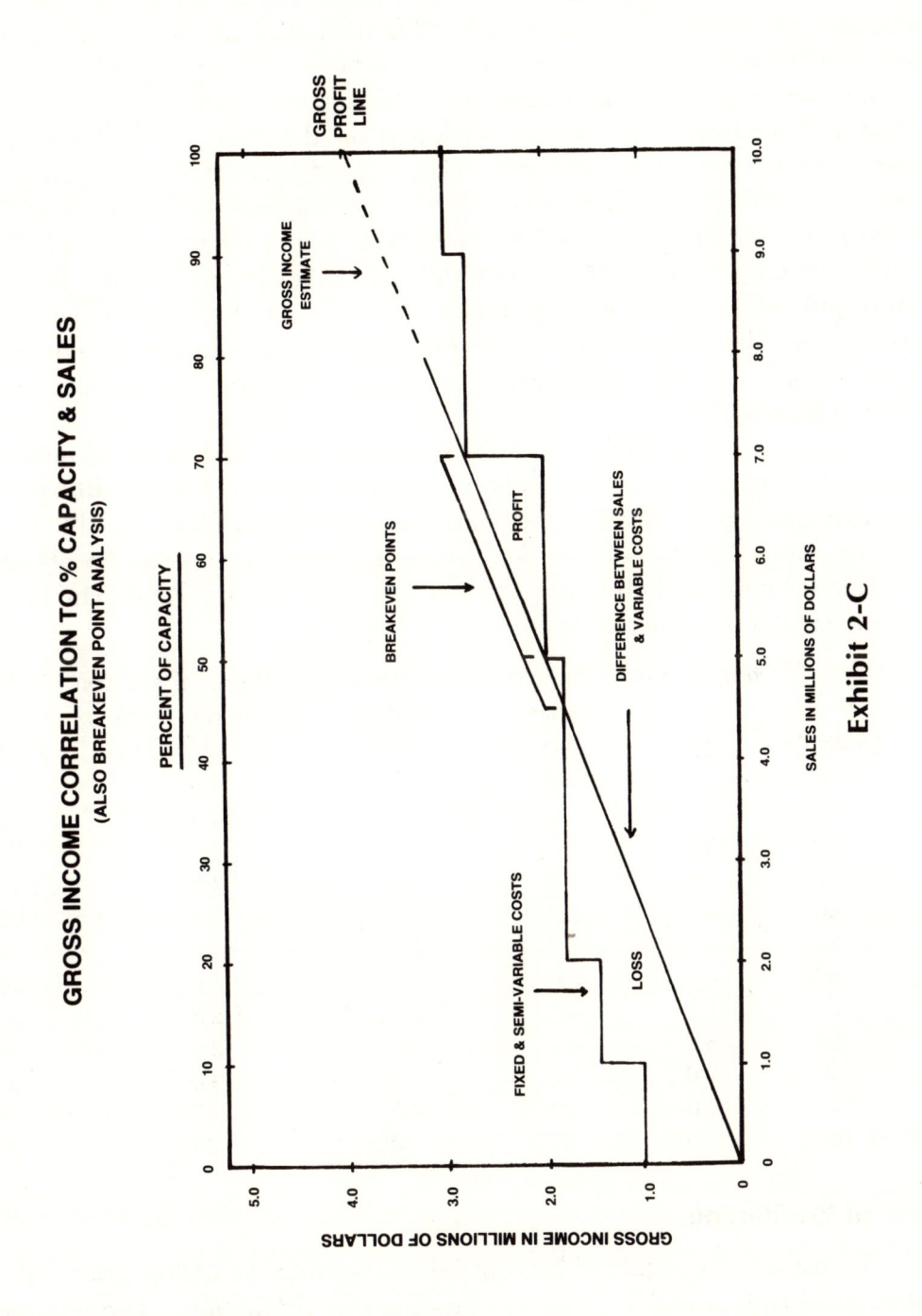

Statistical Techniques for Mechanical Cost Estimating 57

GROSS INCOME CORRELATION TO % CAPACITY & SALES
(ALSO BREAKEVEN POINT ANALYSIS)

Exhibit 2-C

BREAKEVEN POINT ANALYSIS

A number of variations to correlation charts can be used as a basis for data analysis and estimating future trends. This type of charting is generally known as a *profitgraph*. Exhibit 2-C displays a type of profitgraph in which the gross income line represents the difference between sales and variable costs. When fixed and semi-variable costs are included on the chart, then the *profit and loss* values can be determined at varying sales volume levels. The points where the sales and costs intersect on the gross income line are identified as *breakeven* or profitless points. The breakeven points are located at 4.5, 5 and 7 million dollar volumes as shown in Exhibit 2-C. At those points, the inclusion of fixed and semi-variable costs provides the basis for the intersection with the gross income line. Profit and loss are segmented and highlighted. A decrease in fixed or variable costs automatically lowers the breakeven point and increases the profit area.

The percent of plant capacity is tied in with the sales volume which means, for example, that five million sales require 50% of the plant capacity to meet the sales goals according to chart layout on the exhibit.

At volumes of $7—10 million, gross income estimates can be obtained as illustrated by the broken line at the top and right of the exhibit. The data used for the exhibit is tabulated below.

Data for Gross Income Correlation (in millions of dollars)

% of Capacity	Sales	Variable Costs	Gross Income	Fixed & Semi-Variable Costs	Profit
0	—	—	—	1.0	(1.0)
10	1.0	.6	.4	1.4	(1.0)
20	2.0	1.2	.8	1.4	(.6)
30	3.0	1.8	1.2	1.8	(.6)
40	4.0	2.4	1.6	1.8	(.2)
50	5.0	3.0	2.0	2.0	—
60	6.0	3.6	2.4	2.0	.4
70	7.0	4.2	2.8	2.8	—
80	8.0	4.8	3.2	2.8	.4
90	9.0	5.4	3.6	3.0	.6
100	10.0	6.0	4.0	3.0	1.0
% @ 100%	100%	60%	40%	30%	10%

Use of Profitgraph

Profits are the result of varying influences such as selling price, sales volume, fixed costs, variable costs, and product mix profitability. The solution to a poor profit posture may not necessarily be an increase in selling price or sales

Statistical Techniques for Mechanical Cost Estimating 59

volume but rather a decrease in costs and/or changes in the product mix—elimination of less profitable products. The profitgraph can be used as a dynamic tool in *controlling operational expenses*.

Another use of the profitgraph is concerned in analysis of the profitability of the various sales components. This type of analysis immediately isolates the problem area(s) for remedial action. Each product line is plotted on a graph with its direct and/or allocated costs, breakeven points are determined, and their specific profitability is ascertained. These data provide the basis for corrective action through management decisions. The decisions would be concerned with (1) eliminating unprofitable product lines and/or providing substitutions thereof, (2) eliminating customer marginal accounts (possibly due to low volume or profit margin), (3) increasing sales volume or price, (4) and/or adding new product lines with increased profit yields.

RATIOS AND PROPORTIONS IN ESTIMATING

A ratio is used to express the relationship of one kind of data to another. The ratio of two numbers is the quotient of the first number divided by the second. Ratios can be indicated by a fraction line, a colon, or a division sign.

$$\frac{20}{5} = 4; \qquad 20:5 = 4; \qquad 20 \div 5 = 4$$

A proportion is an equality of ratios. If the ratio of one pair of numbers is equal to the ratio of another pair of numbers, the two pairs are said to form a proportion. For example, $20 : 5 = 100 : 25$ — both ratios equal 4; therefore, the results indicate a proportion. A *direct proportion* exists when two sets of numbers are so related that an increase or decrease in one is accompanied respectively by an increase or decrease in the other. For example, at a fixed price per product, the quantity of products sold and their costs are directly related.

In the estimating process, if any three numbers in a proportion are known, the missing number representing a cost estimate can be determined through an equation.

Proportion Application to a Cost Estimate

- *Situation*: If 10 specific part items at a total cost of $50 are required for a product unit, what is the cost for producing 100 units?
- *Proportion*: $10 : \$50 = (100 \times 10) : x$ (cost)
- *Solution*: $10x = \$50,000; \quad x = \$5,000$
- *Equation*: $\dfrac{10}{50} = \dfrac{1,000}{x}; \quad 10x = 50,000; \quad x = \$5,000$

•*Situation*:   In preparing an estimate or a flexible budget, it was determined that at 50% of normal capacity, the direct payroll was $1500 in Task Section A. Estimate the direct labor cost at 75% of normal capacity.
Proportion: 50% : $1,500 = 75% : x (direct labor cost)
Solution: .50x = $1,125;   x = $2,250
Equation: $\frac{.50}{1,500} = \frac{.75}{x}$;   .50x = $1.125;   x = $2,250

The above examples are overly simplified, but the same type procedure would prevail for any magnitude or complicated data providing the proportion is valid. In the mechanical process, varied input would be entered in the appropriate format and the calculations rapidly accomplished.

Proportional Distribution of Overhead

In estimating, budgeting, or actual environment, it is often necessary to distribute a lump sum overhead cost over a number of items in proportion to certain fixed or agreed ratios. Therefore, a number is divided in proportion to two or more given numbers when its parts bear the same relation to the number as the given numbers bear to their total. This situation may be expressed as a *continued proportion*. For example, assume that $5,000 overhead is to be distributed in the following proportions:

$$a : b : c : d = 2 : 4 : 6 : 8$$

The first step is to total the given numbers (2 + 4 + 6 + 8 = 20). The next step is to multiply the $5,000 by the given number's relationship to the total (20); for example, 2/20 × 5,000; 4/20 × 5,000. The $5,000 is then proportionately distributed into the values for a, b, c, d, or $500, $1,000, $1,500, and $2,000.

As a matter of practical convenience, another version of the above process is to divide the $5,000 by the total (20) of the given numbers and multiplying this result successively by the given numbers (5,000 ÷ 20 = 250 × 2 = 500; × 4 = 1,000 and so on). This form of solution is more appropriate when the numbers are large and the distribution extensive. The above proportional distribution approach is commonly used to estimate utility costs by organization, based on area of occupancy.

Inverse Proportion

An inverse proportion exists when two sets of quantities are so related that an increase in one is accompanied by a decrease in the other. For illustration, let us assume that men and machines are about equally efficient and a definite job is to be done. The premise is therefore that the more employees placed on a job, the less time will be required to accomplish it.

Statistical Techniques for Mechanical Cost Estimating

- *Situation*: 20 operators produce 1,000 units of product in 10 days. How many operators would be required to produce the 1,000 units in 6 days?
- *Proportion*: x : 20 = 10 : 6;   6x = 200;   x = 33 operators
- *Situation*: 500 units of a product are produced by 10 operators in 5 days. How long should it take 15 operators of the same efficiency to produce the 500 units?
- *Proportion*: 15 : 10 = 5 : x;   15x = 50;   x = 3.3 days

Ratios and proportions can be very helpful in computing a wide variety of pertinent estimating and distribution tasks. The estimator must be familiar with their usage and relevancy. The procedures above can be mechanized and are ideal for "gaming" various type situations.

INDEX NUMBERS FOR PRICE CORRECTION

The index number represents a statistical tool for measuring changes in groups of data during intervals of time. It is often used as a shortcut in the estimating activities.

If the product for which costs are estimated is complex or if estimates must be made by correcting previous actual costs for price level changes, detailed calculations become time consuming. In many situations, it is possible to avoid a large amount of analysis and adjustment of individual wage rates and material prices. Total labor, material, and overhead costs may be adjusted by means of index numbers.

Price Correction

One of the simplest forms of index numbers is illustrated by the following example:

Year	Total Payroll	Total Manhours	Average Rate/Hour	Index Number of Wage Rates (1979 = 100)
1979	1,440,000	300,000	$4.80	100.00
1980	1,540,000	350,000	4.40	(4.40 ÷ 4.80) 91.67
1981	1,656,000	360,000	4.60	95.83

Use of above index may be illustrated by assuming that 1,000 units of a given product were made in 19X0; the cost sheet for that product lot showed total direct labor costs of $10,000. If another product lot of 1,000 units is produced in 19X1, direct wages may be converted to the 19X1 wage levels by the following calculation:

$$(\$10{,}000 \div 91.67) \times 95.83 = \$10{,}454$$

Errors in Use of Index Numbers

An index number is a representation of an average; the weighting of individual items entering into the index affects it to a marked extent. Therefore, in the case of labor costs above, the changes in the index number are attributed to the following:

- *Changes in proportionality from year to year.* The index can show a decrease in the total average wage rate as indicated above, even though no reduction in specific jobs occurred. The change in average wages could reflect merely a shift in the types of tasks being done during the respective years. In other words, a greater proportion of medium and low priced labor could have been used versus a smaller proportion of high priced labor.

- *Changes in proportionality of specific jobs.* Unless the weighting of the items in the index corresponds to weighting of the items on the cost sheet, inaccuracies can result. A detailed estimate of the specific direct labor operations could result in a total cost considerably above the $10,454 calculated above as an index number correction. The use of index numbers for a specific operation can reflect a change in wage rates which actually did not occur. It may represent for that particular job an assortment of high, medium and low priced labor which is different from that prevailing on other jobs processed in the department.

- *Price level changes.* The error of $454 ($10,454 − 10,000) above is attributed to the fact that the relative increase in rates for high priced labor is smaller than that for low priced labor which was predominantly used in the above assessment.

If all batches of a product require the same proportions of high and low priced factors, the index number method of adjustment entails no weighting errors. If, however, these proportions vary from job to job, index numbers must be used with great caution and discretion.

WEIGHT RATIO THEOREM

It is not always feasible to relate directly future work with past performance because of a number of varying circumstances. One of the influencing factors is as follows:

- Radical changes in product design, particularly in industries where new innovations and technological improvements are constantly being made such as computers, aircraft, and automotive vehicles. The unit product may remain fundamentally the same as the original, but there may be a significant effect on labor hour and elapsed time estimates as well as additional and more sophisticated material requirements.

Statistical Techniques for Mechanical Cost Estimating

In industries that manufacture the larger type commodities, it has been observed in certain compatible situations that product weight, as a common denominator, is a logical estimating tool for predicting changes in labor hours expended and in elapsed time. To further explore this premise, the following discussion is pertinent.

Consideratons in the Use of Weight Ratio

First, material processing tasks in the production phase can only be accomplished on the surface; that is, penetrations (holes) are drilled from the outside inward thus "forming" pressure, or force must be applied on the outside surfaces of material and so on. Therefore, it can be assumed that the work is directly proportional to the increase or decrease of the outside workable surface or area.

Second, it can be ventured that the work done on a small unit is proportional to the work done on a large unit as expressed in *Formula I* below. Since the weight of the small unit is proportional to the weight of the large unit, the work accomplished is proportional to the weight as expressed in *Formula II* below. It is also known that weight is proportional to the volume (*Formula III*) and the volume is proportional to the linear dimensions cubed as represented by *Formula IV*. Based on the above analysis, the following formulas are expressed:

SYMBOL IDENTIFICATIONS

H — Labor hours
A — Area of material
L — Linear dimensions
W — Weight
V — Volume

$\left[\begin{array}{l}\text{A symbol qualified by Sub}_1 \text{ or }_2 \\ \text{indicates a large or small unit} \\ \text{and is represented by:} \\ H_1 = \text{hours, large unit;} \\ V_2 = \text{volume, small unit}\end{array}\right]$

Formulas and Solutions

$$\text{I} \qquad \frac{H_1}{H_2} = \frac{A_1}{A_2} \qquad\qquad \text{II} \qquad \frac{H_1}{H_2} = \frac{W_1}{W_2} \qquad\qquad \text{III} \qquad \frac{W_1}{W_2} = \frac{V_1}{V_2} \qquad\qquad \text{IV} \qquad \frac{V_1}{V_2} = \frac{L_1^3}{L_2^3}$$

Since (weight = volume = linear dimensions)

$$\frac{W_1}{W_2} = \frac{V_1}{V_2} = \frac{L_1^3}{L_2^3} \qquad Then \qquad \frac{W_1}{W_2} = \frac{L_1^3}{L_2^3} \qquad or \qquad \frac{L_1}{L_2} = \frac{W_1}{W_2}$$

Also if (area = linear dimensions and labor hours)

$$\frac{A_1}{A_2} = \frac{L_1^2}{L_2} \quad and \quad \frac{A_1}{A_2} = \frac{H_1}{H_2} \quad and \quad \frac{H_1}{H_2} = \frac{W_1}{W_2} \quad then \quad \frac{W_1}{W_2} = \frac{L_1^2}{L_2}$$

Since

$$\frac{A_1}{A_2} = \frac{L_1^2}{L_2^2} \quad \text{and} \quad \frac{A_1}{A_2} = \frac{H_1}{H_2} \quad \text{then} \quad \frac{H_1}{H_2} = \frac{L_1^2}{L_2^2}$$

Since

$$\frac{A_1}{A_2} = \frac{L_1^2}{L_2^2} \quad \text{and} \quad \frac{L_1}{L_2} = \frac{W_1^{1/3}}{W_2} \quad \text{then} \quad \frac{A_1}{A_2} = \frac{W_1^{2/3}}{W_2}$$

Since

$$\frac{A_1}{A_2} = \frac{H_1}{H_2} \quad \text{Conclusion is} \quad \frac{H_1}{H_2} = \frac{W_1^{2/3}}{W_2} \quad \text{(theoretical weight ratio)}$$

Formula Application

In applying the above premises, assume that the *weight* of the large unit is *10,000 pounds* and that the *one-hundreth unit* produced required *4,000 labor hours*. Management's decision was to discontinue the larger model for a smaller and ligher unit *weighing 5,000 pounds*. What should be the estimated labor hours for the *first unit of the new model*?

Formula (note above) $\quad \dfrac{H_1}{H_2} = \dfrac{W_1^{2/3}}{W_2} \quad$ *Formula Substitution* $\quad \dfrac{4,000}{H_2} = \dfrac{10,000^{2/3}}{5,000}$

$$\frac{4,000}{H_2} = 2^{2/3} \text{ or } 1.334; \quad H_2 = \frac{4,000}{1.334} = 2,999 \text{ hours}$$

The 2,999 figure represents the estimated hours to be expended on the last unit of the new model at the one-hundreth unit. If the learning curve is a .333 slope, then the individual unit curve will be .667.

Using a logarithm chart, the line must be projected back on a .333 slope with dividers from the 2,999 hours calculated above at the one-hundreth unit. The 2,999 individual unit time is comparable to 4,499 cumulative average hours. Projecting back from this point on the one-third slope, it was estimated that the labor hours for the first unit of the new model would be 21,560 hours.

Only through testing historical data can it be determined how valid and realistic the weight ratio theory is to a given organization. A standard mechanical program incorporating the formulas discussed above is the key to reducing time-consuming manual operations and further provides the capability to test varied products for determining the attributes of using weight as a common denominator.

DEVELOPING A MACHINE HOUR RATE

Applying overhead as a rate per machine hour requires the determination of the ratio between the amount of overhead expenses to be applied and the

Statistical Techniques for Mechanical Cost Estimating 65

number of machine hours. Overhead is then charged to the job or process by multiplying this rate by the number of machine hours involved in a specific operation. The computation of the rate may be expressed by the formula:

$$\frac{\text{Overhead expense for a specific machine}}{\text{Machine hours}} = \text{Rate per machine hour}$$

Theoretically, the actual overhead and actual machine hours might be used; however, this practice is generally not followed. Usually the computation is on the basis of *estimated actual expense* or the *anticipated normal expense* for a future period; also, the rate is calculated for machine or group of machines that are identical in cost and operation.

The machine hour rate therefore represents a *predetermined estimate* of the actual overhead cost per hour for operating each machine. This rate, when applied on a time basis to the jobs processed on the machine, should result in the absorption of actual overhead. Differences between actual and absorbed overhead are the result of error in estimating the amount of indirect expenses and/or the number of machine time hours.

Detailed Calculation of Machine Hour Rates

There are three basic steps in computing machine hour rates.

- Determination of the *estimated overhead expenses* for the period by department or cost center. This may be a formal budget in the form of an expense distribution sheet, wherein the expenses are listed at the left of the sheet and various machine identities are entered as columnar headings at the top of the format with their appropriate line item estimated expenses. If the budget is based on normal production, then normal rates will result.

- *Regrouping of expenses into three categories*: (1) specific charges to each machine; (2) building costs, and (3) all other general and service costs. The specific expenses by category are displayed in Exhibit 2-D.

- *Direct and prorated expenses are combined* to obtain the total overhead to operate each machine during the year. The machine rate is derived by dividing this total by the number of estimated operational hours. Some organizations segregate their rates into setup time and running time.

Distribution Basis

There are a number of bases that can be used in overhead distribution; some common guidelines are shown at the top of Exhibit 2-D. The distribution bases are predicated on organizational policy to satisfy specific needs and finite sophistication in expense distribution.

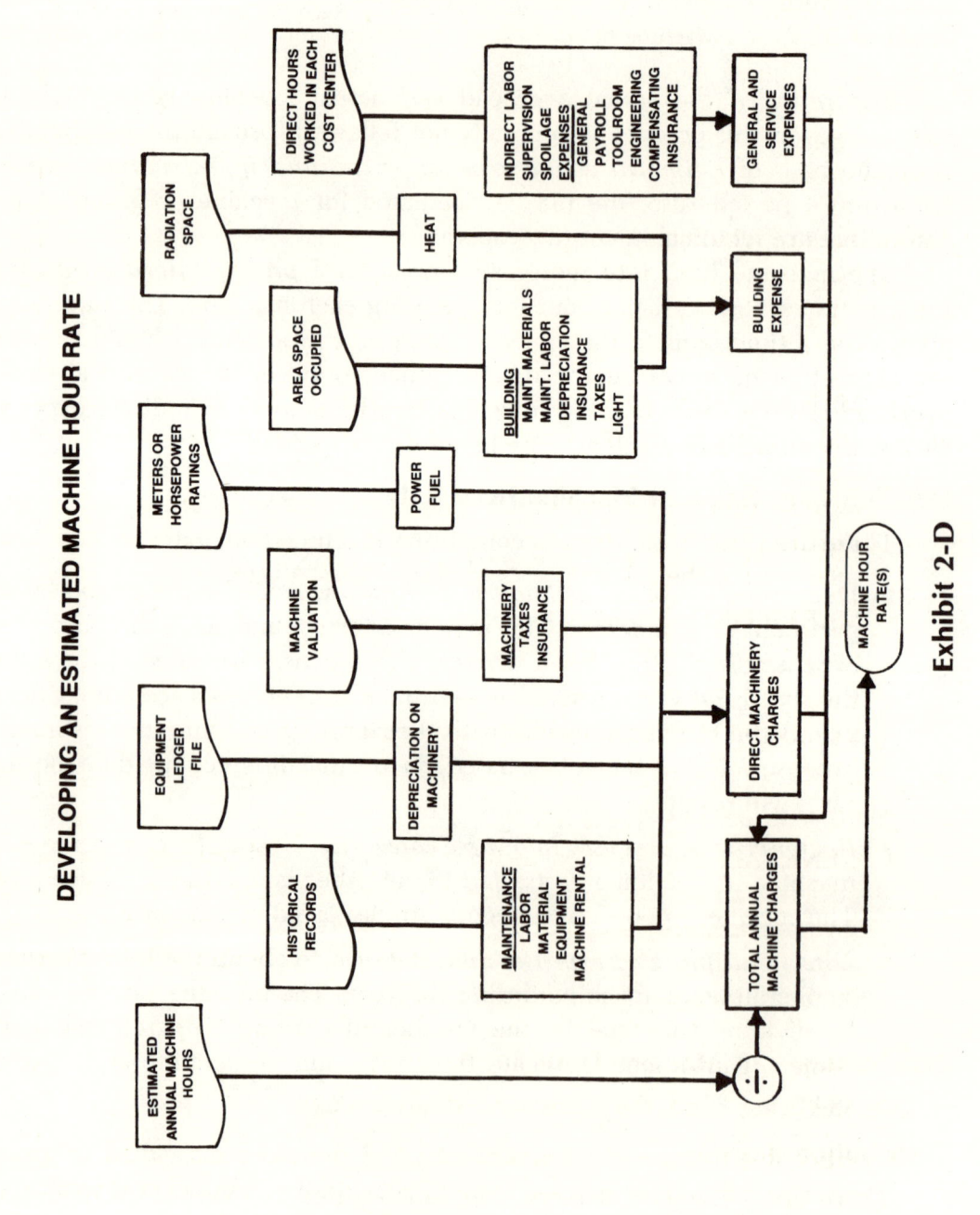

DEVELOPING AN ESTIMATED MACHINE HOUR RATE

Exhibit 2-D

Statistical Techniques for Mechanical Cost Estimating

Over- and Under-Absorbed Burden

Use of estimated machine hour rates may result in over- and under-absorbed burden for the period involved, because actual expenses and actual hours of operation may differ from the estimates. These differences can be disposed of in various ways dependent on organizational policy. Some common methods employed include (1) recosting the jobs through the use of a *supplementary rate*, (2) closing the difference into *cost of sales* or profit and loss, and (3) *prorating the difference* among cost of sales and year-end inventories of work in process and finished goods.

Advantages of Machine Hour Rates

In situations in which machinery is the main factor in production, the machine hour method represents the most ideal approach to overhead application for the following specific reasons:

- MANAGEMENT. Provides overhead costing that is scientific, logical, and realistic in its use. Cost reports are dependable and accurate. Confidence in reliable price quotations to customers—not over- or understated—thus precluding either operating losses or failure to obtain jobs. Further, machine hour rates provide an equitable basis for the measurement of the monthly cost of idle machines.

- MARKETING. Provides a reliable basis for the sales engineer to quote more accurate estimated selling prices for jobs.

- ENGINEERING. Provides a realistic method for estimating the job on a proposed specification and rate sheet with a high degree of accuracy.

- COST ACCOUNTING. Provides the most accurate method of allocating overhead expenses to each job.

- GENERAL. This method uses time as a base in applying overhead. It possesses an advantage over other procedures when one operator tends several machines or a number of operators are required for one machine. Further, a cost center rate is readily determined by combining the operator's pay rate with the machine overhead rate.

Disadvantages of Machine Hour Rates

On the other hand, there are some disadvantages.

- Precludes the use of a blanket rate and therefore individual or group machine rates must be used which increases the detailed cost work.

- Additional detailed data must be gathered such as machine times for each machine. Since this information is not required for other purposes, additional cost is incurred for accounting activities.

- This method is only used for costing those operations performed by machinery and thus is inapplicable in other situations.
- Use of machine hour rates may have to be supplemented with other types of rates; whereas direct labor rates can generally be used uniformly throughout the plant.

SPECIAL TOOLING AND SERVICES

Estimating techniques for special tooling and services can be classified into two prime categories—development and tactical. Included in these groupings are the (1) design, fabrication, and maintenance for project tools and support equipment, and (2) production planning and illustration.

Development Contracts

The planning requirements for tasks that are the first of its type can often be estimated by using the statistics of a previous similar task activity. The similarity must be evaluated to ascertain the percentage of increase or decrease that must be applied to the new item being quoted. This type of information can generally be obtained from task outlines, discussions with capable engineering staff, and previous program directives. Appropriate estimating for an unknown activity is highly dependent upon the capabilities and experience of the planning estimator in his interpretation and use of historical data.

Tactical Contracts

Tactical (production) contracts and follow-on business can be projected with greater accuracy and realism than new activity contracts because more definitive knowledge has been accumulated from the previous product and/or program. Comparisons of the work effort however are mandatory to ensure that similarities prevail and that any new development requirements are ascertained. This is accomplished by a thorough review of historical documentation.

ESTIMATING SPECIAL TOOLING

Special tooling specifically consists of all jigs, fixtures, molds, patterns, special gauges, special test equipment, and other aids that are acquired or manufactured by the contractor for use in contract performance. This type of equipment generally requires substantial modification to meet the peculiar needs of government contracts. The special tooling category does not include items of tooling or equipment that were acquired by the contractor prior to the contract (whether or not altered or adapted for use in contract performance), consumable small tools, or general purpose small tools.

Estimating Technique for Project Tools

The method employed to estimate project tools when tool designs are unavailable is to analyze each tool type relative to the part configuration it is to produce and to its application in the fabrication and assembly processes. The estimating technique used is *evaluating historical data* for each tool type.

The fabrication hour value for each tool type is tabulated and the average hour value is then the basis for estimating tools for a program of considerable magnitude. Charts are prepared for other tool types which highlight the average hour value for tool fabrication depending on the degree of complexity. Tool complexity is classified into categories of simple, medium, complex, and special.

Requirements and Control

Tooling requirements and quantities are established by the pre-planners, manufacturing engineers, and tool planners. Each segment must be analyzed by listing all the parts therein and by itemizing the list of tooling by type and quantity needed to produce those parts.

The control of tooling expenditure is often accomplished by the tool checkbook system. The checkbook record is maintained by production planning and reflects the posting of tools by segment as they are ordered and the fabrication hours estimated to produce the tools. This system provides a control on budget expenditures and is used as a tool to forecast potential budget overrun situations. A weekly status of tool checkbook activity is distributed to affected organizations for review and for corrective actions if needed.

PROJECT SUPPORT (TEST EQUIPMENT)

This category includes items of special tooling used to test, check, inspect, calibrate, appraise, gauge, and measure mechanical, hydraulic or electronic parts, equipment or systems to ensure compliance with all specifications. These items are for in-house, vendor or subcontractor use and are not intended as deliverable end items. They could, however, be transferred to the customer at some later date.

Estimating Technique

The following discussion provides the basic rules and the proposed steps necessary for a sound estimating technique that can be defended in a customer audit.

Condensed estimating standards are used which represent the time required to accomplish a task based on the following assumptions:

- Worker is qualified and properly trained.
- Machines and tools are readily available.

- No unavoidable delays are anticipated.
- No rework is assumed due to engineering and manufacturing changes.
- Normal working conditions and rate of effort.

The procedural steps in estimating new equipment are as follows:

*1. Establish the base type standard hour content (not the shop earned which are generally higher) through the use of an operation sheet and condensed estimating standards.

2. Multiply the estimated actual standard hour value by the performance factor of the respective equipment category (electronics for test equipment and mechanical for ground handling equipment). These factors will be maintained and updated on a continual basis, and the average factor for a sliding three month period will be used.

*3. Reduce the results of Step 2 (standard hours × performance factor) by the estimated variances that can be projected for the specific piece of equipment. The estimated actuals minus the variances represents the true performance factor.

4. Calculate the new performance factor for record purposes.

To illustrate the above steps, let us assume that a piece of equipment requires standard hours of *10.6* for setup and *38.2* for run time; a performance factor of 3.3 and estimated variances of *57* hours.

SOLUTION: Standard hours — Setup   10.6
                            Run   38.2

Step 1   48.8   standard hours
              × 3.3   applying performance factor
Step 2   161.04   estimated actual hours
              − 57.0   variances (would be by
                          detailed item)
Step 3   104.04

Step 4   104.04 ÷ 48.8 (above) = 2.132 revised factor

RECONCILIATION:

48.8 (standard hours) × 2.132 (revised factor) = 104.04 factored standard hours. 104.04 + 57.0 (variances) = 161.04 estimated actual hours.

*To further illustrate the value which is represented by the variance:

Estimated standards	*Estimated standards*	*Variance*
48.8	75.53	161.03
× 2.132	× 2.132	− 104.04
104.04	161.03	56.99

Surface Support Equipment versus Project Support Equipment

Electronic test equipment is defined as that equipment used to check out the product after factory completion and prior to delivery—identified as surface support equipment (SSE). The equipment used to produce and check out the product during manufacture is identified as project support equipment (PSE).

The technique used for *estimating both types* of test equipment is, as described above, the same, but the distinction is made because of their use and organizational placement. SSE is considered a deliverable item which is categorized as special tooling. Identical equipment will appear in both categories.

RATE CAPABILITY OF SPECIAL TOOLING

The purpose of rate capability is to establish tool quantities which will support peak production rate requirements as specified in program directives, task outlines, manufacturing plans, and tooling policies. Consideration should be given to requirements for spares, return for repair items, and needs for evaluation hardware.

Estimating Procedure

The process of projecting tool quantities to meet a specific rate of production requires a detailed assessment of each tool's capability. This is accomplished by computing the tools' productive and non-productive time. A procedure that is commonly used or variations thereof, dependent upon the need and sophistication of the organization is outlined in Exhibit 2-E. Specific procedural calculations are illustrated to augment the text for better understanding of the detail. In Exhibit 2-E, the result is the requirement for *two tools*.

Time Phasing

An important factor in considering tool capability is time phasing for meeting requirements at time of need. Tool need dates are charted on a scheduled rate chart. Tool capability is then determined from the calculations outlined in Exhibit 2-E. Tool fabrication start date would be indicated on the chart by a bar setback from the need position date of the tool which should ensure tooling availability at the appropriate time.

Project Tool Calculations for Increased Rate

    ASSUME— Two shifts @ 40 hours per week; 261 workdays in year less 7 holidays; 80% utilization; 16.8 hours (actual elapsed time); 1.6 learning curve factor (from a curve chart); scheduled peak rate of 38.

    CALCULATIONS— (1) 2 shifts × 40 = 80 hours/week

(2) 261 − 7 = actual workdays/year ÷ 5 = 50.8 equivalent weeks
(3) 80 hours × 50.8 = 4064 hours/year—two shifts
(4) 4064 hours ÷ 12 = 338 hours/month
(5) 338 hours × 80% = 270 available hours
(6) 16.8 hours actual elapsed time ÷ 1.6 learning curve factor = 10.5 hours/unit at rate
(7) 270 available hours/month ÷ 10.5 elapsed time at rate = 25.7 unit capability per month
(8) 38 rate schedule ÷ 25.7 unit capability = 1.5 or 2 tools required

RATE CAPABILITY FOR SPECIAL TOOLING (PROCEDURAL CALCULATIONS)

1.	SETUP HOURS REQUIRED 2 TIMES NUMBER SETUPS PER MONTH	5.0 HOURS (2.5 × 2)
2.	REQUIRED TIME TO LOAD TOOL FOR ONE CYCLE	.2
3.	PRODUCTIVE TIME WHILE PART IS IN TOOL	.5
4.	REQUIRED TIME TO INSPECT PART WHILE STILL IN TOOL STATUS	.4
5.	UNLOADING TIME FOR ONE CYCLE	.2
6.	PERCENTAGE TIME TOOL WILL BE USED FOR IN-HOUSE REWORK	20%
7.	PERCENTAGE OF TOOL DOWN TIME (INSPECTION, REPAIR)	10%
8.	PERCENT OF TOOL YIELD (ACCEPTABLE PARTS PRODUCED)	60%
9.	AVAILABLE HOURS/MONTH FOR TWO SHIFTS—80% EFFICIENCY—ASSUME 270—COMBINE STEPS 6 (20%) AND 7 (10%); DEDUCT 30% FROM 100%; MULTIPLY 70% × 270	189
10.	HOURS PER MONTH TOOL AVAILABLE FOR PRODUCTIVE WORK—MULTIPLY RESULT IN STEP 7 BY PERCENT IN STEP 8 & SUBTRACT SETUP HOURS (STEP 1); (189 × 60%)—5.0	108.4
11.	ELAPSED TIME PER PART—ADD DATA IN STEPS 2 THRU 5; (.2 + .5 + .4 + .2)	1.3
12.	HOURS PER UNIT RATE—DIVIDE RESULT IN STEP 11 BY LEARNING CURVE FACTOR (ASSUME 1.6 FOR THIS PROGRAM (1.3 ÷ 1.6)	.81
13.	UNIT CAPABILITY PER MONTH—DIVIDE RESULT IN STEP 10 (108.4) BY STEP 12 (.81)	133.8
14.	QUANTITY OF TOOLS REQUIRED TO SUPPORT PEAK RATE CONDITIONS—DIVIDE SCHEDULED PEAK RATE QUANTITY (ASSUME 250) BY RESULT IN STEP 13 (133.8)	1.9 OR 2 TOOLS

Exhibit 2-E

Statistical Techniques for Mechanical Cost Estimating

In view of the many tools to be considered for the production process, it is highly desirable that this process be mechanized. The input assumption can readily be changed as required (rate schedule for an example) and records updated with minimal effort. A computer printout would indicate a fabrication start date for each tool and the date of availability for production planning.

EFFORT EXPENDED VS. PROGRAM COMPLETION

Method Illustrations

Projection of "to-go" hours relative to actual hours expended is computed by determining the percent of program completion and by applying the following technique:

- Actual hours expended for the period of time, representing 45% or less of program completion, added to the percentage of forecasted "to-go" as reflected on Exhibit 2-F will represent the manhours required for the total effort. During the time prior to 45% of program completion, many factors must be considered. Therefore, the actuals recorded may not be truly representative during this period for use as a basis of projecting subsequent effort for program completion.

    Illustration I—Projected tooling hours = 10,000
    a. Actual hours at 15% of program completion = 2,800
    b. 15% program completion = 83% of projected hours "to-go"
    c. 83% of 10,000 = 8300 + 2,800 (actual hours expended) = 11,100 hours for total effort. Therefore, 11,100 tooling hours should be negotiated for this program.

- Actual hours expended for the period of time representing 46% or more of program completion applied to the percentage of actual hours "to-go" as shown on Exhibit 2-F will represent the manhours required for the total effort. The same note above applies with respect to using actual hours during this period as a basis for future projections.

    Illustration II—Projected tooling hours = 10,000
    a. Actual hours at 50% of program completion = 7,400
    b. 50% of program completion = 35% of the total hours "to-go" and 7,400 hours represents 65% of the total hours expended
    c. 7,400 ÷ 65% = 11,385 manhours required for this total effort. This is the value that should be negotiated.

Results of Technique Application

Applying the technique to development program actuals, the following results would be obtained by assuming the program was considered to be 50% complete at the time of the negotiations.

Statistical Techniques for Mechanical Cost Estimating

TASKS	% OF TOTAL EFFORT REQUIREMENTS	EXTENDING OVER % OF TOTAL PROGRAM
PLANNING		
ORIGINAL EFFORT	10 - 27%	15 - 25%
PROOFING & CHANGES	40 - 60	30 - 50
METHODS IMPROVEMENT & SUSTAINING EFFORT	20 - 40	25 - 55
TOOLING		
ORIGINAL EFFORT	20 - 40	15 - 25
MODIFICATION & PROOF CHANGES	10 - 30	10 - 20
	22 - 48	10 - 50
METHODS IMPROVEMENT & SUSTAINING EFFORT	5 - 25	25 - 55

% PGM COMPL.	PLNG HRS EXPENDED	TLNG HRS EXPENDED
10	7	20
20	18	35
30	35	48
40	51	66
50	63	77
60	71	82
70	78	87
80	85	91
90	92	95
100	100	100

PERCENTS OF EFFORT EXPENDED VS PROGRAM COMPLETION

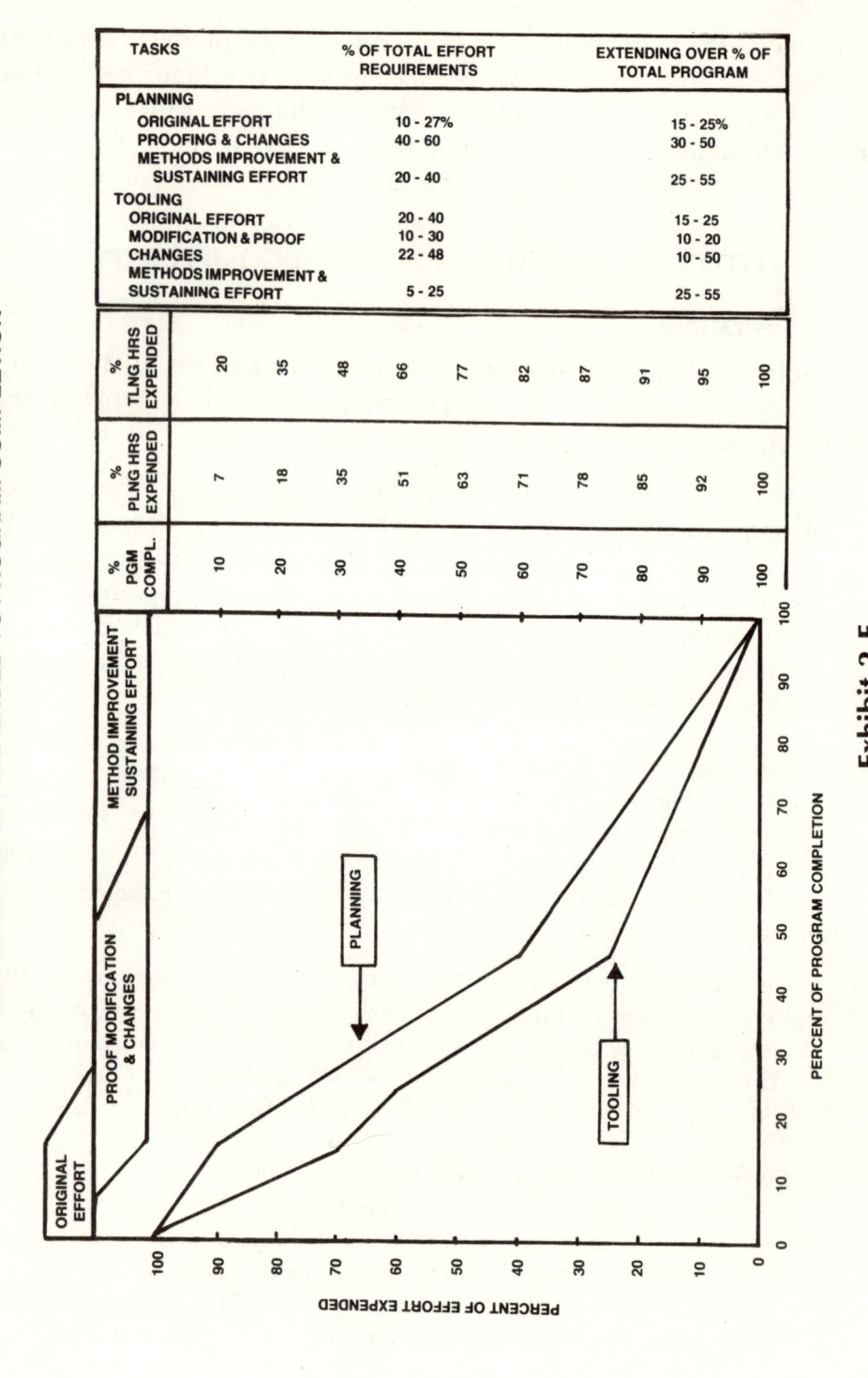

Exhibit 2-F

Statistical Techniques for Mechanical Cost Estimating 73

In view of the many tools to be considered for the production process, it is highly desirable that this process be mechanized. The input assumption can readily be changed as required (rate schedule for an example) and records updated with minimal effort. A computer printout would indicate a fabrication start date for each tool and the date of availability for production planning.

EFFORT EXPENDED VS. PROGRAM COMPLETION

Method Illustrations

Projection of "to-go" hours relative to actual hours expended is computed by determining the percent of program completion and by applying the following technique:

- Actual hours expended for the period of time, representing 45% or less of program completion, added to the percentage of forecasted "to-go" as reflected on Exhibit 2-F will represent the manhours required for the total effort. During the time prior to 45% of program completion, many factors must be considered. Therefore, the actuals recorded may not be truly representative during this period for use as a basis of projecting subsequent effort for program completion.

    Illustration I—Projected tooling hours = 10,000
    a. Actual hours at 15% of program completion = 2,800
    b. 15% program completion = 83% of projected hours "to-go"
    c. 83% of 10,000 = 8300 + 2,800 (actual hours expended) = 11,100 hours for total effort. Therefore, 11,100 tooling hours should be negotiated for this program.

- Actual hours expended for the period of time representing 46% or more of program completion applied to the percentage of actual hours "to-go" as shown on Exhibit 2-F will represent the manhours required for the total effort. The same note above applies with respect to using actual hours during this period as a basis for future projections.

    Illustration II—Projected tooling hours = 10,000
    a. Actual hours at 50% of program completion = 7,400
    b. 50% of program completion = 35% of the total hours "to-go" and 7,400 hours represents 65% of the total hours expended
    c. 7,400 ÷ 65% = 11,385 manhours required for this total effort. This is the value that should be negotiated.

Results of Technique Application

Applying the technique to development program actuals, the following results would be obtained by assuming the program was considered to be 50% complete at the time of the negotiations.

74 *Statistical Techniques for Mechanical Cost Estimating*

TASKS	% OF TOTAL EFFORT REQUIREMENTS	EXTENDING OVER % OF TOTAL PROGRAM
PLANNING		
ORIGINAL EFFORT	10 - 27%	15 - 25%
PROOFING & CHANGES	40 - 60	30 - 50
METHODS IMPROVEMENT & SUSTAINING EFFORT	20 - 40	25 - 55
TOOLING		
ORIGINAL EFFORT	20 - 40	15 - 25
MODIFICATION & PROOF CHANGES	10 - 30	10 - 20
	22 - 48	10 - 50
METHODS IMPROVEMENT & SUSTAINING EFFORT	5 - 25	25 - 55

% TLNG HRS EXPENDED	20	35	48	66	77	82	87	91	95	100
% PLNG HRS EXPENDED	7	18	35	51	63	71	78	85	92	100
% PGM COMPL.	10	20	30	40	50	60	70	80	90	100

PERCENTS OF EFFORT EXPENDED VS PROGRAM COMPLETION

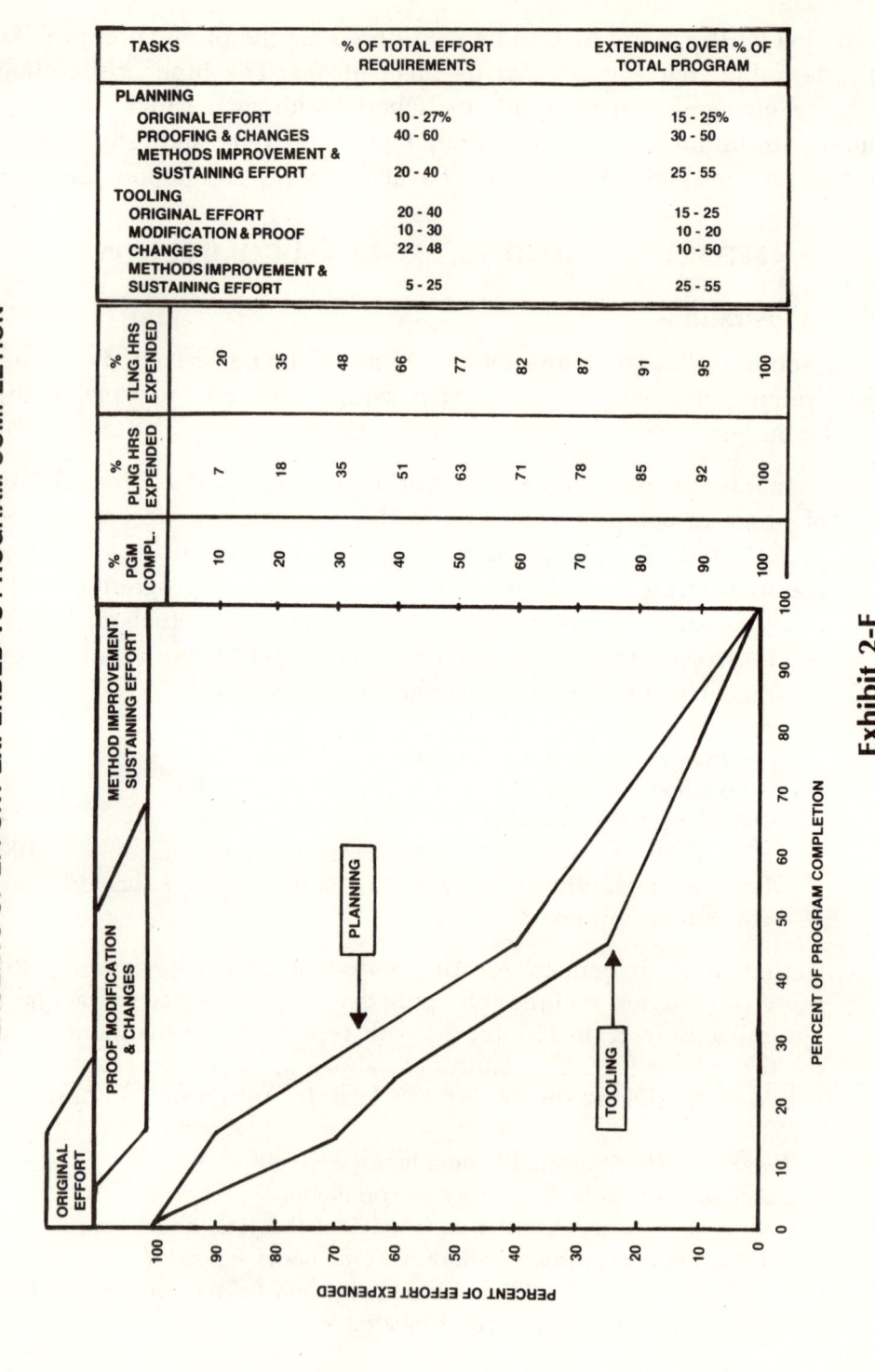

Exhibit 2-F

Statistical Techniques for Mechanical Cost Estimating 75

	ACTUALS	NEGOTIATED FOR TOTAL EFFORT		TECHNIQUE APPLICATION
Mock-up	829	900	(829 ÷ 65%) =	1,275
Project support equipment, fabrication & assembly	1,240	1,511	(1,240 ÷ 65%) =	1,908
Project tools fabrication & assembly	312	480	(312 ÷ 65%) =	480
Project support equipment design	2,199	2,764	(2,199 ÷ 65%) =	3,383
	4,580	5,655		7,046

Projected hours of 7,046 less 5,655 hours negotiated equals 1,391 loss (less than what it probably will take to complete program).

Exhibit 2-F actually represents optimistic figures based on the analysis of the events for which planning and tooling activity is expended. The process of tooling and planning hour expenditures for any given time during the program were predicated on the assumptions displayed on Exhibit 2-F.

STATISTICAL ESTIMATING HIGHLIGHTS

There are many statistical techniques that can be used to provide greater accuracy and realism in mechanical cost estimating and product pricing. The type of estimating procedure and the extent to which it is to be used is dependent on the character of the product to be estimated and the applicability of the technique based on historical experience relevance and accuracies. Some organizations use ratios, correlations, weight theorem, index numbers, machine rates, or statistical formulas. Being aware of the many common techniques discussed in this chapter, it is the task of the planning estimator to select one or more of these approaches for assessing and testing his historical records as to which procedure(s) is most feasible for utilization. Different elements of cost might require their own unique approach as indicated for overhead in this chapter's review. The final determination to a given method's use results from a thorough data evaluation and the assessment of results.

3

Standard Costing for Realistic Cost Performance

Standard costing is not a new discipline, and its utilization is continuing to increase as more costs become standardized. Standard costs represent one form of predetermined costs that are used as a basis for valuation of inventory, development of realistic selling prices, and preparation of cost reports, and also as a control vehicle for measuring cost performance. When properly applied, standard costing is an invaluable management tool for operating a successful business venture.

STANDARD COST DEFINITION

Standard costs represent predetermined costs that are based on past experience and controlled experiments such as are provided by engineering studies and specifications (cost and quantity measurement criteria).

Standards are further predicated on efficient production processes for quantity standards and or projection of market trends for price standards. A fixed dollar amount is specified for basic labor, material, and overhead needed for an estimated quantity of production. The objective of standard costs is to provide an effective means of measuring operation performance in terms of time/labor costs and material quantity usage and costs.

TYPES OF STANDARD COSTS

The two accepted general types of standard costs are current standards and basic or measurement standards.

Current Standard Costs

In current standard costs, standards are modified annually or more often as the situation dictates. This type of standard is representative of what a cost should actually be under current operating conditions. The revisions are to incorporate and update changes in prices and/or methods of production. If the *update* process is not followed, then the standard costs are not truly representative of what the costs should be under prevailing circumstances.

There are two possible *disadvantages* to this type of costing which may or not be relevant in some organizations.

1. Time and expense is involved in periodic revision of standards due to price and technological changes.
2. By changing standards, the comparability of data for different periods is destroyed unless the records are adjusted for compatibility.

Another characteristic of current standards involves the use of cost controlling accounts. Although the stores account would reflect the actual cost, all of the inventory accounts and cost of sales are debited and credited at standard cost; therefore, unless the resultant variances are prorated back to inventories, the dollar value will appear in the balance sheet at the standard cost. Under this situation, the financial statements will not reflect the actual costs and IRS will object to this type of accounting practice.

Basic or Measurement Standard Costs

Under this type of costing, the standards are generally somewhat permanent in nature and are changed only when major revisions occur in specifications and/or production technology. The measurement standard is primarily used as a performance assessment vehicle which compares actuals with anticipated costs.

The theory behind measurement standards is that prices for goods or purchased services are primarily considered beyond the control of an organization and therefore it is assumed that it makes no difference whether the reflected standards are current or historical in nature. The resultant effect is an anticipated increased price variance. The major determination is directed toward the evaluation of the relative efficiency experienced in the use of labor and materials. The price base is considered immaterial under the basic standard costing approach.

It is noted that the standard cost of a part component and/or end product is actually not a *cost* per se but rather an initial projection expressed in standard dollars which are adjusted before they are used for costing purposes.

In valuing inventory and estimating or recording production costs, the adjustment factors reflect anticipated changes of current conditions through the use of cost application ratios to the elements of cost based on actuals. The basic measurement standards, however, remain unchanged.

The prime characteristic of basic standards is that they provide a means for projecting cost trends currently anticipated and actually experienced.

CURRENT VERSUS MEASUREMENT STANDARD COSTS

In establishing quantitative and cost standards, there are minor differences between the two methods *initially* in setting standards. Under the current type, however, the anticipated prevailing prices are used; whereas, in measurement standards, the prices reflect those that existed at the time that the initial standards were established.

In comparing the results relative to revision frequency, each type of standard costing has its advantages and disadvantages.

Current standards permit a more realistic comparison with actual results. With this measurement, however, it becomes more difficult to compare fluctuating actual costs of different periods when the set standards in turn keep changing.

Under *measurement standards*, actual costs are readily compared against fixed standards for successive time periods; therefore, it is possible to measure the trend ratios of actual costs to standards over greater periods of time. Further, current performance can be more effectively compared under this type standard by introducing a ratio or index number which reflects the prices anticipated to prevail for the coming period. Current performance effectiveness can thus be measured without reference to the standard cost sheets. In summary, the following guidelines govern when the measurement standards are used.

- Current standards would be expressed as percentages of the corresponding measurement standard values.

- Actual costs expressed as percentages of measurement standards are compared to current standards to determine the extent of the actual performance variance from what was anticipated. Actual costs would also be compared to the measurement standards to determine the respective trends among periods.

MISCONCEPTIONS RELATIVE TO STANDARDS

There has been a considerable amount of literature written, some contradictory, about the meaning, use, and objectives of standards. Disagreements about the use and determination of standards can be attributed in part to differing organizational policies as to the objectives standards should serve in their particular organization. Some of the more common misconceptions or fallacies about standards are as follows:

- *Standards are representative of average cost conditions.* This is untrue because average costs may obscure poor planning, inefficient operations, inadequate performance, excessive material usage, and spoilage. Realistic standards can aid immeasurably in overcoming the above findings.

- *Standards are a projection of what costs should be under normal working conditions.* It is difficult to predict what normal working conditions should be as most progressive organizations are constantly experiencing some type of change. Examples of changes are development of new products, redesign of current products, update of operating procedures, increase/decrease in sales volume, replacement of equipment, and changes in the economy. The occurrence of one or more of these situations can create deviations from the so-called normal cost trends and thus can invalidate the projected operating environment. Establishing realistic standards could be a desirable solution.

- *Standards represent attainable projections of production planning and associated costs.* This expectation is invalid because attainable projections may not realistically reflect what can be done. It is difficult to ascertain the meaning of the term *attainable*. For example: Is it readily accomplished under loose standards? What type of operating environment must exist? Will actual costs be above or below *attainable* costs? Will production output meet sales demands?

- *Standards represent budget plans and their expectations.* This assumption is not necessarily valid. Budgets are generally predicated on historical cost experience tempered by a forecast of the future operating environment. This may presuppose current operating conditions. Questions arise: Does it reflect improvements in task methods? new equipment? possible substitution of new and less expensive materials? technological advances?

- *Standards represent replacement costs.* Before this statement can be accepted, the term *replacement costs* has to be specifically defined. Does it mean that future market price trends have been incorporated in the price standards for labor, material and overhead? If so, then the price aspect could be considered a standard. Replacement costs do not indicate the degree of efficiency to be experienced in the operating environment.

Before a standard cost system can be effectively utilized, an organization must be secure in the understanding of its objectives and use; otherwise, the effect of operating results in terms of accomplished efficiencies become obscured and overlooked.

CHARACTERISTICS OF STANDARD COSTING

There are two different methods for determining product costs: (1) costs are determined after the work effort has been completed or (2) statistically established prior to work initiation. The latter approach is a characteristic of setting cost standards.

The objective of standard costing is to provide a means for exercising control over the various activities involved in product production and its costs. Standards are recognized as a basic tool in controlling the amount of work effort and quality to be accomplished in the manufacturing operation.

Basic Characteristics

- Basic requisites to establishing standards are the study of and determination of the guidelines which represent an acceptable level of work and cost performance. An approach must be considered as to the most effective means of measuring performance based on the projected plan of operation.

- Standard costs reflect a complement rather than an alternative to actual costs, since their comparison is more useful to management than is either one by itself.

- Some factors in production cost cannot be controlled by management such as prices paid for material and supplies, labor rates, and production volume. Standard costs provide a capability to evaluate costs on the basis of performance efficiency and cost variations due to external factors that are uncontrollable.

- Standards are expressed in terms of quantity and price for each element of cost, and the variances between standards and actuals are analyzed and explained in similar terms.

- Physical standards cannot be used to evaluate the gross profit by classes of production, customer, or marketing operations; whereas, cost standards do provide this capability.

- In organizations that do not employ standard costing, then the complete utilization of quantitative standards is impaired.

- Standard costing can be effective in both the process or job order type of cost accounting which includes all elements of cost.

- Predetermined standards are of significant importance to plant management in those industries involved in bids, proposals and production plans that are formulated far in advance of actual production. Historical costs are generally accumulated too late to be of maximum value.

CONSIDERATIONS IN SETTING STANDARDS

There are a number of factors to consider in establishing product cost standards. In labor standards, effect must be given to time spent on production tasks. Time is priced through labor rate application. In standardizing material costs, effort is directed toward type, quality, usage, and cost. Manufacturing overhead involves support and expenditures for indirect needs such as labor, supplies, utilities, and repairs.

Standard Costing for Realistic Cost Performance 83

Each cost element requires different approaches and considerations in establishing cost trend standards. More detailed aspects in the development of standards are as follows:

Direct Labor Standards

Exhibit 3-A displays an overview of the various considerations involved in direct labor standards. Before standard costs can be considered, the operational environment must be assessed in terms of its contribution to task performance. Since emphasis is placed on the employees' effectiveness, his surroundings can have a major effect on work accomplishment.

As shown in Exhibit 3-A, prime requisites in the working environment include a *logical plant layout,* wherein the flow of work is in sequential order,

CONSIDERATIONS IN SETTING STANDARDS

DIRECT LABOR

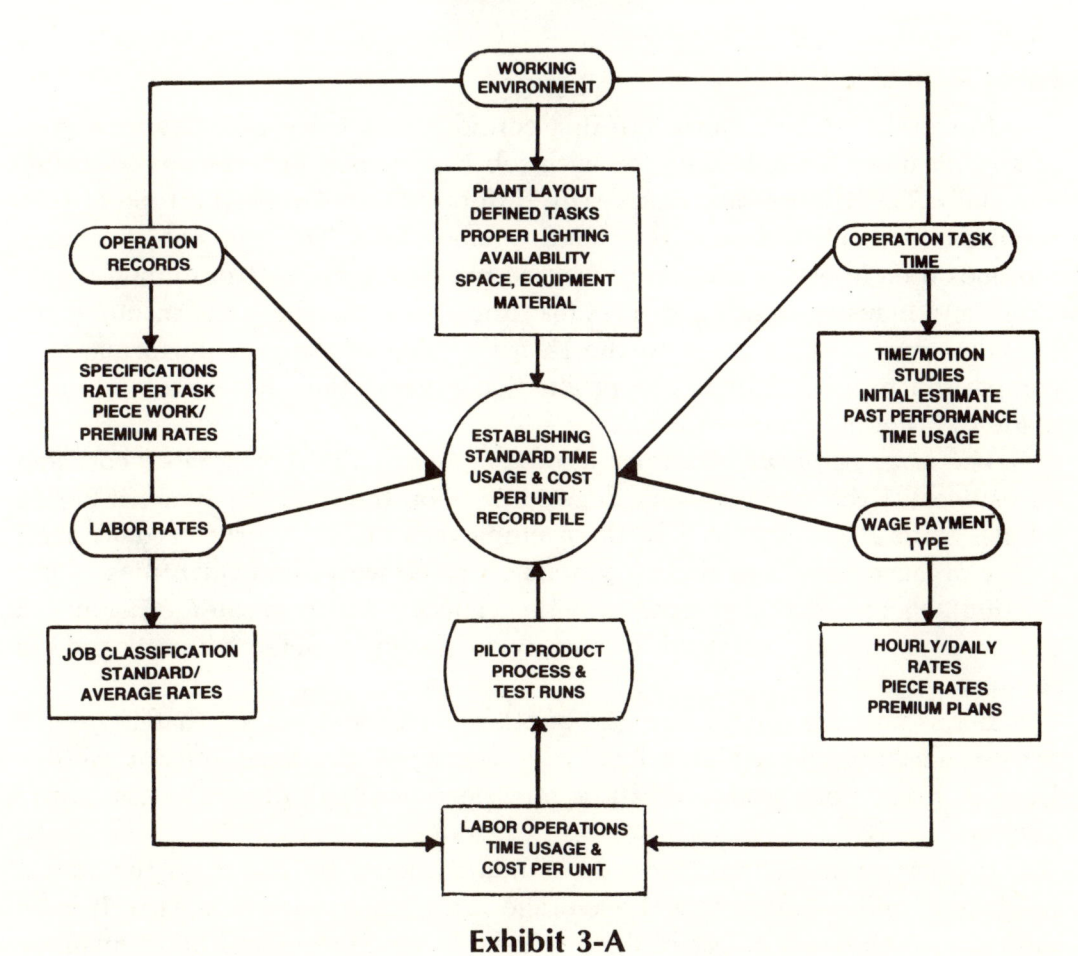

Exhibit 3-A

and sufficient space has been provided for the employee to perform his tasks. Proper *lighting* and *ventilation* are necessary. The specific operational *tasks* must be streamlined, clearly defined, and understood by the employee. *Equipment* must be operable, adequate, and available. Required quality *material* must be available when needed in the manufacturing process.

Time and motion studies must be conducted to determine the elapsed time required to perform each specific task. Each manual and machine operation is reviewed under prevailing working conditions to establish time usage allowance standards. The results are compared to averaged past performance and initial estimates to resolve differences before the standard is finalized. Actual task performance can only be satisfactorily measured by specific methods of operation and conditions that existed when the standards were set.

Engineers generally prepare the *operation record* that specifies the proper procedures and sequence of events in production. A cost rate per task is established. Piecework or premium rates are resolved as they pertain to the effort involved.

Labor Rate Standards

In setting rate standards, the first consideration is job classifications. A set of specifications is established for each job based upon experience, education, and skills. This is necessary in order to differentiate between the type of labor required for each task and the relative labor rate. The two most common methods used in establishing rates are the prevailing results from union negotiations and industry trends and rates for similar tasks. In the latter instance, due consideration must be given to the relative value of the task performance in comparison to other jobs in the production organization. Reference is usually made to historical average rates.

The *wage payment plan* must also be considered in setting labor cost standards because the rate may vary depending upon the type of payment. For example, some organizations pay their employees on an hourly or daily basis. Other organizations base their payment on piece work (unit quantities of production). Piece work payments provide an incentive to greater efficiency in performance but also can lead to poor workmanship in defective parts and material wastage.

Bonus and premium plans are another form of payment that is used to provide incentive for a higher level of efficiency. Using this payment method, labor costs per item produced can be on a declining basis due to increased production.

In most organizations, the rate standard should be based on the rate of production and payment that the average worker is expected to earn. It is the most simple approach to establishing standards. Piece rates and bonus plans require more analytical study to determine the true labor costs and to establish rates for production output cost performance.

Standard Costing for Realistic Cost Performance 85

Historical experience and time and motion studies provide the basis for establishing standard wage rates. On new product development, where different operational processes may be involved, test runs of pilot production are assessed and timed to establish attainable standard labor costs for acceptable production output.

Direct Material Standards

Product design, standards, composition characteristics, production methods, operating procedures, and indirect support are necessary before standardization of material costs can be achieved. Various technical specialists research the pertinent product relevant to the following:

- Type and quantity of raw materials to be maintained in inventory and used for specific parts.
- The task methods to be employed in manufacturing and the sequence of events in product production.
- Description and part requirements to be used in sub-assemblies and assemblies.
- Specific material specifications.

The various considerations involved in setting standards for direct material are noted in Exhibit 3-B and the following:

- Product investigation and determination of the basic characteristics such as size, weight, shape, proportions, and quality required.
- Engineer product design drawings relative to internal manufacture and outside purchases are developed.
- Detailed specifications are prepared for the required type and quantity of raw materials most economical to be used for specific parts as well as usage factors. Part description, manufacturing requirements, part listings for task processes and assemblies would be included.
- Standard raw material part lists are prepared and also part specifications concerned with the type assemblies required.
- Standard usage specifications include the quantities to be used in each manufacturing process.
- Assembled products require additional engineering data in the form of specifications or bills of material.
- Excess usage is used relative to shrinkage, scrap, and waste. A determinant standard factor is developed and included in the standard that indicates unavoidable losses.
- Material price standards reflect the unit cost for each type of material to be used.

CONSIDERATIONS IN SETTING STANDARDS
DIRECT MATERIAL

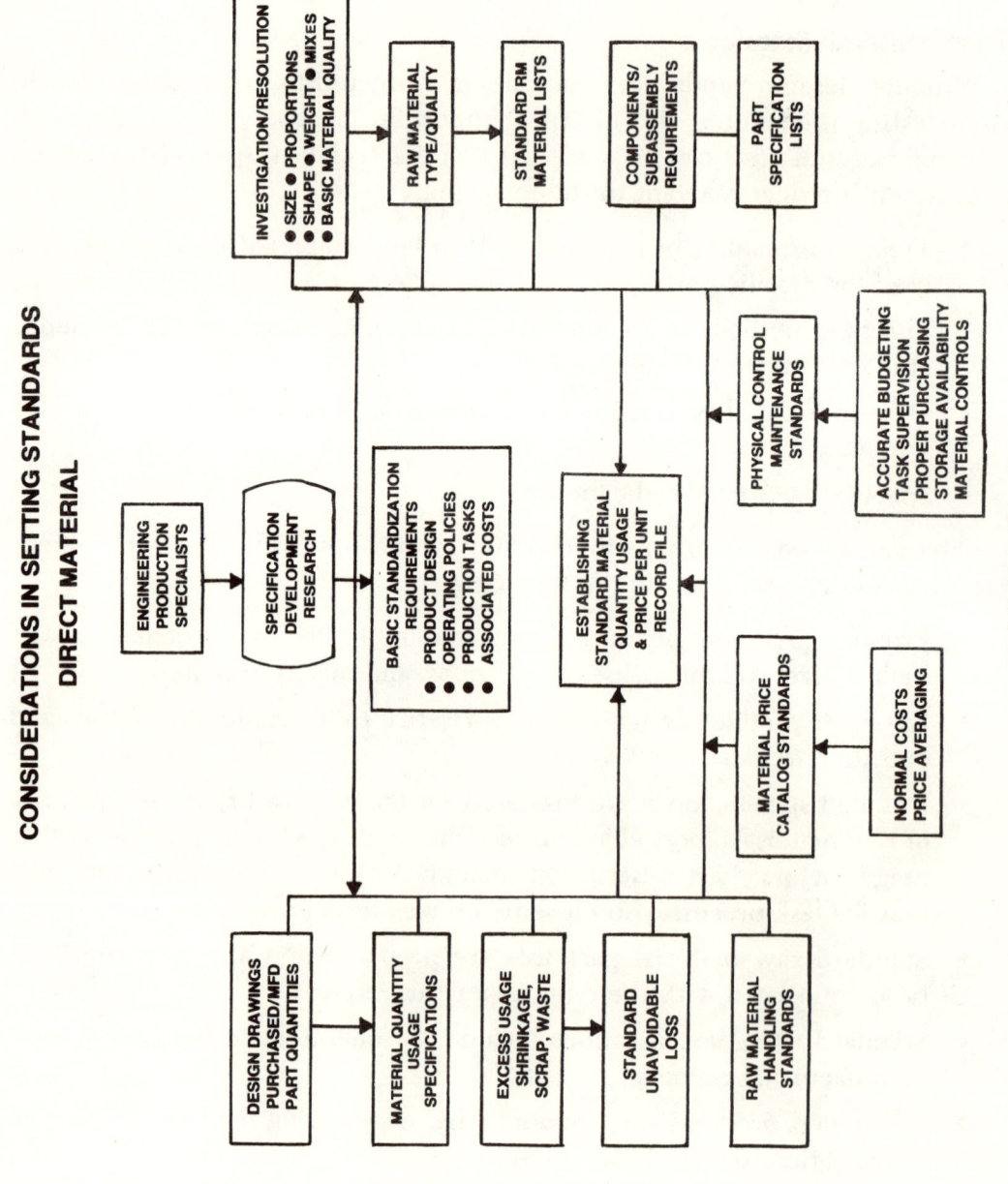

```
                    ┌─────────────────────────┐
                    │  INVESTIGATION/RESOLUTION│
                    │  • SIZE  • PROPORTIONS  │
                    │  • SHAPE • WEIGHT • MIXES│
                    │  • BASIC MATERIAL QUALITY│
                    └───────────┬─────────────┘
                                │
                                ▼
                    ┌─────────────────────────┐
                    │  RAW MATERIAL TYPE/QUALITY│
                    └───────────┬─────────────┘
                                │
                                ▼
                    ┌─────────────────────────┐
                    │  STANDARD RM MATERIAL LISTS│
                    └─────────────────────────┘

                    ┌─────────────────────────┐
                    │  COMPONENTS/SUBASSEMBLY │
                    │  REQUIREMENTS           │
                    └───────────┬─────────────┘
                                │
                                ▼
                    ┌─────────────────────────┐
                    │  PART SPECIFICATION LISTS│
                    └─────────────────────────┘
```

- **ENGINEERING PRODUCTION SPECIALISTS**
- **SPECIFICATION DEVELOPMENT RESEARCH**
- **BASIC STANDARDIZATION REQUIREMENTS**
  - PRODUCT DESIGN
  - OPERATING POLICIES
  - PRODUCTION TASKS
  - ASSOCIATED COSTS
- **ESTABLISHING STANDARD MATERIAL QUANTITY USAGE & PRICE PER UNIT RECORD FILE**
- **PHYSICAL CONTROL MAINTENANCE STANDARDS**
- **ACCURATE BUDGETING, TASK SUPERVISION, PROPER PURCHASING, STORAGE AVAILABILITY, MATERIAL CONTROLS**
- **MATERIAL PRICE CATALOG STANDARDS**
- **NORMAL COSTS, PRICE AVERAGING**
- **DESIGN DRAWINGS, PURCHASED/MFD PART QUANTITIES**
- **MATERIAL QUANTITY USAGE SPECIFICATIONS**
- **EXCESS USAGE, SHRINKAGE, SCRAP, WASTE**
- **STANDARD UNAVOIDABLE LOSS**
- **RAW MATERIAL HANDLING STANDARDS**

Exhibit 3-B

Standard Costing for Realistic Cost Performance   87

- A normal price level is developed for the material based on historical costs, trends, and current price data provided by procurement.

- The costs concerned with handling raw material are added to the unit standard cost. Based on historical experience, a cost factor is developed and applied to the standard unit cost. These costs include freight, receiving, storage, and allocated procurement costs.

- As shown in Exhibit 3-B, this control involves the items listed at the bottom of the exhibit that indicate the criteria for assessing material control processes.

The research and compilation of the data discussed above should provide a valid base to establish quantity usage and price standards. Although the initial research may be expensive in effort and cost, the results in savings, and cost effectiveness exceed the expenditures. The benefits are minimization or elimination of excessive variety in materials, reductions of inventory, better prices for procuring standard items in large volumes, and the avoidance of time delays in the availability of special items that are ordinarily in inventory.

Manufacturing Expense Standards

Manufacturing overhead involves those expenses that are not readily identifiable to a specific product as is the direct cost for labor and materials. Overhead is segregated into various expense accounts dependent upon the needs of the organization for allocation, control, and setting standards. The expenses are segregated by service and productive organizations. Service department expenses are allocated to productive departments on a predetermined and equitable basis which is predicated on historical experience; whereas, production department overhead is a direct charge to production. Manufacturing expense standards are more thoroughly discussed in Chapter 9.

RESPONSIBILITY FOR SETTING STANDARDS

There are varying levels of supervision who are responsible for setting standards, surveillance thereof, reporting, assessing results, and initiating revisions when major changes have occurred in production methods, equipment acquisitions, and product design. Responsibilities are delineated as follows, but they may differ somewhat among organizations due to organization structure and policies.

In some organizations, the standardization tasks are delegated to a steering committee. This committee remains in existence even after the initial standards have been developed. The purpose is to monitor results and make changes as the situation dictates. In smaller organizations, a special committee of concerned executives is established as a surveillance unit over standard cost activities. Department heads are usually charged with the responsibility of establishing standards and enforcing compliance.

Development of material usage standards are assigned to a *technical group* who have the necessary expertise and experience in the proper selection, control, and usage of the product material requirements.

The *procurement organization* is responsible for material price standards. Specialized buyers provide their intelligence relative to the trend of anticipated costs, market quotations, and pertinent history statistics.

The projected labor rates are usually the responsibility of the *controller* in conjunction with executive management. Labor rate changes can result from industrial trends, union negotiations, and anticipated general or merit payroll increases.

Foremen and/or first line supervision are accountable for proper utilization of material expended in terms of set standards. They should not be held responsible for deviations in material quantities used if the situation is caused by increased production volume requirements, product component changes, or management dictated policies affecting material usage. First line supervision should participate in establishing standards, since meeting and enforcing standards will be primarily under their control.

Standard Cost Variance Reporting

Each month or oftener variance reports are produced and provided to the operating management and the first line supervision. The reports provided to each person may vary somewhat in content and substance due to their specific needs. The operating management would receive reports for each organizational unit under their jurisdiction; whereas, first line supervision would only be provided a report relative to their own group in terms of budget or standard allowances, actual costs, and variances attributed to their operation.

COMPARATIVE EFFECTIVENESS IN SETTING STANDARDS

Standards are often classified as to their utilization and control measure objectives. The segregations fall into three prime categories that are often expressed with varying descriptive terms. The more common identifications are ideal, engineered attainable (based on sound engineering planning studies), and liberal or readily attainable standards.

Ideal Standard

This type of standard reflects a high degree of perfection that is generally unattainable on a *sustained basis*. This standard is considered to be ineffective for maintaining efficiency and the involved task-performing employees recognize this fact. On the one hand, the employee believes that reasonable performance was achieved but when the result is not up to management's expectation, it is difficult for either management or the employee to prove their relative position of an ideal accomplishment. The result is a conflict of understanding and frustration which could materialize in the loss of the employee's future motivation.

The problem is that the ideal standards were incorrectly based on the anticipated existence of perfect operational conditions such as efficient processing methods, no material wastage, machine down-time at a minimum, availability of proper equipment when required; in other words, the *ideal* environment.

Engineered Attainable Standard

This type of standard is achieved through the use of proper operational methods, adequate job orientation and training, skilled manpower, adequate equipment capability, and effective performance. Each of these requirements plays a vital role in establishing sound standards. Engineers conduct time and motion studies to determine and resolve existing capabilities described above. Based on their investigative findings, compatible and achievable standards are established. At this point, the engineering fact-finding group may recommend changes to achieve maximum efficiency. These could be changes in manufacturing processing methods, additional training, changes in plant layout, product redesign, material substitutions, or advanced equipment.

Readily Attainable Standard

This type of standard is generally based on possibly inadequate research and uncontrolled past experience and performance which has not been reflected in setting the standards. The standard may include an allowance for abnormal material usage or spoilage and employee time inefficiencies in performing their tasks. Under this type of standard, waste and inefficiencies are perpetuated and the results reflect an abnormal cost performance. It is management's responsibility to seek out and correct the inefficient use of labor, materials, and equipment and to revise the standards to reflect reasonable expectations.

From the above discussion, it is readily determinable that the most successful and effective standards are those that are based on *engineered attainable*. Scientific and statistical techniques by competent personnel have been employed in setting these standards. Equitable goals of achievement are provided for which employees can be held reasonably responsible to meet. This type of standard is very useful for effectively controlling costs and also for valuing inventories, since it includes all of the necessary expenditures for the product being produced and costed.

REVISION OF STANDARDS

Current standards should be revised when there are significant changes in labor rates, material prices, product modifications, or product task processing methods; otherwise, the standard may be invalid or non-representative as a tool for measuring performance.

Other reasons for making revisions to standards are if the original standard was incorrectly set or if it can be proven that the standard was inadequate from the standpoint of attainability. Current standards are generally changed once a year at the time that new budgets are developed or when it is necessary due to significant differences between the actuals and standards.

Procedure for Changing Standards

When standard costs are revised and retroactive, the changes must be reflected in inventory values and the surplus account. If the changes affect only future production, adjustments are unnecessary. Changes in material prices and usage affect only the work performance after revisions are made.

A situation may arise in which current tasks are under the old standards and new tasks will be measured by the revised standards. The most convenient accounting method for these transactions is to set up dual work in process accounts for data recording purposes. Subsequently, the old accounts will be closed upon task completion.

USE OF STANDARD COSTS IN ACCOUNTING

Standard costs can be effectively utilized to complement process cost or job order accounting systems. They are compatible with process costing because of the mass production characteristics that include significant output of standardized, uniform products. The process system is relatively inexpensive to implement. Monthly actuals are accumulated for a comparison to standards, and variances are calculated and analyzed.

Standards can be used with job order costing, but standard costs are more involved and expensive to develop, because they must be constantly revised to reflect the needs of each new type of special order. It is a time-consuming task as jobs have to be considered with relatively small dollar values.

STANDARD COST RECORDS

Individual organizations will differ on the type of cost records required to monitor and report on the standard cost performance. The general content of a manufacturing specification card would undoubtedly include operation task description on a step-by-step basis and the cost segregation of labor, material, and support service requirements to be used. The operation and cost elements are priced at standard cost and recorded on a standard cost card.

The size and complexity of an organization in terms of the number of different operations, parts, sub-assemblies and varying product lines will govern the number of card records to be required. The recording process is a natural for the computer in that masses of data can be manipulated, changed, summarized, and reported.

A typical product cost sheet contains the various labor operations in terms of standard time to be used and the labor cost that results from a standard wage rate application to time. The overhead rate is applied to direct labor hours or dollars to obtain overhead costs. The type material and/or product components are itemized under the material caption in terms of standard quantity to be used, its associated unit of measure, the price, and the dollar cost. Other non-manufacturing types of pertinent expenses are also shown. Operating profit margin plus 100% would be applied to the total cost to obtain a selling price per unit.

Source of Cost Data

Product standard costs are initially based on the manufacture of a prototype or *pilot* product. A series of test runs are conducted to determine and resolve the basic costs involved. The costs are analyzed in depth for consistency and realism. Unit standard costs are entered in the records for future product costing.

ADVANTAGES OF UTILIZING STANDARD COST

There are a number of benefits to be achieved from establishing an effective, reliable standard cost system. Specific advantages are noted as follows:

- Effective management tool in developing product price, cost proposal preparation, and production policies.

- Quantity and time standards represent a consistent unit of measurement for management in evaluating the operating efficiency of employees and organizations during different periods of time.

- Standards are desirable as incentives to employees, supervisors and executives because above standard performance would be a basis for monetary or other types of rewards.

- Standards permit the *principle of exception* wherein the attention of management is primarily directed toward problem areas of superior and below standard performance. The assumption is that if actual performance meets standard time and rate goals, then executive involvement is not required.

- Standard costing provides an economical means of cost accounting and generally results in time and effort savings in record keeping.

- When inventories are priced at standard cost, ledger records can be maintained in terms of quantities only. This situation eliminates clerical effort in pricing and item record reconciliations. Total standard cost of available inventory is readily computed by multiplying standard quantity by standard unit cost. If the average actual cost is required, it is obtained by multiplying standard cost by the ratio between actual and standard cost of the inventory. Both processes lend themselves to *computerization.*

- Using the standard cost approach, requisitions and bills of material can be prepared and priced more rapidly then when the product items must be priced at actual cost.

- Standard cost of finished goods upon completion can be rapidly ascertained by multiplying quantity by standard unit cost.

- Under the standard cost system, each involved employee undertakes his task with prior knowledge of the job standards. If the results do not meet the standard goals, the employee is accountable to supervision for variances from standards.

- Analysis and interpretation of costs can be significantly reduced by elimination of all details except those requiring attention as being unusual variances of actual costs from standards.

PROBLEMS ASSOCIATED WITH ACTUAL COST SYSTEMS

In the past and in some organizations today, too much emphasis was placed on the use of *actual costs* as a measure of an organization's operating efficiency and performance. This is not to say they are unimportant in operating a business from the standpoint of reality in reporting but, in many organizations where price lists, sales proposals, and production plans must be developed far in advance of actual production, actual costs are generally obtained too late to be of maximum value.

Actual costs are not necessarily a true reflection of efficient operations; they can include ineffective labor performance, excessive quantities of material usage, defective parts, idleness, time wastage, and inefficient operating methods.

In a progressive organization, management needs not only actual costs for analysis and reporting but also, more importantly, a means of evaluating and measuring the effectiveness of resource utilization in terms of labor, material, and indirect support costs. The tool most commonly used is the establishment of standards in their operations. Predetermined goals, reflected by standards for cost elements and efficient operating methods, provide a sound basis for developing pricing policies, planning production activities, and assessing the effectiveness of production.

Many cost systems require voluminous and costly record keeping activities that may not be realistically necessary if a standard cost system can fulfill the requirements.

ESTIMATING VERSUS STANDARDS

In *estimating*, emphasis is placed on actual costs which are considered to be representative reliable costs. The success of estimating is measured by the relative degree to which estimated costs coincide with actuals. Estimate revisions are based on actual costs during the pertinent period and the anticipation of changes in cost conditions expected for the future.

When *standards* are used, the emphasis is placed on what costs should be if the plant were operated efficiently with each supervisor, operating employee and relevant piece of equipment functioning at performance effectiveness in production. Standards determined at the beginning of a period are used as the barometer or guideline of efficiency. Standards are not revised unless they have been incorrectly established or unless major changes have occurred; too frequent revisions of standards make them unreliable as a basis for comparison.

STANDARD VERSUS BUDGETED COSTS

Budgeted and standard costs are predetermined costs that are used for performance evaluation. *Budgeted costs* are not true standard costs; they are what costs are expected to be after careful analyses have been made of past and present costs and anticipated future conditions. Budget cost is developed from actual costs that will prevail and be significant in the future if current operating procedures are continued. Minor effort, if any, is pursued to change existing conditions or to make projections of cost-directional changes, even though plant operations were to become highly efficient.

Accuracy of the budget is directly determined by the validity and reliability of cost data used in developing the budget. Standard costs are considered to be a more reliable source of data for budgeting than estimates of cost developed by other means. Budgeting can be of major importance and usefulness in setting material price standards, direct labor, and overhead rates.

Budgets have a greater scope than standard costs since they reflect *all* aspects of costs and income objectives for *all* organizational functions. Standard costs are generally confined to operational costs.

Standard costs complement the budgeting process; the product quantity requirements are determined after the sales forecast and inventory levels have been resolved. The next step is to determine the manufacturing costs as a basis for obtaining the cost of sales for the income statement, and inventory balances for the balance sheet.

ASPECT OF COST REDUCTION

In many organizations, cost reduction programs are not on a continuing basis but rather sporadic and triggered by circumstance(s). For example, it may result from learning that a competitor's similar product is being sold for less; customer negotiations reveal that the overhead rate is too high in comparison with competitors' proposals; there is a *tight squeeze* on maintaining an adequate cash flow; a mandatory edict comes from top management of a 15% cost reduction; profit goals are not being achieved.

When one or more of these situations occur, an all out effort is put forth by those concerned to scrutinize every activity and process to determine cost problem areas to achieve reductions. After the *fire drill* has been completed and necessary reductions effected, complacency returns once again until the next *panic* occurs. To overcome this situation, the cost reduction program must be a prioritized and systematic objective that is constantly under the surveillance of top management. Goals must be continually reviewed, and if accomplishments exceed set *bogies*, the concerned employees should be rewarded.

Cost Reduction Criteria

To effect this type of program, certain criteria must exist and be adherred to such as the following:

- Establish a cost reduction group reporting to responsible management whose prime responsibilities would be to seek out areas where cost reductions could be effected, and initiate the necessary effort to accomplish them. This effort must be on a continuing basis.

- Initiate an employee suggestion program in which employees would be rewarded for cost reduction suggestions that result in actual savings.

- Management must set specific goals for cost reduction and continually review the results.

- All operations must be reviewed and considered as potential candidates for cost reduction opportunities.

- Cost reduction reporting on a routine basis is a *must*, and the results should receive appropriate management review and attention. A means must be initiated to adequately check the results.

Dynamic management must always be seriously concerned with future events that can affect the effectiveness of their operations and profit goals. Although standards play a vital role in cost control, this is not enough to a progressive management who must always have as their prime objective—the search for opportunities to reduce costs.

Significance of the Learning Curve

It is a natural assumption that the employee will improve his effectiveness with time and repetitiveness in performing his tasks. This progress should improve the quality and quantity of the output. *Learning or progress* curves occur among individuals, organizations, and industries. The competent worker improves his proficiency in task performance, and the organization gains in terms of lower costs. As a result of the *learning* process, standard costs should be on a relative declining basis. This favorable situation can only happen from integrating standard cost accounting with advanced concepts resulting from the scientific management approach to planning activities.

ADOPTING STANDARD COSTS FOR SMALL ORGANIZATIONS

In some small organizations, there exists a misunderstanding as to the use and value of a standard cost system. The assumption of both management and the cost accountant is that standard cost is generally associated with large and complex organizations that are characterized by multi-product output and varied operational procedures. In a sense, this may be true. A modified approach to standard costing, as discussed below, may however provide a favorable assurance that this type of costing can also be successfully employed by smaller organizations.

Small Business Environment

In the small business, operational control is primarily effected by the owner. He or she is cognizant of all activities that are occurring in his operation, is involved in each major decision, and conducts his enterprise based on his judgment and experience. As the business expands, he is practically forced to delegate responsibility and authority to others for performance control and decision-making. At this point, the advantages of standard cost become important in establishing realistic product(s) sales price, setting up cost objectives, valuing inventory, and monitoring and controlling costs through cost performance reporting.

In initiating a standard cost system in a small organization, the following approach can be pursued. First, the individual(s) concerned with this project familiarizes himself with the objectives and general requirements of the system. Second, the individual assesses product components and operational tasks in terms of associated quantities, time effort, and costs. This evaluation should lead to establishing initial estimates that might reflect a rough order of magnitude. These estimates are a start and a means for future improvements in quality and accuracy. This effort is pursued in conjunction with qualified operating personnel who know and understand product production. Third, the beginning standard cost system is expanded as required to meet new needs. As time passes, advanced techniques are added for evaluating and setting standards.

Direct Labor Standards

In reviewing the operations, the amount of time required to perform each task and the type of individual skill involved are determined. Wage rates are predicated on standard job classification with allowances for future increases.

Task hours are accumulated by individual, operation and/or machine, product, and organization. The application of the wage rate to the hours will provide standard labor costs.

Actual hours worked by the categories listed above are accumulated both on the weekly payroll card and on the task shop order. In the computerized process, labor is entered into the system from remote terminal input devices for further processing.

Actual labor costs are compared to the standards, and deviations are determined. The variances consist of time and rate differences. An evaluation of variances indicates problem areas for corrective action—inefficient time performance or a need for revising standards in terms of attainable standards. Production time is costed at standard.

Direct Labor Variance Analysis

Exhibit 3-C provides an overview of variance analysis for direct labor in terms of performance or efficiency and wage rates. A description of this system follows:

- *Time standards* are established for each task performance.
- *Standard wage rates* are predetermined for each job classification based on historical data evaluation and future anticipations.
- *Application of wage rates* to the operational time standards results in a standard cost for task performance. Standard hours and cost are further summarized by product.
- A *daily time card* or direct computer input from station keyboard devices provides actual hours spent and prevailing wage rate.
- Information from the daily time card is accumulated weekly in order to compute the direct *employees' weekly earnings* which represent direct labor costs by product. These data are also used for the labor distribution journal.
- The *actual hours expended* and the wage rates by classification are recorded and accumulated in the actual direct labor hour summary file. Standard wage rates are applied at month end to obtain actual hours at standard wage rates.
- *Actual quantity produced* is converted into standard hours that are recorded and accumulated in the standard direct labor hour summary file. The standard wage rates are applied to the standard hours to obtain standard hours at standard wage rates. The derived standard costs are charged to the production inventory.
- The *standard costs* are compared to the *actual hours at standard rates* to obtain the performance variance. The actual hours at standard rates

Standard Costing for Realistic Cost Performance 97

**DIRECT LABOR VARIANCE ANALYSIS
SMALL ORGANIZATIONS**

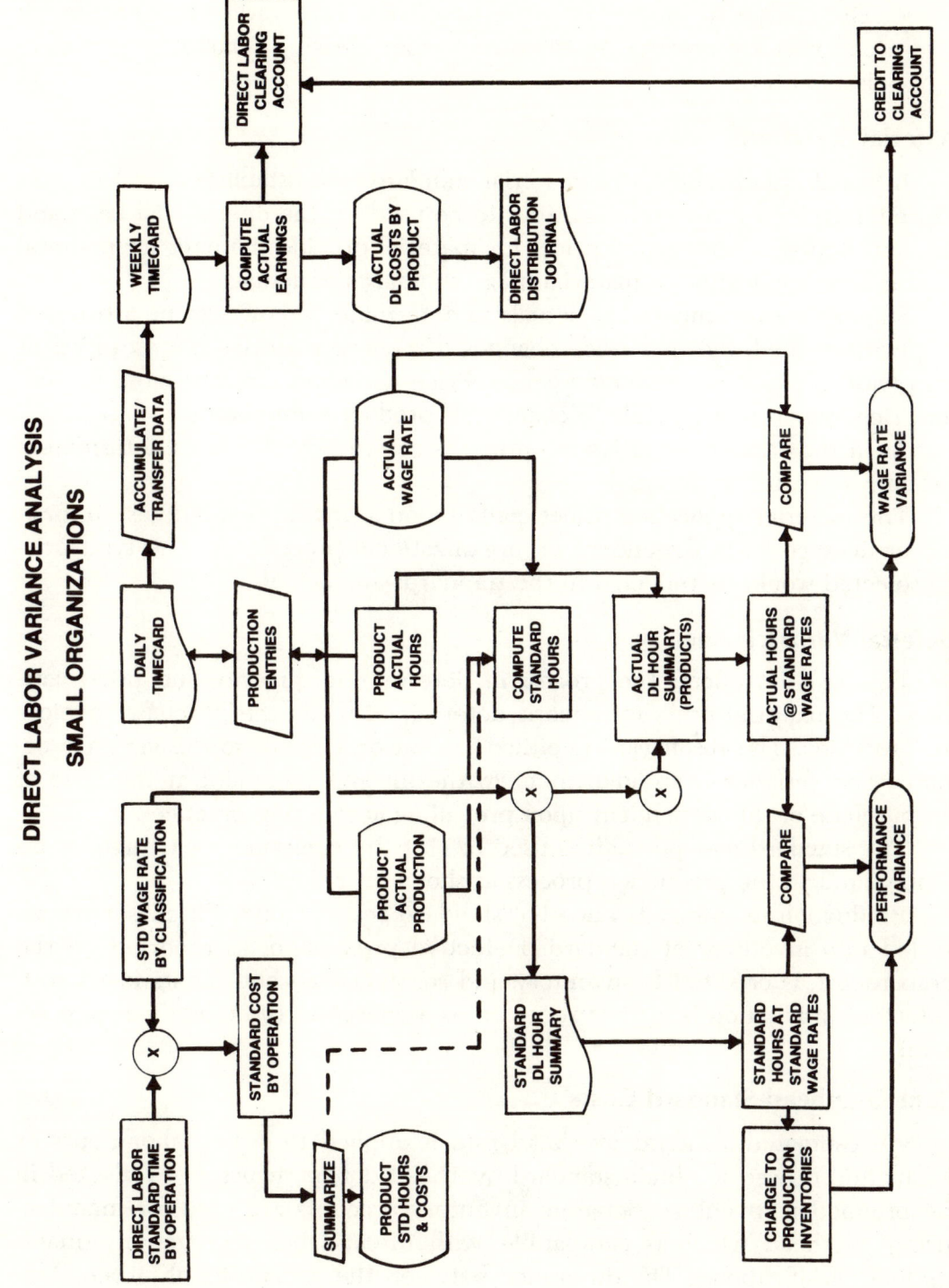

Exhibit 3-C

are compared to actual labor costs by product to derive the *wage rate variance*.

- The charge to *production inventory*, wage rate variances, and payroll earnings are credited to the direct labor clearing account as shown in Exhibit 3-C.

Material Standards

In small organizations, the material standards are established on the basis of predetermined types and quantities to be used for the operational tasks and product. Actual or anticipated prices for material provide the basis for material costing after application to material usage standards or actuals.

Standards are compared to actuals to determine variances to be attributed to quantities used and unit price changes. Excessive material usage can result from wastage, spoilage, or obsolescence. Price variances are attributed to vendor price increases or possibly to changes of product components.

As in the case of direct labor, variances are reviewed, causes determined, and corrective action initiated.

The material application prices could be on a first-in, first-out; last-in, first-out; or average basis, dependent on organizational procedures. The type pricing selected would be reflected in the standards and actuals.

Material Variance Analysis

Exhibit 3-D reflects the process in determining quantity and price variances. The material price variance is determined when the purchase invoices are processed. The result can be either a debit or a credit to the variance account. The variance is an adjustment to the income statement at the time of the purchase or sale dependent upon prevailing accounting practices.

The standard cost per unit is used to cost the component part and/or assembly units in the production process as shown in Exhibit 3-D.

Production inventory is valued at standard cost per unit. Purchases are recorded into inventory at standard. Defective production, as reported on the scrap report, is credited to inventory and so are sales—both at standard cost. Defective production is further reported as a charge to the usage variance account.

Plant Overhead Standard Costs

An estimated standard overhead rate is applied to direct labor hours or dollars and is used to obtain standard overhead dollars, which are reflected in the production inventory. Separate inventory accounts are used for manufacturing overhead which is compatible with direct labor segregations (major product classifications). The difference between the actual and absorbed standard overhead dollars are charged or credited to the overhead variance accounts.

DIRECT MATERIAL VARIANCE ANALYSIS
SMALL ORGANIZATION

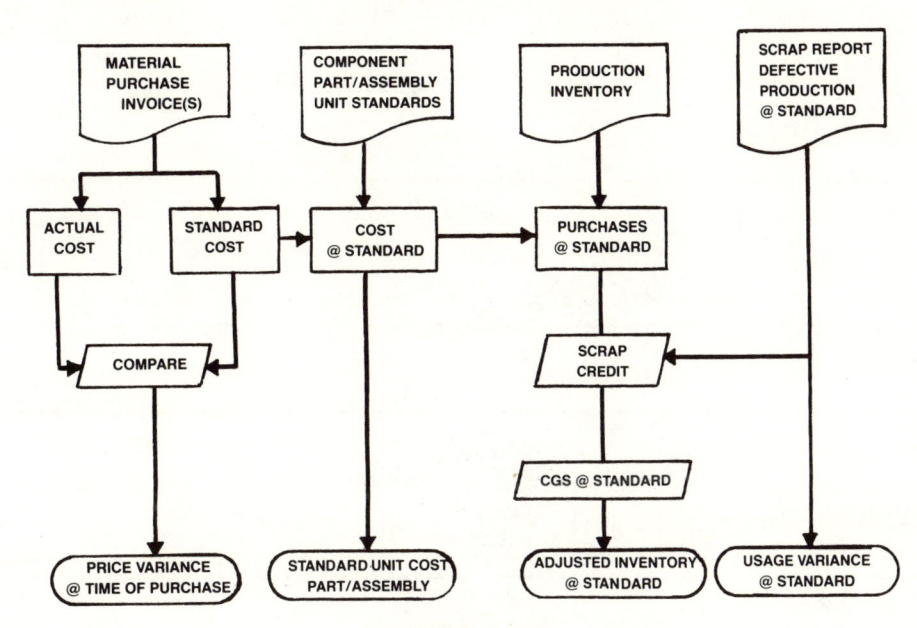

Exhibit 3-D

Summary

The discussion on initiating a standard cost system in a small business provides the basic steps involved. The system can be expanded or contracted according to the needs and dictates of the organization. It is definitely a start in the right direction to achieve operational performance reporting, inventory valuation, and basis for setting selling prices. Using a computerized system will provide management with a reliable tool for evaluating their organization's operational efficiency and gaining greater control over costs.

DIRECT LABOR VARIANCE DEVELOPMENT

In most organizations, labor costs represent a significant part of the total product costs, particularly, when employee benefits are recognized as part of the labor costs. Under the standard cost concept, the prime concern is with actual direct labor expenditures, since employee benefits (as reported in the overhead expenses) can be significant.

Evaluating labor variances requires an understanding of the specific factors involved in standard versus actual labor costs. Standard direct labor costs consist of the total standard time established for performing a task multiplied by a standard wage rate. Actual direct labor costs reflect the actual time expended in performing pertinent tasks multiplied by the actual average rate plus any direct incentive or bonus compensations.

As shown in Exhibit 3-E, there are basically two types of labor variances involved—wage rate and time deviations—which are discussed as follows.

DIRECT LABOR VARIANCE DEVELOPMENT

	HOURS		RATE	TOTAL VARIANCE	DOLLARS
STANDARD	40	X	3.00		120.00
ACTUAL	36	X	3.05		109.80
TOTAL DIRECT LABOR VARIANCE					10.20 (FAVORABLE)

	STANDARD RATE		TIME VARIANCE TIME DIFFERENTIAL		
	3.00	X	(40 − 36) 4	12.00 (FAVORABLE)	
ALTERNATE APPROACH	STANDARD RATE		ACTUAL HOURS		STANDARD DIRECT LABOR
	3.00	X	36 =	108.00 −	120.00 12.00 (FAVORABLE)

	ACTUAL HOURS		RATE VARIANCE RATE DIFFERENTIAL		
	36	X	.05	1.80 (UNFAVORABLE)	
ALTERNATE APPROACH	ACTUAL HOURS		STANDARD RATE		ACTUAL DIRECT LABOR
	36	X	3.00 =	108.00 −	109.80 1.80 (UNFAVORABLE)

Exhibit 3-E

Rate Variance

The difference between the set standard and the actual wage rate represents the variance. The differences can be attributed to a number of prime factors such as:

- Unrealistic or inadequate standard rate development resulting from unexpected union negotiations, general increases, or competitive labor market influences.

- Inappropriate use of higher skilled job classifications for lower level task operating personnel.

- Changes in job skill requirements or mix of tasks in a given organization due to introduction of new equipment or technology improvements.

Standard Costing for Realistic Cost Performance 101

- Initiation of incentive and bonus plans.

In assessing the rate variances, there must be a concerted effort by all concerned to ascertain the specific causes for the differences, so that corrective action can be properly exercised—either operating environment changes or revised standards.

Time Variance

In analyzing labor time variances, there are a number of specific factors which are delineated as follows:

- Insufficient time was allowed in the standard to perform the task efficiently. Standards may have been set too high with no time allowance for machine down-time, rework, material substitutes or unavailability, delays in work flow, and idle time.

- Inadequate time was provided for machine setup. This is a necessity prior to production runs. It should be an added factor to the physical performance of the task.

- Standards should include appropriate time for employees to clean up their immediate areas or tools, obtain further training orientation, assemble materials, and attend approved meetings.

After consideration has been given to the above factors, it can be determined if the variance resulted from efficient or inefficient operations.

Labor Variance Calculations

Exhibit 3-E reflects the process of computing time and rate analyses, which are vital in assessing operational performance. As illustrated, there was a *net favorable variance* of $10.20 which is attributed to the difference between a favorable time variance of $12.00 and an unfavorable rate variance of $1.80. Two approaches are used in calculating the time and rate variances. Possible causes for the deviations are discussed above.

DIRECT MATERIAL VARIANCE DEVELOPMENT

The two major factors in direct material variances are quantity usage and price. In organizations in which material costs are significant, the analysis of the variances is important to measure performance.

Price Variance

Exhibit 3-F displays actual material costs based on inventory and purchase invoice records. Material quantity requisitions or facsimile documentation is the basis for establishing material usage. Both price and quantity can be by

DIRECT MATERIAL VARIANCE DEVELOPMENT

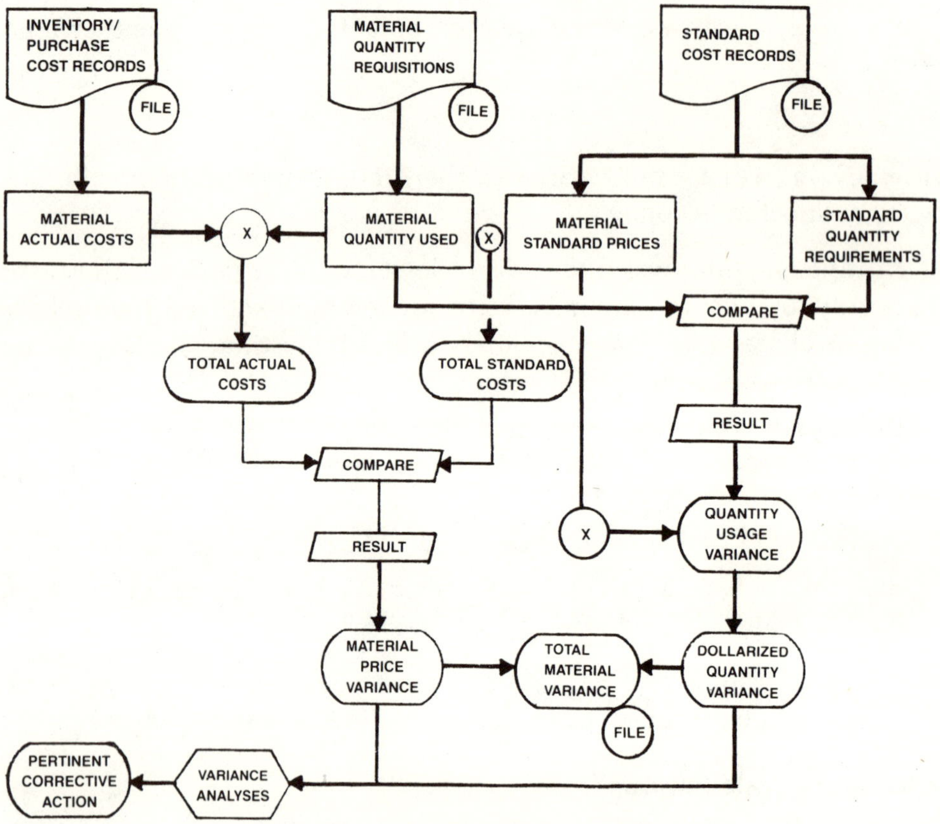

Exhibit 3-F

unit part identity or class of material product line. Standards are developed on a similar basis.

Material quantity used in the unit measure (part, product) required is multiplied by the material price and summarized to total actual cost. Standard cost records include unit price and quantity requirements. To determine the price variance, actual quantity usage is multiplied by the standard price; the difference from the actuals is the variance.

This variance represents either a favorable price variance, wherein purchase costs are less than standard, or vice versa. If the variance is favorable, the appropriate journal entry is to debit materials in process account and credit material price variance. If the variance is unfavorable, then the journal record reflects a reverse entry.

Quantity Variance

As shown in Exhibit 3-F, the actual quantity used is compared to the standard quantity allowance; the result represents either an excess use or a favor-

Standard Costing for Realistic Cost Performance 103

able below standard use. In either case, the quantity difference is multiplied by the standard unit price(s) to obtain the dollarized quantity variance.

The sum of the material price and quantity variances represents the total variance attributed to direct material. Variances are evaluated to determine the cause(s), and corrective action is initiated either to revise the standards if unrealistic or to resolve inefficient material usage or procurement problems.

ADVANCED CONCEPTS ON STANDARDS

Although considerable improvement has been made in the development and usage of standards over the years, progressive organizations are continually *on the alert* for more advanced methods to enhance their standard cost objectives. Generally, predetermined standard costs are used to evaluate the operating supervisor's performance in controlling costs. Under advanced concepts, additional type standards are developed to measure top management's performance in creating an effective environment for further cost reductions, with primary emphasis on cost trends rather than control. This type of standard provides management with additional information as to future cost reduction trends to expect in each operation and product. Further, managers must provide the necessary incentives to make the goals achievable.

Advanced Criteria for Consideration

- Under a standard cost system, historical information is available as to the standard cost for operational tasks and products over a period of years. Properly organized, the records show the directional trends of standard cost per unit. Undoubtedly, the trends reflect increases, decreases, or possibly an *even keel* situation.

- The significance of *cost vectors* (directional trends) can further be emphasized by multiplying the unit standard costs by the annual production to obtain total dollar deviations assessed to operations and products.

- Standard cost increases and static levels should be reviewed and evaluated to determine the causes for this situation. By calculating the rate of change of vectors, an index number can be calculated that reflects the coefficient of change characteristics of the standards.

- In the advanced concept on standards, standard indices of improvement are established as future goals, which indicate the level of efficiency required in the operational learning curve. Management reviews present standards with the new objectives to determine deviations which indicate if cost reductions are following the pattern of the learning curve trends.

Basically, cost effectiveness can only result from the drive, goal-setting, and resourcefulness of a dynamic management.

FUTURE OUTLOOK OF STANDARD COSTING

Undoubtedly, the use of standard costing will continue to grow and expand as more advanced and computerized techniques are explored and incorporated into the system. Management must be more directly involved and be aware of the advantages to be derived from greater cost standardization, visibility, control and improving operational performance. Some common observations on expanding use of standard cost systems are noted as follows:

- Increasing amount of literature is appearing in accounting/planning periodicals relative to new approaches, procedures, and techniques that are being explored, initiated, and/or being used.

- Standard costing philosophy is being applied to other facets of an organization's operation such as (1) planning, (2) data analysis, (3) interpretation and audit, and (4) achievement of exception reporting needs through application of predetermined statistical formulas.

- NASA and DOD costing procedures are placing greater emphasis on standard costing as a means to achieve control objectives on government contracts.

- The standard cost approach is being used for formulating incentive programs on fixed price contracts. Government agencies are becoming increasingly involved in the use of predetermined cost as a basis for evaluating bids and proposals, performance measurement, and compliance to their objectives.

- Management executives are seeking new approaches to capitalize on advanced practices and procedures relative to cost standardization and control.

- Quantitative techniques and applications are being explored and implemented as a means of resolving standard cost related problems. The applications include the concept of cost vectors discussed above.

COMPUTERIZATION AND STANDARD COSTING

The computer has proven to be an extremely valuable tool in operating a standard cost system. After realistic standards have been established and programmed, many split-second solutions to complicated and time-consuming questions can be achieved. The computer provides the capability and flexibility for making timely revisions to standards and calculating variances from actuals for measuring performance results. Data reporting is easily effected. Comparisons between old and revised standards can be made to isolate specific differences and determine the cause(s). Further, new standards can be assessed in terms of the effects resulting from decisions relative to different product output requirements.

Actual cost trends can be plotted by the computer with an overlay of standard cost projections to determine and verify the validity of standards used in relation to actual developments. Computerization is cost effective and provides change flexibility and a rapid means for manipulating standard and actual cost data.

STANDARD COSTING POINTERS

Standard costing is a vital, viable, dynamic tool for predetermining realistic cost data for product pricing and performance measurement. Prevailing fallacies and misconceptions are pinpointed in this chapter relative to the true meaning and objectives of standard costing. The considerations and criteria involved in establishing useful standards are provided to serve as an aid in determining whether standard costing will successfully benefit your operations, and to what extent a computerized approach will effect cost savings. The approach to setting standards is outlined to provide reliable, succinct guidance to an organization pursuing the development of standard costing techniques. Standard costing for small organizations is explored and the significant advantages defined. Advanced concepts on standards and the future role of standard cost usefulness and utilization are highlighted.

4

Procedural Cost Accounting: Prime Tool for Assessing the Cost Estimate

Most organizations engaged in producing a product or performing a service have some form of cost accounting in order to accumulate, assess and record costs as a means to realistically price their product or service. Further, the data provides an analytical approach to establishing attainable operational goals that are essential to effective cost control and performance evaluation. Also, the data is used for various financial records and reports.

This requirement does not necessarily imply that the historical cost statistics and accounting records will be directly associated with their cost estimating activities; however, it is most advantageous if they are interfaced, as appropriate. Cost accounting data are the basic source for detailed operational cost associated with a product and provide a means to establish, monitor, and verify the validity of cost estimates.

Successful cost estimating systems are generally predicated on some form of appropriate relevancy to cost accounting systems and records. This chapter will discuss various accounting procedures that are pertinent to the realistic development and assessment of cost estimate projections.

COST ESTIMATE SYSTEM OVERVIEW

A cost estimating system represents the use of predetermined product unit costs which include direct labor, material, and manufacturing overhead as a basis for (1) costing work in process (WIP), (2) costing finished goods (FG) inventories, (3) reflecting costs in the accounting records, (4) comparing cost estimates with actuals, and (5) computing variances for analysis and corrective action decisions. This type of costing can provide an abbreviated method of product unit costing without necessarily (in some organizations) maintaining formal detailed accounting records.

System Characteristics

Costs are estimated by unit of production and segregated by elements of cost. At the beginning of each activity period, cost estimates are projected for each product and/or product line. During the activity period, the segregated actual costs are accumulated, recorded in summary ledger accounts, and compared to the estimates to ascertain various variances.

Cost data comparisons are made by product total, organization, and/or cost element. It is common in some organizations to make comparisons for all

Procedural Cost Accounting 109

of the segregations above in order to provide a basis for a more thorough analysis and evaluation of the resultant variances. The periodic review and comparison of estimates and actuals provide the means for intelligent revision and updating of estimates as required. Cost of sales and inventory valuations are affected by the cost estimate.

This type of cost system is generally utilized in situations wherein (1) the products are few and comparable in physical characteristics, (2) the manufacturing processes are relatively simple and stabilized, and (3) there are only minor cost fluctuations between accounting periods.

System Requirements

The system requirements include a schedule of estimated costs and inventory as well as a detailed analysis of the cost of sales.

The *cost estimate schedule* is developed by product/product line and detailed by type operation or task relative to time and cost elements. In addition to the basic costs, the summary schedule includes a percent application for G & A/selling expenses and profit to derive the gross selling price.

An *inventory schedule* is maintained in order to cost work in process. A typical schedule format is illustrated below.

INVENTORY SCHEDULE
Work in Process

Department _____									Date _____	
		LABOR			MATERIAL			OVERHEAD		
Product Identification	Quantity	Unit Price	Completion Percent	Sub Total Costs	Unit Price	Completion Percent	Sub Total Costs	Unit Price	Completion Percent	Sub Total Costs
Sub total costs by product are summarized to obtain total WIP.										

Raw material and finished goods ledgers are maintained to provide perpetual inventory records. Physical inventory checks are periodically conducted to verify the book account records. When variances occur and are validated, the required adjustments are reflected in the records. The inventory is costed on the basis of cost estimates and completion stage by element of cost as illustrated above.

As products are sold, a *cost of sales analysis* is prepared and a typical format is illustrated below.

COST OF SALES ANALYSIS

Product Identification	Quantity Sold	LABOR		MATERIAL		OVERHEAD		TOTAL
		Unit Cost	Sub Total Costs	Unit Cost	Sub Total Costs	Unit Cost	Sub Total Costs	Cost of Sales

The inventory schedule is used as a basis for preparing the cost of sales data which is recorded in the accounting records and periodically reflected in the income statement.

ESTIMATE SYSTEM VERSUS STANDARD COST

Cost estimates are often similar in some respects to standard cost objectives relevant to the following common goals:

- Probable product costs are predetermined before labor effort, material, and support costs are committed and expended.

- Product sales decision-making is predicated on future cost anticipations, particularly, with respect to price quotations.

- The effect on future costs is determined when changes are planned in upgrading equipment, material substitutions, and/or revised operational procedures.

- Cost assessment of new products or services is made before production and sales effort are initiated, in order to ensure a profitable return on the contemplated resource investment.

- Both systems involve the establishment of goals for the work effort and cost expenditures in order to control costs and measure performance.

COST ESTIMATE ACCOUNTING PROCESS

The various steps in the cost estimating process are presented in Exhibit 4-A. This exhibit outlines the accounting debit and credit transactions relative to the stores account, work in process inventory, finished goods, and cost of sales. The WIP inventory is also ascertained and verified by a physical inventory which represents a more accurate value, but the time element and cost involved would make this approach prohibitive on a continuing repetitive basis.

After the cost estimates have been reconciled with actuals, the revised data provide new estimate information for use in future projections.

COST DETERMINATION CRITERIA

As a basis for estimating, costs are predetermined through the use of historical accounting records or in terms of anticipated cost approximations. If properly organized, accounting records provide detailed and summary cost data. The detailed records include costs by (1) organization, (2) type of equipment or manufacturing process, and (3) product part (subassembly and assembly). If it is determined that the future operational environment and costs will be comparable to those of the past, then the historical records will provide the

Procedural Cost Accounting

ACCOUNTING PROCEDURE FOR COST ESTIMATES

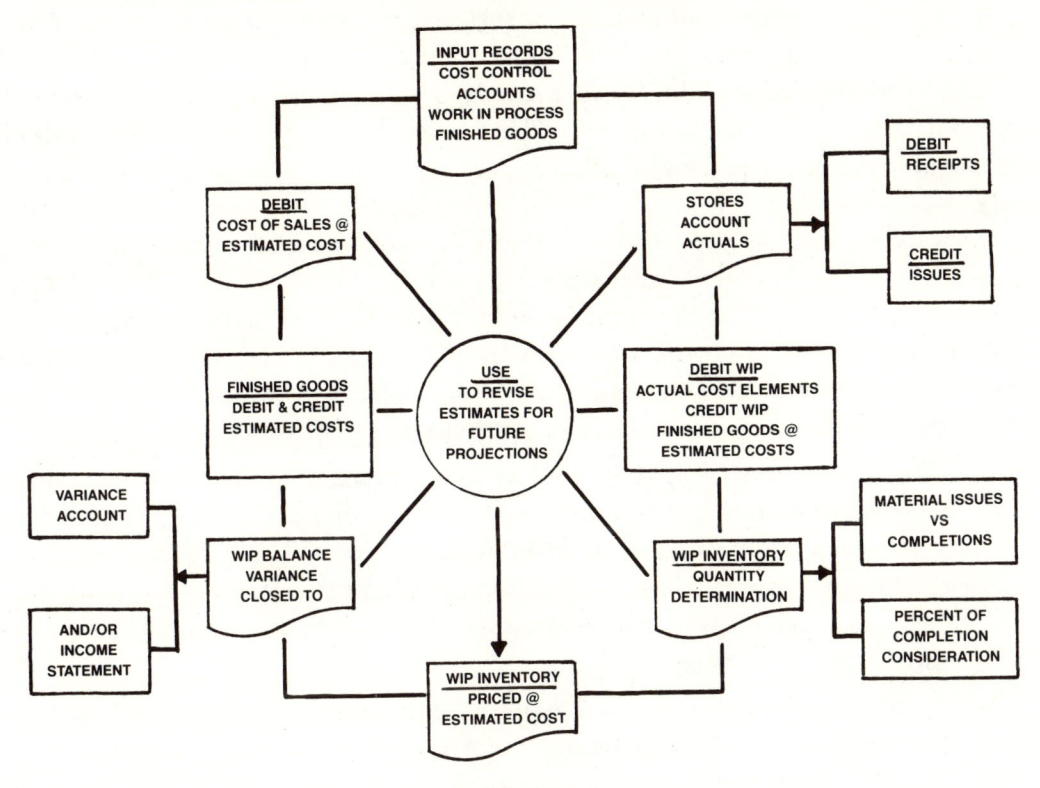

Exhibit 4-A

basis for cost estimating. Any known or anticipated changes are reflected in the projected cost data.

In small and uncomplicated operational organizations, the maintenance of detailed formal accounting records may be prohibitive in terms of practicability and costs; therefore, informal cost approximations may be more compatible to their estimating needs. A compromise would be to make periodic test checks of actual costs to determine unit product costs and trends as a basis for estimating future costs.

Cost approximations represent estimates that may or not be based on formalized accounting records dependent upon the complexity, data availability, and needs of the organization. Product cost assessment can be based on the judgment and experience of the estimator, who associates actual or anticipated cost to the product labor and material requirements. Product specifications are used to establish the needs in terms of material and processing requirements, and anticipated costs are based on historical and current market trend of prices for raw material and prevailing or anticipated employee wage rates and time effort.

PROCEDURAL ACCOUNTING SYSTEMS

A cost system is defined as being a systematic record of all financial transactions relative to the functional activities of engineering, production, distribution, and administration. The basic records involve journals, ledgers, account categories, and operating statements. The design of a cost system is dependent on type of product, equipment in use, and production methods and requirements.

Various accounting procedures are used for cost estimate development and evaluation and also for deriving variances. In some organizations, the cost estimates are independent of the general ledger system, and comparisons are not made on that basis due to the time constraints (monthly reporting). The more formal, analytical approach to cost estimate accounting is to employ prescribed accounting systems or methods such as the following:

- *Continuous process accounting* is used for mass production operations wherein the item output represents similar or standardized type products which are processed in an identical manner. Under this procedure, the produced items lose their singular identity. Separate work in process accounts are used for each element of cost in order to compare cost estimates with actuals.

- *Job order accounting* is used when cost estimates are reflected on production orders and accounting records, for comparative and statistical analysis utilization.

- *Alternate methods* such as (1) separate work in process accounts for each product unit produced, (2) accounts for each element of cost for each production department, or (3) a single WIP account for all cost elements.

A more detailed discussion of the above accounting systems and methods is provided as follows:

CONTINUOUS PROCESS ACCOUNTING

This commonly used method requires the recording of cost estimates in the general ledger accounts. In typical mass production operations, it is costly and impractical to compare estimates and actuals on a daily basis. Generally, average cost per unit on a period basis satisfies the comparison requirements.

Exhibit 4-B illustrates the accounting process relative to using separate WIP accounts for each element of cost. The objectives in this computerized system are to calculate variances by cost element, work in process, and finished goods inventories and also to effect their relief (transfer) to the cost of sales.

The following steps occur in the mechanical process (see Exhibit 4-B).

Procedural Cost Accounting 113

PROCESS ACCOUNTING PROCEDURE (INVOLVING COST ESTIMATES)

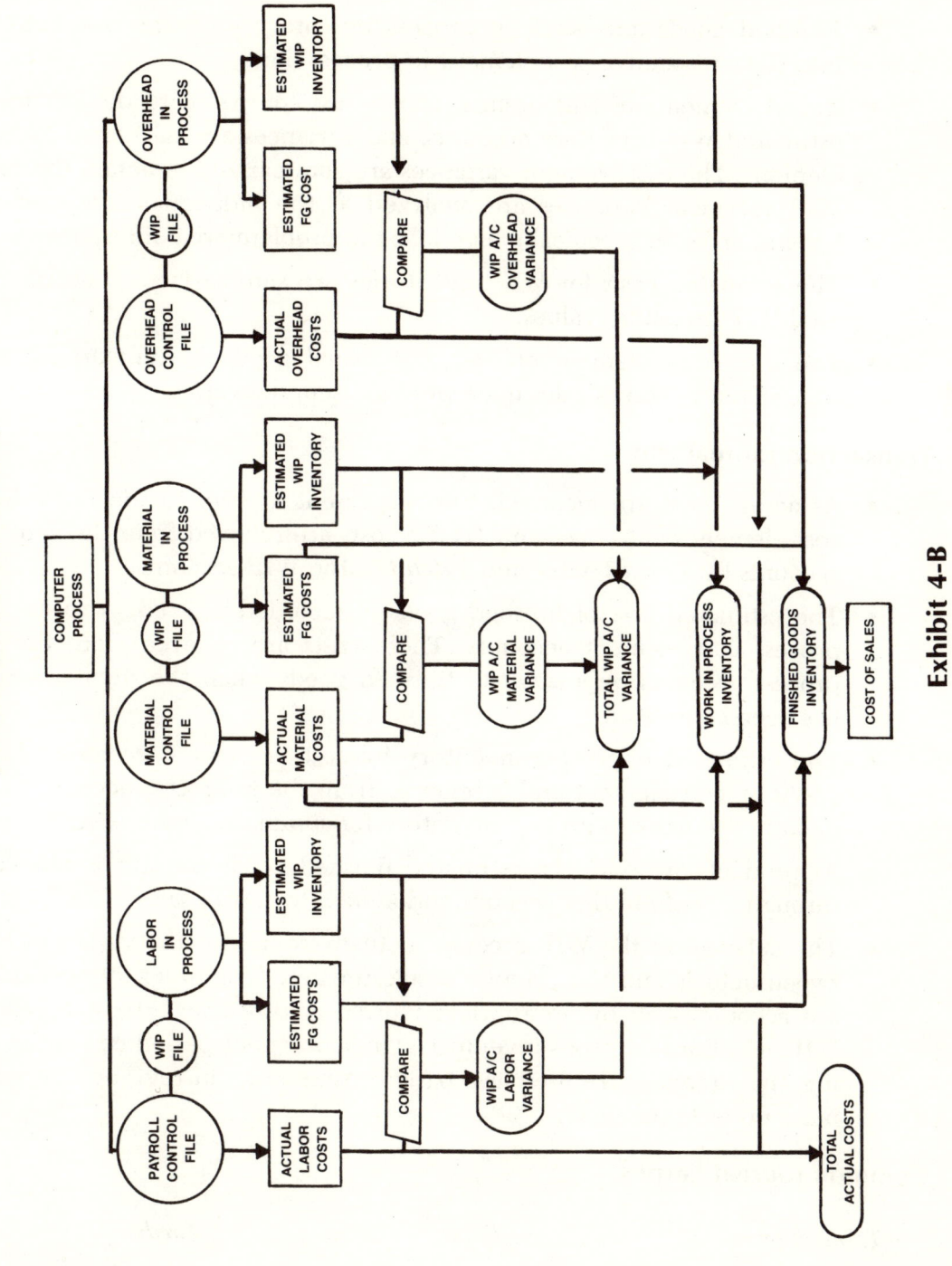

Exhibit 4-B

- Incurred actual costs for direct labor, material, and overhead expenses are accumulated in their respective control files.
- Finished goods and work in process inventory estimates are entered into their respective cost element in process files.
- Actual elements of cost (item 1 above) are compared to the pertinent estimated WIP inventory accounts, and variances are calculated by cost element. The cost element variances are summarized to obtain the total WIP variance. Variances are analyzed at the individual cost element level in order to specifically highlight the problem area differences.
- The estimated costs for WIP inventories are summarized to obtain the total WIP inventory values.
- The estimated element of cost in finished goods is summarized and transferred to cost of sales upon product item deliveries.

Transaction Journalizing

- As actual costs are incurred, they represent a *debit* to the individual cost element control account. These costs are relieved from the control accounts by a *credit* entry and a *debit* to the WIP accounts.
- The estimated cost of finished goods is recorded as a *credit* to the in process cost element accounts. These costs are relieved from the in process accounts by a *debit* to finished goods when the item product has been completed.
- The estimated in-process inventory by cost element is recorded as a *credit* by cost element and is relieved from the in-process account by a *debit* to the work in process inventory for summation purposes.
- As products are sold, the estimated finished goods account is relieved through a *credit* to that account and a *debit* to cost of sales.
- The balances in the WIP accounts actually represent the variances between actuals and the original cost estimates. Disposition of variances are accomplished by appropriate journal adjustments to cost of sales, WIP, and finished goods inventories. In subsequent period cost estimating, the variances are used as a basic consideration in revising cost estimate projections.

Common Journal Entries

Transaction	*Debit*	*Credit*
Incurred payroll costs	Payroll control	Accrued salaries/wages
Material purchases	Material control	Accounts payable or cash
Incurred expenses	Overhead control	Accounts payable/other liabilities

Procedural Cost Accounting

Transaction	Debit	Credit
Completed work in process	Finished goods	In-process cost elements
Recording sales	Accounts receivable	Sales
	Cost of sales	Finished goods
Payroll distribution	Labor in process	Payroll control
	Overhead control	Payroll control
Material used distribution	Materials in process	Materials control
	Overhead control	Materials control
Actual overhead distribution	Overhead in process	Overhead control
Payment of accrued liabilities	Pertinent liability accounts	Cash
Closing in-process accounts to variance accounts	Elements of cost variances	Elements of cost in process

The above general entries are common in most organizations and can be readily programmed for use in a mechanical system.

JOB ORDER COST ACCOUNTING

A job order system accumulates each element of cost separately for each job or order in production. This type of system is generally used in organizations that do special work or that manufacture to a customer's specifications such as shipbuilding, machine shops, missiles, and spacecraft. Organizations using this accounting system have found it advantageous (analysis and control) to record on each production order, before production commences, a forecast estimate of the amount of labor, material, and indirect support that will be required to perform the task. In this manner, a comparison between the actual and estimated costs can be readily effected while the work progresses.

Exhibit 4-C illustrates an overview of the relevant mechanical processing that occurs in a job order accounting system. A brief discussion of the steps involved follows:

- Actual costs are accumulated in the individual control files as they occur. Payroll, material, and overhead expenses are identified to the production order, account number, and specific organization performing the task.

- Estimated elements of cost are inputted into in-process files similarly identified in the manner specified above for actual costs. This is necessary in order that compatible comparisons can be made.

- Actuals are compared to the cost estimates, and variances are derived by job order cost elements and summarized to obtain the total variance. The individual job order cost element variances are outputted for review and analysis.

JOB ORDER ACCOUNTING PROCEDURE (INVOLVING COST ESTIMATES)

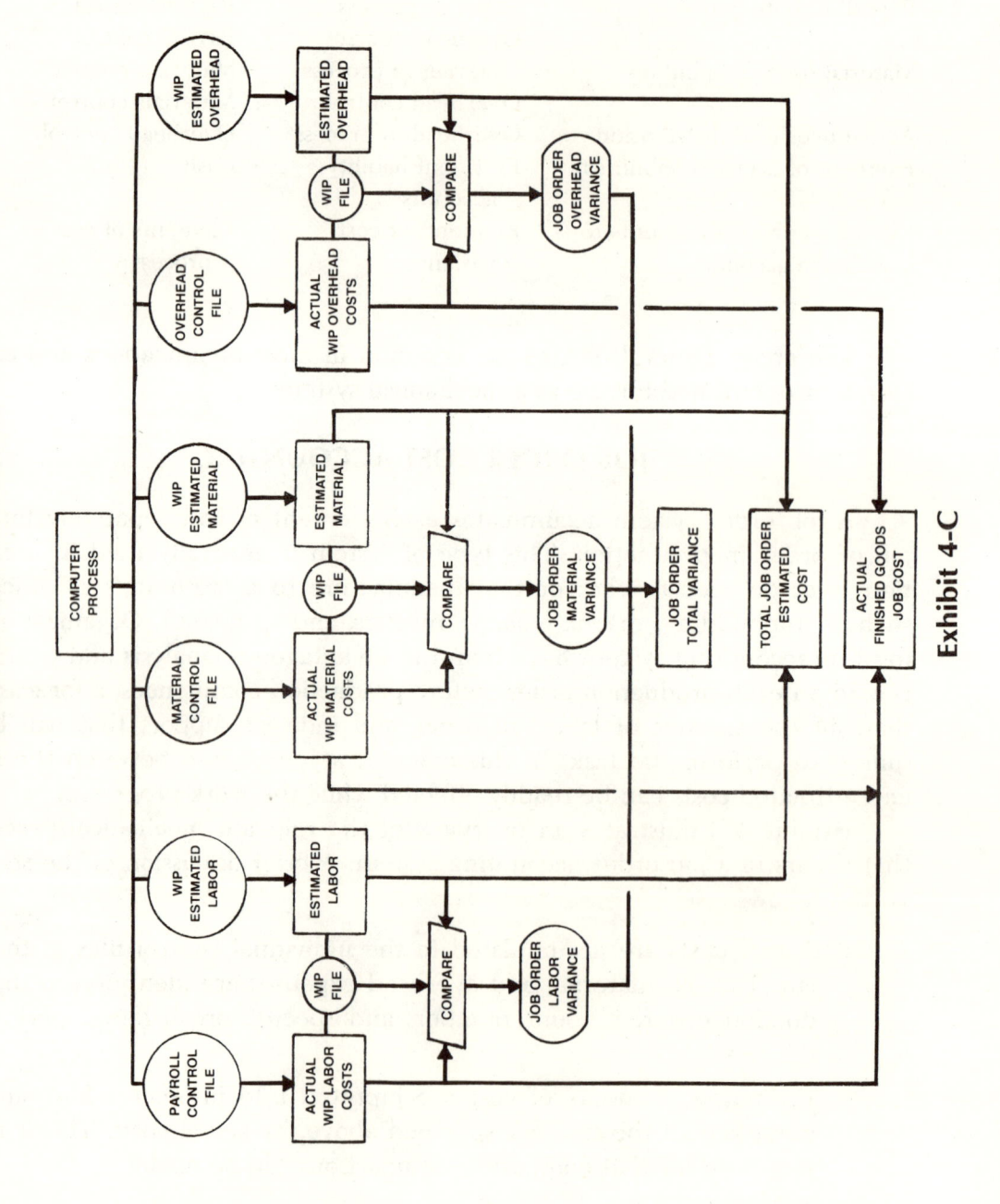

Exhibit 4-C

Procedural Cost Accounting 117

- The actual work in process cost elements are transferred to the finished goods account through a *credit* to the WIP accounts and a *debit* to finished goods.

PRODUCTION DEPARTMENT ACCOUNTING

In the production department accounting system for estimated cost, a separate work in process account is used for each department. Under this procedure, estimated costs are used for the process and operation cost systems.

Exhibit 4-D presents an overview of this accounting procedure, and pertinent comments are indicated below.

- Labor, material and overhead cost estimates are made for each product and production department.

- The cost element control files are used to accumulate WIP actuals as they are incurred in the processing cycle. A separate account is used for each production department in order to cost work in process.

- The WIP account for each relevant department is debited for the actual elements in the period incurred and credited for the estimated cost of completed goods which are transferred to finished goods.

- A typical inventory of WIP in each department is made based on estimated costs and either transferred to WIP inventory accounts or utilized as the beginning inventory balance in the department for the following accounting period.

- As shown on Exhibit 4-D, the estimated finished goods are summarized to a department total and eventually transferred to cost of sales.

- Generally the cost element estimates for each department are revised based on the variance analyses and are reflected in the following accounting work periods.

The above procedure can be effectively accomplished in the computerized environment, particularly, in those organizations that manufacture many and varied products in a number of organizations. Otherwise, considerable manual effort would be required for calculations, summaries, and comparisons. The computation tasks are generally prohibitive on a timely basis. The manual approach can materially affect a timely decision-making process for corrective action.

JOB ORDER VERSUS PROCESS COST SYSTEMS

The job order and process cost systems are different in terms of production objectives and cost accumulation as shown in Exhibit 4-E. There are inherent advantages and disadvantages to each system, but their basic utilization is dependent on an organization's needs.

PRODUCTION DEPARTMENT ACCOUNTING PROCEDURE
(INVOLVING COST ESTIMATES)

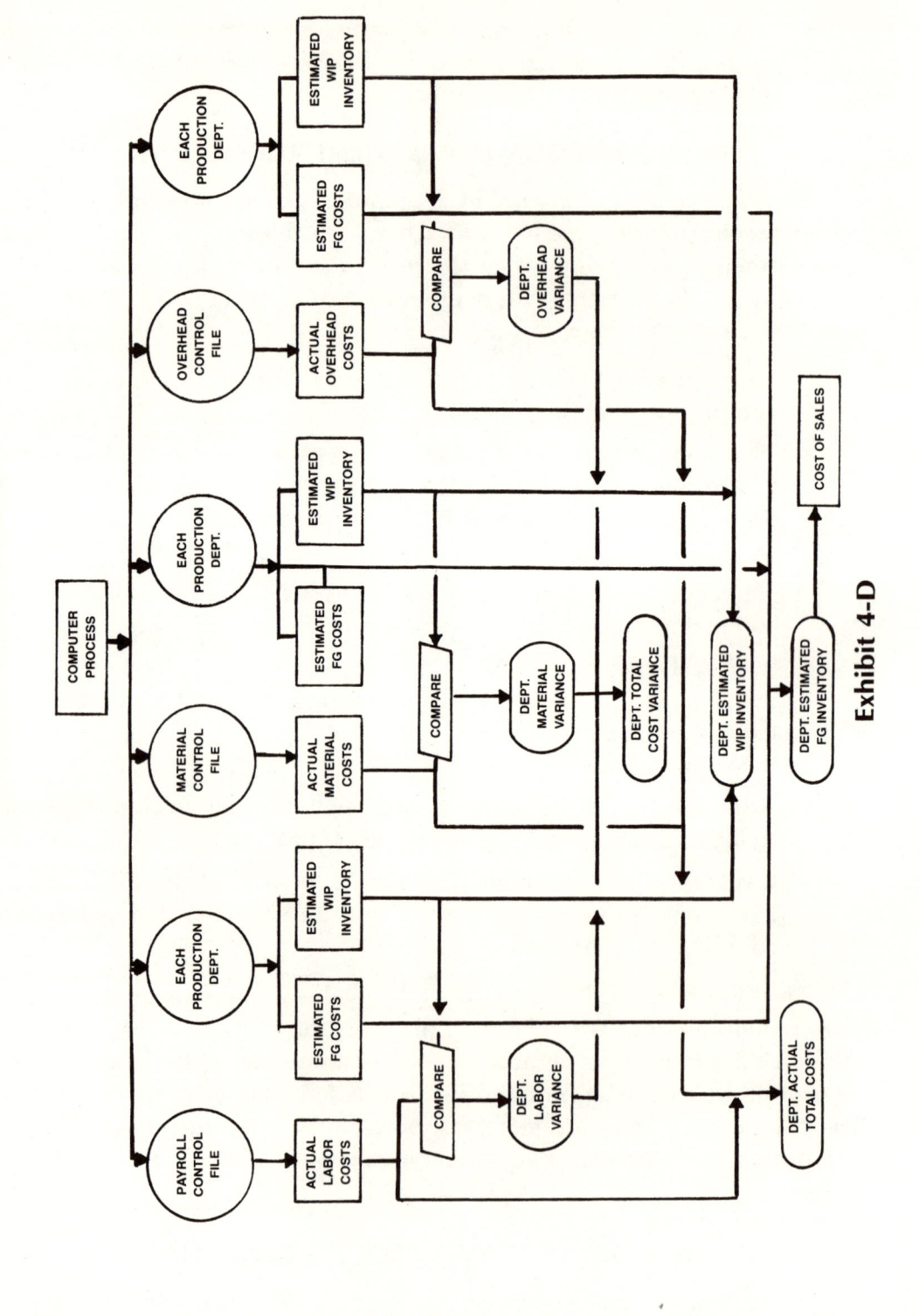

Exhibit 4-D

Procedural Cost Accounting

JOB ORDER VS. PROCESS COST SYSTEMS

JOB ORDER COST ←→ **PROCESS COST**

Operational Objectives

Job Order Cost	Process Cost
SPECIFIC JOB CUSTOMER SPECIFICATION	CONTINUOUS/MASS PRODUCTION PROCESS/PRODUCT STANDARDIZATION HOMOGENEOUS PRODUCTS

Prime Characteristics

Job Order Cost	Process Cost
COST ACCUMULATION BY EOC FOR EACH SPECIFIC PROCESS/JOB ORDER	COST ACCUMULATION BY EOC FOR OPERATION TASKS PROCESS COST AVERAGING TO OBTAIN UNIT COST INTER-ORGANIZATION COST TRANSFERS TO POINT OF PRODUCT COMPLETION

Major Advantages

Job Order Cost	Process Cost
BASIS FOR ESTIMATING SIMILAR TYPE ACTIVITY IN FUTURE EVALUATING JOB PROFITABILITY CONTROLLING OPERATIONAL EFFICIENCY BY ACTUAL VS ESTIMATE COMPARISONS DETERMINING SALES PRICE FOR SPECIFIC JOB ORDER TYPES	BASIS FOR PERIODIC COST COMPUTATION BASED ON ACCOUNTING CYCLE NEEDS AVERAGE COSTS BY PRODUCT UNITS READILY COMPUTED MINIMAL RECORD KEEPING EFFORT AND COST

Probable Disadvantages

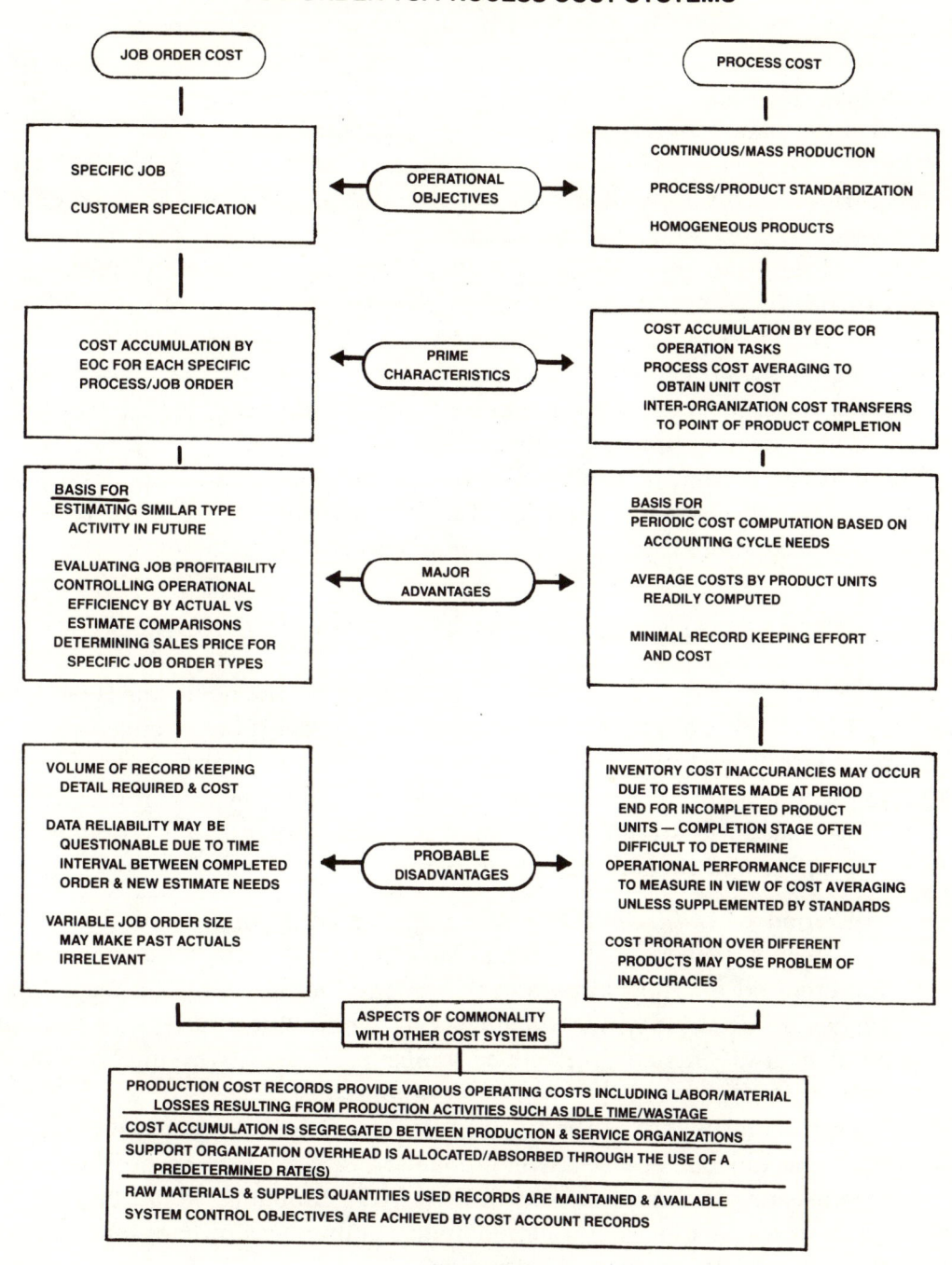

Job Order Cost	Process Cost
VOLUME OF RECORD KEEPING DETAIL REQUIRED & COST DATA RELIABILITY MAY BE QUESTIONABLE DUE TO TIME INTERVAL BETWEEN COMPLETED ORDER & NEW ESTIMATE NEEDS VARIABLE JOB ORDER SIZE MAY MAKE PAST ACTUALS IRRELEVANT	INVENTORY COST INACCURANCIES MAY OCCUR DUE TO ESTIMATES MADE AT PERIOD END FOR INCOMPLETED PRODUCT UNITS — COMPLETION STAGE OFTEN DIFFICULT TO DETERMINE OPERATIONAL PERFORMANCE DIFFICULT TO MEASURE IN VIEW OF COST AVERAGING UNLESS SUPPLEMENTED BY STANDARDS COST PRORATION OVER DIFFERENT PRODUCTS MAY POSE PROBLEM OF INACCURACIES

Aspects of Commonality with Other Cost Systems

- PRODUCTION COST RECORDS PROVIDE VARIOUS OPERATING COSTS INCLUDING LABOR/MATERIAL LOSSES RESULTING FROM PRODUCTION ACTIVITIES SUCH AS IDLE TIME/WASTAGE
- COST ACCUMULATION IS SEGREGATED BETWEEN PRODUCTION & SERVICE ORGANIZATIONS
- SUPPORT ORGANIZATION OVERHEAD IS ALLOCATED/ABSORBED THROUGH THE USE OF A PREDETERMINED RATE(S)
- RAW MATERIALS & SUPPLIES QUANTITIES USED RECORDS ARE MAINTAINED & AVAILABLE
- SYSTEM CONTROL OBJECTIVES ARE ACHIEVED BY COST ACCOUNT RECORDS

Exhibit 4-E

In the job cost system, the disadvantages can be minimized (relative to record keeping activities) in part or total by the use of a computerized system for cost accumulation, data processing, and reporting. The mechanical system improves report timelines and can be programmed to discriminate between order sizes so that the data generated is applicable to varying size estimates.

The process cost system must be complemented by the establishment of realistic performance standards so that the operational efficiencies can be effectively measured. This alleviates the negative results from unit cost averaging. Standard cost determinants at varying stages of product completion have to be initiated to preclude inaccuracies in product segment costing. This can be accomplished by identifying the progression and completion of the product and/or component/subassembly additions to the product. A mechanized program would store the cost determinants to which reference would be made through an abbreviated input identifier.

Noted at the bottom of Exhibit 4-E are the common characteristics associated with any cost accounting system. The commonality aspects are basic to production record keeping, cost accumulation, and cost distribution.

ALTERNATE ACCOUNTING METHOD CONSIDERATIONS

Dependent on an organization's accounting procedure needs for their estimate activities, there are other methods that can be used, but their usefulness is questionable for most progressive organizations. The primary reason for this assumption is indicated below for each type of method. However, this is not to say that the procedures would not be valid for some organizations, depending on their objectives and accounting requirements.

- Utilization of *individual WIP accounts for each product* produced. In this process, each WIP account is charged for the actual costs generated and credited for the estimated product production cost. The major *disadvantage* occur in those organizations where there are a substantial number of diversified products or similar products of varying styles and sizes, as in the case of the shoe or tire industries.

  The problem in this method would be that an excessive number of accounts would be required which could result in costly record keeping, account analyses and cost control. Reporting timelines would be jeopardized in the manual environment but suitable system computerization could possibly overcome this situation.

- Utilization of individual *WIP accounts for each element of cost for each production department.* The possible problem with this procedure would arise in those organizations that have a large number of operating departments, as in the case of the automotive industry or aircraft.

Procedural Cost Accounting 121

A large number of accounts would be required with the obvious disadvantages noted above. If this accounting approach is essential, computerization could provide the solution to a costly record keeping activity and account cost control.

- Utilization of a single *WIP account for all elements of cost*. In this process, the overall WIP account would be charged with the actual costs and credited for the estimated cost of production. The problem is that cost variances could only be developed in total, and thus individual cost elements could not be effectively monitored and assessed. The result would be poor cost control and unavailability of important data detail in preparing an intelligent cost estimate.

  If this procedure is used, some type of alternate satellite system is required to provide the additional data required for operation assessment and control.

DIRECT PRODUCT COSTING

Direct product costing involves the elements of cost in terms of labor, material, manufacturing expense, and other direct costs. These costs are directly associated and identifiable with the actual manufacture of a product or performance of customer services. The importance and the process involved in developing these costs are discussed below.

Direct Labor Costs

Direct labor costs are concerned with the accumulation and payment of salaries/wages for work performed specifically for product production. Costs for labor are based on individual hourly rates and/or composite rates by cost center or department, dependent upon the prevailing accounting/estimating practices within an organization.

Direct labor costing is very important to an organization because costs are identified to specific jobs and operations and thus provide information as to value received from work performed in the production process. Wage payments are based on time or day rates, piece-work rates, and/or premium incentive rates. Direct labor costs are also used as a basis of control in measuring performance based on pre-established standards for production volume and product quality. Further, use of direct labor hours or dollars is a convenient, authentic basis for distributing overhead expense among products and organizations.

Direct labor estimates are developed based on design and product component specifications and historical costs for similar parts/assembly experienced in previous production processes. The product is thoroughly evaluated to ascertain the type of operational processes to be performed and the amount of time required for their accomplishment. Labor costs therefore represent the result of process time requirements multiplied by specific or average wage rates. The rates should reflect the anticipated future trends.

Time estimates for task setup are also included in the overall labor estimate and are analyzed separately to highlight deviation problems. Operation setup time and costs are distributed over the number of units produced. The labor cost estimate record includes such information as date, customer, part number and description, performing organization, type of operation and machine, setup costing, output quantity, and cost. The labor cost estimates are compared to actuals when they become available in order to measure performance results, data validity of the original estimate, and its applicability to future estimates.

Labor Cost Variances

The major causes for actual labor cost variances from standard or estimated are attributed to (1) actual rate paid versus the standard and (2) actual hours used versus the standard hours projected in the production process. Variances are identified as labor rate or efficiency. The formulas used in computing labor variances are as follows:

- *Labor rate variance* equals actual hours expended times (standard hourly rate minus actual hourly rate).

- *Efficiency or usage variance* equals standard labor rate times (standard labor hours minus actual labor hours).

Direct Material Costs

Material costs represent the expenditures for direct materials used in producing a completed part/product. Costs are based on the prevailing or anticipated purchase price including freight charges, handling, and the cost of containers in which the product is to be stored for delivery. Direct material costs become an integral part of the overall product cost. Records are maintained relative to the purchase requisition and order, vendor's invoice and reconciliation, the receipt, inspection and disbursement of materials, plus the inventory-on-hand record keeping.

Different organizations use various methods for production material costing depending upon their established procedures and needs. Some of the basic methods include first-in, first-out; last-in, first-out; specific cost; and the averaging approach in terms of moving, periodic, and weighted. More than one method is used in order to adequately cost materials used. Generally, actual or historical costs of raw materials, work in process, and finished goods are the most acceptable methods, since accounting data is recorded on the basis of costs.

Procedural Cost Accounting

Material cost estimating is based on past quantity utilization and costs for previously produced similar products. For new products, reference must be made as to the type, quality and quantity (possibly weight) of the material to be utilized. Similarly to direct labor, these types of data can be determined from product design drawings and specification details provided by engineering/manufacturing organizations. A product prototype model is of considerable help in defining material requirements and their cost.

Material cost trends are available from the procurement organizations that maintain constant liaison with the concerned vendors that provide specific materials. The cost prices are usually based on the actual cost of delivery to the buyer's plant at prevailing prices for normal quantity lots. The prices should be specific as to type of material, quality, and quantity.

In situations in which cost data is based on estimating standards, it is practicable to cost material on the anticipated replacement basis; otherwise the estimated cost will not reflect valid future costs. Cost projections are adjusted by a percent increase or decrease application.

Material Variances

The prime contributing causes for actual material variance from standard or estimated are attributed to price and quantity usage. Price variances can result from changes in the market price, errors in recording, or improper purchasing events such as incorrect quality and quantity.

Usage variances generally result from spoilage and waste in the production process; changes in product design, machinery, and operational methods; and losses in handling and storage.

The formulas used in computing material variances are as follows:

- *Material price variance* equals actual usage times (standard unit cost minus actual unit cost).
- *Material usage variance* equals standard unit price times (standard quantity of material in the product minus actual quantity of materials used).

Manufacturing Expense

Manufacturing expenses represent indirect support costs in the production. These expenses cannot be specifically identified to product production and therefore cannot be charged directly to product units. In such a situation, overhead must be equitably spread over the production units through the use of an overhead burden application or burden absorption.

Overhead can be applied to the product based on rates established after or before the actual expenditures are experienced. The formulas are calculated as follows:

- *Based on actual costs*
  Application rate equals actual period overhead expenses divided by actual production in terms of units, direct labor hours, or dollars.

- *Predetermined rate*
  Application rate equals estimated period overhead expenses divided by estimated production in terms of units, direct labor hours, or dollars.

- *Prime cost method* (using actuals or estimations)
  Application rate equals overhead expenses divided by direct labor plus material costs.
  Application rate = overhead expense ÷ (labor + material costs)

- *Adjustment for over/underabsorbed expenses*
  Supplementary rate equals actual overhead rate minus the absorbed rate and the result divided by units, direct labor hours or dollars.

Costing cannot be completed until the close of the period, and this delays the determination of costs for work in process and finished goods. This method also poses a problem in providing guidance for future product pricing.

Using the estimated method, product costs can be immediately determined for costing purposes. Most organizations employ the estimated cost method. This method, however, results in a difference between actual overhead and estimated overhead which must be corrected through journal entries and product cost adjustments.

Overhead Variances

The prime variances associated with overhead transactions are classified as expense, efficiency, and volume (capacity or utilization). The *expense variance* results from actual expenditures being greater or lesser than the budget allowance at a specific level of activity. The variance may be attributed to one or a number of expense accounts due to seasonal conditions, inefficiency, or poor control. If the variance results from inefficiency or poor control, then it should be disposed of in the profit and loss account. If it is due to uncontrollable circumstances, the disposition of the variance would be reflected in work in process, finished goods, and cost of sales.

The *efficiency variance* results from the actual direct hours worked being greater or lesser than the pre-established standard production hours. The greater-than-standard variance may arise from material shortages, labor problems, or machine downtime. If the actual hours are favorably less than standard, the cause may be high performance, good supervision, or improved machinery. Disposition of this type of variance is effected through the profit and loss account.

The *volume utilization variance* results from operating more or less than the number of hours in any given budget period. This variance can be attribut-

Procedural Cost Accounting

ed to production problems such as work inefficiencies, non-realization of learning curve expectations, machine failure, or unrealistic standards. The utilization variance may exceed budget goals through improved processing methods or more advanced equipment. Variance disposition would be through the profit and loss account.

Overhead Variance Formulas

The formulas for computing overhead variances are as follows:

- *Overhead expense variance* equals budgeted overhead cost at actual production activity level less actual overhead cost.

- *Overhead efficiency variance* equals (normal overhead rate times standard direct labor hours in product) minus (normal overhead rate times actual direct labor hours in product).

- *Overhead utilization variance* equals (normal overhead rate times actual direct labor hours in product) minus (budgeted overhead cost at actual activity level).

The control of overhead costs through the use of standards and variance analysis differs from that used for direct labor and material because there are a significant number of expense accounts used, some of which are fixed and uncontrollable. It is difficult to define specific control responsibility for many costs because of the complex nature of overhead expenses: their identification to the specific tasks and their being reported on a monthly basis rather than daily or weekly which would permit immediate analysis and corrective action.

In estimating the total manufacturing overhead, detailed expense and production (direct hours, labor dollars, number of units) budgets are developed. The estimated overhead dollars are divided by the designated determinant to obtain an application overhead rate. Dependent upon the basic determinant (labor hours, dollars, units) used, the rate is applied to determine the estimated overhead. If departmental overhead budgets are used, the same procedure as above would apply wherein separate department overhead application rates are used.

COST ACCUMULATION SYSTEM

The primary objectives of the cost accumulation system are to provide the basics required to collect costs effectively, meet data processing criteria, and also serve as a control and reporting vehicle. System principles and requirements are displayed in Exhibit 4-F.

After a new and different contract or sales order has been negotiated, it is necessary to follow specific criteria for accumulating, recording, and reporting costs against the contract and/or product. This includes the delineation of task

COST ACCUMULATION SYSTEM
BASIC PRINCIPLES & REQUIREMENTS

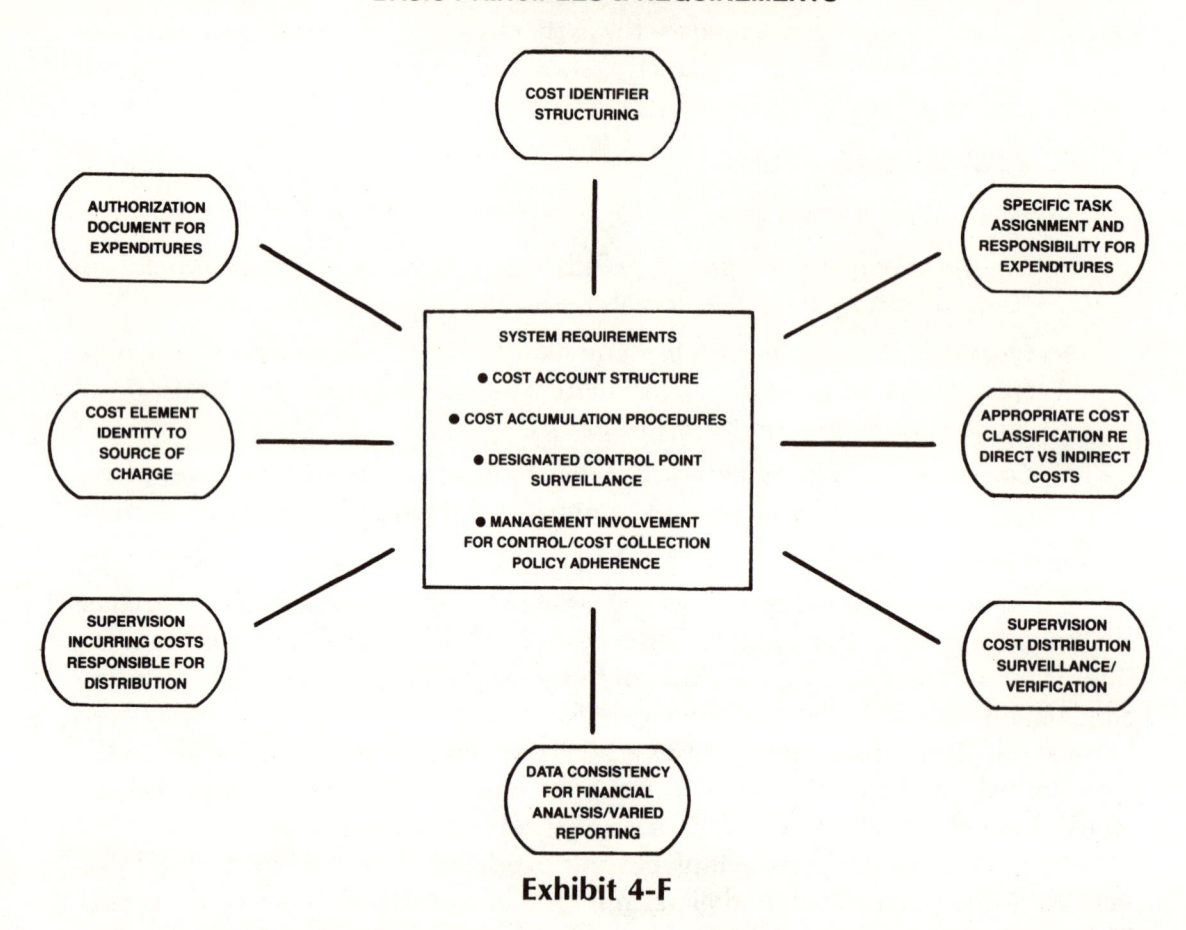

- COST IDENTIFIER STRUCTURING
- AUTHORIZATION DOCUMENT FOR EXPENDITURES
- SPECIFIC TASK ASSIGNMENT AND RESPONSIBILITY FOR EXPENDITURES
- COST ELEMENT IDENTITY TO SOURCE OF CHARGE
- APPROPRIATE COST CLASSIFICATION RE DIRECT VS INDIRECT COSTS
- SUPERVISION INCURRING COSTS RESPONSIBLE FOR DISTRIBUTION
- SUPERVISION COST DISTRIBUTION SURVEILLANCE/ VERIFICATION
- DATA CONSISTENCY FOR FINANCIAL ANALYSIS/VARIED REPORTING

SYSTEM REQUIREMENTS
- COST ACCOUNT STRUCTURE
- COST ACCUMULATION PROCEDURES
- DESIGNATED CONTROL POINT SURVEILLANCE
- MANAGEMENT INVOLVEMENT FOR CONTROL/COST COLLECTION POLICY ADHERENCE

Exhibit 4-F

assignment and expenditure responsibilities, expense authorization approvals, and adherence to pre-established cost element identification and classification. On standard and routine contracts/sales orders, prevailing organization accounting practices generally follow the basic principles outlined on Exhibit 4-F.

The system requirements noted in the exhibit are basic to any advanced cost collection system in most organizations. To be effective however, the system must be flexible, and its work order structure must consider all aspects of data identification needs.

Work Structure Description

The accumulation structure will include the following from the basic level of cost collection to the summary work in process account, product, and budget center. The extent of the identifier requirements are based on the reporting and control needs of an organization.

Procedural Cost Accounting 127

- *Cost code for type of customer*—commercial, government, foreign.
- *Type contract/sales order*—commercial, fixed price, cost plus fixed fee.
- *Product identifier*—development, support, production.
- *Project identifier*—contract cost identity.
- *Work order*—generally a four digit number in which the first two digits identify the project and the remaining two digits designate the major function of the project.
- *Functional activity*—usually a four digit number that further breaks down the identity of the task performed and cost incurred.
- *Organization*—by major function such as R & D, engineering, manufacturing; also, department, cost center.
- *Task*—a four digit number which further defines/identifies the cost or effort to a lower level of reporting for specifically measuring performance, establishing standards, costing the operation.
- *General ledger account*—work in process, contract type, interdivision project identity, contract cost designation.

Work-in-Process Breakdown

Direct elements of cost are identified and summarized to project budget centers (engineering, manufacturing), accounting work orders, contract items and their total and work in process accounts. The cost elements include direct labor hours and dollars, overhead, material, other direct costs, and interdivision activity. Budget centers are created to provide reporting requirements for operation control and performance measurement.

From budget/cost centers, the costs are summarized by accounting work orders and further totalled to the contract or sales item level. The contract item costs are further summarized to the individual contract totals. The values of groups of contracts are then reflected in the work-in-process accounts. WIP account segregations reflect fixed price, cost plus, and commercial type contracts.

Computerized Process

To effect proper cost distribution, the identifiers are inputted into the system from basic source documents such as time cards, shop orders, and material requisitions. The cost data are initially sorted, accumulated, and audited. Internal program controls detect invalid data resulting from incorrect or insufficient identification, and the transaction is rejected to the terminal input station for corrective action. Valid charges are processed, history files updated, and reports generated as shown in Exhibit 4-G.

Procedural Cost Accounting

**COST ACCUMULATION OVERVIEW
COMPUTERIZED PROCESS**

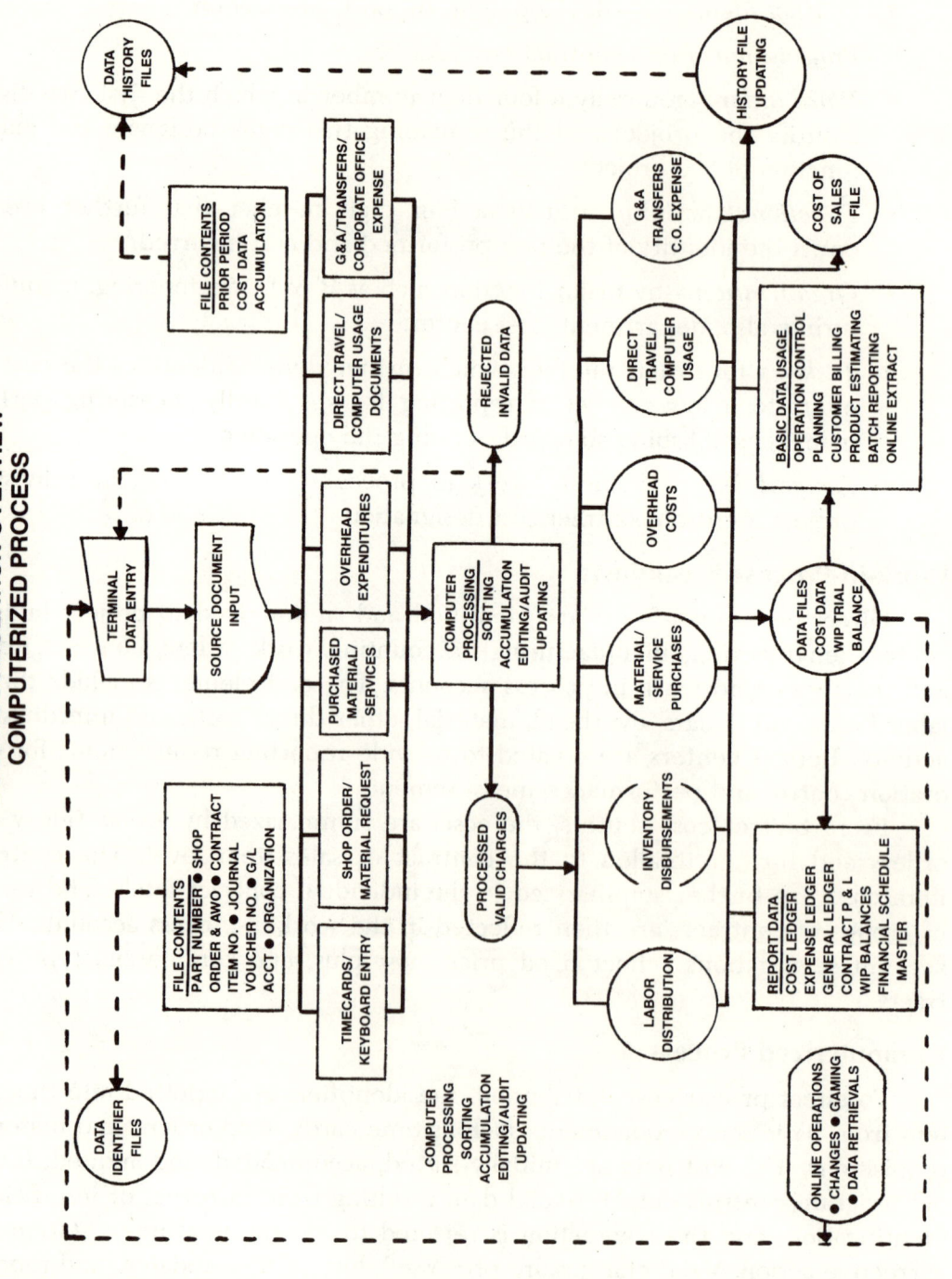

Exhibit 4-G

Each transaction activity is referenced to a journal voucher to permit its proper flow to a general ledger account and subsequently to financial schedules. The transactions include such items as generating a liability (payroll, payables), cash disbursements, customer billing, and contract charges.

Disk data files are updated so that *online operations* are possible in terms of making file changes, effecting "what if" gaming (a supplemental program), and retrieving specific data at the online terminal locations. Information security controls are established to prevent data changes and retrievals except by authorized personnel and/or organizations.

COST COLLECTION REPORTING

There are a number of reports produced from the mechanical cost accumulation system. The primary two cost reports are the cost data ledger and work-in-process trial balance. Other data developed are used for the contract income statement (excluding other income and deductions and pretax profit), expense and general ledgers, and the financial schedule master.

Cost Data Ledger

This ledger reflects for each burden center those costs incurred for the benefit of a center regardless in what organization the work was performed. In the project ledger, however, the costs reported are those for each burden center wherein the costs were specifically incurred.

The report format of the cost data ledger is displayed in Exhibit 4-H. This is a detailed report which provides data summaries by contract, element of cost, project budget center, cost code, accounting work order, and work-in-process account. Transaction journal voucher numbers are shown that indicate to what general ledger account the costs will be accumulated. Direct hours and dollars are reported for labor, and only dollar values for the other cost elements. Information is reported for the current period, year, and cumulative to date. This provides the basis for tracking costs between periods as well as reflects total costs to date by contract and product.

Primarily the cost ledger is maintained for external and financial management requirements, and it provides a reference basis for estimating product cost, billing completed work in process costs, allocating overhead to direct labor dollars, and determining work-in-process trial balance and total contract costs.

Work-in-Process Trial Balance

The cost collection system also provides data requirements for the WIP trial balance schedule which format is displayed in Exhibit 4-H. The information includes total incurred cost by contract or sales order, division cost transfers, G & A, and so on.

COST ACCUMULATION REPORTING (MECHANICAL)

COST DATA LEDGERS*

| WIP ACCOUNT | PRODUCT CODE | CONTRACT IDENTIFIERS (CODE / ITEM / TASK) | ELEMENT OF COST (EOC) | PROJECT BUDGET CENTER (PBC) | COST CLASSIF. CODE (D/I) OR AWO | JOURNAL VOUCHER | CURRENT PERIOD (HOURS / VALUE) | YEAR TO DATE (HOURS / VALUE) | CUMULATIVE TO DATE (HOURS / VALUE) |

WORK IN PROCESS (WIP) TRIAL BALANCE

| CONTRACT (CODE/SALES ORDER, NUMBER/IDENTIFIER/DESCRIPTION) | TOTAL INCURRED COST | COST OF SALES | TRANSFERS TO OTHER DIVISIONS | CORPORATE OFFICE EXPENSE | G&A EXPENSE | WIP BEGINNING BALANCE | CLOSED TO COST OF SALES | WIP ENDING BALANCE |

* SUMMARY TOTALS BY CONTRACT, EOC, PBC, COST CODE/AWO, WIP ACCOUNT

Exhibit 4-H

Procedural Cost Accounting

Cost of sales and expense information is extracted for the organization's income statement and contract status schedule. The work-in-process inventory balance is reported in the balance sheet and inventory status reports.

The WIP trial balance is the top summary report from the cost accumulation system and provides data for cost control surveillance and decision-making relative to contract and product operational cost trends.

Benefits Provided by the Cost Collection System

This mechanical system provides the basic source of data for product pricing, customer billings, and operational control. Its mechanization ensures the capture of information at the lowest level of detail and the summation of information to the hierarchy levels. It further provides the capability for multifile updating and reporting. The system is cost effective, accurate, timely, and versatile.

DIRECT VERSUS INDIRECT COSTS

Basically, all costs are identified and classified as direct or indirect. The *direct costs* are expenditures that can be specifically identified to an organization's product or service. They become an integral part of the product cost and consist of direct labor, material, other direct costs, and manufacturing overhead.

Indirect costs represent support expenditures that are not directly identifiable or contributive to the project/product accomplishment requirements. Typical costs in this category are administration, management, clerical, supplies, and indirect labor support.

Characteristics of Cost Segregations

Direct costs reflect the following criteria:

- Directly *identifiable* to projects and allocated prime cost work orders.
- Tasks are *designated* as direct within the scope of occupation codes and organizational classifications.
- Task performance *authorization* is provided through the use of project work orders.
- Direct labor, material usage, and technical effort are necessary to fulfill the project requirements for physical product manufacture and service support.
- *Allocated prime costs* are classified as direct and are not subject to direct project identification. These costs are incurred for common or joint objectives on a number of projects such as: common minor materials,

common manufacturing planning, product assurance, spares handling, logistics, and technical services.

Indirect costs are characterized by the following criteria:

- Categorized indirect within scope of *occupational codes* and *organizational classifications*.
- *Not directly associated* with or contributive to the accomplishment of project requirements.
- Costs incurred in the *support of* operational activities relative to facility capabilities, financial resources, and control reporting.
- Costs *not subject to consistent and direct economic measurement* and not specifically authorized by project work orders or allocated prime costs.

Problems Associated with Labor Cost Segregations

- *Lack of consistency* in organization structure due to change requirements.
- Possibly *too much flexibility* or ambiguity in occupation code classifications.
- *Extensive diversification* of work activity which poses problems of cost classifications.
- *Continual pressures* on competitive overhead rates that could lead to "stretching a point" in re-classifying indirect labor to direct.
- *Budget pressures* arising from financial management conservatism and need to out-perform projected objectives.

MASTER AUDIT FILE PROCESS

In the constantly changing environment of increasing mechanical processes, the computer has become the major data development vehicle for financial and management reporting. In order to entrust the validity of cost data identification, input, and manipulation to a mechanical process, it is mandatory that a capability be established to control, accept or reject extraneous and inaccurate data. The system program must be able to properly differentiate, through basic identifiers, invalid input and reject it before processing and finalizing the files prior to report generation. This task is accomplished through a master audit file system. Basically, there are two types of program controls.

- *Edit.* These controls include program processing identifiers, data location in files, record length in fields, various codes, file description, transaction designations, and others, dependent upon an organization's control needs.

- *Audit.* The controls are directed toward monitoring the validity of transaction and data identifier input relative to the master audit file usage in the cost collection system. Exhibit 4-I presents an overview of the master file process; a brief description follows.
    1. The file is initially established with the basic input identifying active organizations, contract/projects, work orders, and authority.
    2. Overhead pools are designated as well as general ledger account categories.
    3. Additions, deletions and changes to items (1) and (2) above are inputted on a daily or weekly basis. This is done through reviewing the prior period's output and incorporating known changes.
    4. Valid overhead expense requests, overhead control accounts, and fixed asset order identifiers are part of the system for audit purposes.
    5. File updating is on a weekly basis, and weekly/monthly audits are mechanically performed as shown in Exhibit 4-I.
    6. After the updating and audit processing have been completed, weekly/monthly reports are generated as indicated in Exhibit 4-I.

This type of mechanical audit control ensures that only valid data is processed and reported. Since this system contains many thousands of identifiers, it is most effectively and reliably achieved on a timely basis through computerization. Minimal manual effort is required and invalid charging is significantly reduced.

COST CONTROL REQUIREMENTS

To achieve effective cost control as a criteria for improving cost estimating and performance evaluation, it is ideally necessary to establish certain control points as a means to monitor and validate proposed expenditures. Exhibit 4-J was developed to illustrate the processes involved. A brief description of this exhibit follows.

- Detailed proposals for resource expenditures are submitted to management for task/project authorization and approval. After the proposals are reviewed and accepted by management, an authorization document is issued for project initiation.

- The budget control group assigns the necessary budget and designates the organization(s) responsible for the expenditure.

- The expenditure authorization document is forwarded to the concerned organizations, but before a physical expenditure can be made, a subsequent approval document must be obtained. This process provides man-

134

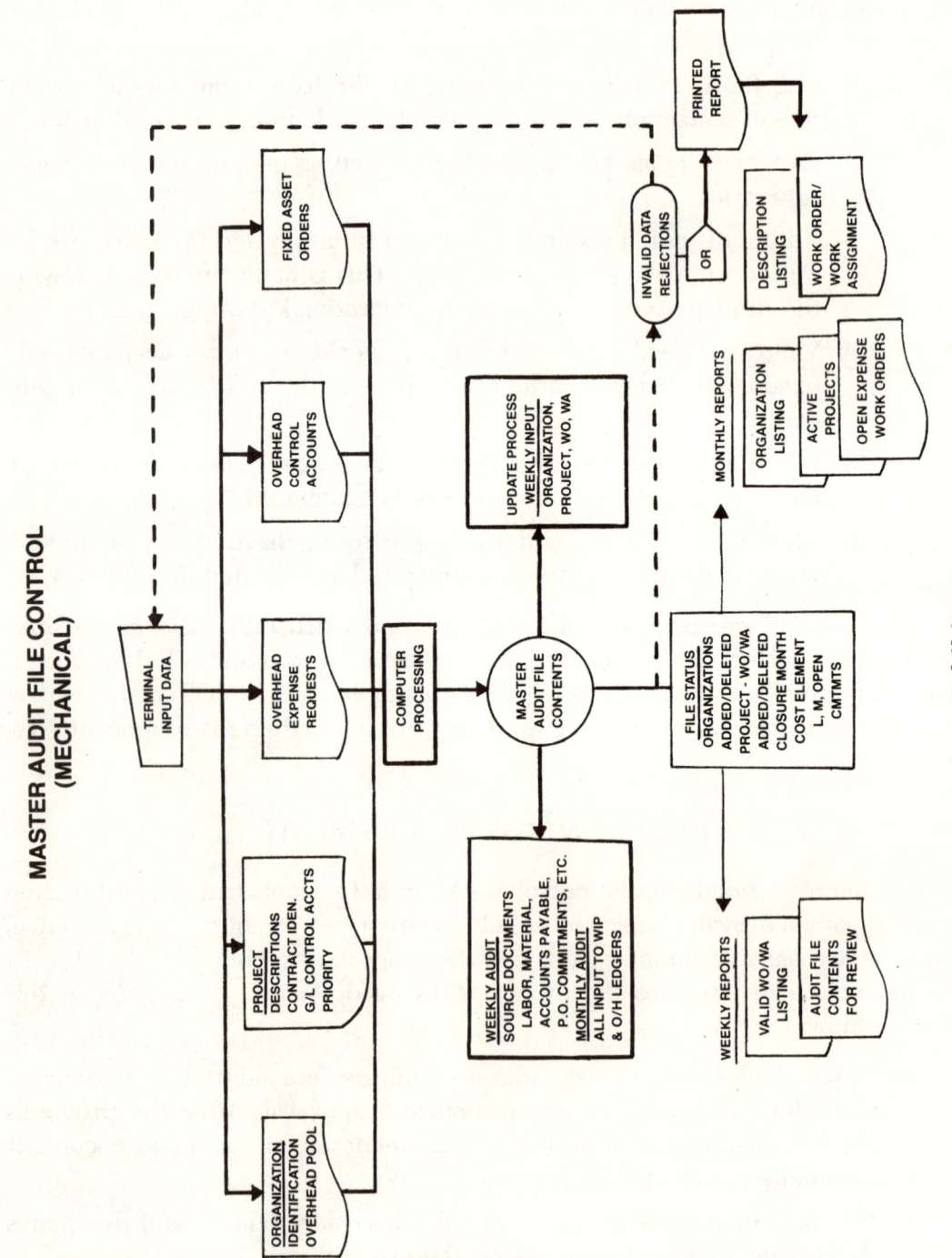

Procedural Cost Accounting

MASTER AUDIT FILE CONTROL (MECHANICAL)

Exhibit 4-1

Procedural Cost Accounting 135

**COST ACCUMULATION SYSTEM
CONTROL PROCESS REQUIREMENTS**

```
* MANAGEMENT              BUDGET CONTROL          *  INVOLVED ORGANIZATIONS  *
  APPROVAL/AUTHORIZATION  ASSIGNS BUDGET &           REQUEST SOURCE
  OF EXPENDITURE          RESPONSIBILITY FOR         DOCUMENT APPROVAL
  PLAN REQUEST            EXPENDITURE                TO COMMIT/SPEND
                          CONTROL                    RESOURCES (RTP)
           │                       │                          │
           ▼                       ▼                          ▼
      AUTHORIZING              AUTHORITY FOR              APPROVED
      DOCUMENT FOR             EXPENDITURE                EXPENDITURE
      PROJECT                  DOCUMENT                   REQUEST
      INITIATION                                          DOCUMENT
                                                              │
                                                              ▼
*  COST DISTRIBUTION       COMPUTER SYSTEM            REVIEWED FOR BASIC  *
   ACTIVITY RESULTS        AUDIT FILE VALIDITY  ◄──   CONFORMANCE TO
   PRELIMINARY DATA    ◄── CHECK & WORK ORDER         POLICY RE PROPER COST
   OUTPUT/REVIEW           LIMITATIONS                CLASSIFICATIONS
           │                       │                          │
           ▼                       ▼                          ▼
      MANAGEMENT              COST ACCUMULATION SYSTEM *  COST DATA        *
      REPORTS                 DATA PROCESS SURVEILLANCE,   CLASSIFICATION
                              CONTROL, AUDIT, &            DOCUMENT
                              VERIFICATION
           │
           ▼
*  BUDGET & COST           COST CONTROL RESULTS       INTERNAL/INDEPENDENT *
   CONTROL ORGANIZATIONS ► PERMANCE MEASUREMENT   ►   & CUSTOMER AUDIT/
   REVIEW/ANALYSIS          BY                        SURVEILLANCE
```

★ SYSTEM CONTROL POINTS

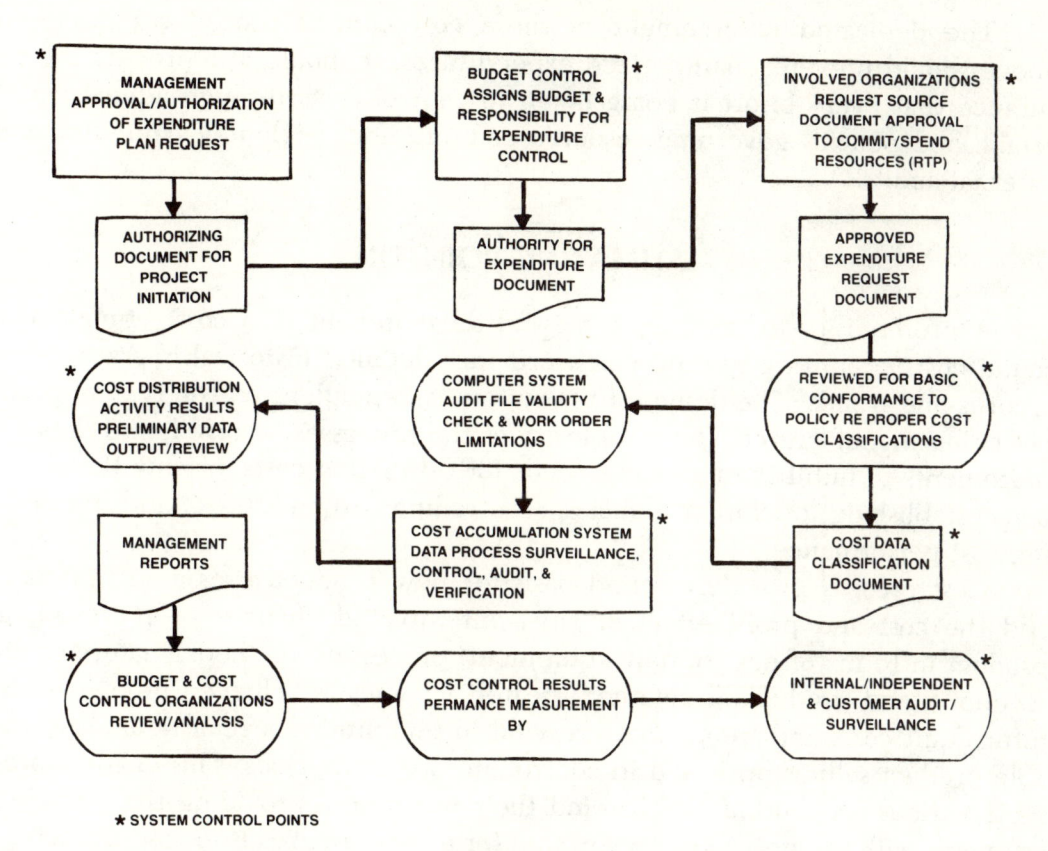

Exhibit 4-J

agement its second opportunity to review and approve project expenditures before they are actually made.

- The approval document is reviewed by the cost/budget control group to confirm that the proper cost classifications have been used and the pertinent data is inputted into the mechanical system. The computer program validates cost identifiers and work order number and budget limitations.

- As expenditures are made, the costs are collected in the cost accumulation system and audited for cost classification charging. Preliminary reports are issued for review prior to the final preparation of various management reports.

- Final reports are analyzed, costs verified, and performance evaluated by the responsible budget/cost control group. Cost performance evaluation reports are provided to management. Based on an organization's policy, a further evaluation of the project's cost and performance results is performed by various audit groups as indicated in Exhibit 4-J.

The dedicated enforcement of these cost control procedures discussed above should prevent unauthorized expenditures. It should also provide the assurance that every effort is being taken to control costs through adherence to established policies governing resource commitments including computer and external audits.

ESTIMATING POINTERS

A prerequisite to realistic, successful development of a cost estimate is a sound cost accounting system which provides detailed historical operating cost records and trends. The design of the system is dependent on the type of product being manufactured, the complexity of the processes involved, and data requirements to fulfill the reporting needs for estimating costs, pricing the product, establishing operating policies, controlling expenditures, and measuring cost performance.

Cost records provide a sound basis for new product assessment, pricing, and the cost and profit effect of any contemplated changes to a prevailing product in terms of design, new equipment, processing methods, material substitutions, and production volume. Greater accuracy is achieved in estimating future unit costs and trends that are vital in establishing a realistic and profitable product selling price and in controlling operating costs. This chapter presents various accounting systems and their utilization, providing the planning estimator with the necessary background for developing realistic cost estimates.

5

The Marketable Manufacturing Cost Proposal

The development of a cost proposal involves a number of relevant factors and the active participation of a number of functional organizations in order to make the process a successful venture that is acceptable to the customer. Exhibit 5-A displays an overview of the requirements when there is a request for a quotation (RFQ). The request represents a formal inquiry from a customer to bid on a proposed product or project.

Organizational structure and data may vary among organizations, but the basics are shown in Exhibit 5-A. They can be expanded or contracted to meet individual organization needs.

REQUEST FOR QUOTATION

The customer communicates his specific requirements to the marketing/sales organization or a responsible functional group. With management's cognizance and approval, the proposal request needs are provided to contract administration or forwarded directly to the concerned functional groups, dependent upon organization policy, to initiate the detailed development of the requirements. At this point, in addition to the customer's outlined request, other pertinent data will be added in accordance with prevailing proposal procedures.

The functional groups then initiate their effort to provide the required data in their sphere of activity which information is outlined in Exhibit 5-A. Continual interface through inter-organization communication is a *must* during the development phase in order to avoid duplicative effort, responsibility encroachment, and problem areas. Organizational coordination is required to achieve a compatible end-result *package*.

When completed, the proposal is forwarded to management for review and approval. The review participants include management, contracts, marketing, and the executive functional staff. This type of combined evaluation group is most logical to resolve data justification, proposed changes, and possible problem conflicts.

PROPOSAL DECISION CRITERIA

The decision to bid on a proposal involves a number of considerations which are reflected in the following relevant questions:

The Marketable Manufacturing Cost Proposal

REQUEST FOR QUOTATION (RFQ) ORGANIZATION INVOLVEMENT

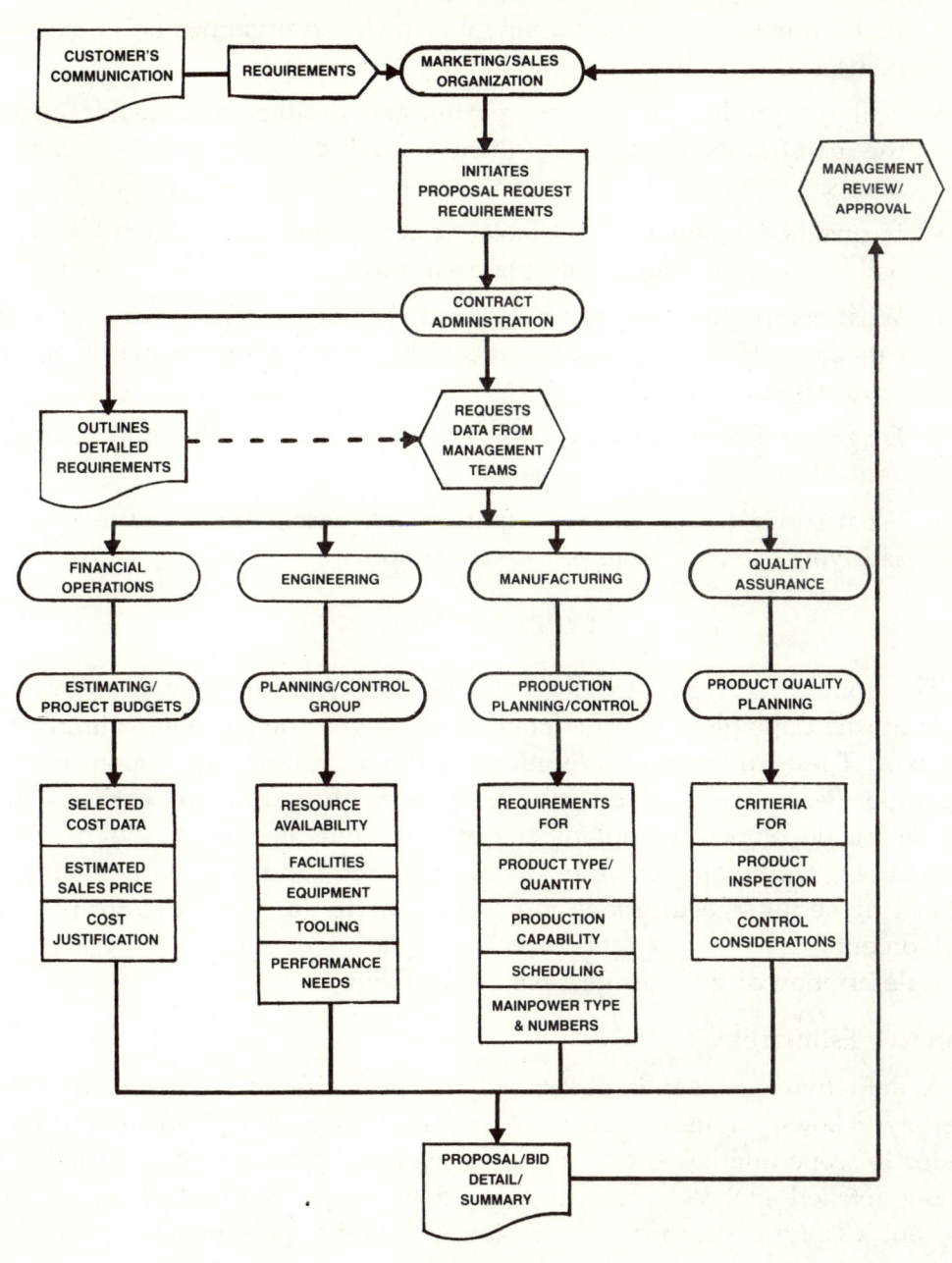

```
CUSTOMER'S                              MARKETING/SALES                    MANAGEMENT
COMMUNICATION  --REQUIREMENTS-->        ORGANIZATION   <-----------------  REVIEW/
                                              |                            APPROVAL
                                              v
                                        INITIATES
                                        PROPOSAL REQUEST
                                        REQUIREMENTS
                                              |
                                              v
                                        CONTRACT
                                        ADMINISTRATION
                                         |        |
                                         v        v
                                  OUTLINES      REQUESTS
                                  DETAILED ---> DATA FROM
                                  REQUIREMENTS  MANAGEMENT
                                                TEAMS
                                                  |
              +-----------------+-----------------+------------------+
              v                 v                 v                  v
          FINANCIAL         ENGINEERING      MANUFACTURING       QUALITY
          OPERATIONS                                             ASSURANCE
              |                 |                 |                  |
              v                 v                 v                  v
          ESTIMATING/      PLANNING/CONTROL   PRODUCTION         PRODUCT QUALITY
          PROJECT BUDGETS  GROUP              PLANNING/CONTROL   PLANNING
              |                 |                 |                  |
              v                 v                 v                  v
          SELECTED         RESOURCE           REQUIREMENTS       CRITIERIA
          COST DATA        AVAILABILITY       FOR                FOR
          ESTIMATED        FACILITIES         PRODUCT TYPE/      PRODUCT
          SALES PRICE      EQUIPMENT          QUANTITY           INSPECTION
          COST             TOOLING            PRODUCTION         CONTROL
          JUSTIFICATION    PERFORMANCE        CAPABILITY         CONSIDERATIONS
                           NEEDS              SCHEDULING
                                              MAINPOWER TYPE
                                              & NUMBERS
              |                                   |                  |
              +------------------+----------------+------------------+
                                 v
                           PROPOSAL/BID
                           DETAIL/
                           SUMMARY
```

Exhibit 5-A

- Does the organization have the necessary technical capability and operating and financial resources?
- Is the product or service compatible with the organization's objectives, plans, and expertise?
- Will the productive capacity permit the product manufacture within the constraints of product quantity and delivery schedule requirements?
- Is qualified manpower available to accomplish the required tasks, or will recruitment and training be required?
- What competitors are involved, what is their contemplated action, and can the bidding organization meet the challenge in terms of product requirements and price?
- Do the profit estimates meet the prevailing goals of the bidding organization?
- What additional or unusual expenses are anticipated to be incurred in satisfying the conditions of the cost proposal?

TYPES OF RFQs

There are three types of requests for quotations which vary in information characteristics dependent on the detail required and the customer's immediate objectives. These requests are definitive, letter of intent, and rough order of magnitude. Each serves its particular purpose in the estimating activity. Sufficient data is developed for pricing the product, but the relative degree of refinement is dependent on the detail required and represented in the engineering design/specifications and the allowable time provided for proposal development.

A description of the classifications are as follows:

Definitive Estimates

A definitive estimate is developed in considerable detail and depth. It generally follows an initial letter of intent and/or ROM which are much broader in scope and based on limited information. The definitive estimate involves a detailed analysis of the projected data which is sufficiently accurate to represent a sound cost proposal for negotiation and to provide a basis on which a product price can be adequately determined.

Letter of Intent

Under certain circumstances, a letter of intent and ROM estimates can be similar in data provision and objectives; however, the letter of intent is normally more formalized and contains more technical detail as an aid in the estimating process. Generally, more detailed specifications must be provided before the final cost data is assembled and appropriately resolved.

Rough Order of Magnitude (ROM)

This type of estimate is developed and based on minimal availability of technical detail and abbreviated time limitations in its preparation. It may provide the basis for initiating work effort on priority projects with a sensitive time schedule requirement. The ROM projection can be used for cost comparisons, performance analyses, and possibly for the budgetary process, but the final cost data must be based on more definitive specifications.

However, the estimate types indicated above are generalized guidelines and can vary in context among organizations and various customer data submissions for proposal development.

MANUFACTURING PROPOSAL ORGANIZATION

A typical manufacturing proposal team and data requirements are shown in Exhibit 5-B. Prime proposal responsibility in the manufacturing functional area lies with the chief executive officer of the organization, who is usually the vice-president of manufacturing operations. Reporting directly to him are the designated proposal coordinator and the functional staff executives at the director level.

Based on the proposal guidelines, the functional areas provide the type of data for which they have responsibility and control. The coordinator's task is to review, clarify, and compile the information into a uniform *package* which will meet the needs of a formal proposal outline. This information is then submitted to the executive vice-president for final review, changes, and/or approval. Depending on the organizational structure and policy, the manufacturing part of the aggregate proposal may be forwarded to the contract group or a centralized estimating function that incorporates it with other input submissions from engineering and finance functions, etc., before releasing it to the negotiating team.

RESPONSIBILITIES OF THE MANUFACTURING ESTIMATING GROUP

The organization of the manufacturing team involved in the detailed estimating process consists of specific type forecasters who have a sound technical background in their particular function such as hardware, test and support equipment, tooling and services, and make or buy considerations. The group's overall functions include the following:

142   The Marketable Manufacturing Cost Proposal

MANUFACTURING PROPOSAL ORGANIZATION

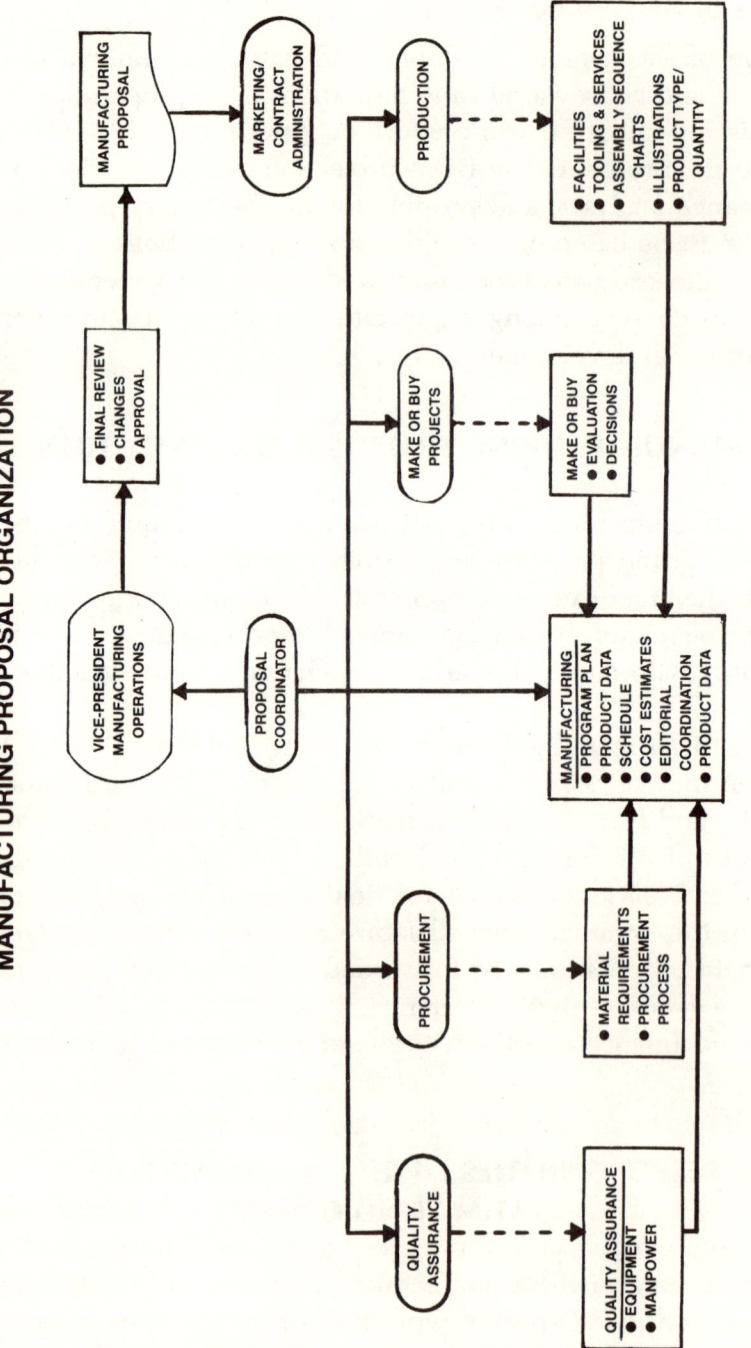

```
                    PROPOSAL
                   COORDINATOR
                        |
    ┌───────────┬───────┼───────┬───────────┐
    │           │       │       │           │
VICE-PRESIDENT │       │       │           │
MANUFACTURING  │       │       │           │
OPERATIONS     │       │       │           │
    │          │       │       │           │
    ▼          ▼       ▼       ▼           ▼
 FINAL      QUALITY  PROCUREMENT  MAKE OR   PRODUCTION
 REVIEW    ASSURANCE              BUY
 • CHANGES                        PROJECTS
 • APPROVAL
    │          ┊        ┊          ┊          ┊
    ▼          ▼        ▼          ▼          ▼
MANUFACTURING QUALITY  MATERIAL   MAKE OR BUY  FACILITIES
PROPOSAL    ASSURANCE  REQUIREMENTS EVALUATION TOOLING & SERVICES
    │       • EQUIPMENT • PROCUREMENT • DECISIONS ASSEMBLY SEQUENCE
    ▼       • MANPOWER    PROCESS                 CHARTS
MARKETING/                                        ILLUSTRATIONS
CONTRACT                                          PRODUCT TYPE/
ADMINISTRATION                                    QUANTITY
    │
    ▼
MANUFACTURING
• PROGRAM PLAN
• PRODUCT DATA
• SCHEDULE
• COST ESTIMATES
• EDITORIAL
  COORDINATION
• PRODUCT DATA
```

Exhibit 5-B

The Marketable Manufacturing Cost Proposal 143

- Provide estimates for effort to be performed by manufacturing relative to product production, design and manufacture of tools and test equipment, support needs, etc., which data are required for the proposal.

- Analyze the effect of any proposed changes on committed projects, and forecast the need for certain facilities and equipment.

- Review proposed manufacturing lot structures for compatibility/production conformance.

- Investigate and evaluate all make-or-buy problems affecting manufacturing and their impact on present/future manpower, material availability, and other relevant capabilities.

- Coordinate and develop production estimates for use by the overall organization in their issuance of pre-contractual work orders.

- Evaluate the compatibility of existing and proposed schedules and production plans with direct labor hour forecasts, and advise affected organizations of the practicability of such schedules and manufacturing plans.

Functional Activity Tasks

The individuals assigned to specific estimating tasks would concentrate on the following requirements relative to their sphere of activity:

- *Product/Product Line.* Project detailed estimates by part number, establish learning curves to the latest product configuration (actuals plus forecasted trends), record current actual product hours in part sequence to assembly, prepare manpower loading charts, and maintain product history and change impact by program/contract.

- *Manufacturing test equipment.* Part numbers are identified to the type of test equipment to be used. A log book is maintained by part number and major changes are recorded. Time standards and actuals are compiled to indicate the equipment performance factor. Equipment usage is coordinated with product schedules and manloading forecasts.

- *Special tooling.* A complete list of special tools is established and cataloged by code and classified by major product segment; maintenance is determined and maintained.

- *Make-or-buy activity.* All make-or-buy items are evaluated, manufacturing recommendations are prepared, and new facilities are coordinated with new processes. All make-or-buy decisions are recorded and coordinated with the appropriate requests for quotes to be negotiated. Manufacturing management is kept appraised of all pertinent recommendations/decisions.

- *Long range forecasting.* The impact of firm and proposed new follow-on programs must be determined relative to manpower requirements.

Manpower would be spread by function, program, and contract and identified as firm, follow-on and anticipated business. Five-year manpower forecasts are projected, and any schedule slippages or gains are reflected on the master manpower chart.

The overall mandate of the manufacturing estimating team is to develop operating forecasts on a current and long range basis. The projections include the direct effort and costs to be expended on current production programs and future anticipated business. This is a necessary prerequisite for developing successful and realistic manufacturing cost proposals on a timely, customer-oriented basis.

NEW PROPOSAL REQUIREMENTS

There are a number of considerations involved in preparing a sound and successful proposal. The tasks are many and varied. Responsibilities must be specifically delineated for their accomplishment. A brief description of the requirements follows:

Manufacturing program plan. The basic program plan includes such data as work statement, product description, operating policies, responsibilities, manpower, and facility needs. Other important considerations in the plan are production milestone charts, assembly sequence drawings and manufacturing operations, production capacity, and schedules.

Critical material and processes. This particular aspect of the proposal is very important since it discloses the technical aspects of the organization. The items include hardware, unique materials, tooling, special equipment, transportation and handling, storage, and processing. This section provides the support to substantiate the fact that the necessary capabilities exist to effectively perform the award terms in accordance with a given plan or any anticipated changes thereto.

Production organization and plans. A manufacturing organization chart is provided indicating the current and/or proposed organizational structure that will be utilized in the award performance. The customer is thus assured that assigned key personnel will not be displaced during the performance of the contract terms. Functions and responsibilities are also delineated.

Cost estimates. This part of the proposal undoubtedly receives the most intense scrutiny by the customer. The cost and estimating techniques must be subject to audit. Although the proposal lists cost computation results, it is also necessary that detailed back-up records be maintained to support all proposal calculations.

Make or buy. Most proposals include a make-or-buy exhibit. The definition, need, procedure, and decision-making process are presented in detail later in this chapter.

Special tooling. Special tools will be provided only to the extent that such tooling will produce reliability, interchangeability, and production rates consistent with overall program economy.

Fabrication and assembly plan. This portion of the proposal includes a well-defined policy covering definition, inplant activities, subcontract and outside production, processing, and quality assurance.

Manufacturing control. The manufacturing control process must be outlined and its utilization defined relative to assignment and report responsibilities which are oriented to the proposal format. Schedule performance, programming, and cost status interfaces are provided in this section of the proposal.

Manufacturing schedules. The policy and manufacturing schedule is included in the proposal with particular emphasis on the initial unit of production.

Manpower. Manpower charts, reflecting the general milestones, permit the customer to ensure that the chart(s) represent the same data contained in the schedule, program plan, and estimates.

Material handling, packaging, preparation. The policy and description must be defined. A chart is included which displays the material flow, storage, turn-around time, multiple use parts segregation, and packaging. Any unique technique applicable to the proposed product should be explained and illustrated in detail.

Manufacturing quality assurance. This aspect of the proposal covers such salient points as policy, definition, manufacturing operation interface, procurement control, liaison, receiving, processing, in-process audits, corrective action, final inspection, preservation, packaging, and any unique system applicable to the proposed product.

Manufacturing standards. The policy, definition, and specified plan relative to the proposed product are outlined. This section also includes the standard type manuals used within the organization.

Facilities. This part of the proposal requires special control so that indiscriminate added costs are avoided wherever possible. Included in this section are the organizational policy, plan definition, present facilities, property owned or leased, capabilities, government-owned equipment, and program interfaces.

Proposal Control Status

After establishing the basic tasks and personnel requirements, it is an excellent idea to prepare a check-off sheet as a control on the status and progress of the proposal development. The priority sequence and activity content listed below may vary among organizations dependent on emphasis and policy.

Priority Schedule	Scheduled Activities
1	Proposal input schedule
2	General manpower load related to current business
3	Preliminary facility layout
4	Initial draft of assignments
5	Preliminary management review
6	Final art work and typing
7	Final review of completed proposal
8	Clean up and publication
9	Customer presentation
10	Negotiation

BID PROPOSAL OVERVIEW

A number of steps are required in preparing a successful bid proposal which involves the participation of affected organizations as displayed in Exhibit 5-C. The activity sequence, processing and varied organization involvement may vary among other organizations depending on proposal complexity and procedures but, generally, this exhibit depicts a reasonable representation of a proposal process that is common to many organizations. A brief description of Exhibit 5-C follows.

- Initially, the customer defines and presents the proposal requirements to Marketing/Contract Administration who assign an identifying cost control proposal number and issue the request for an estimate to the concerned program manager.

- The responsible program manager reviews the request for feasibility of accomplishment and conformity to organization objectives and, if it meets the guiding criteria, approves the request and forwards it to the estimating organization.

- The estimating group further reviews the requirement, adds any supplementary guidelines needed, and forwards it to affected organizations who will participate in the proposal development. If organizational procedures require, the initial estimate may be considered as only preliminary until reviewed and approved by the program manager and responsible management.

- The approved preliminary estimate is provided to the estimating organization for further review and input coordination via a keyboard terminal device into the computer system. In the meantime, Contract Administration assembles the detail in the format required by customer directive.

- Contract Administration negotiates the proposal contents with the customer and, if accepted, issues a sales order to the program manager

The Marketable Manufacturing Cost Proposal 147

DEVELOPMENT OF BID PROPOSAL OVERVIEW

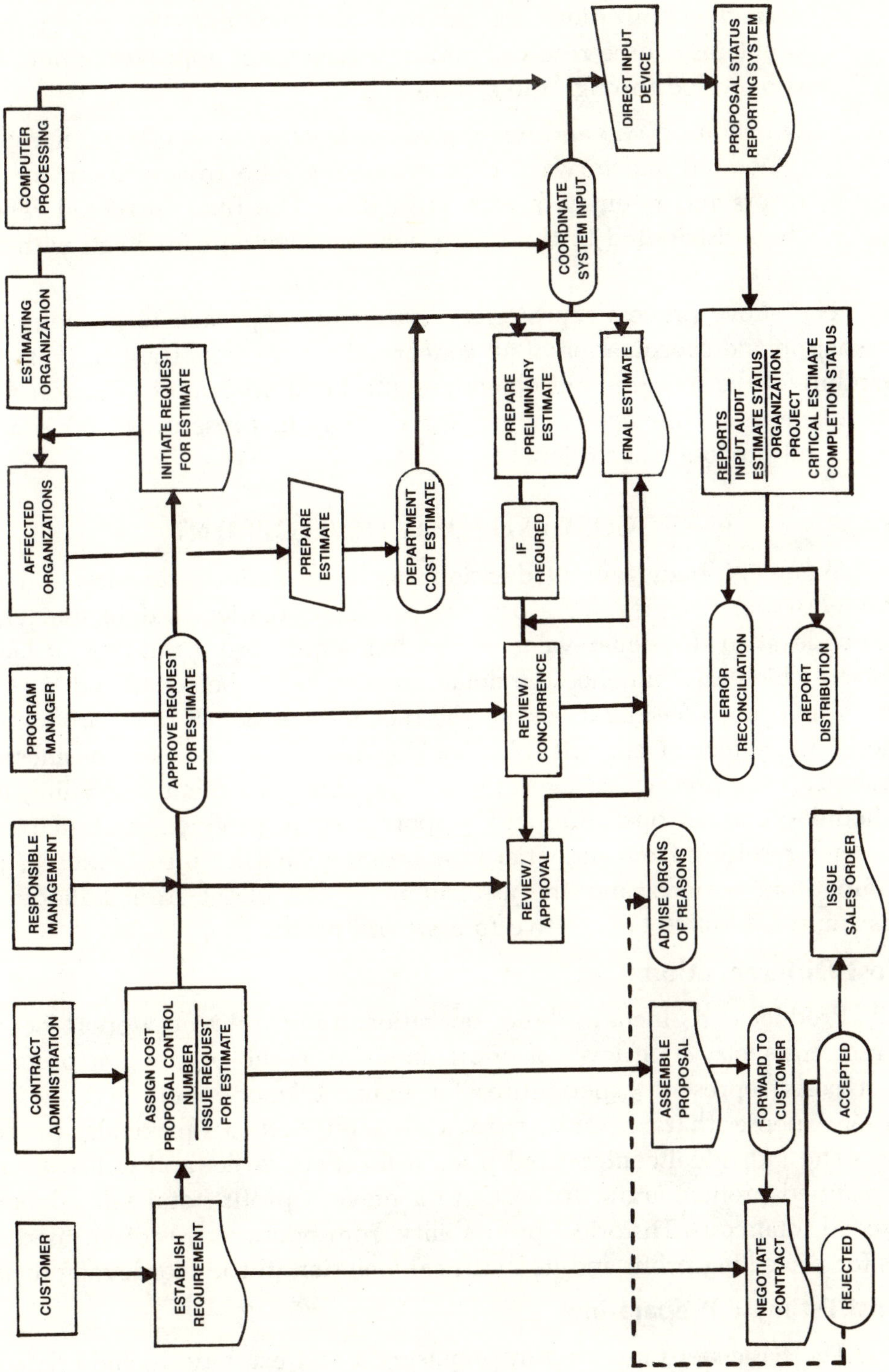

Exhibit 5-C

and estimating function for input into the computerized process for subsequent progress reporting. If the proposal is rejected, the concerned organizations are advised of the reasons for rejection. If the problems can be resolved and if management approves, a new estimate is re-cycled through the system.

- On an approved and negotiated contract, various computer reports are generated and forwarded to estimating who review them for possible errors and re-entry of corrective data. The final corrected reports are then distributed to the concerned organizations involved with the proposal.

The above process represents a systematic approach to proposal bidding; the liaison and coordination of all concerned is very important to (1) the understanding of the requirement objectives, (2) the appropriate reflection of the estimates, and (3) the need for concerted effort in presenting and achieving a successful proposal conclusion.

COST PROPOSAL DEVELOPMENT

When the management decision has been made to develop and respond to a customer's request for a product/service quotation, a determination must be made as to the dollar value of the bid. There are a number of factors involved which can influence the dollar amount bid to be submitted.

The prime considerations are the type of contract (R & D, production, services), the effect of current sales backlog plus proposed new business on the organization's productive capacity and capability to meet prevailing delivery schedules, current operating and support costs of production, anticipated cost changes resulting from potential new business, market intelligence of possible competitors' actions, and the assessment of the effect from adherence to a maximum allowable bid relative to costs and profit.

Cost Differentiation

Product costs include direct operational and indirect support needs. The direct costs vary with level of effort involved in the production process; indirect costs represent expenditures for indirect labor, operating supplies, and other expenses that cannot be specifically identified to a particular product.

The individual contract bid price will reflect direct and indirect costs plus a planned profit margin. In order to achieve a profit, total sales dollars must exceed total costs. Historical profitability from operations is often used as a basis for projecting profit and its statistical inclusion in the bid development.

Cost Estimate Preparation

The basic steps involved in preparing a cost estimate include data investigation, evaluation, and labor hour estimates. A description and discussion of this process follows.

Investigation. In the investigation phase, the basic data is organized and set forth relative to product/project identification, specification reference, quantity to be estimated, and scheduled date of information need. The pertinent engineering organization will provide supplemental data such as design drawings, product capability requirements, change possibilities in product development, anticipated development or design problems, indicated tolerance needs (if appropriate), and a list of drawings required to produce the product.

A make-or-buy decision must be made at this point of the investigation. It must be determined which components and/or assemblies will be manufactured internally and which will be purchased from outside sources.

The manufacturing planning organization generally provides the type and extent of tooling needed to manufacture the product in the quantity required. Other areas of investigation include any anticipated production problems, assessment of the available manufacturing capability, feasibility of achieving output rate of production, unit and type of equipment needs, and the determination of appropriate space and facility requirements. The planning organization usually provides documentation relative to assembly part lists, operation sheets or shop orders, and assembly sequence charts.

The manufacturing control organization is solicited for information concerning the work to be performed by manufacturing, a detailed product description, an overview of the production implementation, the delineation of responsibilities, the test and inspection requirements, and an analysis of critical manufacturing areas.

The production scheduling group provides schedules for commencement of the fabrication and assembly processes, lot structure units in process, planned *build-up* rates and peak rates of production, and anticipated completion of the program.

The planning estimator must also be familiar with the accounting system and how it will be employed in cost identification, accumulation, and data analysis processes. Varied cost-charging structures and practices may be used. As an example, direct manufacturing hours can be classified and accumulated as actual fabrication and assembly, or charged in total against lot quantities. In other situations, the manufacturing hours may be charged and accumulated to a unit indentification number by lot and assembly hours.

The accounting organization also provides a vital role in making available historical actual data of product costs that can be extremely important in preparing estimates and monitoring cost performance.

Estimate evaluation. Upon completion of the investigation, the compiled data relative to the product being estimated must be analyzed in terms of accuracy, reliability, and applicability. At this point in the estimating venture, adjustments and corrections may be required before the basic data can be used. It may be that the learning curve does not reflect the actual hour expenditure experienced on previous similar products. The deviation from the history pattern must be assessed and, if valid, consideration must be given to making the necessary adjustments to meet reality in performance results.

In the analysis process, it is necessary to validate the information compiled relative to the product itself such as composition, production processes, rate of production, availability of manpower, and equipment capabilities. Inaccurate information can lead to poor estimates, inability to meet customer requirements satisfactorily, and loss of business to competitors.

Labor hour estimates. A prime requisite in the estimating process is to determine the number of direct manhours required to manufacture a product in the quantities specified to meet the delivery schedule. A number of relevant approaches can be utilized, but the most common are the manhour estimate and the standard hour method. Variations of these methods are employed to meet individual organization requirements.

The manhour estimate is used when the basic data provided to the estimator is limited in scope as in the case of the ROM estimate. Under this method, the estimator projects the manhours required to produce the initial product unit based on the *learning curve* approach. Using the selected and applicable progress curve, subsequent production unit manhours can be readily calculated.

The *manhour method* is commonly used when the product to be estimated is the first of its type and precise specification data are lacking. The available engineering information is reduced to its lowest definable composition level for comparative purposes to previous products. The levels of comparison can be by component or part, sub-assembly, or assembly. The objective is to establish product and process composition relationships to historical data. Through comparative association of components or other definable characteristics, manhour values can be calculated for each level and process in the production of the product. If the comparisons indicate differences, the projected hours may have to be increased or decreased depending on the circumstances involved. The results of the product composition comparisons will yield individual manhour values which, when summarized, represent the total manhour requirements for the initial product needs. Using applicable progress curve factoring, the cumulative value for specified quantities of production are calculated. Further details of the process are in Chapter 10.

The scope of product information availability would govern whether the estimate would be the basis for final cost negotiations or restricted to budgetary use.

Standard hour is probably the most realistic, reliable method of estimating. This technique is involved with time and motion studies conducted by the appropriate engineering organization. This method is most applicable to mass production of a simple item. Standard hours represent a compilation of basic standard elements (employee operational task time) to provide a standard hour time for layout, punch press, drilling, cutting, milling, and so on.

The Marketable Manufacturing Cost Proposal 151

The *time standards* method is used when there is sufficient basic data provided to permit detailed analyses of the requirements. The steps involved in this process are as follows:

- A detailed standard hour estimate is prepared for each part contained in the engineering drawings.

- Each operating task in the manufacturing process is itemized in terms of part number, description, manufacturing code, item quantities, set-up, run time, and extended run.

- After each operation or series of operations, a standard hour setup and run value is determined and entered on a standard hour summary sheet.

- After completing an estimating form for each part, a summary is prepared separately starting with the top assembly drawing number for the product to be estimated. See the Standard Hour Estimate form.

STANDARD HOUR ESTIMATE

Part Number	Model	Date
Part Code	End Item Quantity	Effectivity

Type Operation	Part Description	Standard Hours	
		Setup	Run
	Unit Standard Hours		
	New Standard Hours		
	Added Standard Hours		
	Deleted Standard Hours		

- A listing is prepared of all drawing numbers, part identification, end item quantity required, manufacturing code, etc. All drawings are listed in sequence showing the next assembly or the sequential assembly pattern. This process enables the estimator to provide a standard hour estimate for any part, sub-assembly, assembly, and total product standard hours.

- From the detailed estimating sheet, the total standard value is entered in the appropriate column opposite the corresponding part number.

The standard hour value to be entered in the *run-extended* column (item above reference) is the product of the *end item quantity* and *run* columns.

- In the case of a single product manufacture, adding the *setup* and *run extended* standard hours would represent total standard hours for that one product.

- Since manufacturers rarely produce one of a product type, the standard hours are naturally affected by the product quantity in each production or the manufacturing lot structure. The lot structure must be determined in terms of the number of lots and products per lot. The lot structure is ascertained through the analysis of such data as *turnaround time* (time between the end of one lot and start of the next) and the required production rate.

- The setup portion of standard hours occurs only once for each production lot, but the *run time* involves each and every production. Therefore, the *setup* hours must be amortized over the lot structure and added to the run time to produce an average standard hour value for each unit of the total production run. The formula for determining average standard hours for any given quantity or units follows.

$$\text{AVERAGE STANDARD HOURS} = \frac{\text{Setup} \times \text{Number of Lots}}{\text{Total Number of Units}} + \text{Run Time}$$

A simplified example of the solution of this equation is shown below based on the following assumptions: 100 units; ten lots of 10 units each; estimated standard hour values for the product are 80 setup hours and 100 run hours.

$$\text{AVERAGE STANDARD HOURS} = \frac{80 \times 10}{100} + 100$$

$$800 \div 100 = 8 + 100 \text{ or } 108 \text{ hours}$$

- The next step in the standard hour technique is determining the *performance factor*. Upon application to the average standard hours, the result will represent the final labor hour estimate for a given program. The performance factor(s) is that value by which standard hours must be extended to produce labor hours—also represented by a progress curve. The factor is obtained by dividing standard hours into actual hours. In the case of a new product, the factor is derived by analysis of historical data for a previously produced product. There are often distinct similarities in product composition and/or operational processes. This subject is discussed further in Chapter 10.

It should be cautioned that irrespective of the technique(s) employed in determining the cost of a product, the method should be considered primarily as a tool to assist the estimator in his projection analyses. Experience and judgment cannot be over-emphasized as major factors in establishing sound, accurate, reliable estimates.

COMPUTERIZED BID DEVELOPMENT

An approach to computerized bid development which can be rapidly achieved and acceptable depends on historical data being fairly stable and representative of future anticipations. A description of the process follows.

1. Ascertain the average historical direct cost per production manhour. Through a thorough investigation, it can often be determined if past history on a similar type product is appropriate and, if so, this data will prove to be a useful guide in providing the rate factor on a new product or one currently being manufactured. A relevant and historical contract status report will provide cumulative direct costs to date and the associated productive manhours expended. Dividing the costs by the pertinent manhours will result in a dollar cost rate per hour. Any anticipated future changes should be reflected in the historical data.

2. Estimated direct cost per manhour is multiplied by the contract manhour requirements to derive the projected total direct costs.

3. Based on historical experience, a G & A/selling rate is calculated per manhour and applied to the projected manhours to obtain G & A/selling overhead dollars.

4. A planned profit rate per manhour is applied to the estimated manhours to obtain the profit margin dollars.

5. The dollar values of items (2), (3), and (4) above will provide an estimated sales (bid) value.

6. As an alternative, the overall manhour application factor would reflect the sum of the rates developed in (1), (3), and (4) above and applied in aggregate to the total manhour forecast to obtain the sales (bid) value. The component sales segregations provide a more detailed means for assessing the reasonableness of the projected direct costs, G & A/selling expense, and profit margin. Further, cost performance analysis and specific corrective action are more realistically achieved by data segregations.

The computer process should be programmed so that the capability exists to calculate the sales bid by an aggregate rate factor application or individual data item (direct costs, G & A, profit) as described above. In some organizations, it may be even more appropriate to use individual rate factors for direct labor, material, and overhead in the direct costs as a more detailed means for measuring cost performance. This type of segregation also permits a more realistic and selective means of data changes in the "gaming" process.

Profit Considerations

On fixed price production contracts, reliable cost estimating is imperative, because if the costs exceed those in the bid price, the result is a direct dilution of the planned profit.

In the case of cost plus fixed fee (R & D) contracts, the organization is usually assured of its planned profit, *but* bid price overruns can seriously jeopardize future business awards from the customer.

BID PRESENTATION EXPENSE

On government contracts, particularly, bid and proposal expense can be a significant cost depending on the complexity of the product or service. Two prime factors influencing the extent of the costs are (1) the urgency of need in obtaining new business and (2) what can be the anticipated effort on the part of competitors in challenging the organization's bid. Proposal expenses can run into many thousands if not hundreds of thousands of dollars depending on its requirements. The bid proposal involves technical and administrative support specifications and physical presentation. One well known organization acknowledged submitting over a *ton* of paper to support its bid proposal.

If an organization's sales business is declining and its stability and/or profits are being jeopardized, it may be absolutely warranted to proceed with the bid effort and expense in order to successfully obtain the contract. Further, the contract may yield additional follow-on business over which the expense can be amortized and a reasonable return achieved. In the case of the anticipated competitor effort (if it can be realistically ascertained), a judgment has to be made as to how much effort and cost will be necessary, and whether it can be absorbed in the attempt to "beat" the competition for the contract award. Past experience on award competition and anticipated results of the organization's effort should provide guidelines on the decision to proceed or not on the bid proposal.

BASIS FOR CONTRACT AWARDS

On government contracts, but not necessarily restricted thereto, there are other considerations involved in addition to the dollar bid which may influence the customer in awarding a contract and/or approving a sales order. One or more criteria noted below could be the basis for proposal rejection or a compromising agreement stipulation.

- Available manpower and technical capability to accomplish the task.
- Record of meeting debt obligations to vendors and subcontractors on scheduled dates.
- Prevailing business backlog that might interfere with the proposal delivery schedule.

- Past history of meeting, slipping, or beating delivery deadlines.
- Experience and expertise in the product or service area of contract needs.
- Past record in over or under-running research and development programs.
- Prevailing average cost per productive manhour on research contracts.
- Continual changes in direct/indirect classifications and their relative ratios.
- Viability of the organization's financial condition.
- Past record of involvement and investment in independent internal research and product development.
- Quality of the physical and detailed specification presentations in relation to the complexity of the proposal requirements.
- Resulting hardship in terms of idle/layoff labor and its effect on the economics of the surrounding community if the contract is not awarded.

Award Rationale

All of the above listed factors do not reflect the same relative weight or consideration in the determination of contract awards. For example, since R & D contracts are cost plus fixed fee, a history of low-cost performance tends to be more important than the actual price bid on a particular contract. On production contracts, however, the bid price is of prime importance. Internal research assumes a greater importance in the awarding of R & D contracts than in the case of production contracts.

Further, R & D experience in a given product area tends to influence the awarding of production contracts in the same product line; however, the converse is not true.

TYPES OF GOVERNMENT CONTRACTS

Due to the varied types of government contracts in existence, different estimating techniques are generally employed. This does not necessarily imply that data projections are *entirely* different among contracts (many facets are the same), but the end objectives can vary to meet certain situations. Types of contracts are as follows:

- *Cost type contracts.* Under the cost plus fixed fee contract, the contractor is reimbursed for allowable cost plus a fixed fee for the completion of requirements under the contract terms. Disallowances such as entertainment and advertising are negotiated but can have an impact on the final profit figure. New product R & D, product capability changes, and redesign are usually on the basis of cost plus fixed fee.

- *Cost plus incentive fee.* This type of contract contains a fee formula for underruns and penalties for overruns. Fees are based on various completion phases, and quality and price performance are of prime consideration.

- *Cost reimbursement without fee.* This type of contract provides for cost reimbursement only, and normally would be applicable to R & D work or facility contracts. The purpose behind the acceptance of this type contract is that it may provide the organization with an opportunity to inexpensively explore new areas of activity and products.

- *Cost sharing.* Under this type of contract, the contractor receives no fee and is only reimbursed for a negotiated portion of the allowable costs. This arrangement occurs on projects which are jointly sponsored by the government and the contractor. This is another form of an *opportunity* contract.

- *Time and material.* This type of contract provides for reimbursement of expended direct labor hours at specified hour rates plus material costs.

- *Fixed price contracts.* This type of contract reflects a firm price to be paid for product(s) to be delivered in accordance with the delivery schedule and/or services performed. The profit to the contractor represents the difference between the contract price and the total costs incurred. This type of contract is preferable to the customer since it places the burden of performance, within contract limitations, on the contractor.

- *Fixed price with escalation clause.* This type of contract provides for the upward or downward revision of the stated contract price upon the occurrence of certain contingencies that are specifically identified in the contract. It is primarily used when serious doubt exists as to the stability of the economic market.

- *Fixed price with redetermination provision.* Dependent upon the terms of the redetermination clause, the contract price is adjusted upward/downward in the prescribed time periods or upon demand of either party during or after the contract period. The adjusted price may involve a potential or retroactive situation or both. The contractor's cost accounting system must be appropriate and adequate if it is to be used as a basis for price redetermination. This type of contract is being de-emphasized and its use is being discouraged by the customer and the contractor except in certain applicable situations.

- *Fixed price incentive contracts.* Under the incentive type of contract, target cost and profit, price ceiling, final profit, and profit adjustment formulas are negotiated at the time of its initiation. It is possible that the contractor would not be entitled to a profit if the actual costs reach the ceiling imposed under the contract terms. However, this type of contract provides for a sharing in the savings of estimated costs as reflected by the actual costs incurred in the performance of the contract.

- *Definite delivery contracts.* Definite quantities of specified products and/or services are provided for a fixed period of time and the deliveries/performance are made to a designated location upon request. The contractor is on a standby basis, and deliveries are scheduled by the placement of customer orders.

The above type contracts and/or variations thereof may be applicable to commercial sales agreements as well.

WORK SCHEDULING

Manpower requirements, long lead time material needs, space, facilities, and special tooling are all based on the manufacturing schedule. The schedule buildup of any product is extremely complex, involving all of the parameters established for a proposal plus a few special schedule assumptions. The manufacturing day schedule is charted and indicates the beginning and ending time spans for procurement, tooling and test equipment, fabrication, assembly, possible modifications, packing, and shipping.

All new programs should be based on standard time spans plus built-in time allowances or contingencies to adequately support any product *unknowns*. The product engineering state of the art should determine the flexibility of the scheduled time spans.

In new proposal preparation and quotations, the manufacturing schedule plays an important part in the prime prerequisites of the manufacturing premises. The quantity delivered per month, the size of the fabrication lots, and the need span for the first article have a major impact on the cost of the product and the type of special tooling policy to be considered.

MAKE-OR-BUY OPERATIONAL CONSIDERATIONS

The make-or-buy decision involves a determination of whether research, development, or manufacturing will be accomplished in the organization or procured from outside sources. Make-or-buy plans are generally based on the following management considerations:

- As appropriate, what is the effect of the decision on price, quality, delivery, and performance of the product?
- Do cost studies indicate it is less expensive to make the product than buy or vice versa?
- Does the contractor plan to broaden his base of subcontractors through competition?
- Will the need for special techniques or equipment make buying more logical?

- Are the necessary competence, technical skills, experience, resources, facilities and equipment available in the vendor organizations?
- Will the production of the item(s) or performance of a service create a requirement, directly or indirectly, for additional facilities to be provided by the customer or the continued use of customer-owned facilities by the contractor?
- Does the contractor propose to ask the customer to provide additional facilities to the work in-plant for which there is capacity elsewhere that is adequately competitive in quality, delivery, overall cost and is acceptable as a source to the contractor?
- Is idle capacity available to absorb additional overhead (a point for "making")?
- Will small volume and capital needs make the investment unattractive from the standpoint of resource expenditure?

MAKE-OR-BUY DATA FLOW

In organizations that have considerable activity in the make-or-buy decision process, a committee of responsible, representative executives is organized to provide direction and formulate policies for make-or-buy decisions.

Implementation of make-or-buy requirements necessitates the participation of all affected organizations in accordance with the responsibilities outlined in policies and procedures and the committee's make-or-buy list. This list identifies basic products and services provided by the organization and also those procured from outside sources.

The make-or-buy activity is basically comprised of two phases: planning and contract performance. The *planning phase* is the preparation of a MOB plan and, when required, a contract MOB exhibit with supporting data as displayed in Exhibit 5-D.

The *performance phase* is the execution of the MOB plan, additions or changes to the plan, and supplemental activity in the form of routine determinations or committee decisions as shown at the bottom of Exhibit 5-D.

MAKE-OR-BUY (MOB) PLAN

The MOB plan is an internal procedure which is the basis for the preparation of a cost proposal and serves as a guide for work placement during contract execution. It is composed of a descriptive list of program requirements for parts and equipment items and assemblies along with the specific decision to make or buy.

A contract MOB exhibit is composed of a listing of the major items as defined by contractual requirments from the MOB plan. It is approved by the or-

The Marketable Manufacturing Cost Proposal

**MAKE OR BUY (MOB) DATA FLOW
SUPPORT TO-REQUEST FOR PROPOSALS**

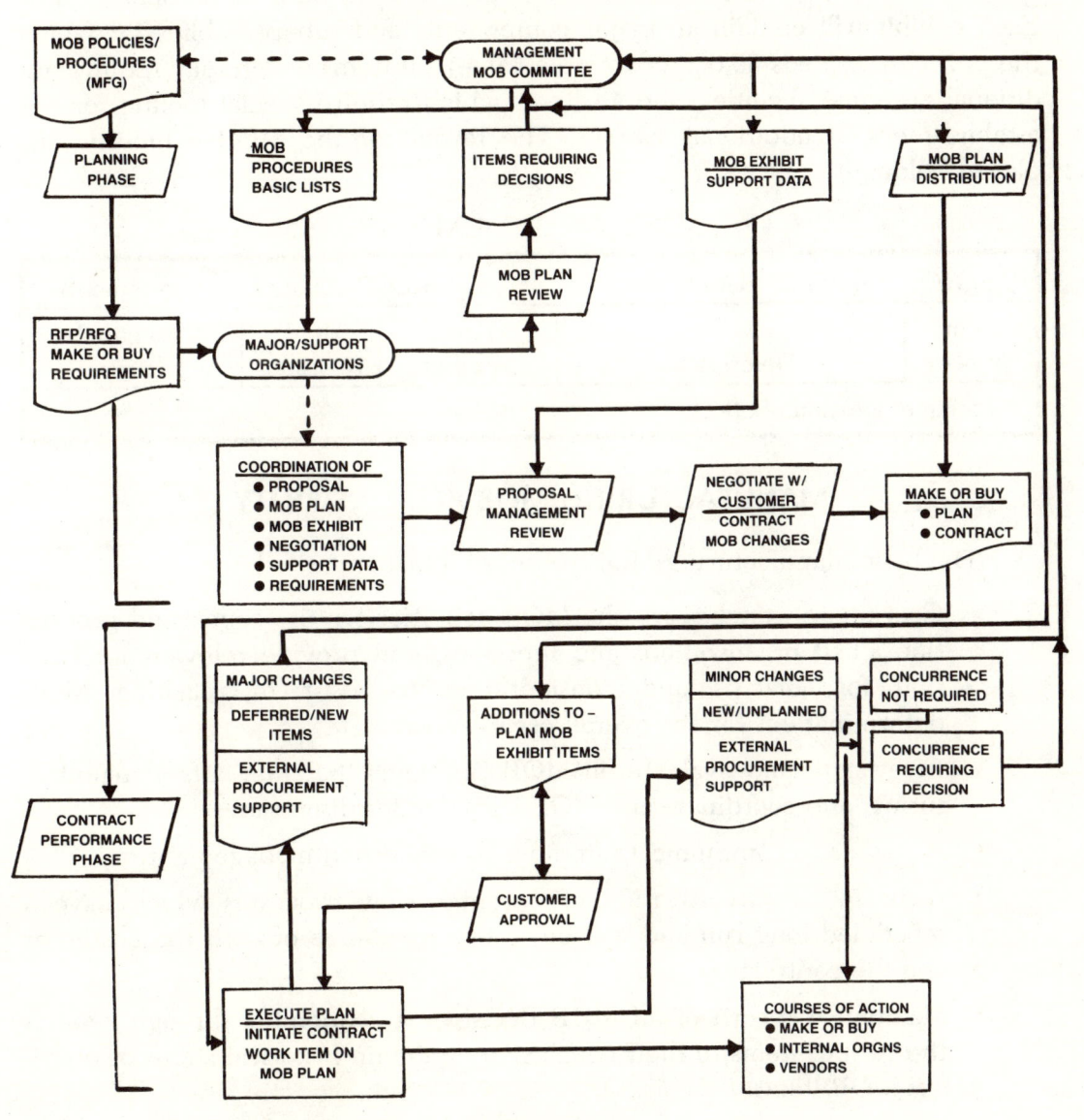

Exhibit 5-D

ganization's MOB committee, submitted to the customer for negotiation, and included in the contract. All proposals for letter of intent or definitive contracts having an anticipated value of a million dollars or more (value will vary among organizations) will include a MOB exhibit.

In contracts having an initial value of less than a million dollars, the exhibit requirements will not reflect a cumulative dollar value basis; for example, each added contract increment will be listed on the basis of its dollar value. Each exhibit will contain all major components and sub-assemblies for which the unit cost exceeds $5,000 (a variable value), all items which may require additional customer facilities, and all items which require special tooling for the establishment of additional sources. The format of the MOB exhibit is displayed below.

MAKE OR BUY EXHIBIT

REFERENCE (product identity):			SUBJECT (Make or buy agreement)	
Item Number	Description	Part Number	MOB Decision	*Potential Source
* Indicates location of effort.				

MANUFACTURING MOB RESPONSIBILITY

The basic manufacturing MOB responsibilities are as follows:

- Coordinate as necessary the MOB activities for the concerned production allied organizations and functions, and provide relevant information for analysis and consideration to assist in reaching MOB determinations for the overall organization.

- Investigate and evaluate all MOB problems that may affect manufacturing, and coordinate any MOB items under discussion.

- Resolve and communicate findings to concerned management.

- Assist in the investigation of potential new processes which have a scheduled long run and will be to the advantage of both the customer and the contractor.

- Maintain a record of all MOB decisions and monitor through reports the various items to their conclusion. Maintain historical status of previous MOB items.

- Collect and disseminate design criteria as far in advance of program schedules as possible. Seek assistance from Value Engineering on matters related to questionable "make" items of peculiar design.

- Maintain knowledge of future programs, types of equipment, processes, and facilities.

- Maintain records of estimates and provide the capability to track estimate progression from rough order of magnitude to the definitive contract.
- Establish program manpower loads to resolve impact on current programs.
- Verify schedule compatibility of item need date and "make" time spans. Consideration should be given to machine loading and department loads when influencing MOB decisions.

MOB AS BASIS FOR RFQs

A request for quotation (RFQ) is a document originated by the Marketing/Sales organization; it is a request for information to be supplied by affected internal organizations. The data provided is the basis for proposal development.

Generally, the Manufacturing Control organization will handle all RFQs involving existing, follow-on, or additional agreements that are derivatives of present hardware or contracts involving the customer. This designated organization will request each involved manufacturing functional area to develop and provide data as required to satisfy the RFQ. The data will be based on the RFQ MOB plan proposal agreed on by the Manufacturing Control and the organizational MOB representative.

The plan provides the basis for estimated direct labor manhour requirements and projected manufacturing schedules including time for planning, tooling, fabrication, assembly, and testing. Overall manufacturing cost estimates are developed and supplied as a part of the quote to the responsible organization. In addition, the *buy* portions of the proposed RFQ MOB plan is the responsibility of Procurement.

It is usually the responsibility of Procurement to coordinate with Manufacturing Control any changes to the Material Organization's quotation that may occur during the development period which may affect manufacturing related data. A copy of the final manufacturing quote is provided to Procurement.

Impact on the Organization

As discussed above, the MOB plan provides the basis for the RFQ and has the following impact on the organization:

- Influences program manpower loads. Through a proper balance of MOB determination, it stabilizes cyclical fluctuations and contributes to the maintenance of organization and technical skills for the benefit of future research and development programs.
- Effectively reduces the ultimate cost of contracts to the customer.
- Enhances community relationships through support of the Small Business Administration program.

- Provides second source for critical items assuring quality, schedule, and supply commitments.

Source of MOB Data

Historical make-or-buy data significantly influence MOB recommendations and decisions. There are three sources of reference to provide this information from computer files:

- *EDP MOB Transaction File.*
  The tape or disk historical file identifies each part by number and description. The appropriate file contains the following information for each contract requirement: RFQ number, contract identity, schedule need date, MOB recommendation, and justification or basis for award.
- *EDP RFQ File.*
- *EDP Actual Cost Data.*
  As actual costs are incurred, they are entered into the computer files and detail/summary records are provided to Manufacturing Control for review, comparison to estimates, and historical reference. All *make* items are identified by a single work order/work authority number. Procurement is contacted on *buy* item costs. These data sources also provide cost analysis information for support equipment. Special tooling is considered to consist of non-end items and is manufacturing's sole responsibility; therefore, it is not subject to MOB plans or exhibits.

FACTORS OTHER THAN COSTS IN MOB DECISIONS

In some organizations a comparative cost analysis of make versus buy data may be sufficient on which to base their decision criteria, but in other organizations there may be over-riding circumstances that can strongly influence the decision-making criteria. The non-cost factors include the following:

- *Confidential or secret projects* may preclude outside purchases as it would compromise new or exotic product design patents which could fall into the hands of the competition such as *toys* in the commercial environment and missiles, aircraft or weaponary on the government contracts which contain secret classifications.
- *Technological obsolescence* may influence the decision to buy externally. This can occur in situations wherein there are substantial changes in product composition which would require continual changes and investment in facilities and special tooling. The additional costs would be difficult to recover in the relevant time frame. Vendor purchases would soften the cost impact and shift risk capital to the seller who may specialize in that type of product.

The Marketable Manufacturing Cost Proposal 163

- *Availability of appropriate facilities*, machinery and equipment can lead to a buy decision if it is determined that the product requirements cannot be accommodated within the prevailing time production cycle without expansion and/or resource purchases with its drain on cash flow and profitability.
- *Quality assurance* can play an important role in the buy decision. In a number of instances, external organizations may have special manpower skills and be extremely specialized with sophisticated equipment/methods in a particular type of product manufacture. Therefore, to achieve the product quality required, it would be significantly advantageous to proceed in the buy direction rather than duplicate a costly resource capability.

PRODUCT COSTING FOR MOB DECISIONS

The specific type of costs to be included in a make or buy evaluation may vary among organizations, but some are basic to all analyses. The investigation of relevant costs are based on vendor quotations and internal historical/projected manufacturing costs. The data are developed on a worksheet format as illustrated below for ease in making comparative analyses.

MOB EVALUATION WORKSHEET

Organization _____ Date _____
Part Identity _____ Decision – Make __
Quantity Required _____   – Buy __

Item Description	Projected Costs	
	Purchased	Manufactured
DIRECT COSTS		
(1) Labor		
Materials		
Purchased Parts		
Subcontract		
Other		
(2) *MANUFACTURING EXPENSE*		
Fixed		
Variable		
Semi-Variable		
TOTALS		

NOTE: (1) Possible segregation by—straight time, overtime, incentive pay.
        (2) Identified to—indirect labor, fringe benefits, supplies, setup.

The costs should include out-of-pocket, incremental and total as appropriate. The direct variable costs will reflect all direct labor, material, and any other costs to be incurred, such as subcontract work that may be required due to tight production capacity.

Relevant to direct material costs, it is a common assumption that the material costs will be the same in the make-or-buy comparison. This may not necessarily be so, for the vendor of parts may procure his material in mass quantity purchases because of his involvement in this type of activity and thus material costs could be significantly lower. The vendor's knowledge of various sources of supply relative to price and quality could be superior to that of the manufacturer. Also, the vendor may be able to buy directly from the processor; whereas the manufacturer may be restricted to distributers.

Direct variable overhead is more difficult to identify as to whether it falls into the category of out-of-pocket or incremental costs. The pertinent expenses can include such items as shown in the "note 2 item" in the above worksheet. Any unusual costs incurred as a result of exceeding the norm of existing plant facilities should be included under variable overhead costs as well as special tooling.

Semi-variable costs for incentive pay and shift premiums are reflected in the long-run make or buy decision analysis. Other semi-variable expenses include additional storage facilities, preparation of engineering drawings, and increased procurement activity.

All make-or-buy decisions should be completely evaluated periodically to preclude production stagnation. Management should specifically outline a systematic approach to MOB analyses and decision-making criteria. The application of MOB principles should not be allowed to obscure the evaluation of other more complicated problems confronting management in its day-to-day operations. The analyses developed for a make-or-buy decision should never be the basis for the cost computations required to increase the gross profit percentages on sales production lines.

PROPOSAL STATUS REPORTING SYSTEM

To effectively control the continuing status of a proposal, particularly, in organizations that have a large volume of activity, a computerized system lends itself to efficiently achieving this objective with minimal effort and cost. A description of this type of system follows:

System Proposals

The type of proposals involved in this reporting system are identified as follows:

The Marketable Manufacturing Cost Proposal

- All management-authorized estimating and bidding efforts which are identified through their assignment of a Cost Proposal Control number and on which a bid decision has been approved.

- The related estimates may be firm, projected, or area type associated with either solicited or unsolicited quotes to customers or potential customers.

The proposals that are not normally included in this particular reporting system are as follows:

- Estimating and/or bidding activity that is not officially authorized or identified by a CPC (control) number.

- Internal estimates for management information only.

- Estimates for internal planning purchases such as make-or-buy decisions, budgetary adjustments, and long range forecasting.

System Input

Three types of input records are entered into this system as shown in Exhibit 5-E. Two of the forms are concerned with the original cost proposal identified as to the control number and title nomenclature; the other form provides department and project code numbers and titles. The *transaction identity* classification indicates type of specific input being entered and the *transaction activity* signifies the type of action to be performed by the computer program such as additions to the file records, changes, and/or deletions.

Proposal Control Output

There are five output reports as displayed in Exhibit 5-E. A brief description of the contents are provided as follows:

- *Input audit listing.* This report lists all of the transactions entered into the system and identified as to type and the cost proposal title. An internal computer audit is performed and a further output on this report lists the errors plus deletions and an abbreviated message as to the reason for file record rejections.

- *Department estimate status.* This report lists by department all the estimates in process by individual organization. The estimate with the earliest due date will be printed on the first line, the next scheduled for completion on the second line, and so on. Each estimate will have a CPC number and title line, a line for *due date*, a line for *anticipated date* if the due date cannot be met, and a line for *completion date* when the activity is completed. As soon as an estimate has been completed and reported, it will be dropped from the report.

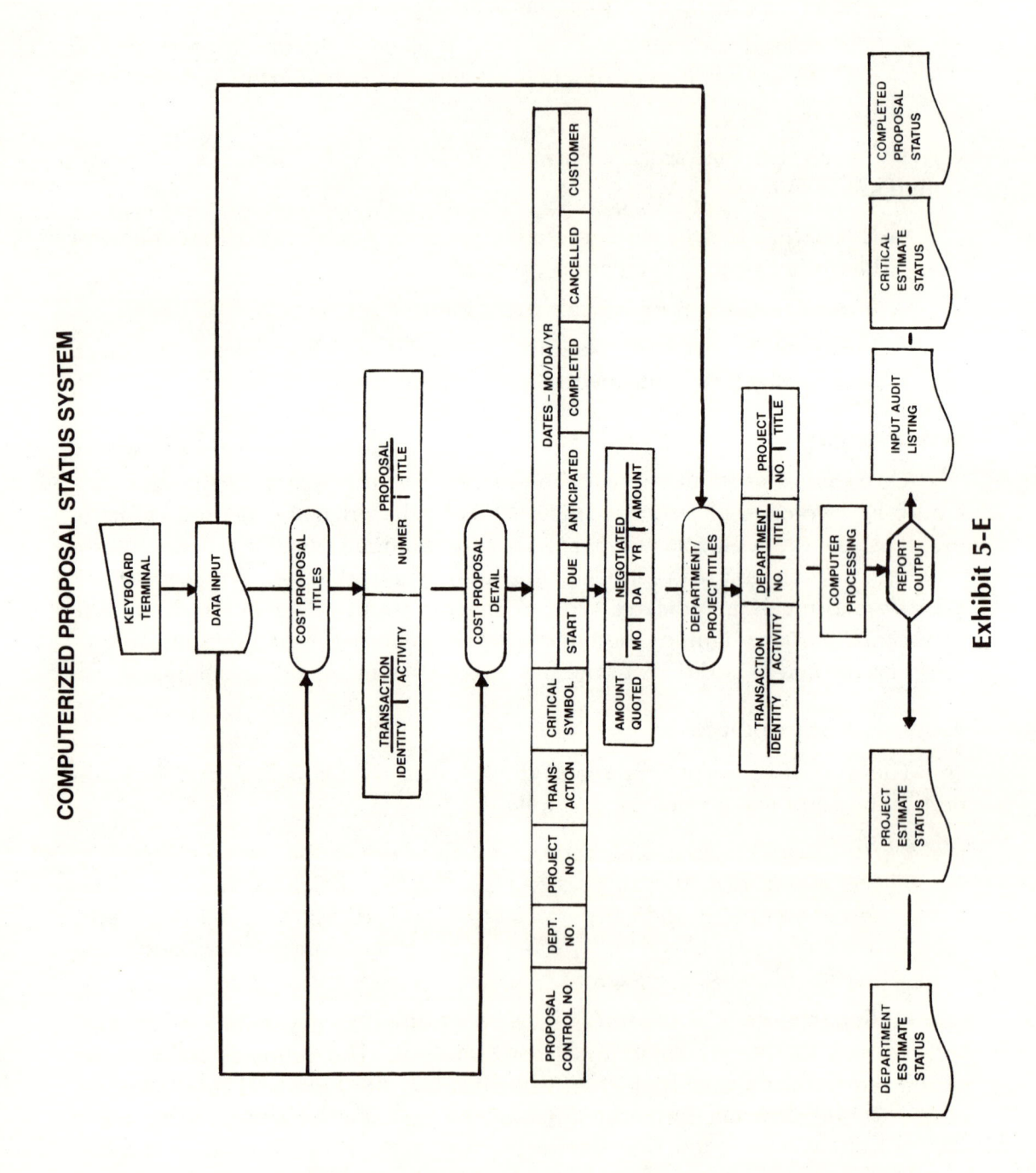

166 *The Marketable Manufacturing Cost Proposal*

Exhibit 5-E

- *Project estimate status.* This report contains a list by project of all the estimates in process—one project per page. Estimates are listed in sequence based on the estimating organization's *due dates.* The listed estimate is identified by a heading containing the cost proposal control number (CPC), its title identity, the action start date and, if applicable, a critical identifier.

  Grouped below the heading is a listing of each department having action to be performed on the listed estimate and the status information applicable to each department. The listed estimate will be dropped from the report as soon as the estimating organization reports a completion.

- *Critical estimate status.* This report lists status information for estimates identified as critical. The print format and the information to be reported for each critical estimate are identical to the requirements described for the *project estimate status* discussed above.

  A critical estimate is defined as an estimate in which management has expressed a particular interest or one which is competitive and has a mandatory completion date or one which must be expeditiously completed and therefore has been scheduled for completion in a minimal period of time.

- *Completed proposal status.* This report lists all of the cost proposals that have been completed but not negotiated. When a CPC is negotiated or cancelled, it is dropped after it has been reported. The report shows amount quoted, the date the CPC was forwarded to the customer, date and amount negotiated, or date of cancellation.

The above computerized system has proven to be effective, inexpensive to operate, timely, and an important tool in controlling cost proposals and their status.

ESTIMATING POINTERS

There are a number of salient points in this chapter which provide an overall understanding of the considerations involved in developing a comprehensive and salable manufacturing cost proposal. The proposal commences with a request for a quotation from the customer; the types and their requirements are highlighted. Responsibilities of the manufacturing estimating team are delineated.

The basis for contract awards is explained. Prevailing characteristics of various government contracts are defined. Make-or-buy considerations are outlined, and the pros and cons for the decision criteria are discussed. A mechanical cost proposal system for controlling the day-to-day status of each proposal is described; its use should preclude the possibility of any proposal being neglected through inappropriate action during the course of its development and processing within the system. The information provided in this chapter will aid the planning estimator in understanding the many aspects involved in the cost proposal preparation and presentation to the customer.

6

Computerized Product Pricing Techniques

Product pricing is an extremely important activity in all organizations because of its impact on the growth of the organization through expansion of sales volume, extent of profitability, and adequate return on investment. It provides a sound basis for inventory valuations. Further, product pricing provides management with essential data to make decisions and establish policies involved in controlling *what products can be effectively produced and at what cost* and *what products can be realistically sold and at what price*. The optimum profit results from maintaining proper balance between these two considerations. Concentration and emphasis must be placed on the most profitable products; otherwise, the sales department may unwittingly promote the sale of less profitable items with resultant profit dilution.

In many organizations, computerized techniques have been developed for various pertinent systems relative to cost accumulation, interpretation, recording, and reporting. The addition of the pricing factors discussed in this chapter will significantly enhance the cost estimating process, improve realistic product price establishment, and permit extreme flexibility in making price changes as required.

PRICING—ART OR SCIENCE?

Realistic product and/or service pricing is considered to be a complicated *art*, but is of vital importance to an organization's success. The use of mathematical formulas has not always been proven to be satisfactory. There often is a significant difference in the theoretical approach and its successful application in achieving sound results. Pricing has yet to become a recognizable *science* that can be effectively used on a continuing basis for accomplishing the ultimate results required and sought by management.

Involvement of the Pricing Team

The *accountant* is oriented to thinking that the establishment of prices for products or services is primarily dependent on a markup on costs to produce a satisfactory profit. The problem that arises with this contention is that the markup then generally represents a *calculated guess*. Costs alone are not sufficient information to establish a sound and intelligent price. The accountant's role would indicate that his prime contribution to pricing would be through the use of his knowledge and experience relative to the effect of volume on costs.

The *marketing and contract administrators* are the prime members of the pricing team. They can provide the planners with the necessary marketing intelligence as obtained from field representatives and/or customers relative to the prevailing market climate, competition, and prices.

Operation research specialists are trained to recognize opportunities for application of their art to the appropriate pricing strategy. This field of research involves the investigation and conclusions relative to a number of variables such as effect of price on volume, volume on costs, and price change on sales expenses and also counter measures to be taken when sales price changes are initiated by competitors.

The *economist* believes that all phases of pricing lie within his sphere of knowledge. He can generally provide applicable theories. In free competition, sufficient data for application of these theories usually is unavailable to any individual competitor, but nonetheless theories can be valuable aids in understanding the basic forces that govern pricing. With this knowledge and practical ingenuity in empirical application, pricing policies and practices can be developed which should contribute substantially to an organization's profitability.

Dependent upon the type of organizational structure and products, many organizations have an *estimating group* who research and develop costs for costing a product. This team of specialists are thoroughly familiar with the product requirements in terms of raw material and quantity and the operating tasks to be performed. They collaborate with designers, engineers, time study specialists, production planners, and project managers in the preparation of their cost estimates. Other data required are often provided by the type of team members described above.

Executive management is the logical choice to lead the pricing team. The executives review and integrate the different viewpoints and objectives of the team members. The pricing policy, however, must be determined and based on the pricing strategy to be followed in the near-term and its long range effect. Management is charged with this most important responsibility.

CONSIDERATIONS IN THE PRICING PROCESS

The normal market is a buyer's market unless the product/service is unique and a "sole source." The buyer rather than the seller often determines the price. The seller may quote a price but the buyer, in the long run, determines what that price will be or what product quantity will be accepted at any price. The average buyer is usually uninterested in what the product cost is to the seller (the opposite is generally true on government contracts). The price the buyer is willing to pay can depend on several factors: (1) availability of substitutes and their relative cost and usefulness, (2) expected future cost, (3) the advantages of possessing the product in terms of necessity and usefulness in their product or business, (4) prestige, and (5) prospective profit or savings from its use or resale.

Pricing Approach

When there is a lack of information concerning the market for a product, an acceptable markup on costs may be necessary for new and unique products or competitive bids on unusual contracts relative to construction and government defense (missiles, aircraft). Consideration must be given to the long range strategy as to what the market will accept. Should the price be high in order to recover development costs rapidly and, at the same time, run the risk of encouraging new competition by reason of high profit margin, or should the price be low in order to discourage new competition and recover development costs over a much longer period?

A competitive bid is often set at an amount believed to be sufficiently low but no lower than considered necessary to obtain the contract. If this bid will not provide the usual margin of profit above cost, the bidder must decide whether the attendant need or prestige of acquiring or performing the work or the necessity of keeping his organization employed warrants the acceptance of a smaller profit or possibly even a limited loss. Cost plus a standard markup is a particularly vulnerable practice in contract bidding. It may result in a needlessly low bid or, if used habitually, may reveal to competitors the organization's pricing method.

Return on Capital Employed

One objective method of determining a suitable markup on cost and its pitfalls when applied to competitive business is pricing for return on capital employed. It may not be always feasible to determine the optimum price to ask for a manufactured product, but it is relatively simple to ascertain the earnings or rate of return on capital required to attract new investment to the organization, as required, for expansion or new product exploitation. A price can be established at a rate that will provide a satisfactory return on capital employed. This principle is generally followed in regulation of public utility rates.

The above approach, however, may only be practical in some situations. Although total revenues of a regulated public utility are established on the basis of costs plus return on investment, the rates for individual classes of services

Computerized Product Pricing Techniques

are actually based on other considerations, particularly, elasticity of demand. Large industrial electric customers may have to be offered rates that do not reflect full allocations of joint fixed costs. Otherwise, they would install their own power plants and the costs to the remaining customers would be higher.

In non-regulated industries, it is obvious that the inefficient high cost manufacturer cannot charge a higher price than his efficient competitor in order to earn the same rate of return. Further, an attempt on the part of any organization to earn the same rate of return on all products probably would fail since it would price some products out of the market. Additionally, fluctuations in supply and demand make consistent application of this method impractical.

PRICING ECONOMICS FOR ACHIEVING PROFITABILITY

A significant element in pricing is an understanding of the economic theory of prices which serves as a guide in this task. A common observation pertinent to any product or service transaction at a *point in time* indicates that a lower price will generally result in sales of a greater quantity. However, at *different times* both price and quantity sold may be higher or lower.

Elasticity of Demand

The relationship of changes in sales volume consequent to change in price is a measure of *demand elasticity*. If the percentage change in quantity sold is greater than the percentage change in price, demand is considered to be *elastic*; if less, it is said to be *inelastic*. If a change of 5% in price results in a change (opposite direction) of 10% in quantity sold, then demand is elastic with an elasticity factor of *two*. If a change of 10% in price results in a change of only 5% in volume, the elasticity factor is *one-half*. An elasticity factor of less than unity represents inelastic demand. Generally, where demand is elastic, there are lower prices and profit margins with greater volume of sales yielding higher profits. Where demand is inelastic, there are higher prices and larger profit margins with lower volume yielding higher profits. Obviously, the benefit resulting from higher volume at lower unit profit margins is most apparent where fixed costs represent a relatively large proportion of total cost and may be realized to the extent of available capacity or low-cost addition to capacity.

The above situation would provide a simple pricing formula if only elasticity of demand could be measured with sufficient accuracy and provided also the elasticity factor was fixed for price movements in any amount and in either direction. Unfortunately, such is not usually the case.

Relative to price increases, they sometimes result in a substantial immediate loss of volume, followed by a gradual recovery later as customers adjust to the higher prices. A gradually increasing industry-wide price structure often stimulates current sales at the expense of future sales as customers increase inventories to anticipate the price rise.

Effect of Competition

The action of competition generally contributes to the intensity of effect on volume of a price change. However, the tendency will exist with or without direct competition, action by competitors, or similar action by all competitors. When demand for its product is elastic, an entire industry can price itself out of the market or it can increase its total market by appropriate price actions.

The classical economic theory of the most profitable price following these tendencies is that profit will be maximized highest at the price wherein marginal revenues and costs are equal. In further explanation, each reduction in price results in increasing the quantity sold and, when there is elastic demand, the quantity increases at a greater rate than the decrease in price; therefore, an increase from total revenues from sales will result up to a certain point. Beyond this point, they will decline. The net increase in *total* revenues from each successive price reduction before the point of diminishing returns is reached is termed the *marginal* revenues.

The above situation is similar with costs. Depending on the ratio of fixed to total costs, unit costs will decrease as volume is increased (within the limits of existing capacity), but aggregate costs for the entire quantity sold will increase. The net increase in aggregate cost from each successive price reduction is identified as marginal costs.

Price Influences

In summary, the primary challenge in effective pricing is to determine the supply of the product or service to be priced, the prices at which it is being offered, and the demand or market for the product or service at various prices. Costs may play an important or limited role. Costs primarily indicate whether the product can be made and sold profitably at any price. Costs do not indicate the amount of markup on cost that will be accepted by the buyers in the market.

There always is a lack of adequate information available concerning open markets and, as a result, pricing theory cannot be applied directly in most cases. Application of sound and practical judgment along with some ingenuity is required.

COST FUNDAMENTALS AS A PRICING BASIS

Product price planning is primarily concerned with the future. Historical and/or current costs cannot be effectively used in pricing unless the future operating environment and the price levels are expected to be similar to the current or past climate. This similarity is not likely because of periodic inflationary trends and changes in the market economy. Therefore, future product pricing should reflect provisions for increased salaries/wages (merit and cost-of-living), anticipated material price commitments (economic trends), realistic overhead rates to cover projected expense increases, and adequate allowances for fixed asset depreciation which are based on current replacement cost of the capital assets being employed in the operations.

Principles Involved

Effective pricing policies should consider *each product* on an individual basis. Product costs should include the costs for manufacturing, product research and development, marketing (advertising and selling expense), administration, and possible allowances for production losses resulting from defective or improper material, inadequate employee training, machine "downtime," high setup time resulting from short run production volumes, changes in product design or fabrication processes, and material substitutions.

Pricing policies should be based on *planned processing time* which reflects the hours to be utilized by the employee and the appropriate wage rates. Quantity and type of material to be used (as determined from past experience and/or engineering specifications) and application of adequate overhead rates to the projected labor base must also be considered.

Product costs should be segregated into the *individual direct elements of cost* as well as planned indirect labor, setup, etc. This detailed analysis and segregation of costs permits rapid changes to the cost items as required due to changes in production volume; it further provides a means to compare actuals to price estimates in order to measure performance and ascertain whether estimate planning requires correction.

Burden rates can be by operation, product/project, cost center, department, and division. A rate can be applied by machine or equipment hour and, more commonly, direct labor hours or dollars providing manhours or machine time coincide with product processing time. Some organizations have a material rate per hour to cover such expenses as receipt, storage, issuance, and handling of materials. Material rates are used if there is a significant difference in material costs as compared to labor costs in the individual product.

G and A and selling expenses are usually fixed and on a continuing basis, and they have no direct relationship to the total cost of the product being manufactured. Most organizations develop a rate per direct hour or dollar to spread these expenses over products/projects, or the rate can be a percent of sales, depending on whether the material element is proportionate to total costs. These expenses are further identified as *period costs*.

Margin contributions. At times, competitive price conditions may not permit the complete recovery of the normal product cost. A knowledge of the approximate direct cash outflow, which is incidental to production and marketing, will disclose the lowest price at which the product can be sold. This disclosure reflects the margin in excess of the direct cash outlay.

Under the above circumstances, it is very important to know the values for fixed and variable overhead. By excluding fixed expense from each overhead rate which is generally not affected by the rise and fall in production or sales volume, the resultant variable rate is used for computing product cost cash expenditures. This knowledge then represents a basis for making intelligent decisions relative to whether some part items can be more economically purchased on the outside versus internal manufacture, also as to changes in product mix, elimination of an unprofitable product, addition of new items, and effecting more stringent cost control procedures.

In summary, product cost data provided to management for establishing selling price policies should represent the planned cost so that knowledge may be gained in advance about relative profit by product in the future market environment. Pricing and planning cost information cannot be obtained from historical records without adjustments to cover probable changes in cost levels and anticipated changes in operating conditions. The objective in pricing is to project in advance the net profit margin after recovery of the full costs on a current dollar basis as should be provided for in the selling price.

IMPACT OF COSTS ON PRICING

Product costs have a definite impact on pricing, but they do not represent all of the determinants in establishing a product price. This is because of the dynamics of supply, demand, and competition in the business environment. The prime utilization of cost data is to establish the minimum requirements for pricing goals and further to provide the basis for ascertaining profit results stemming from varying price decisions.

Pricing Policies

In establishing pricing policies, management provides the basic guidelines in setting product prices such as overall corporate growth objectives, increased earnings per share, profit maximization, suitable return on investment and expanding market penetration plans. Relative to the physical pricing decisions, considerations involve organizational pricing policies and procedures, projected sales volume, capital investment evaluation, and plant capacity utilization.

Historical costs and revenue data are primarily used as a basis to assist and improve on the future estimating process in price setting. Projected future costs and revenues, however, are the most important criteria in product price development, taking into consideration the factors outlined above.

DIRECT COSTING IN PRICING DECISIONS

Advocates of absorption costing generally assume the following viewpoints:

- Direct costing is only useful for one-product type organizations because multi-product firms do not cost individual products adequately.
- They point out that usually there are many products that use different proportions of the time of costly facilities.
- They question whether each product is assigned its fair share of overhead if fixed manufacturing costs are not allocated to products.

Under the standard direct cost system, period costs are allocated to all products or product lines as part of the profit planning operation at least once a year. The allocation is made in total for the planned volume and sales mix. They are never unitized. Direct cost advocates indicate that it is the unitizing of period costs that makes absorption costs confusing to operating managers because the unit costs are only valid with the *assumed* volume and mix. By showing the allocation in total with the projected volume and mix, confusion is avoided. Further, operating management can readily see and understand the true inter-relation of prices, costs and volume.

In Defense of Direct Costing

The profit plan for the ALPHA organization shown below illustrates the comments above. In addition to the allocation of period charges to product lines, the cost distribution for capital employed is also shown. This procedure permits a realistic appraisal of both short-term pricing and long-range planning. By carefully selecting the product lines, the profit plan will show not only whether each product is bearing its fair share of burden but also if it is providing an adequate return on capital employed. This is the true measure of profitability according to direct costing advocates.

Note in the illustration on page 178 that the profit plan has a column for idle plant which permits the use of a long range volume basis for product pricing while, at the same time, providing for realistic profit plans for the coming year. This column would show a profit in any year in which the planned volume is above the selected normal percent of capacity and a loss in a year when it is below normal. This is reflected in the display.

ALPHA COMPANY
PROFIT PLAN (000s $)

Description	Product A	Product B	Idle Plant	Total
Sales Forecast	15,000	25,000	0	40,000
Direct Cost				
Direct Labor & Expense	4,500	7,500	0	12,000
Material	3,000	10,000	0	13,000
Total	7,500	17,500	0	25,000
Gross Profit Margin	7,500	7,500	0	15,000
Period Costs	3,750	5,000	200	8,950
Net Operating Profit	3,750	2,500	(200)	6,050
Gross Profit % Sales	50	30	—	37.5
Net Profit % Sales	25	10	—	15.1
Capital Assets Employed	10,000	12,500	2,000	24,500
% Return	37.5	20.0	(10.0%)	24.7

Day-to-Day Pricing Decisions

Direct costing data can be very useful in determining the target selling price. One procedure is to divide the estimated direct cost of the product to be priced by the complement of the profit/volume ratio for that product line. For example, the appropriate price for a new product which is to become a part of Product Line X and has an estimated direct cost of ten dollars per unit would be calculated as follows:

$$\text{Computed price} = \$10.00 \div (1.00 - .20) = \underline{\$12.50}$$

In actual practice, markup which also reflects the discount structure is generally computed in advance, so that the suggested selling price is determined by multiplying the direct cost by the proper markup factor. In organizations having direct product costs, there are various factors that can be used for selecting markup percentages that will yield a target return on capital employed for a relative ratio of conversion cost to material cost.

In summary, under the direct costing approach, only the variable manufacturing direct costs and selling/administrative expenses are utilized in the product cost. It does not include the fixed overhead, which could be highly significant in the product cost if considerable fixed resources and plant capacity are involved in product production.

COST ABSORPTION APPROACH TO PRICING

In organizations that *do not have* direct cost available, the most common procedure used in determining costs for pricing products is identified as *absorption costing* and described as follows:

- Production cost centers are established by machine type and/or processing method.

- All departmental labor and expenses, service department allocation or charges, and fixed manufacturing expenses are distributed to the cost centers.

- Costing rates per unit (usually manhour or machine hour) are established for each cost center based on either the normal level of activity or the projected level.

- The cost estimate for a given product details the manhours or machine hours for each cost center and the material quantities required per unit.

- The manhours or machine hours, extended by the costing rates, and the quantities, extended by the estimated prices, are totalled to obtain the overall manufacturing cost.

- To the above total, a percentage is added to cover selling and administrative expenses as well as another percentage to provide for a profit margin.

Aspects of Absorption Costing

Generally, the accounting function monitors the overhead rates. When production volume fails to absorb the total cost of a given cost center, the rates are increased and, conversely, when the volume over-absorbs the burden, the rates are reduced. Utilizing the logic of this method of competitive pricing to an extreme, one of two situations must result:

- The product is priced below the competitive level and volume is increasing. Burden rates are reduced because the factory burden is being over-absorbed. This results in lower prices that cause volume to increase faster until the point is reached at which orders exceed capacity.

- Or, the product is priced above the competitive level and volume is dropping. The costing rates are increased to absorb the burden on the lower volume. This situation results in higher prices; the product becomes even less competitive and volume drops more rapidly. Costing rates will again be increased and so on until the volume is zero and the costing rate is infinite.

In the first situation, the organization failed to maximize profits within plant capacity and, in the second instance, the organization is forced out of business. In view of these results, it would seem ridiculous to assume that management would increase prices when the organization is losing business to competitors and conversely reduce prices while taking business away from competitors.

A Solution to the Dilemma

A number of organizations resolve the above problem by using a long range volume or capacity basis for setting burden rates. Management's pricing objectives are to obtain prices for its products which would recover all costs and provide an acceptable return on capital invested. It has been determined that the long run normal or average cost of a product constitutes a more appropriate guide than does the cost that prevails in any given short period. A basis for this direction is that unit costs predicated on short period volume increase when volume declines and decrease when volume increases.

For example, if management should follow short average costs in pricing, it might expect a serious reduction in its share of the market potential if it increased selling prices at a time when industry activity was declining. On the other hand, to lower prices when a temporary rise in volume occurs destroys the opportunity to recover losses in periods of low volume. The above disadvantages can be minimized by developing product costs in which the fixed costs are spread evenly over the number of units produced during a period of sufficient length to average out short period volume fluctuations.

Direct Cost Viewpoint

Using direct costing techniques, however, for pricing products generally eliminates the above confusion and complexity. With direct cost data, most pricing decisions can be made by non-accounting executives simply through the use of basic arithmetic.

The decision of which costing method to use is dependent upon the organization's policy, the economic climate, and other influencing factors that can be known only by detailed analysis of their advantages and pertinance to effective pricing.

COST ASPECTS IN COMPETITIVE PRICING

Costs play an important role in competitive pricing decisions. Following are some situations in which competitive pricing decisions are made; costs reflect a different role in each.

- Cost for *customized products* (made to order) have a direct effect on prices. The bid price is determined by certain markups on cost estimates. When too many bids are lost, the markup factors are reduced and, conversely, they are increased when it is determined that an adequate share of the market can be obtained in spite of the higher prices.

- Prices on *general competitive products* are predicated on a cost markup. The leader in that particular field sets the price. The rest of the industry follows, and its costs are used for selective selling.
- In the situation in which the *product price is set by custom*, costs determine the weight or quality of the product that can be offered. The usual procedure is to take the retail price and work backwards in order to determine the basic costs which in turn governs the type of product that can be profitably offered. The resultant effect from this procedure is that it may force the development of more efficient processing methods and/or the use of quality comparable substitute material.
- Relative to *products of standard quality and form*, costs indicate to management whether or not to produce a product. The marginal manufacturer's cost at a given level of demand determines the market price.

In the situations discussed above, direct costing techniques provide better data for pricing decisions, make possible the achievement of capacity levels, and maximize profit by selective selling after capacity is reached. Total or direct estimated costs, however, represent only the initial starting point in determining the selling price.

SALES PRICE DETERMINATION FACTORS

There are several approaches that can be used in developing a sales price based on estimated cost and profit requirements. One common approach, discussed below, involves the use of the computer capability for calculating the required data and, upon availability of actuals, outputs a report indicating cost performance results.

Cost Estimate Development

Labor and overhead input data are based on historical experience by cost center. The prime reasons for estimating costs at the cost center level are that the work is performed at that level (labor estimates are more realistic) and, further, in cost performance analyses, variances can be pinpointed specifically to the area of occurrence and responsibility.

Historical *labor rate averages* are adjusted for anticipated increases that could occur during the future production periods. Consideration is also given to the learning curve factor in sustained production increases.

PRICE DETERMINATION FACTORS
PRODUCT COST DEVELOPMENT

DESCRIPTION	PLANNED PER UNIT COST	PLANNED COST FOR 100 UNITS	ACTUALS	VARIANCE
LABOR				
COST CENTER 1	5.00	500.00	AS THEY	CALCULATED TO
COST CENTER 2	8.00	800.00	BECOME	EVALUATE COST
S/T	13.00	1300.00	AVAILABLE	PERFORMANCE
OVERHEAD				
COST CENTER 1	7.50	750.00	COSTS ARE	
COST CENTER 2	8.00	800.00	ACCUMULATED	ACTUALS CAN
S/T	15.50	1550.00	BY 100 UNIT	BE REDUCED
MATERIAL	40.00	4000.00	LOTS	TO PER UNIT
OT PREMIUM	.50	50.00		COST BY COST
PRODUCTION COST	69.00	6900.00		ELEMENTS BY
TOOLING	5.00	500.00		DIVIDING BY
G&A (10% × $69.00)	6.90	690.00		100
TOTAL COSTS	80.90	8090.00		

Exhibit 6-A

Overhead expenses reflect past experience by detailed accounts and are translated into overhead rates which are applied to direct labor hours or dollars.

The *quantity and type of material* to be used in the product are carefully ascertained based on detailed design specifications and results from a pilot (prototype) development product. Procurement, with their vendor contacts, provides the necessary raw material prices for costing purposes. Cost savings on material can generally be achieved by quantity purchases.

Past experience has indicated that inevitably *overtime* will be required to meet scheduled deliveries. This factor is calculated to be *fifty cents* per unit based on total labor hour correlation.

Tooling replacement, upgrading, conversion, and possible site rearrangement expenses must be considered in the estimate. These are based on past production experience. The factor of $5.00 (in Exhibit 6-A) per unit used is predicated on a 2,000 unit production schedule at a historical and/or planned $1,000 cost. The writeoff of the cost is spread to each unit produced.

Consideration is given to anticipated expenditures for *G & A and selling expenses*. Based on a detailed assessment of the individual expenses, it is determined that 10% of the production costs is a representative expense value for the cost estimate. Some organizations develop the G & A rate based on direct labor hours or dollars. Either correlation method is acceptable based on relevancy and organization practices.

Profit/Selling Price Development

A major consideration in establishing a realistic product price to achieve a reasonable return concerns the profit requirements. Excessive profit objectives can lead to a non-competitive total product price with the resultant loss of sales and the threat to the survival of the organization. Conversely, insufficient profit can impair (1) organizational growth potential, (2) ability to meet its liability commitments, and (3) ability to improve or replace its machinery and equipment for advanced operational efficiencies. It can also have a negative effect on production capacity and preclude dividend payments to stockholders who invested capital in the organization. Sound profit planning is therefore a "must" to a successful business venture. Important factors to consider in developing profit requirements are as follows:

- Due to continual *improvement in equipment technology*, allowance must be made to amortize the cost of existing and planned equipment requirements. This is accomplished through the application of a reliable depreciation rate, based on the useful life of the property, to the prevailing gross property investment and planned new facilities and equipment. This is generally done by individual item and translated into a calculated composite and weighted depreciation rate. In Exhibit 6-B, a 15% rate is considered to be representative based on historical experience.

- Most organizations have *long term debt commitments* that must be met from profits. The indebtedness is created from bank or other institutional loans, bond issues and/or other credit borrowing instruments. Sinking funds are established to which annual contributions are made over a selected time period to meet the scheduled date of repayment in the future. The sinking fund is generally always financed by present and anticipated profits; therefore, an allowance must be made in the product price to accommodate the fund requirements.

- *Dividends* are of important concern to organizations that issue capital stock to support their operational requirements and growth. Most prospective non-speculating stockholders review an organization's dividend payout history before they purchase stock. Dwindling sales and profits may preclude or reduce dividend payments that could make the stock unattractive for acquisition with a consequent fall in market value. Disgruntled stockholders and/or board of directors could have an adverse effect on how the organization will operate in the future and could lead to the replacement of responsible management executives and their staffs. Poor stock performance can also lead to severe problems in financing an organization's current operations as well as its future stability and survival. Therefore, most organizations make allowances in their profit planning to include dividend payments. Most utility organizations particularly pay an attractive dividend rate since they are constantly seeking additional capital to exploit new natural resources and to expand facilities.

PRICE DETERMINATION FACTORS
PROFIT/SELLING PRICE DEVELOPMENT

EQUIPMENT REPLACEMENT	000s	DIVIDENDS	000s
GROSS INVESTMENT		CAPITAL STOCK	
PLANT/FACILITIES	$20,000	MARKET VALUE	$12,000
REQUIRED EXPANSION/		PLANNED DIVIDEND	
EQUIPMENT	300	RATE	.05
TOTAL GROSS		DIVIDEND OUTFLOW	$ 600
INVESTMENT	$20,300		
ANNUAL		REPAYMENT OF LONG TERM DEBT	
DEPRECIATION RATE	.15	LONG TERM DEBT	$1,800
ANNUAL		ANNUAL REDUCTION (10 YEARS)	180
AMORTIZATION VALUE	$ 3,045		
		SALES PRICE DEVELOPMENT	
SUMMARY		$3,825 ÷ 48 = $7,969 (BEFORE TAXES)	
EQUIPMENT REPLACEMENT	$3,045	$7,969 ÷ $20,300 = .3925 (PROFIT %)	
DIVIDENDS	600		
DEBT REDUCTION	180	PER UNIT COST (ABOVE)	$ 80.90
	$3,825	PROFIT ($80.90 × .3925)	31.75
		SALES PRICE PER UNIT	$112.65

Exhibit 6-B

The dividend rate selected in the illustration in Exhibit 6-B is 5% which is very conservative in an economic inflationary environment and is only being used for illustrative purposes—yet even now, some organizations are paying less or nothing at all.

For reasons stated above, the three factors discussed are used in developing a realistic profit rate for reflection in the product price.

Calculating the Product Sales Price

After the above pertinent data have been extracted from financial records and other factors have been determined (depreciation, sinking fund, dividend rate), the computer program in the mechanized process performs the following calculations to derive a selling price:

1. Gross property investment and planned expansion and acquisition projection values are totalled and a composite depreciation rate is applied to obtain the annual depreciation.

2. The annual reduction rate of the long term debt is entered into the computer. The rate is derived by dividing the debt amount by the number of years required to accumulate the total debt value. In Exhibit 6-B, the debt of $1.8 million is divided by the ten year period for payment, or $180 thousand is the annual contribution to the sinking fund reserve. It is presumed that the interest has been included in the overall total.

3. The dividend rate is entered into the system. It will be applied against the number of shares of stock outstanding.

Computerized Product Pricing Techniques 185

4. As shown in Exhibit 6-B, the sum of the above three figures is capitalized by dividing by 48% to give effect to the before-tax basis (assuming 52% corporate tax).

5. The result from the prior calculation above, item 4, ($7,969,) is divided by the gross investment ($20.3 million) to obtain a profit rate percent of 39.25%.

6. The profit rate percent is applied to the total cost per unit ($80.90) to obtain the profit dollars ($31.75) which, when totalled with the costs, results in a projected selling price of $112.65 per unit. This price is reviewed by the marketing organization to determine whether it is compatible with competitor quotations and customer acceptance. At this point, management makes a decision on any changes, up or down, based on market intelligence appraisal and other pertinent considerations.

COMPUTERIZED PRODUCT PRICING

Mechanical cost collection, financial record file retrievals, factor development, and varied data manipulations are common practices in many organizations. The computerized system is fairly simple to develop and has great potential in significantly improving realism and accuracy in product price determination. The program has extreme flexibility in making data changes, recalculating new prices as the occasion demands, testing alternative courses of action, and, most importantly, considerably reducing the manual effort and cost involved in achieving price setting objectives.

Customer Price Lists

Price lists can be prepared mechanically and will reflect the influence of the learning curve aspect. This is done by determining the midpoint on the learning curve and calculating the selling price for a specific quantity. Naturally, the smaller productive units will reflect reduced profit margins as opposed to larger productive lots wherein the learning curve influences production output in terms of increased quantity and reduced unit cost. Aspects of the learning curve are discussed in depth in Chapter 10.

The selling price can be calculated at various points on the curve which will indicate a declining selling price as quantity units of production are increased. The learning curve interval points can be selected at any quantity levels, for example, 50, 100, 150, to prepare a realistic customer price list.

Product Cost Development

Exhibit 6-C illustrates the mechanical system in developing cost estimates which is the first step in determining a selling price. An abbreviated discussion of this system follows. The product planning estimator provides the basic input into the program after consultations with engineering, manufacturing, and financial personnel who have access to and knowledge of product requirements in terms of design specifications, operational processes, and historical costs and projections.

Input

- Average wage rates and operational time involved in producing a product unit are entered into the program by cost centers.

- Average overhead rates by cost center are inputted and based on historical experience, which is adjusted for any known or anticipated changes in production support expenditures.

- A representative quantity lot is a direct input for costing a quantity lot.

- Type and quantity of material to be used for the product unit and associated costs are entered into the program.

- The overtime rate factor per direct hours is entered, based on past production experience and management objectives.

- The financial function provides a projected G & A and selling expense percent which is based on historical correlation to total manufacturing cost per unit.

- Manufacturing provides tooling replacement costs, based on history and the anticipated future costs, and their amortization is calculated to provide the value to be charged against each production unit.

Computer Processing

The processing steps involved in this price determination system are outlined as shown on Exhibit 6-C.

1. Cost center labor costs are obtained by multiplying the operation time per product unit by the average wage rate in the specific center. The labor cost per unit is multiplied by 100 to derive the cost for a 100 unit lot by center. The cost center labor costs are summarized to obtain the total labor costs for the units of production.

2. The individual cost center overhead rates are applied to their respective cost center labor hours to obtain the overhead costs per unit. Overhead rates will vary among cost centers dependent upon the amount of indirect support and expenses involved. The overhead dollars by unit and cost center are multiplied by 100 to determine the cost for 100 product units. The cost center overhead is summarized to obtain the total overhead costs for 100 units.

3. Labor costs and overhead expenses are combined for each cost center to obtain the total basic cost by cost center for 100 units.

Computerized Product Pricing Techniques 187

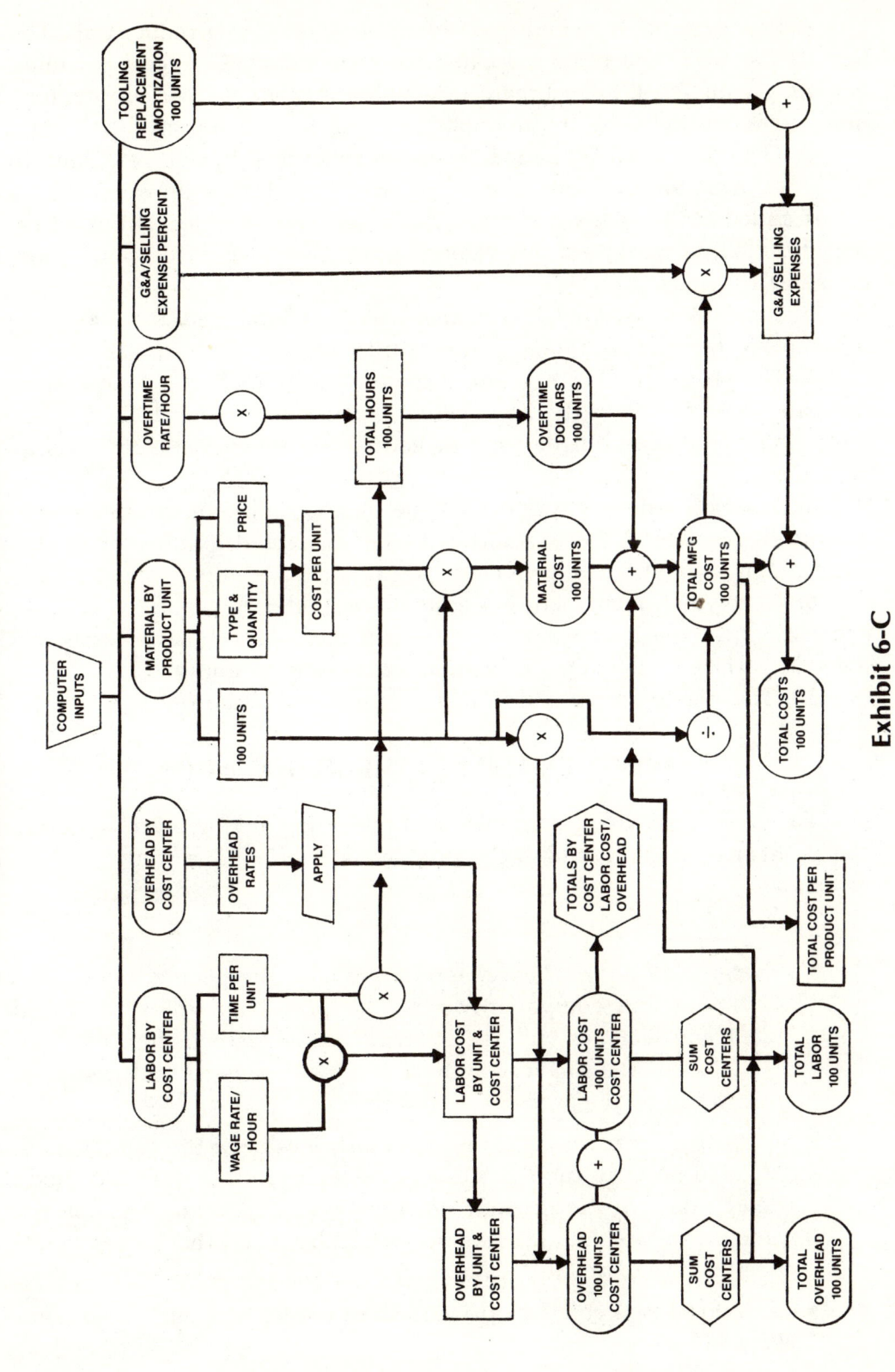

**PRICE DETERMINATION FACTORS
COMPUTERIZED PRODUCT COST DEVELOPMENT**

Exhibit 6-C

4. Raw material type and quantity are projected by product unit. The anticipated and relevant price is applied to obtain the material cost per unit. It is generally impractical to segregate raw material by individual cost center. The unit cost is multiplied by 100 to obtain the costs for the 100 product units.

5. The operational time used by unit is multiplied by 100 to obtain the total direct hours for 100 units. Through correlation studies, an overtime premium is added for each hour of direct labor worked. It is determined that the factor is $.50 per unit, and this value is multiplied by 100 to obtain premium costs per 100 units.

6. Total labor, overhead, material, and premium costs for 100 units are summarized to obtain the total manufacturing costs.

7. The projected G & A/selling expense rate is applied to the total manufacturing costs to obtain the anticipated expense dollars for 100 units. Direct labor hours or dollars can be used in lieu of total manufacturing costs as the base.

8. Based on historical experience, the tooling replacement cost projections are developed. This value is amortized over a selected number of production units and, in Exhibit 6-A, the value used was $5.00 per unit.

9. To the total manufacturing costs is added the developed G & A/selling expenses and tooling amortization to obtain the total estimated costs for 100 units. This value divided by 100 results in the cost per unit.

10. The system output and format is shown on Exhibit 6-A.

PROFIT CRITERIA IN THE SELLING PRICE

Exhibit 6-D provides an overview of the processing involved to determine the profit margin and establish the product sales price. The steps involved are as follows:

Input

- *Property Administration* generally provides the planned and projected expansion and equipment costs. The prevailing gross investment in plant and facilities and the average annual depreciation rate are obtained from the financial history records, reviewed and inputted into the system by the property organization.

- *Financial Operations* provides the market value of the capital stock at a selected point in time or number of shares outstanding, planned dividend rate, long term debt amount, annual debt repayment reserve amount or rate, and tax rate reciprocal based on the tax rate (52% reflected in the Exhibit 6-A illustration).

- The developed cost files provide the product cost and the quantity to be sold.

Computerized Product Pricing Techniques   189

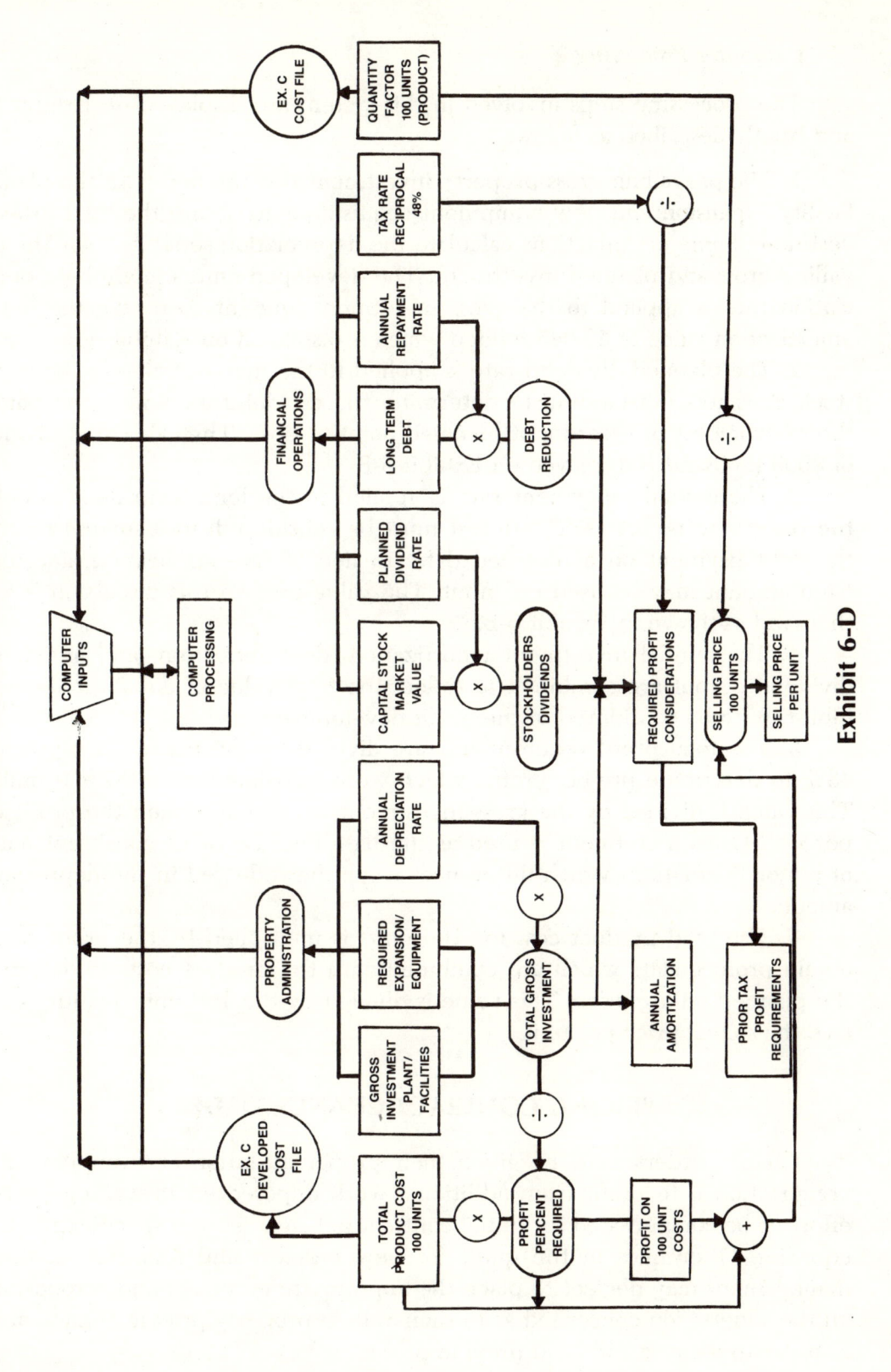

Exhibit 6-D

PRICE DETERMINATION FACTORS
PROFIT CRITERIA & SELLING PRICE

Computer Processing

The processing steps involved in this system are displayed on Exhibit 6-D and briefly described as follows:

1. The prevailing gross property investment is combined with the planned facility expansion and new equipment acquisitions to obtain the total gross investment. Some organizations calculate the depreciation separately for the prevailing gross and planned investment. The developed annual composite depreciation rate is applied to the gross investment amount to derive the annual amortization value of $3.045 million which is displayed on Exhibit 6-B.

2. The planned dividend rate is applied to the market value of the capital stock or shares outstanding to determine the dividend amount to be paid to the stockholders of record at a specified point in time. The calculated dividend of $600 thousand is displayed on Exhibit 6-B.

3. The annual repayment rate is applied to the long term debt to obtain the reserve to be set aside (interest must be considered) in a sinking fund for the debt payment on a specified date. In lieu of rate application, an annual fixed amount may be used for input. The value used in this discussion is $180 thousand as shown in Exhibit 6-B.

4. The annual investment amortization, debt reduction, and anticipated dividend payout are combined to reflect the total value of $3.825 million (Exhibit 6-B) to be considered in the profit development.

5. The total profit requirements are divided by the tax rate reciprocal of 48% to determine pre-tax profits which were calculated to be $7.969 million. This value is divided by the gross investment amount to obtain the profit rate percent. Gross investment is used as the base because of its consistent nature of minor fluctuations which differences would be reflected in the depreciation amount.

6. The total product cost for 100 units is multiplied by the profit rate to obtain profit dollars which are combined with the product costs to determine the planned selling price. This value is divided by the 100 unit quantity to derive the selling price per unit.

PRICING CONTRACT CHANGE ORDERS

Change orders must be given their proper attention and emphasis if an organization is to profit from additional work imposed on prevailing contract effort or be compensated for initial contract deficiencies and specification inadequacies. Oftentimes in the quest for new business and follow-on contracts, management may neglect to place the appropriate emphasis and responsibility on the supervision concerned as to their role in properly pricing change orders in order to recover costs and provide profit.

Formal Change Orders

Two types of changes in contract effort performance are formal and constructive. The formal change involves the customer's request for a change in product/equipment specifications in terms of design, re-direction of engineering effort, supplemental characteristics and/or capabilities, quantities, and revised production requirements. Under these circumstances, it behooves the contractor to prepare a formal change order for approval by the contracting officer. Some of the changes may be minor in nature and others of significant importance relative to the work performed and/or impact on future effort and costs.

When faced with this situation, the contractor should insist that sufficient time and effort be expended by qualified organizational planners, estimators, and others concerned to make certain that the change orders are realistically estimated and priced. There should be a detailed procedure for proper follow-up on the original estimate versus the incurred costs to determine how well the estimate was prepared and as a basis for improved future pricing. Half-hearted effort and use of a "secondary" pricing team often leads to an erosion of profits and an inadequate recovery of bonafide costs; this result can only be attributed to poor management direction and control.

Constructive Change Orders

This type of change order ordinarily results from some act or omission (after-the-fact contract change) of the contracting/negotiating representative, requiring the contractor to expend effort and change material components/processing from that originally defined in the contract. The changes requested may be oral, in the form of a letter, or another type documentation. In essence, additional requirements to a contract present an implied change or redirection to the negotiated contract terms and should be treated as such.

Constructive change orders can be attributed to a variety of reasons. The problem may arise from misinterpretation of the contract specifications. If the contracting officer's interpretation of the terms is incorrect and he instructs the contractor to perform differently than what was intended, the contractor has recourse for any ensuing problems in terms of contract overruns. Incomplete or inadequate specifications can lead to a constructive change order. In situations where the contracting officer rejects work that is in accordance with the specification terms and requests rework, the additional costs are reimbursable. If the contracting officer requests that the work be performed in a manner contradictory to the contractor's allowed choice in the contract terms, he then is charged with the responsibility for the costs and thus a constructive change is effected. There may be other grounds for constructive change actions, and the negotiated contract terms provide the basis for additional cost reimbursement with its attendant profit.

Pricing the Changes

In pricing constructive change orders, detailed support cost and pricing data must be compiled in terms of disruptive time and events involved, cost in additional material, and the affected work areas involved. Other elements in the reimbursement include claim preparation costs, interest on borrowed money to effect changes, and the appropriate profit on costs.

Diligent attention to the effect of constructive change orders and taking the appropriate action when necessary can often prevent overruns as in the case of fixed price contracts and lead to a significant improvement in profit.

PRICING INTER-DIVISIONAL TRANSFERS

The growth of decentralized organizational units due to acquisition activities and mergers have created problems in effectively and realistically establishing inter-organizational prices. A primary source of the problem is the accumulation of overhead in inventory.

When a product is transferred from one division to another, the acquiring division generally costs its inventory at the transfer price and the cost is treated as a *direct cost* even though the transferring division has been credited with a certain amount that reflects period costs and profit. Therefore, the overall true margin of a given end-product to an organization is often obscured. The detrimental effect is that management cannot accurately evaluate which products to exploit through increased advertising and promotion and further determine where additional resources should be provided to effect growth potential.

Approach to the Problem

Using *direct cost formulas* can often eliminate the above problems. The procedure is to price inter-plant transfers at direct cost and maintain material costs separately from the other direct costs by selected product lines. The markup on direct conversion and material costs would be calculated for each product line to meet the objective return on capital employed.

The *markups* are applied to the totals transferred during an accounting period, and the total margin above the direct costs are credited to the period costs of the transferring division and debited to the period costs of the acquiring division. This can be accomplished on a monthly basis or on a twelve month moving average cycle.

Using the above method, the finished product will always reflect a realistic overall profit margin, there will be no inter-divisional profits to be eliminated, and the detailed accounting clerical effort will be kept to a minimum. Further, much internal dissension can be avoided because prices are based on mathematic computations that are indisputably fair to both divisions.

FLEXIBLE PRICING FOR COMMERCIAL PRODUCTS

In most businesses, two sets of factors must be considered in pricing a product—cost and market. Several types of cost factors are discussed below.

Cost Factors

One type consists of easily measurable costs such as direct labor, purchased materials, normal factory labor, selling and administrative expense, financial charges, and customer discounts. There are unique cost element variations in each product which cannot be easily measured such as procurement, special tooling, inspection and handling, and R & D costs. Value added by manufacturing is another type cost factor. Products with a high proportion of manufacturing costs to material often command a larger margin on sales than those with a low proportion of manufacturing costs. The amount of investment is another cost. Different products require varied inventories and fixed investment.

Although variations in cost and investment required are more difficult to measure than processing costs, it is practical to consider these factors in the development of a pricing formula.

Pricing Formula Development

Cost factor application to pricing at times and in some organizations represents itself as being a simple task. There is a tendency to emphasize a pricing formula based on percentage of margin on sales which supposedly produces the right price on the selling prices of the competitor's products. It is more realistic to use a series of formulas rather than a single formula for each product, in order that the factors which are difficult to measure may be taken into consideration.

The first step in developing a formula is to determine the normal relationship between sales, costs, and expenses. Since the formulas will be used to price new products to be sold in the future, it is important, whenever possible, to forecast sales, costs, and expenses rather than to use historical data. In this situation, pricing formulas are determined at the same time the budget is developed and are adjusted when the budget is revised.

Costs and expenses should be segregated between fixed and variable components. This can be accomplished by using *scattergraphs* which provide an analysis of each component of cost and expense or mathematically by using the *method of least squares*. The latter is preferable because it avoids unnecessary argument as to which expense items are fixed or variable. The method of least squares also has its shortcomings. It is important that the price and cost levels be comparable throughout the period analyzed. Varying relationships of sales to production can also distort the figures.

194   *Computerized Product Pricing Techniques*

Calculating Fixed and Variable Costs (Least Squares Method)

An illustrative format and procedure for calculating fixed and variable costs using the least squares method is as follows:

Monthly period	(1) Sales Budget	(2) Cost & Expense Budget	(3) Sales Times Costs	(4) Sales Times Sales

PROCEDURE

a. Enter data for columns (1) and (2) from the developed budget.
b. Multiply column (1) by (2) and enter in column (3).
c. Multiply column (1) by itself to obtain values for column (4).
d. Summarize monthly values for all columns used to reflect all periods.
e. Multiply columns (3) and (4) by the total number of periods used and enter values in (h) and (i) computations below.
f. Multiply total annual sales (column 1) by annual cost (column 2) and enter value in column (3).
g. Multiply annual sales (column 1) by itself and enter result in column (4).
h. Subtract value developed the (f) item above from result in (e) item from column (3).
i. Subtract value developed in the (g) item above from result in (e) item for column (4).
j. Divide result from (h) item by result from (i) item to obtain variable cost and expense percent (70% was calculated in the above process).
k. Fixed expense equals total cost and expense budget less variable cost and expense (sales budget value times factor developed in item (j) above) or $3,000 developed from data used in the above procedure.

The next step is to determine the projected relationship of standard variable cost of sales to sales. For purposes of this illustration, the projected cost of sales will be 60% of sales.

Next, it is necessary to determine the sales volume level that will be used for pricing purposes; this value is $15 million. This volume may be the same (and often is) as the sales budget providing no major changes are contemplated in the projected year; otherwise, the revised value is used for the sales budget.

Using $15 million sales volume, 70% application for total variable expense, 60% for cost of sales, and the developed $3 million for fixed expense, it is possible to develop the overall projections that will be the basis for a series of pricing formulas. The overall projection data is displayed below.

Computerized Product Pricing Techniques

	VALUE IN 000's $	PERCENT TO SALES
Sales (less returns)	15,000	100.0
Cost & Expense		
Standard variable cost of sales	9,000	60.0
Other variable expense	1,500	10.0
Total variable expense	10,500	70.0
Fixed expense	3,000	20.0
Total cost and expense	13,500	90.0
Profit Before Taxes	1,500	10.0

Multiple Formulas

Having determined from the above the percentage relationship of fixed expense to sales, the varying formulas can be constructed using different relationships of standard variable cost to sales instead of the 60% average. The varying relationships will result in different percentages of profit to sales as shown below.

	PERCENT TO SALES				
Sales (less returns)	100.0	100.0	100.0	100.0	100.0
Cost & Expenses					
Standard cost of sales	70.0	66.0	62.0	58.0	54.0
Other variable expense	10.0	10.0	10.0	10.0	10.0
Total variable expense	80.0	76.0	72.0	68.0	64.0
Fixed Expense	20.0	20.0	20.0	20.0	20.0
Total cost and expense	100.0	96.0	92.0	88.0	84.0
Profit before taxes	0.0	4.0	8.0	12.0	16.0
Formula % to apply to standard cost to obtain net price (% Sales ÷ Standard cost) *Example*: 100 ÷ 70 = 1.43	1.43	1.52	1.61	1.72	1.85
Formula % to apply to standard cost to obtain list price assuming 20 & 5% trade discounts (Net price formula ÷ 75%) *Example*: 1.43 ÷ 75 = 1.91	1.91	2.03	2.15	2.29	2.47

Modifying Results by Other Cost Factors

As displayed above, five separate prices for markup factors to obtain list price (1.91, 2.03 etc.) have been developed to apply to individual products on a judgmental basis. The data are readily developed in a computerized program, and many other varying formulas can be easily calculated dependent upon need.

Each factor will provide a different selling price based on projected average costs and expenses with different margins. The results provided by these formulas do not, however, consider variations in costs, value added by manufacture, or investment required. Therefore, it is recommended that the variations be either formally or informally considered before the final price is selected.

Return on investment can be readily incorporated at this point. Assume that your organization has established a goal of a 25% return, before taxes, on the assets employed. Since capital is turned over twice a year, the average margin on sales would be 12.5%. Suppose that the organization is faced with the problem of pricing a new product that requires additional capital, has a higher ratio of manufacturing costs to material costs, and requires certain special handling and promotional costs. Under these circumstances, the estimator would select a pricing target in the 15–20% range. Conversely, if the cost of the variations was below average, the pricing target would accordingly be below average.

Adjusting Results for Market Factors

Costs represent only part of the selling price. Sales prices must be weighed against both the long- and short-term capacity of the market. One approach to measure market capacity is a thorough market research in a test area. The researcher may select alternative selling prices and, by interviewing a representative number of prospective customers, determine how many customers indicate they would purchase at each of these prices. By multiplying projections of these quantities by the fixed expense and margin in each product, it can be determined which selling price will produce the greatest contribution to profit. The cost of the capital required should be deducted from this contribution to determine which selling price will provide the largest net contribution.

Another method of obtaining the same information is to actually test-sell your product at different prices in comparable non-competitive markets. Each of the above methods of determining the most profitable selling prices is time-consuming and expensive; therefore, the methods must, in a practical sense, be limited to a few items which have a large potential sales volume.

Computing Price Changes

Generally, there are two types of circumstances which warrant changes in selling prices. The most common is a blanket increase that passes on to the customer the upward trend of costs. This type of increase usually *applies across the board* or to large classes of products. The second type of price change is effected in order to increase the profit contributed by a single item or groups of items. The latter changes are more difficult to effect than blanket adjustments because they reflect changes in the nature of the product and market climate or possibly errors in the original pricing.

Although judgment and trial and error cannot be entirely avoided when decisions are made relative to individual items, it is possible to analyze and resolve the economics involved by comparing the profit margin in a specific product to its sales volume.

Pricing Criteria

In the ideal environment, a product should be priced before it is designed. It is amazing how much funds and resources can be expended on the development of a new product that may subsequently be found to be unprofitable. It is recommended that the proposed selling price and an estimated sales volume be included as a part of each engineering project authorization for a new product. Since the sales organization has the responsibility for selling a certain quantity of the product at a given price, it would seem to be a function of the market research/sales organization to make the *initial* determination of price and volume figures.

The controller and his staff have the responsibility for providing the information required to work back from proposed selling price and profit targets to cost figures. Engineers also need various tools to estimate rough costs in order to design within the specifications of the project authorization. Due to the tendency to overlook certain elements of cost such as payroll taxes and benefits, insurance, and other indirect expense, it is important that cost-finding tools be developed and/or reviewed by the controller's staff.

After a product has been designed, many other functions become involved. It is necessary to prepare bills of materials and to determine production and inventory requirements, cost and source of materials, tool design, manufacturing methods and schedule requirements, advertising and promotional programs. The selling price and cost estimate for the product should be re-examined and redetermined at this time.

Using the information provided by other participating organizations in the pricing/sales cycle, it is the function of the controller's staff to determine the cost of the product and recommend a range of selling prices that will meet cost and profit goals.

PRICE CONSIDERATIONS ON DEFENSE CONTRACTS

In recent years, the Defense Department has been exerting extreme pressure on contractors to reduce their selling prices. Their weapons have been and are very astute price negotiations at the time of the contract award and further the disallowance of certain costs after performance on cost-reimbursement contracts. Because of the fierce competition for defense contracts, the Defense Department has begun to favor those contractors who have a proven record of efficient performance with reasonable cost boundaries. Since contract cost performance is the key criterion to achieving contract awards, significant emphasis is being placed on the pricing functions in organizations that are defense-oriented.

Problem Factors in Contract Pricing

Most defense industries experience difficulties in contract pricing because of various inherent peculiarities in their type of business which preclude the use of an inflexible pricing formula. Some of the prime negative factors involved are as follows:

- Exotic products and their complexity in the state of the art advancement.
- Constant changes in technology require continual engineering planning changes.
- Unique products often involve misinterpretation of the requirements.
- Volatile volume is often created by change requirements and this situation can often lead to contract terminations and inefficient production planning.
- Short production runs often result from rapidly changing technology.

The above factors are only representative of the many peculiarities of defense contracting that make it mandatory for management to establish control over the complete pricing cycle in order to protect the organization's assets and assure profit and growth in the future.

The Pricing Cycle

There are two separate tasks to be performed during any pricing action—cost estimating and pricing. Cost estimating involves a detailed evaluation and analysis of the contract tasks to be performed and the compilation in a systematic manner of an estimate of the various direct costs necessary to accomplish the requirements.

The pricing function generally consists of adding overhead costs to the direct costs, and adding a reasonable profit to arrive at a *formula-established* price.

Management must then apply the judgment factor to obtain the final price to be quoted to the customer. The first task must be performed before the second can be considered. There are instances in which sales-oriented organizations have reversed the cycle to gain immediate results. However, these types of organizations will not pose a competitive threat for long to the more stable, progressive organizations that pursue a systematic approach to contract pricing.

The accepted and proper approach to pricing would encompass, but not be limited to, the following major sequential steps in the pricing and control cycle.

1. Preparation of the direct cost estimate.
2. Application of overhead costs.
3. Establishment of the selling price (profit inclusion).
4. Negotiation of the contract price.
5. Establishment of internal contract cost controls.

Controller's Role in Pricing

As applicable to defense industries, a study of the pricing cycle has shown that if profits are to be realized from work performed under defense contracts, every phase of the pricing action must be controlled with the objective of maximizing profits. The peculiarities of defense industries requires that each pricing action be subjected to diligent financial review, since the data developed at that time determines the selling price of the product, and it also provides the basis for internal control during the performance of the project. Because of this interrelationship of all phases of pricing, the controller and his staff are faced with full responsibility for maintaining a constant control over each major function in the pricing cycle.

In order to accomplish the above, the controller's staff must be familiar with the techniques used to develop the basic direct labor estimates for all bid proposals. The internal review of these estimates is under the immediate supervision of the controller, but, if this is impracticable, the reviewing authority must receive functional guidance from the controller.

PRODUCT PRICING HIGHLIGHTS

Computerized product pricing techniques significantly aid estimators/planners in their pricing endeavors. This chapter has explored the various considerations, economics, and influencing factors involved in the price determination process. The role of historical, current and future costs has been discussed in detail relative to their impact on product pricing, competitive considerations, and pricing of inter-divisional transfers. Computerized systems have been described for price development on defense contracts as well as flexible pricing for commercial products.

This chapter encompasses the many facets and criteria that are so vital to effective product pricing and establishing a sound selling price that will not only achieve planned sales volume but also acceptable profit goals and return on investment.

7

Mechanical Manpower and Labor Cost Planning in Product Price Estimating

One of the prime costs to be considered in estimating a product price involves the direct and indirect manpower required in effectively producing a saleable product to meet scheduled delivery requirements. The same situation prevails in providing customer services. Varied skills are required to achieve production and allied support goals and activities.

Manpower planning and costing is the most significant factor in the aggregate product price estimating; therefore extreme accuracy is required in developing a reliable, realistic manpower forecast plan and its costing.

AN APPROACH TO MANPOWER PLANNING

Most progressive organizations prepare an operational plan which presents guidelines and direction for conducting their future business activities. The developed plan is commonly identified as the annual budget or a long range forecast covering a five year period or more, depending on the nature of the business and its needs. In most organizations, the use of time-span plans are common. The plan is periodically updated and/or revised depending on the extent of changes that occur in the business climate.

Manpower planning is one facet of the overall budget or estimating plan, but its importance cannot be minimized because of its impact on (1) effective and skilled production of a successful, saleable product or service, (2) extent of facility and equipment investment requirements, and (3) other costs of salaries, wages and associated benefits that are included in overhead expense. Manpower is generally the major cost in operating a business enterprise and involves all types of personnel—management, administration, marketing, engineering, and manufacturing.

Planning Responsibility

Each organizational entity develops a manpower plan on which labor costs and various payroll expenses are based. In a divisional structured organization, each division submits a summary of its annual plan on specified formats to the corporate management for review, approval, and consolidation with other organizations. Included in this plan is a manpower projection of the number of employees required to meet the planned operations; the data is presented by monthly periods.

On the corporate level, the financial aspects of the annual plan are generally administered by the financial planning organization under the direction of the corporate controller or vice president of finance.

The controller in each division has a counterpart on his staff similar to that of the corporate budgets and planning director. The division controller is responsible for measuring performance against the plan and publishing periodic reports comparing actual to planned headcount at various levels of responsibility. Variances are analyzed and also reported with causes for differences noted.

Functional Manpower Projections

The *administrative and sales* departments plan their manning and departmental expenses based on their approved fixed expense budgets and manpower projections. Department planners develop basic data relative to their organization activity levels from which reasonable estimates can be made as to the number of employees required.

The *engineering* departments plan their needs within the framework of the anticipated engineering projects which have been authorized. The plan also includes the requirements for general research programs and specific customer engineering applications.

The *manufacturing* departments' plans are based on the unit sales projections which reflect inventory levels and objectives and stated requirements for interdivisional activity. The manufacturing function generally includes packing, receiving, and shipping. Functional structure may vary among organizations.

A MANPOWER PLANNING PROCEDURE

Exhibit 7-A displays an overall manpower planning data flow which shows the sequence of events used in transmitting basic data to the production organization for planning the sales/inventory manufacturing forecast, determining the direct labor input requirements for assembly and test hour calculations, and recording manpower needs by specific skills for the department manning schedule. Specific requirements are shown for the dollarized payroll expense budget and the division manpower plan.

Sales/Inventory

Division management provides sales and inventory requirements data to production management. The production staff then plans the production schedule based on the monthly unit sales forecast, beginning product inventory status, and turnover objectives. The detailed schedule includes the forecast of deliveries, beginning inventory, and planned sales to inventory ratio.

Based on the three elements of data outlined above, the manufacturing department plans monthly production deliveries by specific product(s).

Assembly and Test Hours

As indicated in Exhibit 7-A, a projection is made of the assembly and test direct labor hours for one delivery unit, and this is extended to obtain total hours. Included in this schedule are the monthly deliveries as reflected on the production schedule which is represented by the *Sales/Inventory* caption of the exhibit.

For the product being manufactured in this organization example, the direct labor lead time is assumed to be less than one month; therefore, input and output coincide in time. The extended unit hours (hours per unit times number of units) are summarized to reflect total hours by period for assembly and test. A factor is added to the totals to reflect direct labor for spare parts and accessories which were itemized in the sales forecast. This factor is based on historical experience and modified, as necessary, by the forecast dollar value of items in this category. The plan provides the direct labor hours required by the two prime producing departments in a manufacturing plant.

The calculated hours are plotted on a time scale by months to determine whether any unusual requirements will occur in specific months. In situations of unusual fluctuations, the data is "smoothed" by projecting the abnormal differences into adjoining periods, and a representative trend line is then drawn on the graph.

The monthly labor and expense budgets generally reflect the *smoothed* labor hour plan rather than projections on an actual labor level which can fluctuate by period. Average "levelling" is used during periods of sharp decline which are followed by a vertical drop to a lower level at the end of a specific month. This has a stabilizing effect on manpower projections as well as actual employee increases and decreases during abnormal periods of time.

Production Department Forecast

The manpower for a production service department includes the employees in that organization by job description or classification number, payroll category (monthly, salaried, hourly), and number of employees at the end of the budget year. Additions or deletions are shown by month. Monthly or hourly rates are provided for each classification plus a planned percent for wage increases during the year, which is identified to a specific starting month so that the appropriate payroll dollars can be computed and projected by period.

Payroll Expense Budget

Displayed in Exhibit 7-A are the requirements for a payroll expense budget. The projected manpower labor dollars described above are recorded

Mechanical Manpower and Labor Cost Planning 205

MANPOWER PLANNING FLOWCHART

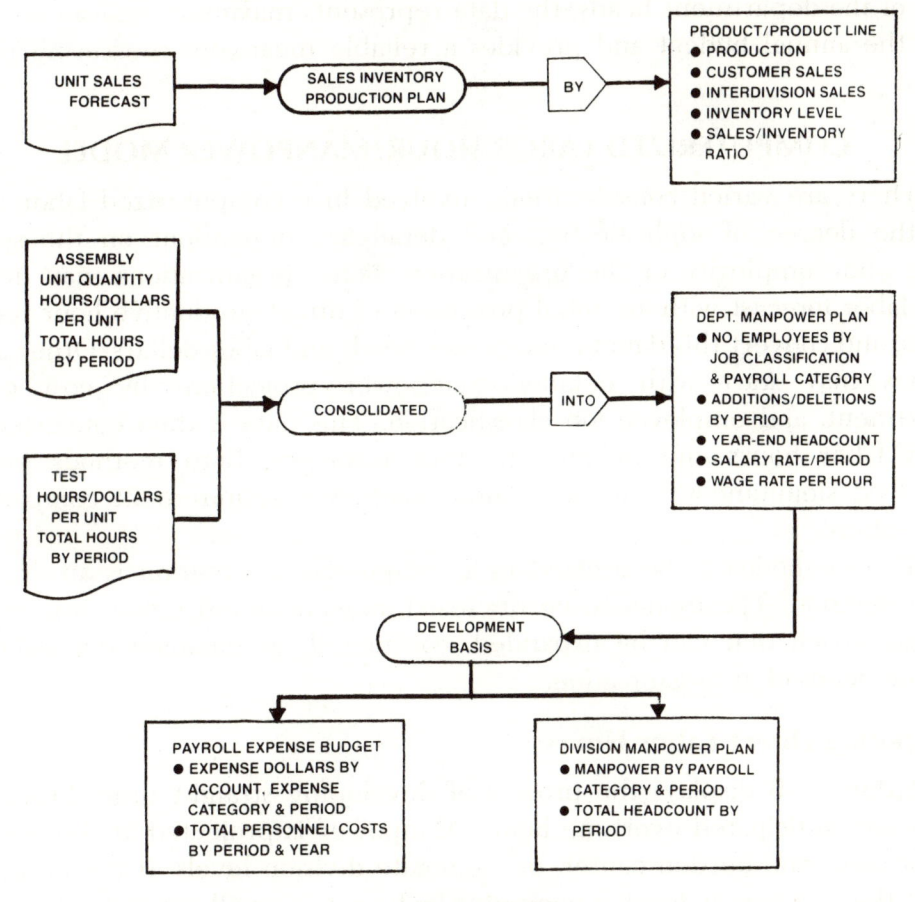

Exhibit 7-A

monthly. Other overhead expenses including fringe benefits are line itemized for each specific organization. Monthly payrolls are dollarized by dividing the pay per month by 173 (40 hours a week times 52 weeks and divided by 12) and multiplying that value by the number of working hours in each period. Fringe benefits and other expenses are based on historical factor application.

Division Manpower Plan

The division manpower projections represent a summary of the departmental data. A consolidation is made by payroll categories and period. However, the manpower is developed in detail by job classification and individual organization. The segregations and summations are readily achieved by a computerized program with minimal clerical effort.

This approach to manpower planning is a fully integrated procedure which is achieved by a series of simple steps as shown in Exhibit 7-A. The sequence of events may vary among organizations, but the principles are applicable in most instances. Since the manpower planning is based on the basic plans of the department heads, the data represents maximum realism and utility in the annual budget and provides a reliable means for measuring performance.

COMPUTERIZED LABOR HOUR/MANPOWER MODEL

There are varied considerations involved in a computerized labor model and the degree of sophistication and detail are dependent on the specific needs and complexity of the organization. Some organizations may develop their labor forecast with an initial projection of direct productive hour requirements, and convert this data to manpower needs and labor dollars. Other organizations may start with detailed manpower projections by cost center, department, and employee job classification. This data is then converted into direct labor hours and dollars. In other instances, both methods may be employed simultaneously to determine manpower requirement compatibility and realism.

The method(s) to be utilized in a computerized program is an organizational decision. The model to be discussed and illustrated below is a generalized approach that can be expanded, contracted, or changed depending on specific needs of an organization.

Computing Direct Labor Hours

Exhibit 7-B displays the process of developing straight time direct labor hours and anticipated overtime hours. Manpower is projected at the cost center, department, burden center, or aggregate division levels. If the projections are at the cost center level, a computer look up table will associate the centers with departments for summation purposes. The sequence of the mechanical processing is as follows:

- The direct manpower projections are multiplied by the straight time hours per day per employee (generally, this factor is 8.0 hours/day). The result represents *total straight time hours per day.*

- The straight time hours per day are multiplied by the number of workdays in a period. This factor will vary among organizations depending on their established accounting month period which will give effect to holidays, calendar month workdays, or a cycle of four, four and five weeks in a quarterly period. The result is *total straight time hours* by period.

- *Productive hours per day* are obtained by multiplying straight time hours by a historical factor application which gives effect to non-productive time. In some organizations, the productive hours per day are established at 7.5 but this figure can vary depending on past and antici-

Mechanical Manpower and Labor Cost Planning

**COMPUTING DIRECT LABOR HOUR PROJECTIONS
COMPUTERIZED MODELS**

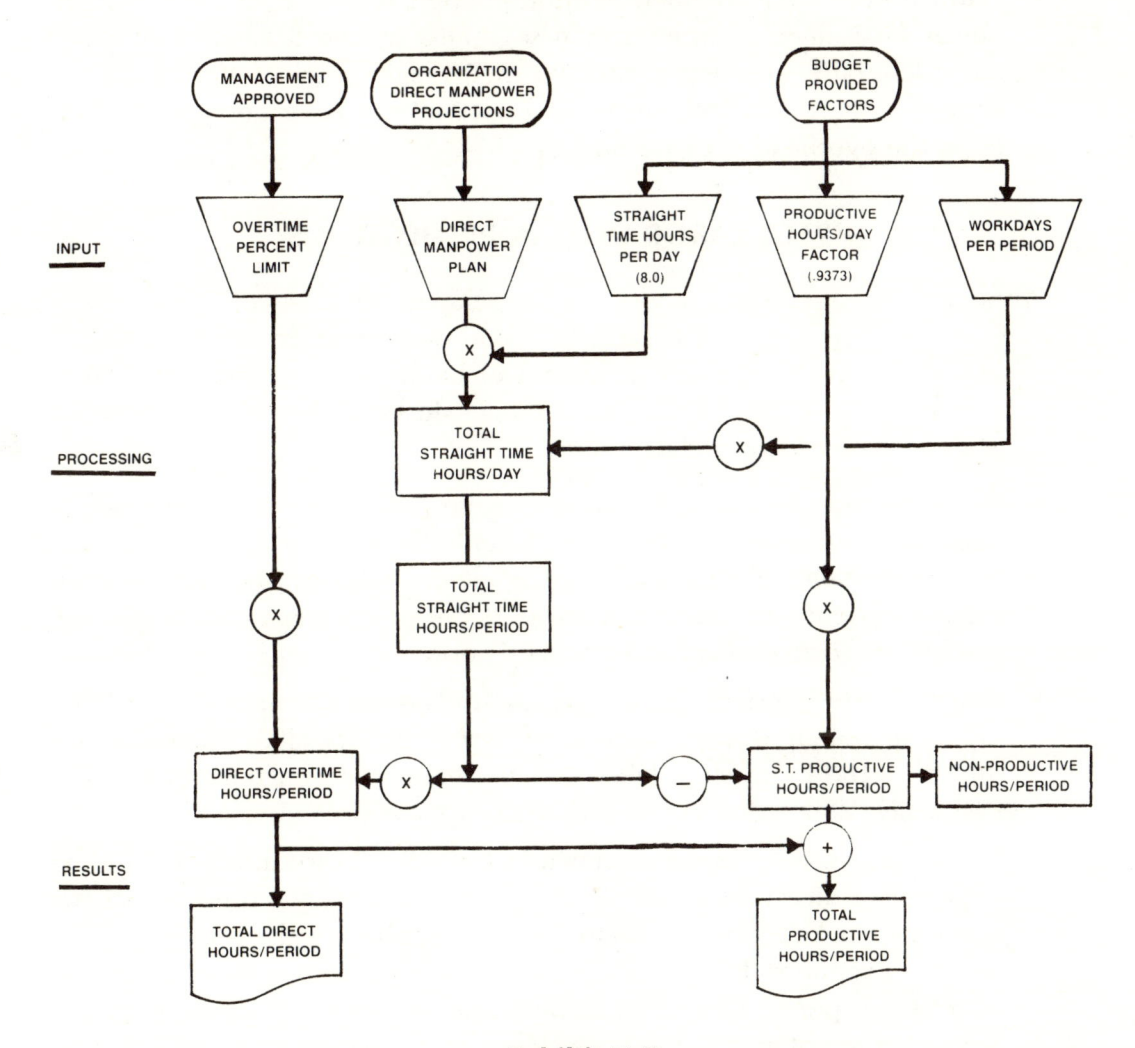

Exhibit 7-B

pated projections. The half-hour difference from the 8.0 hours represents time allocated to sickness, union meetings, training, idleness, etc. The factor on the exhibit of .9375 was derived by dividing 7.5 by 8.0 hours.

- *Overtime hours* are based on straight time or productive hours depending upon organization policy. Many organizations use straight time as the basis. The overtime factor is predicated on historical experience, projected need, and/or management edict. The factor application to straight time hours results in projected direct overtime hours by period.
- The computed overtime hours are combined with straight time or pro-

ductive hours to derive total hours per period as shown in Exhibit 7-B.

- *Indirect hours*, are obtained by multiplying the projected indirect manpower for individual organization segments by the 8.0 hour factor per day. Generally, the non-productive hour segregation is not made, except for special analyses, since the total indirect labor costs are reflected in the overhead expense budget.

DIRECT LABOR DOLLAR PROJECTIONS

Although this aggregate model was developed to calculate direct labor dollars as a logical sequence of events, the computer program can be changed rather simply to compute the direct manpower based on projected direct labor hours as displayed in Exhibit 7-D. This subject will be discussed subsequently. The process for direct labor dollars follows:

- Based on the data developed in Exhibit 7-B, the period productive hours are multiplied by the direct labor rate by organization (cost center, department). Planned average or cluster rates can be used or even rates by specific job classifications. In detail or summary, the result represents *productive direct labor cost* by period.

- Straight time hours by period are multiplied by the appropriate labor rate(s) to obtain *straight time direct labor* dollars. This value(s) is reduced by the productive labor cost to obtain the *non-productive labor cost* which is included in the overhead expense projections.

- Projected overtime hours as shown in Exhibit 7-C are multiplied by the appropriate direct labor rate to determine the straight time cost of the overtime. An overtime premium factor is applied to the hours to calculate the premium dollar cost for the overtime which is included in the overhead expense. The straight time and premium overtime costs are combined to obtain the *total overtime* costs by period.

- Direct labor straight time and overtime (excluding premium) are combined to derive total straight time labor costs.

- Productive direct labor and straight time overtime costs are combined to obtain *total productive labor costs* by period. These values become an element of cost (direct labor) in the cost of sales budget as shown in Exhibit 7-B.

DIRECT MANPOWER FORECAST BASED ON HOURS

This module is a programmed routine in the overall computerized model. The manpower module can be used for two purposes:

Mechanical Manpower and Labor Cost Planning 209

DIRECT LABOR DOLLAR PROJECTIONS

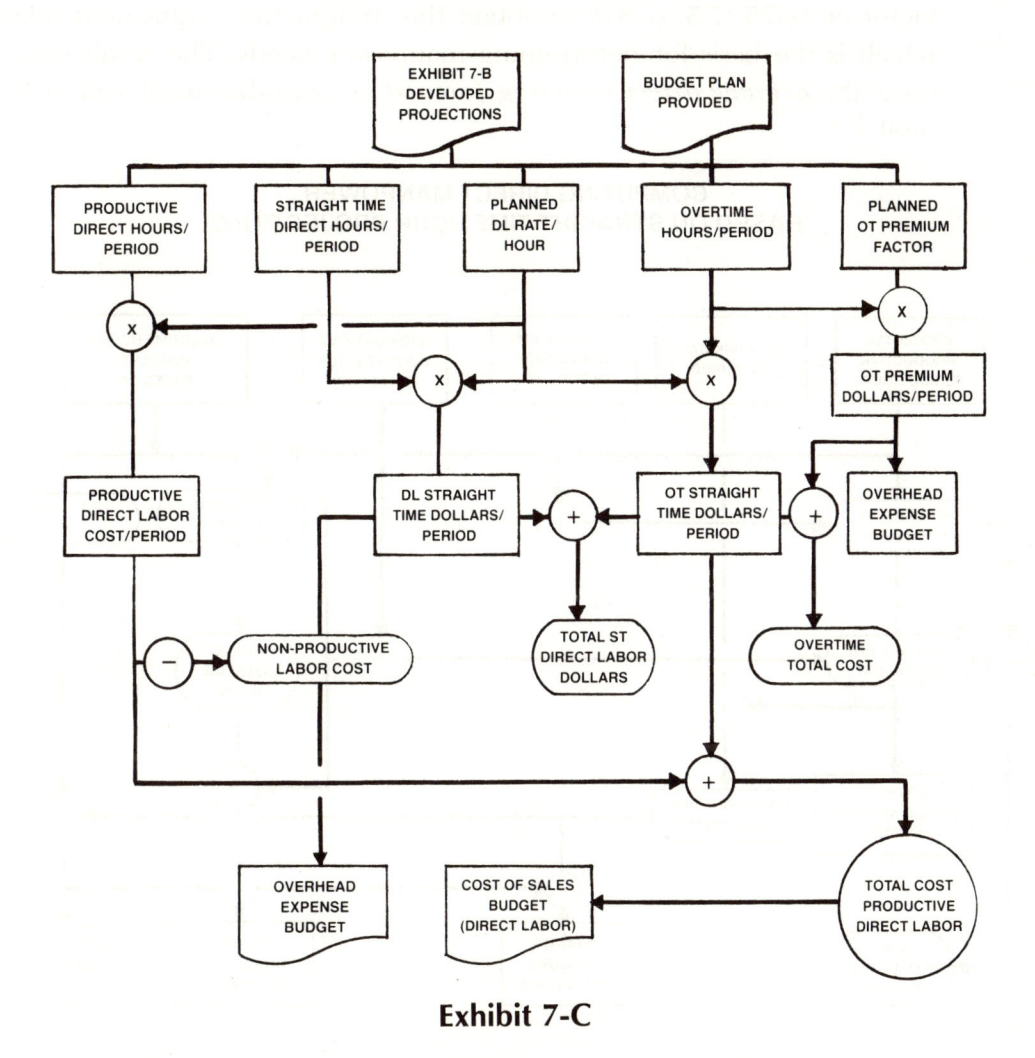

Exhibit 7-C

1. Converting projected straight time hours developed in Exhibit 7-C to obtain a manpower forecast which can be used to check the reliability of the initial manpower input (if the forecasting procedure requires a manpower input). This will verify whether the program is performing its routines in accordance with the developed computer instructions.

2. More importantly, independently developed straight time hours are translated into a period average manpower forecast. The processing procedure follows.

- Projected period productive hours are divided by the established number of workdays in the period to determine the *daily* productive hours required.

210   *Mechanical Manpower and Labor Cost Planning*

- The daily productive hours are divided by the straight time conversion factor of .9375 (7.5 ÷ 8.0) to obtain the straight time equivalent hours which is the basis for determining manpower needs. The result represents the *average direct manning forecast* by period as displayed in Exhibit 7-D.

**COMPUTING DIRECT MANPOWER
BASED ON STRAIGHT TIME HOUR PROJECTIONS**

[Flowchart with the following elements:
- PROJECTED PRODUCTIVE PERIOD HOURS
- NO. WORK DAYS BY PERIOD
- STRAIGHT TIME CONVERSION FACTOR (.9375)
- STRAIGHT TIME HOURS FACTOR PER PERSON
- OVERTIME HOURS PERCENT BASED ON
- PRODUCTIVE HOURS/DAY
- PRODUCTIVE HOURS %
- S.T. HOURS %
- *STRAIGHT TIME HOURS/DAY
- PERIOD OVERTIME HOURS
- PROJECTED PERIOD AVERAGE MANPOWER
- STRAIGHT TIME HOURS/PERIOD
- NON-PRODUCTIVE HOURS/DAY
- TOTAL OT/STRAIGHT TIME HOURS
- TOTAL PRODUCTIVE PERIOD HOURS
- PERIOD OVERTIME HOURS]

★ MANPOWER CONVERSION BASED ON S.T. HOURS BASE

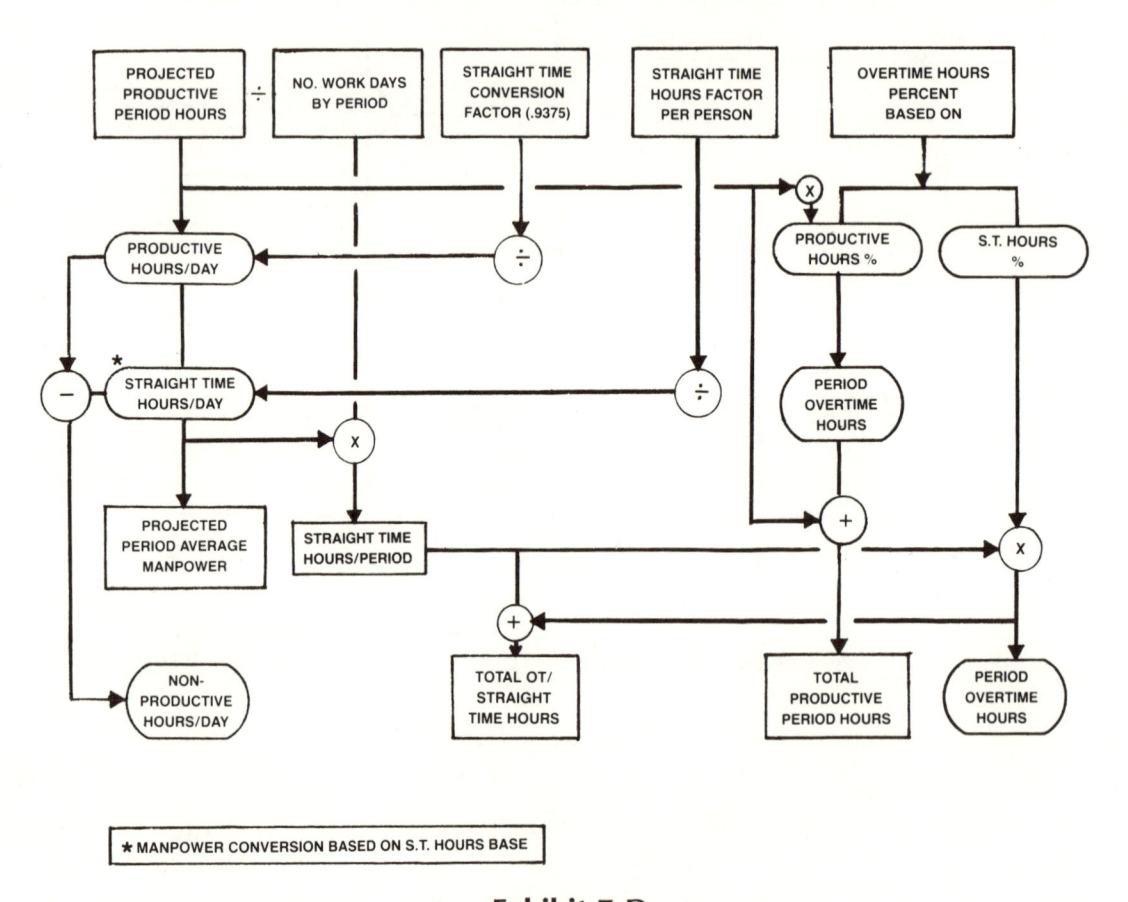

Exhibit 7-D

- Another approach to achieve the same result would be to divide the period productive hours by period and then dividing this value by the number of hours in a day times workdays in a period to obtain period manpower. An example follows:

Productive hour requirements—150,000 ÷ .9375 = 160,000 straight time hours

160,000 ÷ 160 (8 hours/day × 20 workdays in period) = 1,000 employees by period

Mechanical Manpower and Labor Cost Planning

- Depending on organizational procedure, overtime hours can be projected on the basis of a percent application to either period productive or straight time hours as shown in Exhibit 7-D. Many organizations use straight time hours as the primary basis.

- The direct hours can then be converted to labor dollars based on the routine described for Exhibit 7-C.

If overtime hours have been included in the productive hour projections, then they must be eliminated in order to derive straight time hours and manpower projections. The overtime factor included will be an input to the system. An example follows.

Projected productive hours by period with overtime included—*159,000*
Overtime factor reflected in above hours—*6%*

159,000 hours divided by 1.06 (100% + 6%) = *150,000* hours without overtime

Mechanical Model Flexibility

The computerized labor model discussed above has considerable flexibility in that it provides the capability of converting manpower into hours and dollars, or dollars into hours, and hours into manpower projections. It permits the calculation of overtime hours and dollars based on productive or straight time hours. Overtime premium hours and dollars can be computed. Non-productive hours and dollars are readily calculated for in the overhead budget. Dependent on organizational needs, other variation requirements can be incorporated into this system. This model can be an effective manual time-saver yielding extremely accurate data, if the input and processing instructions are reliable and valid.

INDIRECT LABOR MANNING

Indirect manpower is projected by the concerned organizations. The forecast can be developed in considerable detail, which is vital for cost control and performance measurement. The data is usually representative of the lowest organizational level (section, cost center, etc.) and summarized to department and division totals. Again the degree of detail is dependent on organization policy and needs. Management may establish a planned ratio of indirect to direct personnel based on historical experience and/or organizational budget objectives.

Indirect manpower is priced by applying planned wage rates by job classification, organization unit average, or cluster rates (more than one organization unit average). The indirect labor costs are reflected in the overhead expense budget, as contrasted to direct labor which is reflected in the cost of sales labor element. This process is conducive to mechanization.

ESTIMATING OPERATING LABOR TIME

Generally, the estimation of labor cost on mechanical products involves more calculations then those required in estimating the cost of material and overhead expense. The cost estimator must have a thorough knowledge of the detailed operations to be performed. To estimate labor with any degree of accuracy requires that each labor operation be recorded in detail on specifically prepared formats and that the operations be listed in processing sequence. If the item to be manufactured is composed of various minor assemblies, then each assembly is broken down in its component parts and the labor operations on the individual parts are listed in detail.

In situations in which time and motion studies are unavailable, the time estimate should be prepared in conjunction with the responsible foreman who has first-hand knowledge and experience with the specific tasks to be performed. Where a complete job evaluation program based on scientific time and motion studies does exist, wage differentials may be established to reflect specific skills, responsibility, work output, and working conditions. The manufacturing time required is dependent on the machines selected for the task, the production methods employed, and the efficiency of the operator.

Setup Cost Estimates

If machinery is used in the production process, the list of operations includes the types and sizes of machines on which the work is to be accomplished. If special machine setups are required, then this information should also be listed on the estimate sheet. In estimating setup time, the cost estimator should have available in his files the standard setup costs on all ordinary products being produced. In special cases or if there is any doubt as to the time and costs involved, the estimator should consult with the production department specialists before making a setup cost estimate. The estimate sheet should reflect realistic time estimates from all of the steps involved in the production process.

DIRECT LABOR TIME STANDARDS

Expenditure of time is the basic criterion in determining direct labor costs. Establishing time standards is ascertaining the time required to perform each productive operation on each product in a standard operation. Time is expressed as a unit of labor quantity required to produce a level of product unit output such as "100 parts completed within a one hour time span."

Labor expenditure standards must reflect productive effort which has been tempered for non-productive time losses due to employee idleness (machine down-time, waiting for material or equipment, etc.), sickness/vacation factors, coffee breaks, and training.

Establishing Time Standards

Various methods or combinations of methods are employed in setting time standards. The most common procedures involve time and motion studies, past performance, and projected estimates.

Time and motion analysis. This method is an analysis of each individual operation to determine the motions and time required to perform each independent task. In the engineer's study of the task motions, consideration must be accorded to "wasted" motions resulting from inadequate placement of material in the working area, poor work-flow sequencing, and improper working environment which is not conducive to efficient operations. Other considerations are inadequate tools or equipment, lack of or poor employee training, outmoded operating procedures and machinery, employee morale and fatigue factors, and possibly inattention or lack of supervision. Many of the above undesirable conditions observed by the time engineer may be eliminated, but those that cannot be must be reflected in the time standard that is established; otherwise, the standard would be of negligible value.

The time and motion evaluation requires that each operation be segregated into its component parts and the appropriate times established for each part. The standard for the complete operation represents the sum of the time spans for all parts. Formulas can be developed which can be readily adjusted for changes in equipment type, operating procedures, and/or material substitutions. New or different tasks can be accommodated by using the standards for similar type tasks, and the changes in terms of additions or reductions to the standard time would be predicated on estimate projections.

Time and motion studies are particularly applicable to those organizations where the production process can be segregated into a series of simple and highly repetitive operations on a single product or a few basically compatible products.

Past performance. Generally, in a job order cost system, cost sheets are maintained which reflect the actual time performance for each operation. An analysis of the cost sheets will reveal any marked time deviations from the norm relative to the same end product. Any unusual differences must be eliminated before relevant averages can be established for the time standards.

This method is based on averages experienced in the past. The procedure is most applicable in organizations producing one product or a few stable products that experience little change in operations or components. Time standards on new products or changes to present ones cannot be established under this method until experience data is available and assessed.

Projected estimates. This method of establishing time standards requires a thorough analysis of relevant data pertinent to the operations to be performed in producing a product. The information is based on past experience with similar types of effort. The projections must reasonably reflect all factors that can influence the operational time performance. This procedure for establishing time standards is most applicable in situations where the product and task operations are generally non-repetitive, such as items that are made to customer specifications and are unique in nature. The cost estimates thus projected provide the basis for establishing the product sales price.

The major problem with this procedure is that it is dependent upon the estimator's judgment and experience; the human element can be fallible with its impact on the extreme validity of operational time standards.

LABOR QUALITY STANDARDS

Labor quality standards are usually synonymous to job evaluation and description. In most organizations of any size, various types of labor are required to perform the many production tasks. As the employee population increases, there arises a need for more varied types of labor with different levels of skill and experience.

Job evaluation requires specialists for describing task functions and the type of individual needed relative to education, experience, and training. Labor grade classifications must be established with their appropriate wage differential. Precaution must be exercised to preclude the use of higher- or over-qualified employees than the task warrants. This situation inevitably creates dissent, morale problems, reduced labor effectiveness, and increased labor costs which cannot be justified nor tolerated in a cost conscious organization. An employee's background, skills, and experience must be compatible with the task requirements.

LABOR RATE STANDARDS

Labor rates are established by employee job classification. The rate should be appropriate for the relative skills and qualifications required for a specific job(s) and equitable/comparable in terms of other prevailing jobs in the organization. Some of the major factors in establishing rate standards encompass the following: historical average rate experience with adjustments to reflect current conditions, the local competitive market rates being paid for comparable labor classifications (supply and demand aspect), wage rates being paid nationally in similar industries for comparable labor grades, union contract agreements (if applicable), and special employee/employer negotiations.

When piece-rates and premium plans are utilized, the standard average rates are determined in a different manner. Relative to piece rates, the employees are paid a set rate per piece (part) produced regardless of production quantity. Therefore, the labor cost per piece or operation is a uniform amount and that rate represents the standard labor price.

Mechanical Manpower and Labor Cost Planning

When premium plans are used as a means of compensating workers, the problem often arises as to whether or not the additional earnings should be considered in establishing the standard wage rate. If the decision is made to include this factor in the standard, the amount to be added must be resolved by a study of premiums made during past periods, and an average amount per labor operation must be computed.

LABOR COST ESTIMATES

Primarily, labor estimates are developed on the basis of costs of similar parts previously produced or by estimating from drawings, layouts, specifications, and other descriptive data. After the project has been analyzed to show the specific operations to be performed, labor time estimates are defined in terms of those outlined operations. The labor cost of any task or operation must include the operation time required and the wage rate to be paid.

Since time estimates are expressed in terms of specific operations on particular types of machines, the prevailing rates for indicated tasks are applied to the time estimates to obtain the direct labor cost in dollars. Piece rate wages eliminate the need for direct labor time estimates; however, estimates for costing setup time must be included.

Cost Estimate Sheet

The cost estimator can obtain information relative to the future cost of labor from the personnel/payroll organizations and current trade publications. The detailed labor cost estimate sheet should include the following data: estimate ID number and date, customer's name, part and drawing numbers, and a brief description of the part and material required. Department numbers should be shown for each of the organizations in which the operations are to be performed. The name and number of the operations to be accomplished and types of machines to be used are also entered on the estimate sheet. The task operations are listed in the sequence of their performance.

Space is also provided on the estimate format to show the cost of operating labor and production output on which the labor cost estimate is based. This section of the estimate sheet indicates the specific wage rates paid for the different labor operations and usually the cost per thousand pieces. Sub-totals are provided for the total labor in each department so that the burden rates can be readily applied.

MANPOWER LOADING FOR RFQs

In responding to a customer's *request for a quote* (RFQ), the projected hours must be translated into a manpower loading plan in order to appropriately distribute the forecasted hour requirements by period. The manload is included with each manufacturing reply to an RFQ.

Manloads are usually expressed in terms of equivalent men, which are derived on the basis of actual work hours per man per week. This factor is based on historical experience and will vary among organizations. The average among organizations is usually 36.0–37.0 hours per week; the difference from the normal 40.0 hours is attributed to training, sickness, personal time off, and union meetings.

The hours per month are converted into equivalent men by dividing the monthly hour projections by 160 hours in a four week month, 200 hours in a five week month (if four, four, five weeks are used for accounting periods) or calendar workdays in a month. The hours worked factor by month is predicated on the prevailing accounting periods.

The prime manloading technique employed is based on the equivalent units produced (in process) method. Historical manloading table calculations are usually used in loading small quantity, short run type development. Equivalent units produced are generally used to compute a production load, particularly, when a manufacturing time span exceeds twelve months. Graphic projections are most ideal and relevant to a high production volume rate and long span product items when immediate manload requirements must be determined.

Development of Manning Tables

Manloading tables can provide an effective means of ascertaining and spreading manpower requirements by designated time periods. This is accomplished by analyzing historical production model lots and creating separate representative tables for periodic and continuous production flow lots. Total product hours including outside production are reflected in the calculations to develop the tables.

Table Calculations

The direct labor hours for each product are converted into equivalent head-count and plotted cumulatively by average months to actual completion date of the last unit in each lot. Each data set (cumulative labor hours versus total elapsed time) is next translated into a common denominator of labor hours percent of elapsed time. The historical progress curves are then plotted together for each product function, and a line of "best fit" (least squares method) is calculated for each. From the cumulative percent values, the incremental increase for each five percent (which is variable) of elapsed time is computed.

The final step in the above process is to convert the percent of elapsed time into calendar periods of manufacturing time spans of 4 weeks through 52

Mechanical Manpower and Labor Cost Planning

weeks at two-week intervals. At this point, the tables are ready to use for each product through application to the production schedule.

Other Approaches

There are other methods that can be employed in developing manloading tables; their use is dependent on appropriateness to an organization's operation and procedural policies. The approaches are derivations of the work-in-process concept and are predicated on statements of the general formulas as demonstrated below.

Direct hours = Unit progress curve values

Equivalent men = Unit progress curve values *divided by* equivalent manhours conversion factor

Equivalent units produced is a rapid means of developing a manload accurately which reflects the schedule and further indicates the projections. This method has the advantage of requiring fewer calculations than the tables because it is based on the total rather than on a lot basis. A problem with this method is that the planning estimator must estimate the date at which one-half of each unit hours are scheduled to have been expended. Under some circumstances, the estimate may be difficult to determine, and thus a degree of inaccuracy may occur. The magnitude of possible error varies inversely with the quantity to be produced. For example, in one organization, a small unit quantity manload varied up to 6 percent, but the manload for a large volume unit production varied less than 1 percent. This situation can be overcome by a percent factor adjustment for the anticipated deviation if historical data experience and results have proven to be accurate in projecting the deviation factor.

Graphic manloading estimating is another technique which is used in some organizations. It is particularly adaptable to loading high rate production items that have an extended manufacturing time span. This is a useful tool for monitoring the effectiveness of shop performance; it is particularly relevant to optimum level manloading in a competitive market environment.

OPERATING DEPARTMENT MANPOWER PROJECTIONS

Equivalent direct manpower projections for operating departments are often developed as shown in Exhibit 7-E. The approved sales forecast is provided to the Production Planning/Scheduling department that uses it as a basis to project part/product requirements to meet customer deliveries on scheduled dates. The Inventory Control department provides the current part/product quantities available and also the requirements for maintaining an adequate pre-established inventory stock level.

EQUIVALENT DIRECT MANPOWER PLANNING
OPERATING DEPARTMENT PROJECTIONS

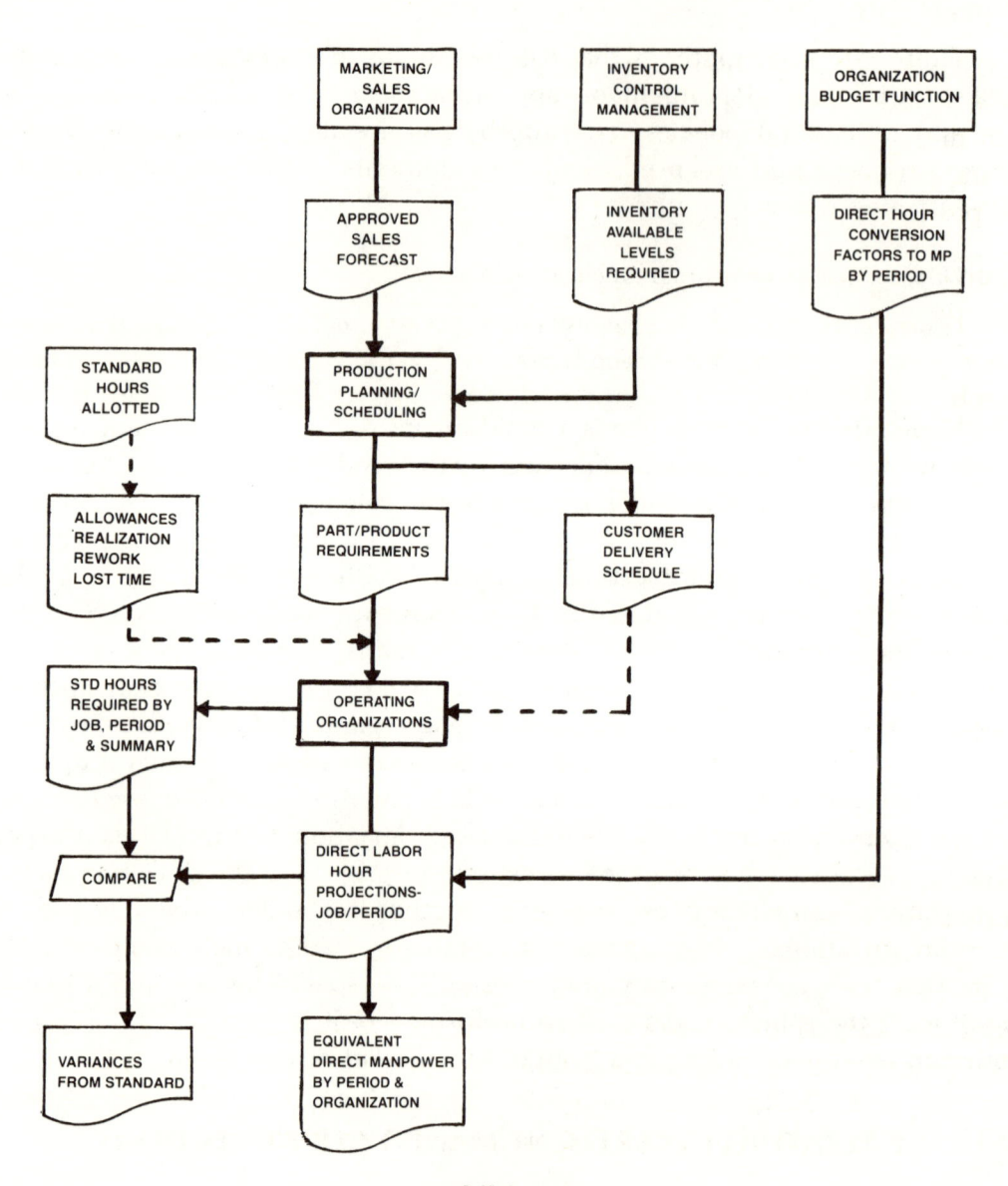

Exhibit 7-E

Production Planning translates the sales forecast and inventory requirements into part/product needs and provides this information along with the customer delivery schedule to the operating departments. They also indicate the standard hours to be allotted for producing the output needs. The standard hours to be used also reflect allowances for work realization based on learning curves, anticipated rework, and lost time.

Mechanical Manpower and Labor Cost Planning 219

The operating departments segregate the standard hours by task and period; they also project the anticipated straight time direct labor hours based on past experience as displayed in Exhibit 7-E.

The projected direct labor hours are compared to the standard hours to determine the variations from standard in order to ascertain if either set of data must be adjusted before completing the direct labor hour forecasts. As actual direct hours are accumulated by period, this data is compared to direct hours, both standard and straight time projections, to determine the variances for possible corrective action.

Equivalent Manpower

Equivalent manpower by period is derived from the straight time direct labor hours which represent the number of working hours in a day times the number of workdays in a given period. An example of the calculations follows.

Assume: 8.0 straight time hours per day
20 workdays in a specific time period
32,000 projected direct labor hours required in period

Calculations: 20 × 8 = 160 hours in period
32,000 hours divided by 160 = 200 employees projected

Allotted standard hours cannot be used for conversion into equivalent manpower because they have been adjusted for allowances as shown in Exhibit 7-E; therefore they do not reflect the total hours to be utilized in a working day by an employee.

The case for using straight time labor hours is that they have not been adjusted for the non-productive factor which could make a significant difference in determining the equivalent manpower requirements.

The calculations required for determining projected manpower as shown in Exhibit 7-E are readily accomplished in a computerized system which provides the added advantage of making changes readily and playing "what-if." The system can be programmed to start with manpower forecasts by period and task and translating this information into direct labor hour requirements and cost. This type of program was discussed earlier in this chapter.

DIRECT MANPOWER FORECAST BY PROJECT

Exhibit 7-F illustrates a detailed manpower forecast by project and period. These projections can be developed by knowing the actual headcount assigned to projects by department or calculated from the project direct labor hour requirements.

The graphic display is developed by cumulating period projected headcount by project, program or product line—whichever represents an organiza-

DIRECT MANPOWER FORECAST BY PROJECT

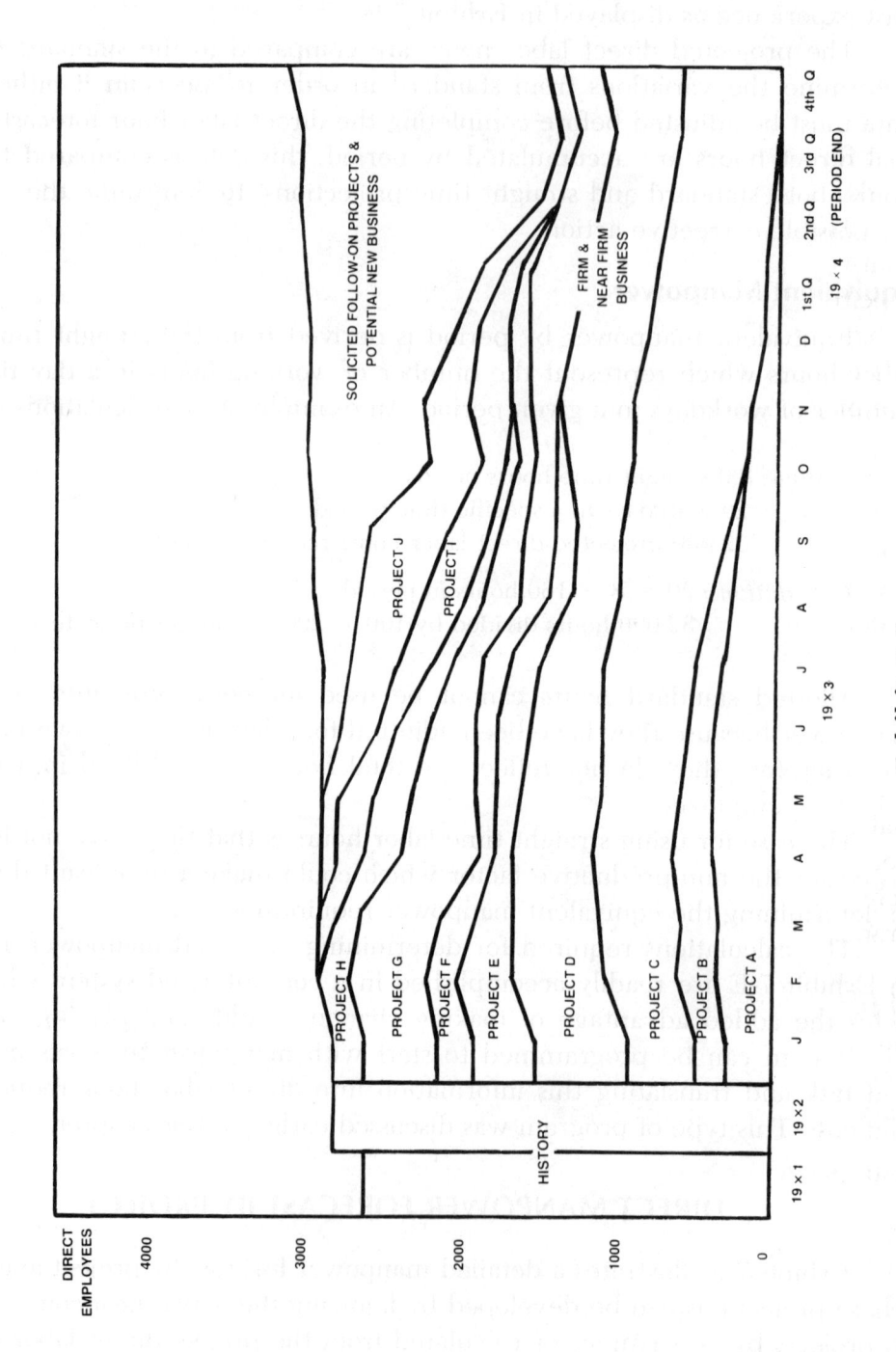

Exhibit 7-F

tion's operating projection requirements. The data is plotted on a "building block" basis to reflect the total direct employees projected by period.

As shown in Exhibit 7-F, follow-on business on current projects in-house and potential new business is reflected; otherwise, the assumption is that the organization's future activities will be drastically reduced. Conceivably, this could be a realistic situation, but rarely will a progressive organization concede that follow-on and potential new business will not result in increased sales and work activity.

This type of display succinctly indicates to management and operating executives the anticipated direction of the work flow activity, and it highlights specifically where increased marketing activity is required on projects being phased out. It points out projects requiring work extension negotiation with the customer and new product needs if the work force is to be maintained at the present level.

Exhibit 7-F also presents a comparison of prior year's actual year-end direct headcount as compared to the two years' future projections. This information reflects an organization's growth status or anticipated decline if the sales objectives are not met. The difference between the top line on the chart and the next line below it indicates the magnitude of new business requirements in order to maintain headcount growth or declines.

SPECIAL TOOLING AND SERVICE MANPOWER

All manpower loading is based on product schedule requirements and the lead time necessary to provide tooling and services to meet those needs. Special tooling is scheduled for completion prior to the start of the product component fabrication. Tool design must precede tool make, and planning must be achieved prior to the tool design process. This chain reaction must be programmed far in advance of production start dates.

Manloading for tooling and services will create lines on a base line chart of peaks and valleys throughout the entire period of a given program. Much of this can be attributed to engineering changes which may cause radical variations to the tooling and services base line chart and simultaneously result in varying changes to the product production tasks.

Estimating Techniques by Contract Type

The methods employed in this type of estimating are generally classified as development and production. Each request for a quote may differ somewhat and be characterized by its own uniqueness; therefore the techniques to be described should be considered as guidelines rather than a strict rule approach.

Special tooling and services include the following task categories: project tools, project support equipment, manufacturing planning, tool and support equipment, design and maintenance, and production illustration.

Development contracts. The planning effort for an activity that is the first of its kind may be estimated by utilizing statistics of a similar type of activity. The similarity must be evaluated to determine the percentage of increase or decrease that must be applied to the new item being quoted. Information of this type may be derived from program directives, task outlines, and discussion with knowledgeable engineers. The planner must be apprised of the quantity of job and part releases that Engineering proposes to initiate. The releases are evaluated in terms of similar items previously produced. If photo prints are available, they are screened, and both the tooling and planning effort may be more readily assessed and determined by an experienced estimator. Interpretation and utilization of historical data is very important in realistically estimating an unknown activity.

Production contracts. Production and follow-on activity may be projected with more confidence than development effort. An expanded definition, process description, and statistics are available for production programs since greater knowledge of the subject had been accumulated during the development phase. A comparison must be made between the two processes to ascertain what development effort will be repeated on the production program. This is usually accomplished by an analysis of engineering job assignment memos and a thorough review of the intended use of the special tooling.

A more detailed description of this technique is as follows:

- Engineering changes create and necessitate planning effort. New effort and/or change releases experienced on a similar program are illustrated in Exhibit 7-G. The trend has been projected through the period of time representing the area to be covered in the new forecast. The planning activity necessitated by engineering changes was recorded by the planning departments through the reporting of document releases. This is a weekly report which can be tabulated as indicated at the bottom of the exhibit. It displays the equivalent men per month expended by the planning activity for the selected period of time.

- To forecast a similar type of effort, all conditions must be relative and reflect an analysis of the past compatible environment. For example, it was determined in one organization that the actuals over a period of several months indicated planning expenditures of 45% for allocated prime costs. Using this factor, the projected planning effort to be expended was determined for the selected time periods. Further, the level of engineering changes affecting planning effort and occurrence of changes was forecasted based on past experience results and their association to future anticipations.

- To support the forecasting technique used for planning, an analysis of the recorded documents on Exhibit 7-G is an essential requirement. A

Mechanical Manpower and Labor Cost Planning

**ENGINEERING CHANGES
EFFECT ON SPECIAL TOOLING**

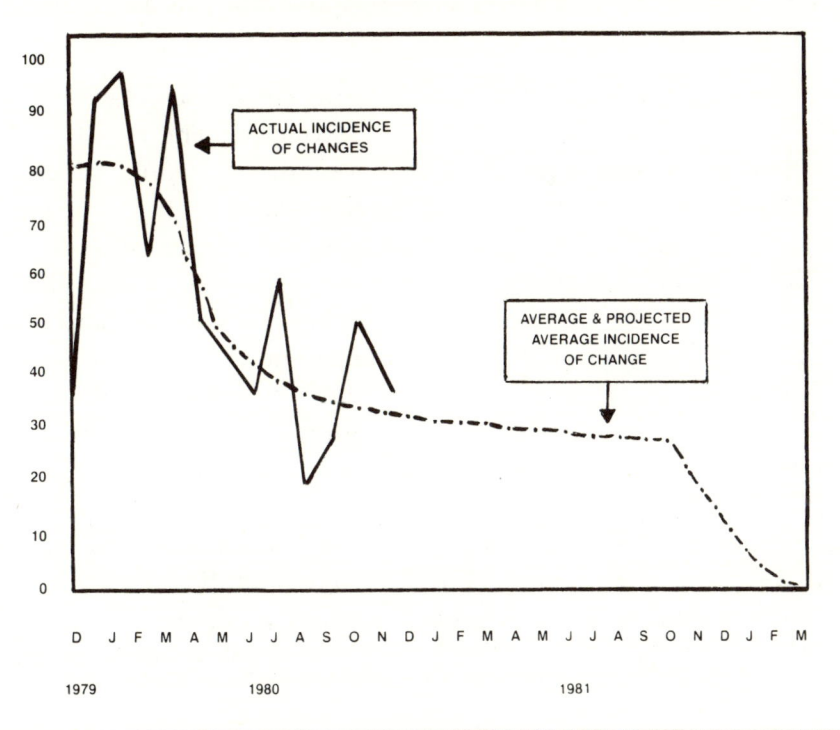

[Graph showing actual incidence of changes and average & projected average incidence of change from 1979 through 1981, with values ranging from 0 to 100 on the y-axis]

PLANNING DOCUMENT REPORT (SIMILAR EFFORT)													
	JAN	FEB	MAR	APR	MAY	JUN	JUL	AUG	SEP	OCT	NOV	DEC	JAN	FEB
EQUIV. MEN EXPENDED	10	13	17	25	30	43	46	47	52	60	61	69	79	78
NEW ENGINEERING														
RELEASES	8	—	4	11	13	—	—	3	5	9	—	—	—	—
DOCUMENTS	284	—	52	65	27	—	—	10	8	25	—	—	—	—
CHANGE RELEASES	16	12	16	13	16	34	31	25	99	93	35	57	105	103
DOCUMENTS	32	118	36	92	55	62	116	163	226	111	83	87	145	166
ENGRG JOBS PLANNED	14	17	22	23	25	34	30	20	110	94	42	37	95	108
TOOL ORDERS RELEASED	6	96	146	56	100	74	113	125	161	172	124	231	85	151
OPERATION SHEETS ISSUED	14	122	84	206	383	380	364	675	849	555	607	293	789	826
TOOL DISPOSITIONS	4	30	87	33	41	4	23	12	25	35	29	42	13	45
LOG BOOKS ISSUED	—	2	—	3	1	2	—	86	178	115	265	200	274	66
OTHER ITEMS —	COULD INCLUDE STOP ORDERS/RELEASES ISSUED. MISC. DOCUMENTS. ETC.													

Exhibit 7-G

time standard hour value for each type of document was applied to the documents produced. A factor representing the department's efficiency was applied to determine the hours required to produce those documents. The results of this evaluation is compared to recorded actuals for a similar time period in which the documents were produced. This comparison has been proven to be valid on many occasions (in one selected organization) and is conducive to an audit check.

- The next step is to determine the number of equivalent men required to effect the recorded changes discussed above. A period of time for past similar effort can be charted to ascertain the hours to be expended for work performed.

As an example, a time span of six months can be selected which would include the same type of effort which is to be quoted. The results of the analysis would indicate that one equivalent man per month would process two engineering changes per month. A chart display would reveal that, based on incidence of change line for the period of time included in the "to be quoted" effort, 250 engineering changes would be required. This value would be obtained by adding the number of changes by the specific period of time. After counting engineering changes per month and dividing the values by a historical factor, the basis for constructing the time phasing of equivalent men required can be determined for the new effort. Calculating the available hours per month times the equivalent men per month would result in the total manhours required.

An exhibit can be constructed to visually determine the equivalent men required for project tools, project tool design modification and maintenance, project support equipment, and project support equipment design and maintenance. Historical experience is the basis for chart development and reflection of future projections.

PRODUCTION PLANNING PROCESS

Initially, a unit production plan is developed and the required input for labor, material, and expense is projected. Since the task of planning manpower for the manufacturing organization is generally the most difficult, the planning procedure in one organization which manufactures products for sale is described below.

1. In this organization, a significant quantity of the products is sold from inventory rather than manufactured to order. The problems of having sufficient stock of each item to sell, inventory investment objectives, and risks of obsolescence have to be carefully considered in the planning process. Consequently, sales must be accurately predicted in advance of a production decision.

2. The number of products sold in any one specific product line can create problem fluctuations in the overall sales production independently of total volume. This situation can adversely affect the type of sales units to be produced and their appropriate scheduling.

3. The plant manager provides the necessary authorization to the factory relative to what items are to be produced and their quantity. The authorization is released only after due consideration has been given to historical and

Mechanical Manpower and Labor Cost Planning

projected sales and inventory requirements. This document also contains the monthly delivery schedule.

4. A production schedule is published each month by the manufacturing planning/control group which contains projected monthly unit deliveries to finished goods stores throughout the year based on the approved authorizations received.

5. Each month immediate range revisions to the monthly quantities to be delivered are made after considering the most recent sales inventory projections. In this manner, the appropriate effect is given to the most current situation in the market; therefore, because of variable market conditions, the mix in actual factory deliveries in a given month may not follow the plan formulated prior to the start of the year.

6. The lead time from the receipt of the authorization to the delivery of products varies with the individual product being considered. In this particular organization it averages three to four months.

Manpower Projection Technique

The unit sales forecast is the basis for developing the production plan for the annual budget. It could reflect a downward or upward trend in factory direct labor. This can be caused by seasonal marketing effects or by the transfer of work/products among divisions to stabilize their workloads. Rather than budget expense for a different labor level each month, many organizations have adopted a "step plan" for direct labor to reflect the decrease or increase being accomplished through two intermediate levels, with the annual total costs being controlled by the forecast plan. In this situation, it is necessary that the manufacturing planning staff determines which expense elements are relatively fixed, variable, or semi-variable. On this basis, indirect labor reductions or increases can be planned to occur when direct labor levels increased or decreased in both the manufacturing departments and in the associated manufacturing service areas. The indirect labor levels are determined by consultation and resolution among the plant manager's staff and the various department heads.

For each department in the plant, a manpower plan is prepared which reflects the beginning-of-year status and monthly changes in each job category. The plans are priced by using job classification rates, planned wage increases, and number of workdays in the month. The consolidated budgets for the manufacturing plant thus represent a step approach to the planned work force reductions or increases on a realistic basis.

Direct labor, consisting of production, assembly, and test personnel, is developed from the manufacturing activity required to support planned sales. Support labor reductions or increases are budgeted to occur when the direct labor changes are given effect. The resultant manpower plan is therefore completely integrated within the framework of the annual plan and is developed in depth at the department and section levels.

Manufacturing manpower is combined with engineering, sales, and administrative projections to produce monthly figures by payroll categories to show how many personnel were planned for the division. It is recognized that the actual direct labor level in the plant may fluctuate up or down from the plan in the immediate time span because of actual production deliveries required in a given future period. However, if sales follow the planned pattern, it is reasonable to assume that actual results will conform to the plan over a period of several months.

The manpower plan is required prior to the development of the expense budget. This is logical since 65% or more of the expenses are payroll related, particularly when one considers the ever-expanding costs for fringe benefits. Generally, the labor expense budgets are based on a plan for specific employees required in the future rather than the projection of historical dollar ratios. The above type plan would include all elements of data necessary to analyze and isolate any manpower variances that occur in the projected periods.

MANPOWER AND LABOR COST DEVELOPMENT FOR SALES PROJECTIONS

The initial requirement in an estimated cost buildup to projected sales is concerned with a manpower forecast. The forecast is developed by the various organizations by future periods based on current business volume "in-house" (backlog) and anticipated new sales orders correlated to the business economic trends and marketing intelligence. The direct manpower is associated with a specific contract, product, and/or product line needs.

The organizational manning provides a means to further summarize the headcount to major project budget centers as identified through a computer "look-up" table record. An indirect to direct manpower ratio is projected by individual organization based on historical factors and/or management edict relative to the overall operating plan objectives. The above process thus provides the total manpower requirements to meet specific sales goals.

After the data is developed, it is forwarded to the responsible budget control group for review and consolidation. The budget group further develops factors for the number of direct labor hours to be worked by the employees and associated with project, product and period. This is important because the organization may be on a calendar month reporting cycle or on a four week per month basis for the first two months of a quarter and then five weeks for the third month. Manpower conversion into direct labor hours reflects the production activity required to meet sales objectives.

Labor rates are predicated on historical experience plus planned wage increases. Labor rates can be developed with a computer program using the least squares projection. Historical direct labor dollars by organization are correlated to direct labor hours, and a formula is derived for application to projected direct labor hours. The formula is adjusted to reflect planned wage increases and other judgment factors. The computer process is particularly appropriate for the larger and more complex organizations due to the volume of detail involved in the calculation process. In small organizations, the input would probably consist of projected individuals, their specific classifications, and associated labor rates for computing labor dollars.

The direct labor dollar cost forecast reflects a major element of prime costs in the cost of sales which indicates the price to be paid in producing sales requirements.

As indicated above, a computerized system for translating manpower projections into labor hours and dollars is a most effective means of developing the detailed data required on a timely basis and provides the capability for making changes rapidly. The mechanical system also provides the capability for comparing actuals with the forecast at the lowest level of detail required.

LABOR COST ESTIMATE POINTERS

In order to effectively project manpower needs and labor costs, the planning estimator must be thoroughly familiar with the multi-detailed tasks involved in producing the end product. He must know the time span requirements in terms of hours to produce a part, sub-assembly and assembly, depending on the complexity of the product(s) being manufactured. The estimator must be aware of both the physical tasks as well as the equipment/machinery capabilities and requirements.

The above data is translated into direct hours and employee needs in terms of skills and numbers which are identified to organizational units and projects/products.

The information is summarized by specific time periods and priced through the application of projected labor rates. Since labor costs are generally the prime cost in producing a product or performing a service, extreme care must be taken in developing a realistic manpower forecast.

Computerization of the tasks involved in this activity will significantly reduce the manual effort required and improve timeliness and accuracy. Further, the system will provide the capability of flexibility in making changes that are inevitable during the process of finalizing manpower requirements.

8

Computerized Planning for Projecting Material and Other Direct Costs

Various classifications are used in identifying and describing specific types of materials that are utilized in the product and/or its support processing. The more common materials are direct, raw, indirect, supplies, stores, and finished parts.

This chapter, however, is primarily concerned with estimating *direct materials* and other direct costs that are associated with the material prime cost element.

DIRECT MATERIAL AND OTHER DIRECT COSTS

Material is considered to be a direct cost if it can be readily identified with and charged to a specific product, production order, or process. It represents a component part of the finished product and/or is used directly in manufacturing, converting, or processing such materials or parts. The cost for containers used in packing the product for customer delivery are also considered to be a part of the direct material cost element.

Raw materials are often used synonymously with *direct materials* because the finished product in one production process may become the raw material for the subsequent phase in production. For example, finished parts purchased from the vendor represents his completed product but, to the purchaser, that part/product is considered to be raw materials in his processing activity.

If the material cannot be specifically or economically associated with a given product, then this type of material should be categorized as *indirect* and the costs should be allocated over production on an applicable overhead distribution basis.

Other Direct Costs

These costs (other than labor and overhead) are directly associated with the product cost and include outside production, direct travel, computer usage, reproduction (technical manuals), and consultants. Classification of these costs may vary among organizations depending on their accounting policies and practices as well as customer dictates, particularly in the case of government contracts.

ACCOUNTING FOR MATERIAL COSTS

Under the *job order cost* accounting system, direct material costs are identified by specific job during each phase of the production process. This procedure includes the time period from when the materials are requisitioned from the stockroom, through the production phase, until the finished goods are completed. Indirect materials and supplies must also be accounted for from the time of issuance until appropriately charged or applied to production and service departments' standing orders.

Material control and accounting require a number of subsidiary ledgers in which are recorded detailed material costs. Control accounts are used to summarize periodically material costs as they are incurred, and the data are reflected in the general ledger. Mechanical subsidiary records include stock ledgers, material requisitions, production orders, and inventory reports. The general ledger control accounts include materials control, material in process, and finished goods. Indirect material usage is reflected in the plant overhead control account.

Material Purchases

The purchase of raw materials and supplies for *inventory* is the most common means of material acquisition. Material purchase vouchers are recorded in a register file and reflect a journal voucher entry of a *debit* to Materials Control and a *credit* to Vouchers Payable. In the subsidiary ledger, an entry is also made in the *received* section of the specific stock account.

There are occasions when a production department may require special, non-inventory stocked items and, under these circumstances, procurement action is initiated to meet these requirements. These types of material purchases are generally handled on an emergency basis due to immediate need in the production process. To do otherwise, could lead to work disruption and/or stoppage. When this type of materials or supplies are received, they are delivered directly to the production department concerned. The recording entry is a *debit* to Materials in Process and a *credit* to Vouchers Payable. A subsidiary record entry is made on the production orders for the cost of the special purchased raw materials and/or finished parts.

Direct Material Issuance

When material requisitions are prepared, they will differentiate between direct materials to be used in the production processes and indirect materials to be used for general purposes. The foremen or supervisors of production departments are responsible for determining which materials are direct or indirect. The requisition form contains two columns—one for direct material entries and the other for indirect.

Two copies of the material requisition are prepared or outputted from the computer. One copy is priced and returned to the requisitioning department and the other is filed by the stock ledger clerk as evidence of the material issue. The departmental copy of material requisitions is used as a basis for recording the material direct cost in the appropriate section of the production order. The cost of the materials used are reflected by a journal *debit* entry to Materials in Process and a *credit* to Materials Control.

Materials in Process

The materials in process account is a controlling account in the general ledger which summarizes the cost of materials as shown on production orders. This account is charged for the total amount of direct materials that are requisitioned from Stores and used in production. The materials required for each job are entered in the materials section of the job production order. The Materials in Process account is *credited* for the cost of materials shown in completed production orders and the finished goods account is *debited* for a similar amount. The cost of materials shown on the completed production orders is transferred to the finished goods subsidiary ledger.

At the end of each accounting period, the balance of the Materials in Process account should be equal to the total material costs which represent work in process charged to production orders that remain uncompleted. The balance of the Materials in Process account represents the cost value of materials in process inventory.

The planning estimator should be familiar with the accounting procedures relative to material costs since it provides him with a logical flow of events pertinent to purchases, issuance, and materials in process recordation. These data sources may prove to be invaluable in providing historical information for future material estimate activities.

METHODS USED IN PRICING REQUISITIONS

Material issues are controlled through the use of properly authorized requisitions or bills of material. The different methods employed in *estimating* or pricing stores issues produce varying costs of jobs and products as well as inventory values.

There are several methods used in pricing material requisitions. *Some* of these methods can also be used in estimating material requirement costs as well. A brief description of each follows.

- *Weighted Average.* In situations where it is most practical that *like material* be intermingled for storage purposes particularly, the weighted average method is most suitable. In calculating unit costs, any additional quantity received is added to the inventory on hand, and also the cost of material received is combined with the cost of materials on hand. The total cost of the above materials is divided by the total quantities to obtain the average unit cost. This process is repeated as inventory changes occur. Because of the numerous calculations involved during periods of frequent price changes and increased purchasing activity, it is *most* appropriate that this process be computerized.

- *Periodic Cost Average*. Under the *process cost system*, requisitions are held until the end of the month for costing because production costs do not have to be ascertained for the individual job orders. New average material costs are calculated once a month rather than after each purchase. To obtain average unit costs under this method, the beginning inventory for the month is combined with the total purchases for the period and divided by the total quantity available during that period. Using this procedure reduces the clerical workload even in the manual environment, but the *major disadvantage* is that the computations are accomplished at month end when considerable effort is required for closing the books and preparing the financial statements. This problem can be alleviated by using the prior month's pricing for the current period's activity.

- *Specific Cost Method*. Under this procedure, each lot of materials purchased are stored separately and records are maintained for each lot or major unit. When materials are issued, the associated costs can be readily determined.
  This method is commonly used when special or non-standard items are purchased for unique orders or when significant unit cost values are involved. Exact identification by serial number is possible.

- *Last-in, First-out (LIFO)*. Under this method, it is assumed that the last items purchased will be the first to be used; therefore, requisitions are priced based on the most recent purchase(s). This procedure reflects material costs at the most current market prices and inventories are costed on the basis of earlier purchases.
  The *major problem* with this method is that inventories may vary considerably from current market value. The pricing objective is to match current costs against current revenues and thus avoid unrealized inventory profits.

- *First-in, First-out (FIFO)*. Under this procedure, the assumption is that the various lots of a material are used in the same relative sequence as they were received. Materials from each lot are charged out at the price that they were originally placed in stock.
  This method is appropriate when there are comparatively few purchases at varying prices.

- *Standard Cost.* Using this procedure, material requisitions are priced at a predetermined or standard cost. Under this method, only quantities of receipts and issues need to be recorded in the stores records. As materials are received, the Stores control account is charged at standard and the difference between actual and standard is credited to a *Material Price Variance* account. The standard cost of materials to be used on each job is recorded in advance on a cost sheet. The variation in quantity used is ascertained at periodic intervals of time and the difference is recorded in the *Material Use Variance* account.

  The *advantage* of this type of pricing is its simplicity; material control is achieved through maintaining price and quantity use variance accounts that highlight the relative efficiencies of material purchases and use. Cerical costs are reduced by eliminating repeated unit cost calculations.

Selecting the Appropriate Pricing Method

Generally, *no one method* of requisition pricing is universally used. Two or more methods may be utilized based on certain relative considerations such as: pricing objectives, type of industry, material quantities used and price fluctuations, length of inventory turnover period, and requirement for reflecting current prices in cost data.

Industry surveys indicate that the two most frequently used pricing methods are first-in, first-out and average cost. Irrespective of the above method(s) to be employed, computerization of the tasks involved (which is common in most major industries) will significantly reduce clerical effort and their costs plus improve data accuracy and timeliness.

ANALYSIS OF MATERIAL COSTS

The primary effort involved in analyzing costs is to make a comparison between actual and standard costs to obtain variances. Some of the possible causes for variances can be attributed to the following problems or events.

- *Material usage.* Changes in the design of the product, machinery, and processing methods. Spoilage and waste. Losses in storage or damage in receipt or handling. Errors in accounting charges.

- *Price variance.* Changes in market price, particularly, in inflationary period purchases. Problems with procurement in terms of incorrect quantity or quality. Errors in recording data entries.

Unfavorable variances should be thoroughly investigated in order to establish responsibility and provide the basis for corrective action. *Favorable variances* should also be analyzed as they may reflect savings and cost avoidance which were obtained at the expense of losses sustained elsewhere in the

Projecting Material and Other Direct Costs

operating environment. Further, *favorable variances* may result in the need for adoption of new procedures or techniques for improving operational activities and procurement practices.

Material cost variances resulting from procurement activities should be segregated from those resulting from production events since the former reflect price variations and the latter, material usage differences.

MATERIAL USAGE VARIANCE

When the actual quantity of direct material used is different from that established as standard for a level of production, the variance is attributed to *material usage*. The variance can be calculated in terms of physical quantities such as pounds, pieces, and units or in dollar values. The latter results from pricing both actual and standard quantities at the standard unit price. Using this approach, it is possible to measure the cost differences due to material usage and price differential. An example of the computations involved are as follows:

Material Type	Unit Price Standard	Usage Quantity Standard	Usage Quantity Actual	Std. Quantity @ Std. Price	Act. Quantity @ Std. Price	Usage Variance
X	$2.00	400	450	$ 800	$ 900	$ −100 UF
Y	2.50	200	180	500	450	+ 50 F
Z	3.00	300	320	900	960	− 60 UF
				$2200	$2310	$ −110 UF

The unfavorable (UF) variances displayed above are attributed to the *actual quantity* at *standard price* being greater than the *standard quantity allotted* at standard price.

Actual versus Standard Quantities

Actual and standard quantities can be determined by various means. A common method is to prepare a requisition for the quantity specified in the bill of materials. If additional material is required to complete the production order, then another requisition would be required. The excess quantity requisitions would be extended at the standard price in order to determine the material usage variance. The *excess* requisitions also highlight the fact that the standard was not being met and therefore an analysis is necessary to determine the reason(s) for this problem.

Another method is to enter on each requisition the standard quantity to be produced. The actual production is also reported. A difference represents the material quantity variance which, when multiplied by the standard rate, yields the dollar variance.

MATERIAL PRICE VARIANCE

The price variance between the standard and the actual cost of direct material costs can result from paying a price for material that is above or below the established standard price. This can be attributed to a number of factors such as: market price fluctuations, odd lot purchases, unfavorable purchase terms, or even losses in discounts. There are always the possibilities of excessive shrinkage or losses in transit and higher than anticipated transportation costs. If the price variance is significant, it should be analyzed in terms of the above factors to determine the cause(s) for possible corrective action. The invoice document and/or contact with the procurement organization will provide the clues for price variances.

Computing the Price Variance

The price variance can be computed by multiplying the actual quantity by the difference between the standard and the actual unit costs or by multiplying the quantity by the standard unit cost and calculating the difference between the standard and the actual costs as displayed below.

Purchase invoice provides the following data:
Item A—1,000 connectors, Type X, @ $ .50 each = $ 500
Item B—2,000 connectors, Type Y, @   .60 each =   1,200
Item C—3,000 connectors, Type Z, @   .70 each =   2,100

Established material price standards:
Connectors: Type X—.40; Type Y—.65; Type Z—.60

Computing variance:

Type Item	Standard Cost	Actual Cost	Price Variance
X	$ 400	$ 500	$ −100 UF
Y	1,300	1,200	100 F
Z	1,800	2,100	−300 UF
	$3,500	$3,800	$ −300 UF

In the above example, the price variance was determined at the time of purchase and receipt of the material. The variance is computed during the process of checking the extensions on the vendor invoices. At this point, the quantities are multiplied by both the actual and the standard unit costs to determine the differences in the price variance.

Some organizations do not compute the variances until the materials are *actually used* rather than at the time of purchase. Under these circumstances, the actual quantity used becomes the basis for calculating the variance. The prior method, however, is more commonly used.

Disposition of the Price Variance

Under the procedure wherein the Stores account is *debited* at standard cost, the price variance is segregated from the actual costs when materials are charged to Stores. A *primary disadvantage* to keeping material inventories at standard cost is that price variances generally do not appear in the same period in which materials are actually placed into production.

If variances are charged to the income statement at the time purchases are made, there could be an adverse effect on income that is not directly attributable to production and sales activity. This can be rectified by setting up a suspense account at the time the invoices are recorded and, as materials are issued, the suspense account is adjusted. Suspense account balances are treated as valuation items which are added to or deducted from the standard stores values.

PROJECTED BILL OF MATERIALS

Prior to the initiation of a new product as a production item or making changes in design of a prevailing product, it is necessary that a complete analysis be made of the requirements and their costs. A number of concerned departments may be involved in this task evaluation such as engineering, manufacturing, marketing, estimators, and management. All contribute their specialization expertise to the "go-ahead" determination and decision. A test model is developed to ascertain the feasibility and the possible problems that could result from new production pursuits and changes to current products.

Design Drawings and Specifications

Based on engineering design drawings and specifications of the product model being estimated, either new or current product being changed, a bill of materials is required and developed. This bill encompasses a listing of all the materials required with their description and part numbers. The responsible supervision specify which materials and components will be produced within the plant and which will be obtained from outside sources.

The requirements are forwarded to procurement for their input on material availability and source and estimated cost. The response from procurement may also indicate a need for further design changes by engineering due to the non-availability of the specific part(s) or their prohibitive cost.

The estimating function in conjunction with manufacturing operations would provide on the original document the quantity required for production planning and scheduling; procurement would provide catalog number, vendor name, delivery date and unit cost; accounting would calculate the total costs; and inventory control planning would recommend the minimum and maximum inventory stock levels based on organizational policy and operational plans.

Production Planning

During the process of structuring a new product or making changes to a current one, the engineering personnel must maintain liaison and coordinate their efforts with production planning in order to ensure that the product objectives are feasible and that the requirements coincide with sound manufacturing standards and practices. Production planning can provide engineering with considerable expertise relative to the ultimate in manufacturing process efficiencies—even to the extent of recommending modifications to the drawings and specifications.

After the proposed engineering innovations have been approved and adopted, the production planning organization translates the specifications into manufacturing terms and practices. This includes the material type and quantity to be used for each part, description of the operational processes involved, machine(s) to be used, tool requirements, possibly new machine needs, tolerances, the estimated setup and run times, and labor costs.

The above detailed data provided by manufacturing becomes the basis for estimating the effort and costing future sales proposals. In the mechanical process, the factors involved in the bill of materials become a part of the computer file and, as the need arises, further pertinent input is provided to the program for processing proposal requirements.

Production Material Requirements

The analysis of historical data of comparable tasks provides the most logical source for information to develop an estimated bill of materials. The data is adjusted to compensate for changes in design and/or complexity. Comparisons are made to actual cost history to establish material usage and price change factors. Adjustments may be applied to product cost increases due to the material price index as a result of quantity breaks and trade discounts.

R & D MATERIAL FORECAST

On research and development contracts, it is often necessary to develop other means of estimating material costs due to the lack of definitive documentation on which to base estimates. This can often be accomplished by developing *material rates per hour or pound* based on actual relationships recorded on similar or related programs. This approach may have to be supplemented by additional estimates for unique items that were not previously contained in any historical data.

OTHER DIRECT COST PROJECTIONS

Other direct costs such as direct travel, computer usage, reproduction, and location allowances will vary among organizations. Some of these costs

Projecting Material and Other Direct Costs 239

may even be treated as overhead depending on organizational procedures and practices. Where these costs are direct charges, the estimating procedure can vary significantly depending upon the type of cost and its dollar volume.

For example, it is extremely difficult to estimate realistically the amount of travel required on a major program of one or two year's duration due to the limited knowledge available on the number of trips required and the probable destinations. One approach is to develop a *rate per direct labor hour* based on actual experience from similar programs. Actual rates can be plotted each month against the forecast and, as with direct labor rates, evaluated periodically. As required, revised forecasts would be established.

Based on historical experience, another approach to estimating other direct costs is to develop either a percent of sales or prime costs. Using the correlation technique, this estimating method can be readily tested as to its reliability and usefulness.

ESTIMATING DIRECT MATERIAL COSTS

Material cost estimates are based on the quantity of each type of material to be used in each product or class of product and also on the anticipated future material prices during the estimated periods. Material quantity estimates are generally based on historical experience in conjunction with an intense analysis of each operation in the overall productive process. Determining the initial quantity of material per product unit is usually an engineering task. The results from a pilot product model and/or experience from a similar product can often provide the criteria for estimating the quantity of pieces or the pounds or feet of material to be required. Material specification records are often supplemented by test runs to verify the material need in each processing step and to determine the allowance for spoilage and shrinkage.

Estimating the total quantities and type of material required and the price to be paid are directly contingent on the production and purchasing budgets. Historical records, relative to material prices, are often helpful in establishing price trends, but they cannot be the exclusive basis in estimating future prices. Procurement's contact with vendors often provides a sound foundation on which to base future prices.

As a general rule, prices will vary in proportion to the quantity of purchases and the amount of vendor discounts.

Material Categories

Material is often categorized into (1) *special types* that are governed by detailed specifications and (2) material that can be purchased on the *open market*. Special materials are purchased with a fairly long lead time interval and therefore are not subject to rapid price changes. Contract prices and recent quotations are used in conjunction with quantity requirements in the production budget to determine future period costs. Based on this information, procurement can generally provide reasonable estimates for future costs.

Relative to material that is purchased on the open market, price estimates are developed from an analysis of the prevailing market conditions and a projection of the probable market environment for the forecast periods. In estimating material costs, transportation and handling costs should be included in the estimate; they are based on historical records and current rate scales.

The total estimated material costs and quantity by specific type items should be inputted into the computer file records for purposes of reference, retrieval, and development of future estimates.

MATERIAL PRICE TRENDS

Material cost trends and anticipated future prices are usually available to the estimator through reference to trade journals, vendor contact, internal and external procurement organizations, and customer intelligence.

Relative to predetermined standards, the prices should be based on prevailing prices for normal quantities and should be specific in terms of quality and grades. When costs are based on standards, it is highly desirable to place them on replacement cost basis. This is accomplished by converting costs to anticipated price levels in terms of percents of increase or decrease to the base price. Using this procedure, the detailed price lists will not require frequent changes, and cost estimate standards are readily adjusted.

MATERIAL USAGE RATIO

Material usage ratios are calculated by dividing the standard cost of the *actual quantities* used by the standard cost of the *standard quantities*. An example of the calculation follows.

Assume:	(1) Standard cost of *actual* quantities used:	$578
	(2) Standard cost of *standard* quantities:	550
Calculations:	$\frac{578}{550} = 1.051;\ .051 \times 550 = (28.00)$ Loss (rounded)	
	$550 - 578 = (28.00)$ verification	

Alternate method. The same ratios can be computed by an alternative method described and illustrated below (ratios and variances based on actual and basic standard rates).

- *Compute overall ratio.* Divide *actual* quantities at *actual* cost by *standard* quantities at *standard* cost.

- *Compute price ratio.* Divide the *actual* unit cost by the *standard* cost.

Projecting Material and Other Direct Costs 241

- *Compute usage ratio.* Divide *overall* ratio (price ratio × usage ratio) by the *price* ratio.

(1) *Assume:*		Basic standard rate: $.50; Actual rate: $.75; Actual hours: 1,500.
Calculations:		Ratio = .75 ÷ .50 = 1.50 or 150% Percentage variance = 150% − 100% = 50% Actual hours @ standard rate = 1,500 × 50% = $750 Dollar variance = $750 × .50 = $375
(2) *Assume:*		Actual quantity: 1,500; Standard quantity: 1,440; Actual price: .75; Standard price: .80
Calculations:		(material variance ratio) Actual quantity (1,500) × Actual price (.75) = $1,125 Standard quantity (1,440) × Standard price (.80) = $1,152 Overall ratio: 1,125 ÷ 1,152 = .9765 Price ratio: .75 ÷ .80 = .9375 Usage ratio: .9765 ÷ .9375 = 1.04

SHRINKAGE, SCRAP, AND WASTE

An important consideration in setting material usage standards that can also be applied in the estimating process concerns shrinkage, scrap, and waste. Many materials are subject to unavoidable deterioration while in storage or in the production process itself. For example, shrinkage could occur in material yardage loss during the dyeing process; meat curing generally results in a weight loss, and scrap can result from punching discs out of sheet metal. Material wastage can also occur from inaccurate, careless, or inefficient work as the material is processed.

In the determination of standards, the first step is to ascertain whether the material loss is due to improper processing methods and avoidable carelessness or is an inevitable result of the material process itself. Since standards represent what should be routinely accomplished, any unavoidable loss of materials is realistically considered in establishing the standards. When *avoidable* losses do occur, they represent unfavorable variances. Therefore, the *material usage standard* should reflect an anticipated minimum scrap loss factor which represents a consistent result of the material processing activity.

Minimum Scrap Loss

Material usage standards must be increased by the amount of the estimated scrap loss. When the loss occurs while materials are in storage due to evaporation or deterioration, the price at which materials are charged out to material in process may be increased sufficiently to cover the amount of the loss, or an expense account may be charged. When losses occur while material is being processed, then the usage standard must be increased by the estimated amount.

Unavoidable Material Loss

Determining unavoidable material losses is a difficult task since it is dependent on worker and machinery efficiencies. It is necessary that a distinction be made between losses that cannot be avoided in spite of the best of care and those that result from carelessness, inattention, and faulty work. Some material wastage can be attributed to the inherent lack of absolute perfection both in men and machines. The allowed standard usage should include an estimated factor for this type of loss; however, all waste from other causes should be reflected as material usage variances.

Establishing a Standard for Waste and Scrap Material Usage

The level at which a standard is actually established is determined by the type of standard in use. If a standard represents what is *actually anticipated*, the allowable waste is estimated from the projected results of operational processes. If the standard is *normal*, then the average amount of waste experienced under similar working conditions should be used. If an *ideal* standard is set, the level is established at the very least that is believed possible.

The setting of standards requires an analysis of historical results and an averaging of the data in order to obtain the most probable value for a waste allowance estimate.

Experimentation under controlled conditions and with selected operators has also been proven to be very effective in estimating material losses that are to be reflected in standards. The experimental method is particularly desirable if there have been changes in processing techniques wherein the prior data is no longer comparable, representative, or attainable under the changed processing conditions. In many cases, however, new product standards can be developed synthetically by using the historical experience for operations that are similar to those previously performed and making allowances as required for any known differences that have been introduced. These standards are generally revised at some future date when actual experience has been accumulated.

MATERIAL PRICE STANDARDS

In estimating material costs, reference is made to established material price standards. These standards reflect the unit cost for each type of material to be used and is in the form of a catalog of standard material prices. Pricing the standard material specifications depends on the nature of the standard to be used.

Basis of Standards

If the standard specifies expected *actual prices*, the process of establishing the standard is dependent upon the projection of anticipated market prices for each type of required materials. Many organizations contract for their material requirements long in advance of the contemplated usage; therefore, the contract price becomes the standard material cost. In other situations, it is customary to stock rather large inventories of raw materials; thus the price actually paid is available as the standard cost.

If the standard is based on *normal costs*, the process of establishing standard prices is dependent upon a statistical determination of the normal price level. The procedure may simply be an averaging of prices paid for a period of years with the elimination of periods reflecting extraordinary circumstances such as recessions, military conflict, and extremely high inflationery periods. Establishing price estimates and standards involves an element of individual judgment because even the best price projections that prevailing techniques can produce have a wide margin of error. This fact however does not vitiate standards, for they still serve a useful purpose as a check upon efforts of the purchasing organization and also as a readily available estimate of excess material prices.

Ideal Price Standards

The basic principle underlying the establishment of *ideal standards* necessitates setting price standards at a figure below that at which it is expected purchases can actually be made. While this practice may serve to some extent as an incentive to the procurement organization, the market price of materials is rarely influenced by the actions of an *individual buyer*; therefore, setting ideal standards does not serve any useful purpose.

Another *disadvantage* of ideal standards is that inventories are often valued at standard; thus, using ideal standards leads to lower inventory valuation. This result may penalize the organization because of the effect of decreased profit and lower current ratio with its effect on credit rating. Although ideal standards can be used for other applicable purposes, it seems preferable to use an anticipated *actual* or *normal* price standard.

Realistic Price Standards

The level at which price standards are set under the basic type of standard is unimportant as long as the price is considered to be realistic. Current prices at the time the standard is established or prices that represent normal conditions are the basic guidelines to material price standards. The material element in inventories is priced at actual cost as an accounting practice; therefore, there should be no problems involved in the effect of the standard price on inventory values reflected on the balance sheet schedule.

MAKE-OR-BUY ASSESSMENT

A make-or-buy plan is an internal plan. It is the basis for the preparation of a cost estimate proposal and serves as a guide for work placement during contract execution. It encompasses a descriptive list of program requirements relative to specific parts, assemblies, and equipment items. A determination is made from the assessment study as to whether the development and/or manufacturing requirements will be a function of internal or external (vendor) effort.

Considerations in the Make-or-Buy Assessment

Make or buy decisions must be made periodically by affected organizations because of their effect on production operation efficiency and profitability. Exhibit 8-A displays the various criteria involved in the make-or-buy decision making. As shown on the exhibit, there are many relevant factors to be considered during the evaluation process. Some may not be applicable to all organizations dependent on internal priorities and practices.

Various organizations are involved in the make-or-buy evaluation in order to achieve a coordinated, comprehensive, realistic assessment. Cost, quality, capacity, available skills, processing technology, and required resources must be considered in the make-or-buy analysis. The advantages and disadvantages of the *buy decision* must be outlined and verified in terms of their impact on internal operations, employee morale, costs, and profit.

The primary objective of the make-or-buy decision is to resolutely determine which direction will result in greater savings with the least effect on operational efficiency and profit dilution.

PROBLEMS ASSOCIATED WITH MATERIAL PROJECTIONS

Generally, the costing of materials required for a given task is the simplest part of the estimating process. The detailed analysis of the project will reveal the specific types and quantities of materials required. This data is presented in the form of a bill of materials, estimating sheet, or categorized list of needed items. Application of current prices to the items listed usually results in a fairly precise statement of material costs. There are, however, certain complicating factors for which allowances must be made relative to material quality, abnormal quantities, scrap, and wastage. Some of the common problems involved are noted in the following discussion.

Projecting Material and Other Direct Costs 245

MAKE OR BUY ASSESSMENT & DECISION-MAKING

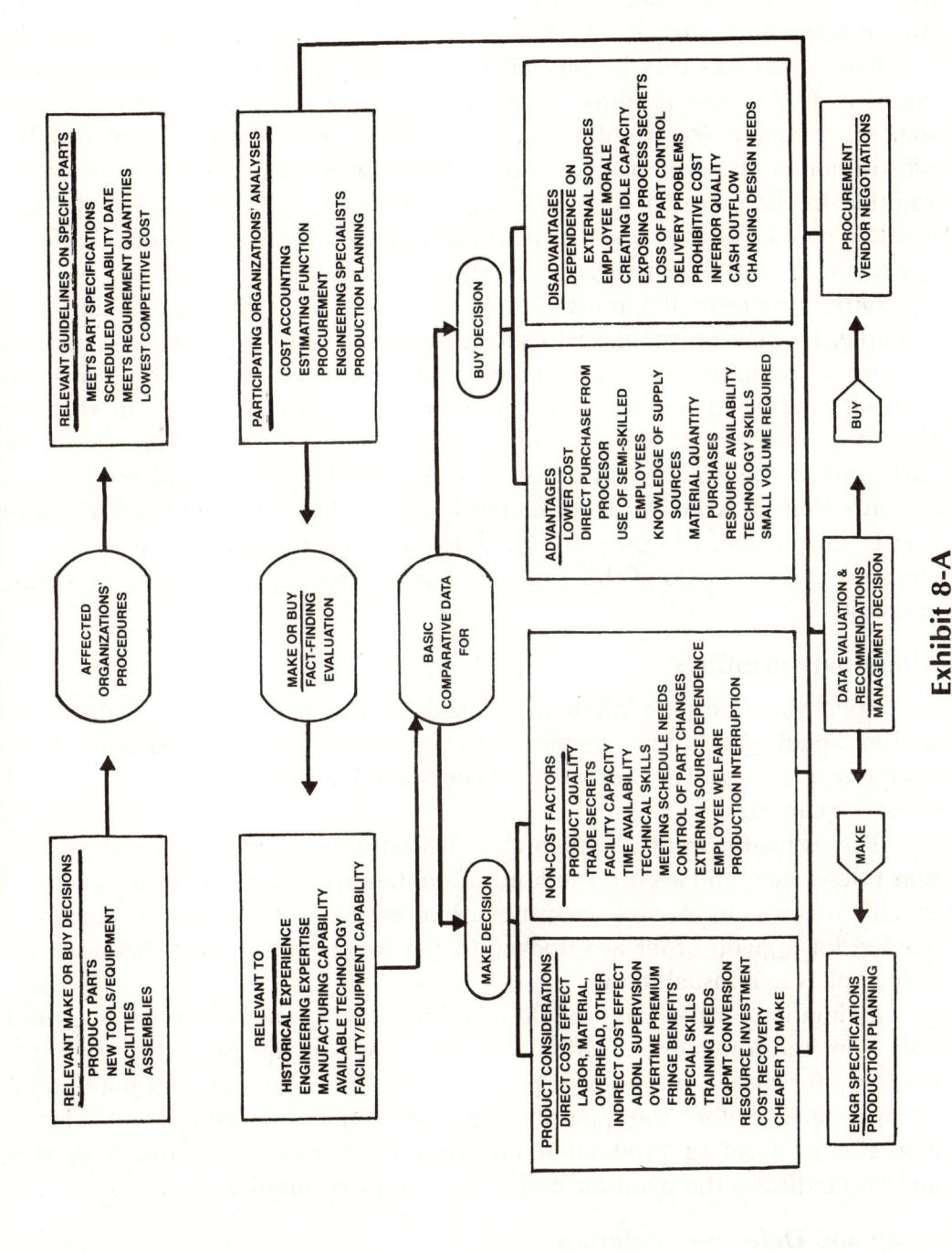

RELEVANT MAKE OR BUY DECISIONS
- PRODUCT PARTS
- NEW TOOLS/EQUIPMENT
- FACILITIES
- ASSEMBLIES

RELEVANT GUIDELINES ON SPECIFIC PARTS
- MEETS PART SPECIFICATIONS
- SCHEDULED AVAILABILITY DATE
- MEETS REQUIREMENT QUANTITIES
- LOWEST COMPETITIVE COST

AFFECTED ORGANIZATIONS' PROCEDURES

PARTICIPATING ORGANIZATIONS' ANALYSES
- COST ACCOUNTING
- ESTIMATING FUNCTION
- PROCUREMENT
- ENGINEERING SPECIALISTS
- PRODUCTION PLANNING

MAKE OR BUY FACT-FINDING EVALUATION

RELEVANT TO
- HISTORICAL EXPERIENCE
- ENGINEERING EXPERTISE
- MANUFACTURING CAPABILITY
- AVAILABLE TECHNOLOGY
- FACILITY/EQUIPMENT CAPABILITY

BASIC COMPARATIVE DATA FOR

MAKE DECISION / *BUY DECISION*

NON-COST FACTORS
- PRODUCT QUALITY
- TRADE SECRETS
- FACILITY CAPACITY
- TIME AVAILABILITY
- TECHNICAL SKILLS
- MEETING SCHEDULE NEEDS
- CONTROL OF PART CHANGES
- EXTERNAL SOURCE DEPENDENCE
- EMPLOYEE WELFARE
- PRODUCTION INTERRUPTION

ADVANTAGES
- LOWER COST
- DIRECT PURCHASE FROM PROCESOR
- USE OF SEMI-SKILLED EMPLOYEES
- KNOWLEDGE OF SUPPLY SOURCES
- MATERIAL QUANTITY PURCHASES
- RESOURCE AVAILABILITY
- TECHNOLOGY SKILLS
- SMALL VOLUME REQUIRED

DISADVANTAGES
- DEPENDENCE ON EXTERNAL SOURCES
- EMPLOYEE MORALE
- CREATING IDLE CAPACITY
- EXPOSING PROCESS SECRETS
- LOSS OF PART CONTROL
- DELIVERY PROBLEMS
- PROHIBITIVE COST
- INFERIOR QUALITY
- CASH OUTFLOW
- CHANGING DESIGN NEEDS

PRODUCT CONSIDERATIONS
- DIRECT COST EFFECT
  - LABOR, MATERIAL, OVERHEAD, OTHER
- INDIRECT COST EFFECT
- ADDNL SUPERVISION
- OVERTIME PREMIUM
- FRINGE BENEFITS
- SPECIAL SKILLS
- TRAINING NEEDS
- EQPMT CONVERSION
- RESOURCE INVESTMENT
- COST RECOVERY
- CHEAPER TO MAKE

DATA EVALUATION & RECOMMENDATIONS MANAGEMENT DECISION

→ *MAKE*: **ENGR SPECIFICATIONS / PRODUCTION PLANNING**

→ *BUY*: **PROCUREMENT / VENDOR NEGOTIATIONS**

Exhibit 8-A

Material Quality

If material needs can be purchased to exact specifications and rejected if they do not meet the specified standard quality, then the remaining problem is that of scheduling. Proper scheduling is a *must* to avoid delays and bottlenecks.

Some materials may be unavailable to meet specifications exactly or grading of materials may produce wide variations in quality. Under these circumstances, consideration is often given to the use of substitute materials. A substitution of one type or quality of material for another affects other items in addition to the material costs. Shifting from one specification for materials to another may involve changes in manufacturing methods which could affect labor and overhead costs to a greater extent than the material cost.

Often, the estimator must be able to plan a job as well as estimate it. For example, he may be required to select items of material to be used in such a manner as to minimize costs. Of course, this task would have to be coordinated with all concerned (engineering, manufacturing, procurement). In this situation, it is necessary to make comparisons between sizes, thicknesses or other variations of specification in order to select the best of a number of choices. Organizations in which cost estimating is significantly extensive and important, find it advantageous to prepare schedules showing variations in price for various sizes and thickness of the same item or differences in shipping procedures and cost.

Abnormal Quantities

Price variations are often influenced by the quantities of material purchased. Small quantity lots generally dictate higher prices and large orders reflect lower prices. The quotation sheet should indicate the price scales for varying quantities.

The estimator must maintain close liaison with the procurement organization to ascertain and secure the kind of quotations which are applicable to the specific material items and quantities required. Since the majority of materials needed for a given order are stocked in the regular inventory, this precaution only applies to unusual items.

Estimating forms should be designed to allow space for a *stock position* report from the stores organization. The advantage of this procedure is that the necessity for special purposes or price inquiries may be seen and noted on the estimate sheet before the quantity and cost estimate are completed. This process aids in avoiding production interruptions because of material shortages and also indicates the need for new or special price inquiries.

Scrap and Defective Materials

Scrap resulting from production is generally reflected as an offset to direct material cost to the extent of its recovery value. This value may be a market

Projecting Material and Other Direct Costs 247

price less estimated or actual realization costs or an estimate of the useful value of scrap materials in other productive operations. The *major problem* relative to scrap or defective materials is that the cost of a particular lot or product may be significantly affected by variations in their amounts. For estimating purposes however, only a *normal allowance* for scrap is included in the cost analysis.

Defective material may be allocated to overhead and applied to all production on a uniform basis when the products are of a sufficiently similar nature to result in approximately the same amount of defectives per number of units produced. If the intricacy of the castings to be produced or machining operations cause significantly more defectives to occur on one type of product versus another, then more equitable costing results from charging defectives to the involved product, rather than spreading the cost to all products through a common overhead application rate.

Some basic guidelines to scrap costing are as follows:

- The percentage of process scrap to be used in the determination of a standard cost should be based on a *normal year's record* of production and scrap.

- A related *separate percentage* should be used for each size, lot or material quantity.

- If *two or more types of equipment* are utilized to manufacture the same kind of product with a resultant different percentage of material yield, then mangement policy should dictate whether to adopt the higher yield as standard and reflect the *lower yield as an excess* or to adopt the lower yield as standard and reflect the *higher yield as a gain* resulting from efficient operations.

- The percentage of spoilage to be used in calculating standard material costs should be those percentages which prevail after all experimentation and development have passed and production is proceeding normally at the standard volume and the standard rate for machine and labor performance.

- In calculating the percentages for waste and spoilage, the deduction should be made by department. In other words, the resulting yield should be calculated against the full cost of product entering a department for processing and should include a *calculated loss* for material, labor, and burden up to and including the burden center where the loss occurred.

Although these guidelines are primarily pertinent in establishing a standard for scrap, they are also relevant to the estimator in estimating activities.

MATERIAL BUDGETS

The procurement organization is generally responsible for developing the material purchase budget which must be consistent with organization policy relative to the levels of inventory to be maintained, economical purchase lots, available financial resources, and status of the market at the time of purchase. The procurement organization is usually the most qualified to develop a program of planned purchasing based on material requirements, with due consideration accorded to the criteria noted above.

Control of Inventory Additions

In controlling additions to raw material inventories, there are four approaches, or combinations thereof, that can be used: detailed budget guidelines, establishing maximum stock limits, speculative purchasing, and purchasing to specific customer orders.

The basic raw materials are purchased in accordance with the detailed purchase budget which is predicated on a production budget. Secondary materials and supplies are procured on the basis of purchase requisitions issued by a stock clerk when any item reaches the minimum set by the stock records. In today's computerized environment, the mechanical system provides the *alert* when items approach minimum levels and, in addition, provides a complete purchase order addressed to the vendor indicating quantity required and other pertinent data. The purchase order is reviewed and approved by procurement before its release.

In industries in which the basic raw material is subject to wide price fluctuations, *speculative purchasing* may be one answer to the problem, but it is rarely accepted as an "on-going" standard practice.

In job order oriented industries where production is of the assembly type, some basic materials are stocked on the basis of a *purchase budget* or through the use of stock limits. Parts and materials that are special to each job are purchased only after the customer's order has been received and accepted.

Dollar Estimate of Purchases

Irrespective of the procedure in providing raw material, an estimate of purchases in dollars by period is essential if a complete budgetary control plan is to operate effectively. Cash requirements and projected balance sheet data are dependent on estimated purchases spread over monthly periods.

Generally, the purchase budget is segregated into two parts: one covering direct materials and the other, supplies. The cost of anticipated *supply usage* is included in departmental expense budgets.

When an organization is producing standard articles for inventory, it is possible to place a substantial part of the procurement on a *detailed budget* basis. By adjusting the estimated material required for the planned production by

Projecting Material and Other Direct Costs 249

the desired inventories at the beginning and end of a period, the required purchases can be determined. These requirements are then modified by the procurement organization relative to the considerations outlined above for the purchase budget. The budget is always subject to change whenever there is a significant change in planned production.

Maximum and Minimum Limits

The most common method of inventory control in the past was the use of stores cards with maximum and minimum limits and order quantities. In the *computerized* environment, the limits and order quantities by inventory item are stored in the computer file. As stock transactions occur, they are inputted into the system, matched against relevant file data, and reconciled; when the limits have been reached, appropriate mechanical action occurs. If the *maximum limit* has been reached, the procurement organization is apprised of this situation and purchasing of the concerned item(s) is stopped. If the *minimum limit* has been reached, an automatic purchase order to the vendor is created showing the order quantity that has been pre-specified in the program.

To be effective, the limits must be constantly reviewed and modified as required to meet production trends. Since the computerized stock file records, rather than a detailed purchase budget, indicate when material is to be ordered, the budget is usually not analyzed by types of material but rather by dollar amounts for all materials.

Although, in most instances, the stock file records are used as a basis for notifying procurement when the stock of raw material is becoming low, this does not necessarily mean that the computer-prepared requisition order will actually be issued to the vendor. By reference to the purchase budget, based on production requirements, procurement controls and issues the orders predicated on an adequate inventory as a whole to ensure that stock levels are in an acceptable relationship to sales volume. Using the purchase requisitions, procurement selects those that are most urgent to the extent of the purchase allowance available.

For materials purchased only on receipt of *customers' orders*, there is little necessity for a purchase budget except possibly for an estimate of cash requirements. Usually, historical experience can be utilized to provide a ratio of material costs to either sales or cost of sales and a percentage applied to either the sales or production budget. In either case, it should be recognized that some allowance must be made for the *lag* due to the time materials are in process.

ESTIMATING POINTERS

In many organizations, the material cost element is a significant cost that must be emphasized in estimating, costing, and control. In the planning process, consideration must be given to the various aspects involved in standard usage and price plus the anticipated variances. Proper pricing of material requisitions is very important to ensure realistic material cost estimates. Computerization of this process is a must to effect accuracy and timeliness of data.

The impact of shrinkage, scrap, and waste must be considered in establishing material standards and estimates. The make-or-buy decisions can seriously affect material costs, production efficiency, and organizational profitability. There are inherent problems associated with material cost planning and estimating. This subject is discussed in depth in this chapter, and ideas and solutions are presented to resolve problems before they occur.

9

Manufacturing Overhead Accumulation, Distribution, and Application in Cost Estimating

Manufacturing expenses include all incidental production costs other than the prime costs associated with direct labor and material. Even though these general expenses are incurred in the manufacturing process, they cannot be *specifically* identified and charged to a given product relative to such items as maintenance, supervision, and production control.

Overhead costs represent those expenses which have been applied and charged to work in process. These costs may reflect actual expenditures by period which are charged to production. In other instances, predetermined rates are applied to direct labor to ascertain the charges to be made to a product. In this latter situation, the expenses may be greater or less than the actual expense, but this application method is a convenient means of allocating overhead costs on a timely basis.

MANUFACTURING EXPENSE ACCUMULATION

Initially, manufacturing expenses are accumulated as a total and then distributed to the proper operating organizations (production and services) and the product itself based on prevailing organizational procedures. The steps in accumulating expenses are as follows, and the manual effort involved has been significantly reduced in the *computerized environment*.

- Expense transaction analyses are made to determine the appropriate account classification (this must continue as a manual effort).
- Transaction recordations are made in subsidiary accounts for analysis and appropriate summations to the control account level.
- The expense transactions are mechanically entered in journals.
- Balances in plant and service expense control accounts are reconciled with the total of the subsidiary ledger account balances.

Expense Classifications

There exist various guidelines for classifying manufacturing expenses; the method(s) used are governed by organization policy and practices. Plant expenses are commonly classified according to the following criteria.

Manufacturing Overhead Accumulation and Distribution

- Primary accounts are predicated on the expense objective (requirement for indirect labor, for example).
- Functional activity relative to the organization's operations (providing maintenance and repair, etc.).
- Expense behavior relative to the degree of variability (shop supplies, power).

Exhibit 9-A illustrates the type of detailed expenses that fall under the primary manufacturing control accounts. The data is recorded by subaccount detail and summarized to the control account level. Expense control accounts are, in turn, summarized to obtain the total manufacturing expenses. The resultant value is divided by estimated or actual direct labor hours or dollars to derive the *overhead application rate*.

The expense types displayed on Exhibit 9-A are fairly common, but their specific classification is subject to organizational practices and the chart of accounts. Varying types of organizations have their own unique accounts that are pertinent to their operations.

EXPENSE CHARACTERISTICS

Manufacturing expenses are also categorized according to their relative degree of variability. Expenses are segregated into three types: fixed, semi-variable, and variable. The distinction between these groupings is as follows:

Fixed charges. Fixed expenses are those charges that remain fairly constant from period to period and do not change appreciably with production volume fluctuations. When plotted on graph paper, this category of expenses is represented by a *straight horizontal line* over the varying time periods.

The product unit cost for fixed expenses would only be reduced by increased production within the prevailing limits of plant capacity. Increased capacity would undoubtedly result in increased fixed expenses due to expanding facilities.

Fixed charges include depreciation, rentals, leases, taxes, insurance, and amortization. Variable expenses represent a *constant* sum per product unit, but fixed expenses are expressed as a *constant value* per accounting period.

Semi-Variable Expenses. These expenses vary partially with production volume within certain limits, but they also remain constant during some stages of volume changes. Plotted on graph paper, semi-variable expenses are represented by a horizontal, vertical, then horizontal step line. In other words, these expense items tend to increase in incremental steps as production increases from minimum to higher volume levels.

Supervision and clerical labor and their associated costs are examples of semi-variable expenses because these expenses increase at particular peaks of production volume output.

MANUFACTURING EXPENSE CLASSIFICATIONS

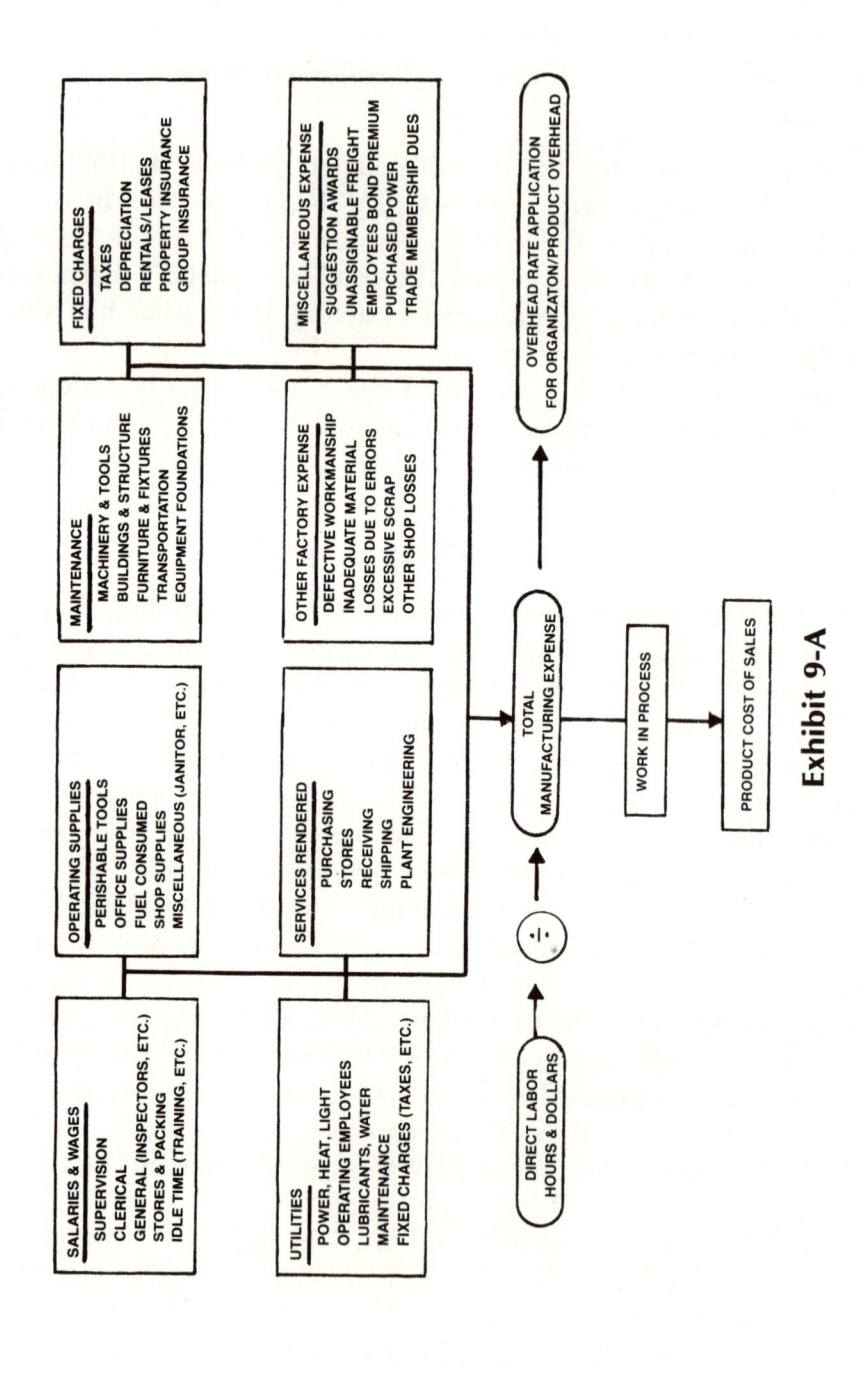

SALARIES & WAGES
- SUPERVISION
- CLERICAL
- GENERAL (INSPECTORS, ETC.)
- STORES & PACKING
- IDLE TIME (TRAINING, ETC.)

OPERATING SUPPLIES
- PERISHABLE TOOLS
- OFFICE SUPPLIES
- FUEL CONSUMED
- SHOP SUPPLIES
- MISCELLANEOUS (JANITOR, ETC.)

MAINTENANCE
- MACHINERY & TOOLS
- BUILDINGS & STRUCTURE
- FURNITURE & FIXTURES
- TRANSPORTATION
- EQUIPMENT FOUNDATIONS

FIXED CHARGES
- TAXES
- DEPRECIATION
- RENTALS/LEASES
- PROPERTY INSURANCE
- GROUP INSURANCE

UTILITIES
- POWER, HEAT, LIGHT
- OPERATING EMPLOYEES
- LUBRICANTS, WATER
- MAINTENANCE
- FIXED CHARGES (TAXES, ETC.)

SERVICES RENDERED
- PURCHASING
- STORES
- RECEIVING
- SHIPPING
- PLANT ENGINEERING

OTHER FACTORY EXPENSE
- DEFECTIVE WORKMANSHIP
- INADEQUATE MATERIAL
- LOSSES DUE TO ERRORS
- EXCESSIVE SCRAP
- OTHER SHOP LOSSES

MISCELLANEOUS EXPENSE
- SUGGESTION AWARDS
- UNASSIGNABLE FREIGHT
- EMPLOYEES BOND PREMIUM
- PURCHASED POWER
- TRADE MEMBERSHIP DUES

DIRECT LABOR HOURS & DOLLARS ÷ TOTAL MANUFACTURING EXPENSE → OVERHEAD RATE APPLICATION FOR ORGANIZATON/PRODUCT OVERHEAD

TOTAL MANUFACTURING EXPENSE → WORK IN PROCESS → PRODUCT COST OF SALES

Exhibit 9-A

Variable Expenses. These expenses generally vary in proportion to changes in production volume. Certain variable expense items, however, have a higher degree of variability in some organizations than others; the reason is primarily attributed to the *degree of expense control* exercised and the *increased rate* of output. For example, if two or three shifts are used, then some variable expenses will not increase in the same relative proportion as production volume. When plotted on graph paper, the slope of the line will represent a steep or gradual curve dependent upon the type of expense item and its increase or decrease resulting from production volume fluctuations.

Examples of this type expense are heat, light, power, lubricants, perishable tools, and operating supplies.

Importance of Classifying Expenses

The classification of expenses according to their behavior is of considerable importance in controlling expenses, developing a manufacturing expense budget, calculating realistic predetermined overhead rates, and understanding the effect of overhead on the unit cost of production.

The following observations and comments are noted relative to expense behavior.

- *Variable expenses* are more effectively controlled than fixed charges.

- Factory expense budgets (1) reflect expenses according to their degree of variability, (2) represent the prime source of data for developing predetermined burden rates, and (3) serve as a cost control tool.

- *Predetermined burden rates* should reflect a segregation of variable and fixed expenses. This is necessary if over- and under-absorbed overhead is to be analyzed effectively for determining the amounts applicable to controllable (variable) expenses versus volume variances (fixed charges).

- *Unit costs of production* are influenced by variable expenses which increase in proportion to production volume; therefore, the *unit variable expense* remains fairly constant. Since fixed expenses remain fairly constant, the *unit fixed expense* tends to fluctuate as production volume increases or decreases.

TRANSACTION RECORDS FOR EXPENSE COLLECTION

Two methods, or variations thereof, are used in accumulating overhead. Expenses can be collected in a *single manufacturing control* account or segregated into *separate departmental expense* accounts. Under the first method, expense transactions are journalized and recorded in a single control account. Supporting this account may be a departmental expense ledger or an expense distribution sheet indicating the distribution of the department's primary expense charges.

Under the second method, expense transactions are accumulated, journalized, and posted to separate departmental expense accounts. In the computer environment, both methods can be effected simultaneously through a sorting routine. The expense accounts are identified in the files relative to manufacturing control and department expense accounts. Segregated report records can be produced simply and effectively.

Basic Expense Source Records

The primary records used to obtain factory expenses include stores requisitions, time cards, purchase vouchers, petty cash vouchers, and maintenance/repair orders. A brief explanation of each follows.

Stores requisitions. The requisitions indicate the charges made for expense items drawn from the stores and supplies inventory and are identified to an account, code number, and requisitioning department. In most organizations, this is a mechanical process.

Time cards. These records are maintained to indicate the time worked by indirect workers who are paid on an hourly rate basis. Pertinent data is entered so that the proper factory expense accounts can be charged for the time worked. The information would include the employee number, indirect labor occupation name, expense account number, part number (if applicable), and concerned department.

Many organizations, particularly the larger ones, have the above process mechanized. An employee's token ID card is inserted into a remote station terminal device and the balance of the required information is keyboarded into the system. The computer calculates the elapsed time worked by part number and employee's earnings (hours worked times the rate). The hours worked record is maintained and reconciled by week and month. An employee's summary by department is reported. The file can be queried via the input device at any time for data retrieval as the situation demands.

Purchase Orders. These vouchers represent a record of factory expense transactions that are charged to the current month's operations. The charges create a liability to outside vendors known as accounts payable. The vouchers are supported by purchase delivery documentation and vendor invoices. The charges are classified and distributed in accordance with the chart of accounts. Where possible, the expenditures are further identified to a specific department.

In most organizations, the above process is computerized and identified as the accounts payable system. Pertinent *purchase order* data is keypunched on cards or keyboarded directly into the mechanical system via an input terminal device. When deliveries are received from the vendor, the *receiving department* inputs type of item, quantities received, and purchase order reference number. When the *vendor invoices* are received, an expense account distribution (indirect expenses) is made and the data is inputted into the system along with other identifying information, such as purchase order and invoice numbers, quantities, item description, and dollars payable. The computer process reconciles the above three inputs and outputs detailed and summary reports as well as a discrepancy listing of any differences among the purchasing, receiving, and vendor invoice inputs.

Petty Cash Vouchers. In certain situations, factory expense transactions are recorded on petty cash vouchers. These transactions are usually for small dollar amounts covering such items as local travel, office and operating supplies, stamps, and entertainment.

In many organizations, cash receipt and disbursement transactions are computerized. A resultant cash flow report is outputted by account number and organization. Expense account data flows directly into a mechanical expense ledger system for processing and reporting.

Inventory Expense Accounts. The transactions under this category involve stores issues for such expense items as fuel, operating and office supplies, perishable tools, and repair materials.

In the mechanical system, the requisition requirements are inputted directly into the system. The information involves requisition number, date, requesting organization and item quantity, and description. As the items are issued, stores inputs item(s) and quantities issued, expense account number, cost, requisition reference number, receiving organization, and issue date. Periodically, a report is outputted indicating the status between item requisitions versus issues, open orders, and stock balances. When inventories approach minimum required balances, a report is issued to procurement as a guide to purchasing requirements. The expense data flows into the expense ledger system.

Maintenance and Repair Orders. Special service repair orders are used to record factory expense transactions relative to maintenance and repair work. The data contained in the order include date, order and expense account numbers, work description, and estimated cost for labor and material. When the work is accomplished, the estimated costs are revised to reflect actual costs.

In the mechanical environment (similar to expense accounts above), the request for maintenance/repair service is the initial input into the system. As work is accomplished and actual costs become available, this information is also inputted. A reconciliation is made of the above two inputs and a status report is mechanically outputted. The actual expense values and account numbers flow into the expense ledger by organization.

ACTUAL VERSUS PREDETERMINED OVERHEAD RATES

Distribution of overhead expenses over production is significantly important as these types of costs cannot be specifically identified to any particular item produced. Therefore, an appropriate means for applying overhead must be established. This is necessary in order to preclude possible problems relevant to timely and competitive bids and estimates, proper product pricing and inaccuracies in inventory and period profits.

Overhead rates may be applied to the product on the basis of rates developed either before or after the expenditures are actually determined. The calculation formulas are noted as follows.

> *Actual application rate* = *actual period overhead* dollars divided by the *actual period production* in terms of units produced or direct labor hours or dollars.
>
> *Predetermined O/H rate* = *Estimated period overhead* dollars divided by *estimated period production* in terms of units produced or estimated direct labor hours or dollars.

Use of Actual Overhead Expenses

When actual overhead is used, the costing procedure cannot be accomplished until period end. This delay is disadvantageous because the final costs on completed production cannot be determined for some time after the order is finished. This results in unacceptable delays for the accounting function. Further, the value of the results are frequently open to serious question and possibly of negligible worth in providing appropriate guidelines for future policies. Using the actual overhead method, however, does result in all overhead being costed to the period production.

Use of Estimated Overhead Expenses

When overhead is estimated in advance and applied to production, then product costs may be determined immediately on order completions. Further, seasonal peaks and valleys are smoothed which makes it possible to recognize in overhead costing the varying rates of production due to cyclical factors. At the close of the period, however, there is a difference between actual and estimated overhead. This variance is commonly known as *under- or over-absorbed overhead*.

Concept of Predetermined Overhead Expenses

The predetermination of expenses is based on actual or estimated period expenses. The application of actual overhead expense by period to production generally results in highly fluctuating unit costs. When an estimate of actual overhead for the year is determined in advance and applied on a uniform rate basis, the costs are smoothed out by period. Thus, the resultant unit costs reflect average costs and, for that reason, are more representative than the actual costs.

Predetermined normal overhead costs indicate what the unit costs might be under controlled spending conditions relative to capacity operation, even though the plant may not operate at that level. Present and future trends indicate greater use of predetermined rates; however, if production volume can be maintained at a consistent level over a period of time and there are no other major disadvantages, actual rates should be used.

OVERHEAD DISTRIBUTION PHILOSOPHIES

Generally, the most complex problem in cost accounting is the measurement and distribution of overhead costs. The bases used in distributing overhead are constantly being reviewed and assessed in order to determine and verify the most equitable, logical method to apportion those costs to products, operational tasks, and organizations. Since overhead costs cannot be identified specifically with units of production and since there are no accounting means of *exact allocation*, each element of overhead must be thoroughly analyzed to determine its appropriate distribution.

Common Methods of Distribution

There are four philosophies that are used as a basis for distributing overhead: (1) service or use, (2) analysis of prevailing applicable conditions, (3) efficiency, and (4) ability to pay. Some organizations find it appropriate in their particular operations to use two or more of the above methods. A description of the methods follows.

Service or use. This is probably the most common procedure in use. It is predicated on the concept that the service or benefit provided can be readily measured, and the greater the service received from a particular overhead activity, the larger the amount of overhead should be assigned to the benefiting organization. The facility overhead is apportioned on the basis of *space occupied* by each organizational unit; production units are charged an amount of departmental overhead relevant to the *time required* for processing or servicing those units; and depreciation, taxes, and insurance on and maintenance of equipment is charged to departments relative to the *time each organization* used the concerned equipment.

Although this method is considered to be equitable and consistent, it does require *more accounting and record keeping effort* because each piece of equipment must be identified with each department and the *time element* must be accounted by organization, production orders, or product units. Examples of service department distribution bases are as follows:

- Payroll department expenses are distributed on the basis of total *labor hours* or *number of employees* in each department.

- Employment department expenses are distributed on the basis of *labor turnover rate* or *number of employees* in each department.
- Maintenance and repair department expenses are charged directly on the basis of the *hours worked* for each department.

Analysis of prevailing conditions. This distribution method is based on the analysis of prevailing conditions to determine the most logical basis for apportioning certain types of overhead. It may be that certain expenses are not closely related to organizations and production units; therefore, some arbitrary and equitable means must be determined for overhead distribution. For example, the salaries of the corporate president and senior executives cannot be directly identifiable and distributed to a specific organization because of their diversified activities. However, a survey of their expended time may reveal that a major portion of their time was concentrated on research, production, or sales activities. Based on these facts, it is logical that the larger share of their salaries should be distributed to the benefiting functions.

Generally, corporate salaries are a part of the overall corporate expense pool and are allocated to the divisions on one or more of a predetermined equitable basis, such as sales volume, headcount, direct labor hours, and profitability.

Surveys of activities have proven to be of considerable help in determining how services can be realistically apportioned. Utilities, maintenance, and equipment repair are other examples of service expenses that lend themselves to this type of analysis for overhead distribution.

Ability to pay. In some organizations, certain expenses can be distributed on this basis. Under this theory, the organizations with the largest sales or income would bear the greater proportion of the applicable expenses. The smaller struggling organizations would thus be given a "break" in their burden assessment. Although the ability to pay method is rather a simple application, its major disadvantage is that it penalizes the efficient and most profitable organizations to the advantage of the inefficient operations.

Although there are certain limitations to adequate overhead distribution, cost accounting serves as an important function in accumulating, recording, and analyzing data as a basis for establishing procedures for equitable overhead allocation.

PRIMARY OVERHEAD DISTRIBUTION

The initial phase in accounting for manufacturing expenses is their accumulation and this process is followed by their identification to departmental expense accounts. Therefore, the primary expense distribution involves spreading the direct overhead charges over the producing and service departments to which they apply and further segregating into the categories of variable, semi-variable, and fixed.

The estimator must be familiar with this process in order that his estimate will be compatible with the accounting procedures and will permit appropriate comparisons for analysis and reporting.

Basic Data for Primary Distribution

Pertinent data must be recognized relative to plant expenses and their applicability to the various production and service departments. Examples of the type data required follow.

- *Plant layout.* A blueprint should be available of the entire ground area occupied by the plant. Consideration is given to driveways, storage piles, building foundations, walks, etc. Departments' occupancy of each building in terms of area dimension used and cubic content must be determined to achieve effective specific type expense distributions.

- *Plant and equipment ledger.* Records must be maintained to provide the location and other pertinent data relative to each unit of machinery and equipment. The purpose of this information is to enable the cost department to allocate depreciation and property insurance to the proper departments when the period primary expense distribution is made.

- *Property insurance register.* This record contains policy premiums paid to cover all buildings, machinery and equipment. Monthly insurance can thus be identified with the applicable property. Additionally, accurate monthly expense charges are available for monthly distribution of property insurance.

- *Patents register.* This record reflects the cost of each patent purchased or developed by an organization. Further, the record indicates the department wherein the patent is applicable to manufacturing operations and provides the monthly patent amortization charges.

Defining Allocation and Proration Expenses

Department expense distribution falls into two categories:

- Expense items that can be directly identified with specific departments; this process is known as *expense allocation.*

- Certain *joint expense items* that must be distributed among two or more departments; this distribution is called *expense proration.*

In the accounting environment, the terms allocation, proration, and distribution are used more or less synonymously. Overhead expenses are accumulated into the following groupings: indirect labor, indirect material and supplies, repairs and maintenance, depreciation, insurance, taxes, fringe benefits, and miscellaneous.

Using various type proration methods, the above expenses are first distributed to production department overhead and then to the cost of the product associated with the department. In distributing overhead, the cost elements are considered to be organization direct, proratable, or general overhead.

Direct Allocation of Expenses

Expenses allocated directly to specific departments are (1) expenses recorded on original records and (2) expenses accumulated on summary records. Through this identification, it is possible to measure exactly the benefit derived or penalty incurred by each department. *Purchase vouchers* represent an example of original records and identify the items purchased by an organization. *Indirect labor* distribution is an example of a summary record, and the labor classifications are the identifying criteria to the specific organization to be charged.

Proration of Joint Manufacturing Expenses

Some plant expenses are shared jointly by a number of organizations. Expenses that cannot be directly allocated to specific departments must be prorated among the production and service departments. For example, plant expense prorations are prepared from summary worksheets. The building depreciation expense summary record provides the basis for prorating the building depreciation to specific occupying organizations based on the space occupied.

The most common bases used in prorating expense items are: floor space (depreciation); cubic content or square feet of radiation (heat); and kilowatt hours or direct labor hours for power expense distribution.

SECONDARY EXPENSE DISTRIBUTION

Secondary expense distributions are redistributions of the total expenses of each service department to the production and other service departments. This type of distribution constitutes a redistributed charge to the departments receiving the services. The ultimate objective is for all expenses to be absorbed by the production departments because the physical product travels *only* through those organizations.

Distribution Bases for Service Department Expenses

In some organizations, service department expenses are distributed *directly* and entirely to production departments only. In other organizations, service expenses are distributed to other *service organizations* before the final distribution of total expenses are made to the producing departments.

Regardless of the procedure followed, the major factor is to use a proper *basis for distribution* of specific service department expenses. Two considerations are involved (1) the type of service provided by the service department and (2) the number of departments that utilize such services.

Some of the bases for distributing service expenses and examples thereof are indicated below.

- Number of employees, total labor hours, or dollars (employment, medical, etc.).
- Relative floor space area (general factory expenses, fire department).
- Direct charges to productive departments (factory and cost accounting).
- Machine hours (utilities).
- Specific application to repair or new work orders (tool room and machine shop).
- Engineering estimates and meter readings (power costs).
- Charges to general ledger control (shipping and warehouse expenses).
- Additions to cost of material and supplies (purchasing and receiving departments).

Service Expense Distribution to Production Departments

Under this procedure, all service department expenses are distributed to the production departments only. This method provides the simplest, fastest, and most accurate means of allocations since the number of distributions are limited only to the number of production organizations.

Elaborate distributions have the following disadvantages:

- Service expense distributions are an unavoidable task, and generally the simplest distribution is considered to be the most accurate and acceptable.
- To fulfill control requirements, it is sufficient to know the service department expenses.
- A more confused mixture of expenses results from interdepartmental distributions.

Secondary Distributions on a Nonreciprocal Basis

Under this method, services provided by certain service departments are in part utilized by other service organizations and thus distributions must be made accordingly. The nonreciprocal basis does not provide for a two-way distribution of expenses between two service departments. In actual practice, this would mean that, for example, power plant expense would be distributed to the tool room because it is provided with power services, *but* no tool room costs would be distributed to the power plant, even though services were rendered. The principal arguments *for* using this procedure are as follows:

- Failure to charge a given service department with the cost of services provided by other organizations creates an understatement of costs for operating the department receiving the service.

- If the expenses of each service organization are controlled through the use of budgets, then the cost of services provided to it by other service departments should be reflected in their budgets. Only in this manner can the operational efficiency of a particular service department be measured.

The arguments *against* this method are that a greater amount of work is required in its use and that no real increase in cost accuracy is achieved.

Secondary Distribution on a Reciprocal Basis

Under this procedure, recognition is given to the fact that services provided by certain service departments are in part utilized by other service organizations; distribution becomes a problem in determining the amounts to be allocated to each other. The problem is that two involved organizations are interdependent and it is impossible to know the total expenses of one organization until the distribution has been completed for the other concerned organization.

Arguments *for* using this method are as follows:

- If a given service department receives services from another department, the receiving organization should be charged. If two service departments provide services to each other, then each organization should be charged for the services provided.

- The full operating expense of a service department cannot be determined unless it is charged with both the direct expenses resulting from the primary expense distribution and all indirect expenses resulting from secondary expense distributions. This would include all interdepartmental service expense transfers.

- Control of service department expenses should include the budgeting of both direct charges and interdepartmental transfers.

Arguments *against* this procedure are as follows:

- It involves more accounting work than either of the two preceding methods.

- It is questionable whether the above method provides any more accurate product costs.

Manufacturing Overhead Accumulation and Distribution

RESOLVING THE RECIPROCAL DILEMMA

There are three methods that can be utilized in making the necessary computations: trial and error, continued distribution, and simultaneous equations.

Trial and Error

Under this method, the objective is to determine by successive trials, the total of each service department's account before distribution. This also includes the allocations from other service organizations. This is an expedient method in situations in which there are more than two or three service departments affected by interdepartmental service transfers.

The primary expense in each service department is the starting point in the calculation process. The percentage of additional expense allocated from other service departments is applied to their *primary expenses* and the new results are obtained. After the first trial distributions interdepartment transfers are completed, the process is repeated by multiplying the new expense totals by the same percentage as previously. The computation results are then added to the original expense totals. Successive trial distributions will be continued until there is no difference between the totals of the last and next to the last trial distributions. An example of the plant service department follows with the services' cost input from factory accounting and the powerhouse.

	1st Trial	2nd Trial	3rd Trial	4th Trial
Plant Service Department	$2,200.00	$2,200.00	$2,200.00	$2,200.00
Factory Accounting (1.6%)	33.60	35.46	35.49	35.49
Powerhouse (.3%)	36.00	36.45	36.48	36.48
	$2,269.60	$2,271.91	$2,271.97	$2,271.97

Continued Distribution

This procedure involves closing and reopening service department accounts by successive distributions. The process is described as follows:

- Apply the given percentage to *prorate the primary total* in the first service department. The account is closed and prorated amounts are charged to other organizations.

- Apply the given percentages to the second service department whose total reflects primary accounts plus proration from the service department above. This closes this account with the charges being made to the other service organizations including the above department.

- The above procedure applies to all other service departments.

- A second cycle of operations is repeated starting with the first department whose total consists only of amounts prorated from other departments. The service department totals become smaller and smaller with each cycle of distribution.

- Stop the process at any point where it is felt that the resulting figures are too small to be of any consequence.

Solution by Simultaneous Equations

Using an expense distribution table, a series of simultaneous equations can be formulated. This method parallels the dollar amount manipulations, and the results obtained are similar to the above two methods. The equation, however, is impractical when there are more than three reciprocal transfers of interdepartmental service expenses.

Final Steps After Distribution

After all service department expenses have been distributed, the total service expenses are allocated to the production department accounts which then represent the direct producing department expenses and the distributed indirect service expenses. The totals can be converted to expense rates for ease of application in charging production.

METHODS FOR OVERHEAD APPLICATION

A number of methods can be used for overhead; see Exhibit 9-B for relevant examples. Some are more applicable to certain organizations depending on their objectives and type of operations. Overhead rates may be applied in plant aggregate (post-determined actual costs), department (pre-estimated actual costs), and cost center (pre-determined normal costs). The centers would include building units, functional operations, individual machine, or machine groups. In the standard cost system, standard rates are based on standard direct labor hours, dollars, and machine rates.

Overhead Formulas

As referenced above, Exhibit 9-B illustrates types of applications, their calculating formulas, and the utilization considerations (pro and con). The types most commonly used in industry are actual direct labor hours, direct labor dollars, machine hours, and standard direct hours. The other methods are employed in special applicable situations.

Criteria for Selection of the Appropriate Formula

Guidelines used in selecting the most appropriate application are:

- The *primary productive element* should be used in the specific manufacturing operation as the base in developing the application rate. In

Manufacturing Overhead Accumulation and Distribution

OVERHEAD FORMULAS & THEIR APPLICATION

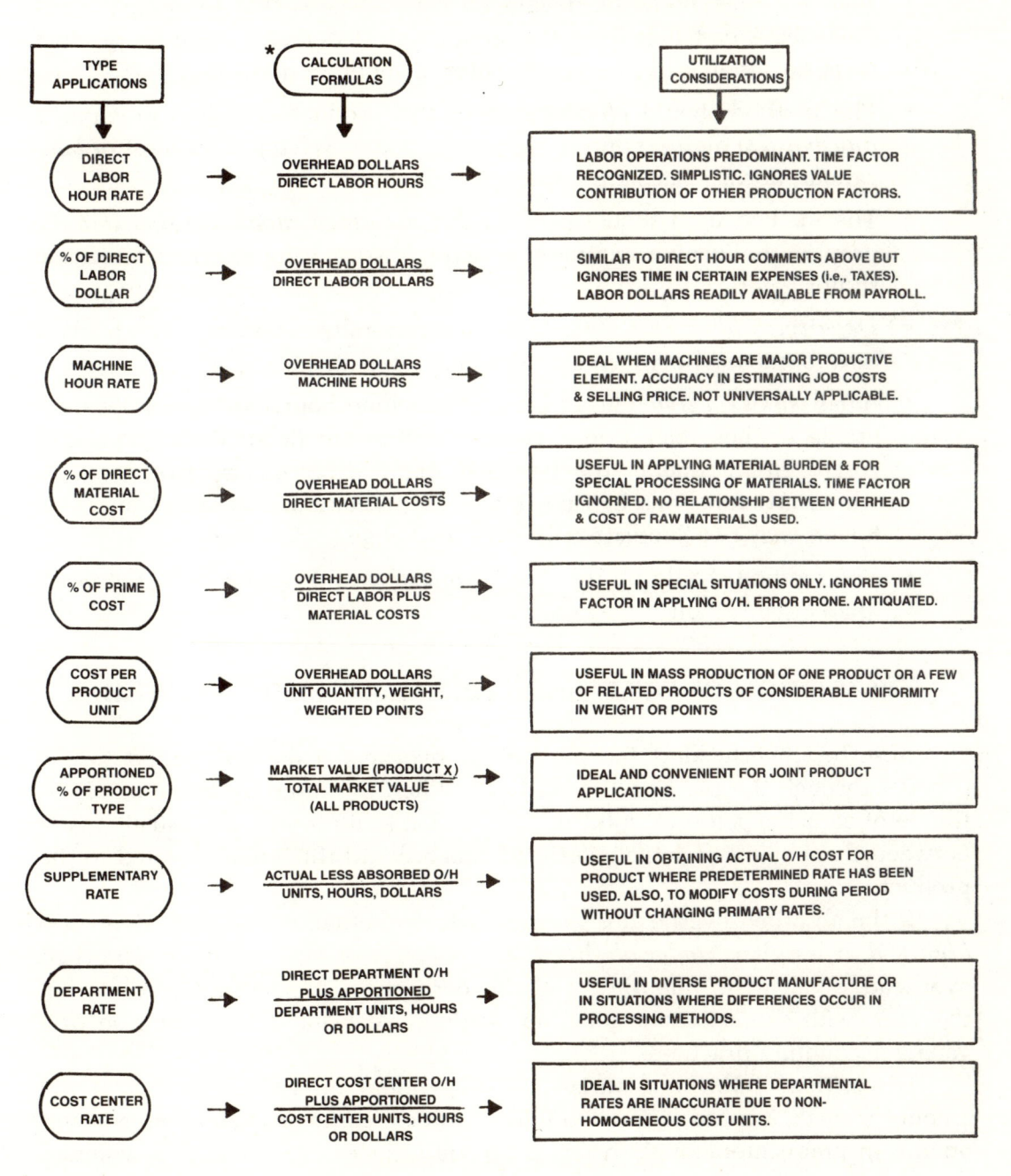

TYPE APPLICATIONS	CALCULATION FORMULAS*	UTILIZATION CONSIDERATIONS
DIRECT LABOR HOUR RATE	$\dfrac{\text{OVERHEAD DOLLARS}}{\text{DIRECT LABOR HOURS}}$	LABOR OPERATIONS PREDOMINANT. TIME FACTOR RECOGNIZED. SIMPLISTIC. IGNORES VALUE CONTRIBUTION OF OTHER PRODUCTION FACTORS.
% OF DIRECT LABOR DOLLAR	$\dfrac{\text{OVERHEAD DOLLARS}}{\text{DIRECT LABOR DOLLARS}}$	SIMILAR TO DIRECT HOUR COMMENTS ABOVE BUT IGNORES TIME IN CERTAIN EXPENSES (i.e., TAXES). LABOR DOLLARS READILY AVAILABLE FROM PAYROLL.
MACHINE HOUR RATE	$\dfrac{\text{OVERHEAD DOLLARS}}{\text{MACHINE HOURS}}$	IDEAL WHEN MACHINES ARE MAJOR PRODUCTIVE ELEMENT. ACCURACY IN ESTIMATING JOB COSTS & SELLING PRICE. NOT UNIVERSALLY APPLICABLE.
% OF DIRECT MATERIAL COST	$\dfrac{\text{OVERHEAD DOLLARS}}{\text{DIRECT MATERIAL COSTS}}$	USEFUL IN APPLYING MATERIAL BURDEN & FOR SPECIAL PROCESSING OF MATERIALS. TIME FACTOR IGNORNED. NO RELATIONSHIP BETWEEN OVERHEAD & COST OF RAW MATERIALS USED.
% OF PRIME COST	$\dfrac{\text{OVERHEAD DOLLARS}}{\text{DIRECT LABOR PLUS MATERIAL COSTS}}$	USEFUL IN SPECIAL SITUATIONS ONLY. IGNORES TIME FACTOR IN APPLYING O/H. ERROR PRONE. ANTIQUATED.
COST PER PRODUCT UNIT	$\dfrac{\text{OVERHEAD DOLLARS}}{\text{UNIT QUANTITY, WEIGHT, WEIGHTED POINTS}}$	USEFUL IN MASS PRODUCTION OF ONE PRODUCT OR A FEW OF RELATED PRODUCTS OF CONSIDERABLE UNIFORMITY IN WEIGHT OR POINTS
APPORTIONED % OF PRODUCT TYPE	$\dfrac{\text{MARKET VALUE (PRODUCT X)}}{\text{TOTAL MARKET VALUE (ALL PRODUCTS)}}$	IDEAL AND CONVENIENT FOR JOINT PRODUCT APPLICATIONS.
SUPPLEMENTARY RATE	$\dfrac{\text{ACTUAL LESS ABSORBED O/H}}{\text{UNITS, HOURS, DOLLARS}}$	USEFUL IN OBTAINING ACTUAL O/H COST FOR PRODUCT WHERE PREDETERMINED RATE HAS BEEN USED. ALSO, TO MODIFY COSTS DURING PERIOD WITHOUT CHANGING PRIMARY RATES.
DEPARTMENT RATE	$\dfrac{\text{DIRECT DEPARTMENT O/H PLUS APPORTIONED}}{\text{DEPARTMENT UNITS, HOURS OR DOLLARS}}$	USEFUL IN DIVERSE PRODUCT MANUFACTURE OR IN SITUATIONS WHERE DIFFERENCES OCCUR IN PROCESSING METHODS.
COST CENTER RATE	$\dfrac{\text{DIRECT COST CENTER O/H PLUS APPORTIONED}}{\text{COST CENTER UNITS, HOURS OR DOLLARS}}$	IDEAL IN SITUATIONS WHERE DEPARTMENTAL RATES ARE INACCURATE DUE TO NON-HOMOGENEOUS COST UNITS.

*HORIZONTAL LINE REPRESENTS A DIVISION FUNCTION

Exhibit 9-B

other words, the bases should relate indirect factory expenses to the product in a logical sense.

- *Separate rates* should be developed for each area that represents a homogeneous cost unit from the standpoint of deriving accurate product costs, i.e., overall blanket, cost center, or operation rates.
- The method should *eliminate* from the product cost any anticipated *unusual fluctuations* due to significant volume changes. In most organizations, normal rates are required.
- The method used should provide the *necessary capability and data* to prepare the income statement which realistically represents operational results.
- *Departmental or cost center rates* are generally superior to the blanket rates because of their greater flexibility in changes and use.
- *Rates based on time* (direct labor or machine hours) are generally preferable to those based on a variable cost factor (labor dollars, material costs). This is due to the fact that many expenses are fixed charges which are functions of time (taxes, depreciation, insurance) and cost factors may not fluctuate with overhead change direction.
- The method should be *practical, applicable* and *conducive to the needs* of an organization.

DISPOSITION OF OVER- AND UNDER-ABSORBED OVERHEAD

Absorbed overhead is the amount of overhead expense applied to the product through the use of overhead rates. When the rates are based on an estimate of actual expense for a future period, some difference will usually result between the amount of actual overhead expense and the amount costed to the product.

If the absorbed overhead is greater than the actual, it is identified as *over-absorbed*; if less, it is *under-absorbed*. The amount of over- or under-absorbed overhead is calculated monthly, and the differences are accumulated during the year, with its disposition generally made at year-end—depending on prevailing accounting practices.

Disposition of the final variance is dependent on various factors. If the amount is small, it is usually carried under Other Income or Deductions account on the income statement. Further, if the differences are small, it is assumed that the original estimates are fairly accurate. If the variances are significant, it indicates that overhead and/or production estimates were considerably in error. In these circumstances, adjustments are made to the cost of sales and inventory in the same ratio that the overhead cost was initially applied.

Supplementary Rates

When it becomes evident during the projected year that the difference between absorbed and actual overhead will be excessive, some organizations compute *supplementary rates*. These rates are used in conjunction with the regular overhead rates which were established at the beginning of the projected period. Other organizations change their regular rates at any time during the period when it is determined that the rates were unrealistic. When this action is taken, it is necessary to close out the previous monthly balances of unabsorbed overhead into the profit and loss account.

SETUP AND OPERATING RATES

When a high degree of accuracy is required in the cost estimate, it is common practice to establish *setup burden* as well as *operating rates* for overhead costs in a given production center. In addition to segregating setup from operating overhead, it is at times necessary to break down the operating rate for machine overhead into two parts. This is to give recognition to the fact that some overhead items do not change significantly when the rate of output or activity fluctuates. The fixed and variable costs would be segregated and two rates or calculations would be used for overhead costs. A standing *machine rate* would be calculated from the relationship of fixed overhead to available operating time and a *running rate* would represent the relationship of variable overhead to the time the machine is operated at regular speed.

In making cost estimates to aid in price or output decisions, it is important that some segregation of these two dissimilar types of costs be made. The establishment of both standing and running machine rates makes possible precise estimates for purposes in which differential rather than normal costs are required.

FACTORY OVERHEAD UNDER GOVERNMENT CONTRACTS

Factory overhead consists of indirect productional expenses that are not directly identifiable with product costs but which are incidental to and required for contract performance. The major categories are reviewed below.

Indirect labor. This category includes all wages and salaries that are chargeable to factory operations except those that are classified as direct labor. In production departments, this would include foremen, timekeepers, inspectors, shop clerks, machine adjusters, and janitors. In service departments, indirect personnel would include those working in storerooms, receiving, shipping, and factory offices.

Material and supplies. This expense classification includes all of the supplies required for general use in the factory such as lubricants, fuel, cleaning and anadizing supplies, perishable tools, and factory supplies. The general term "supplies" encompasses a wide variety of miscellaneous materials that are needed for shop operations rather than becoming a part of the product.

Service expenses. This expense group includes all normal service and maintenance expenses other than those specifically set forth above or in the subsequent discussion. Included are power, heat, light, water, gas, and ventilation. Separate expense accounts are created for the service departments which further encompass all charges for labor, material and supplies.

Fixed charges. Under this category, recurring charges, associated with fixed assets used for production requirements, would include rentals, leases, property and plant taxes, insurance premiums, depreciation, and depletion of natural resources. Amortization of *unrealized* appreciation of asset values and depreciation of excess facilities *are not admissable.*

Depletion is generally calculated on a unit basis which is intended to amortize the estimated content of a mineral deposit or other natural resource over the period of its expected life.

Miscellaneous factory expense. This expense class would include miscellaneous costs that are necessary and incidental to services, operations, and plant and equipment involved in the performance of a contract. Examples of these types of expenses are ordinary and normal rearrangement of facilities, vacation pay, factory employee pensions and retirement payments, employers' payments to social security and unemployment, and factory accident compensation.

Indirect engineering expense. These costs are a part of general plant expenses, categorized as engineering overhead, and would include labor (engineer fees and supervision), material supplies, and miscellaneous expense (maintenance and repair of engineering equipment and external purchased services for blueprinting, drawings, computer time, and reproduction).

DISTRIBUTION COSTS UNDER GOVERNMENT CONTRACTS

This category of expense includes the costs for distribution, servicing, and administration. They are a part of the general expenses used in determining the cost of performing a contract and encompass bid and proposals, general selling and distribution, general servicing, employees' compensation for personal services and other expenses. A brief description of these types of expenses follows.

Bid and proposals. These expenses represent ordinary costs that are incurred in preparing and submitting bids and/or proposals which are involved with the negotiation of estimated costs. They do not include any experimental or development work that precedes bids or negotiations.

General selling and distribution. These expenses include any other costs of selling and distribution that can be justified as properly incidental to and necessary for *contract performance.*

General servicing. Under applicable circumstances, these expenses constitute a part of the cost of performing a contract and are incidental to the delivery or installation of items requiring ordinary adjustments of minor defects. These expenses would not include *guarantee or direct charge expenses.* Guarantee expenses generally include costs incurred after delivery of the product or installation of a construction project.

Employees' compensation for personal services. These costs include salaries and other compensation of the general office. Examples of these expenses are:

- Salaries of corporate officials, executives, and department heads.
- Salaries and wages of administrative clerical and office service employees.
- Employers' payments for unemployment, social security, and pensions.

Other expenses. These types of expenses cover corporate general and administrative costs. Included are the following: general office and administrative (supplies, rentals, equipment repairs and depreciation), consultant fees and expenses, employees' welfare (pensions and retirement), ordinary and necessary contributions to charitable organizations, state and local taxes excluding income taxes, compensation insurance premiums, and dues and memberships in pertinent trade associations.

UNALLOWABLE COSTS UNDER GOVERNMENT CONTRACTS

The government has outlined certain guidelines for determining whether certain costs are allowable or unallowable for reimbursement. The criterion is whether the expenditure represents a *bona fide requirement* in the performance of a contract. Exhibit 9-C displays examples of common types of disallowances; however, under certain unusual circumstances, some or a part thereof of these expenses could be renegotiated depending on the situation. It behooves the contractor to set up his chart of accounts in such a manner that suitable analysis can be made to differentiate between allowable and unallowable costs.

COST CONSIDERATIONS UNDER GOVERNMENT CONTRACTS

Proper cost consideration in government contracts is only the first step in providing necessary cost details. Costs must be analyzed and segregated into civilian and individual government agencies. Further, the costs must be allocated to specific contracts.

Production Cost Analysis

The principles involved in allocating indirect production expenses to contracts are specified in government directives. With respect to factory indirect

272 Manufacturing Overhead Accumulation and Distribution

UNALLOWABLE COSTS UNDER GOVERNMENT CONTRACTS

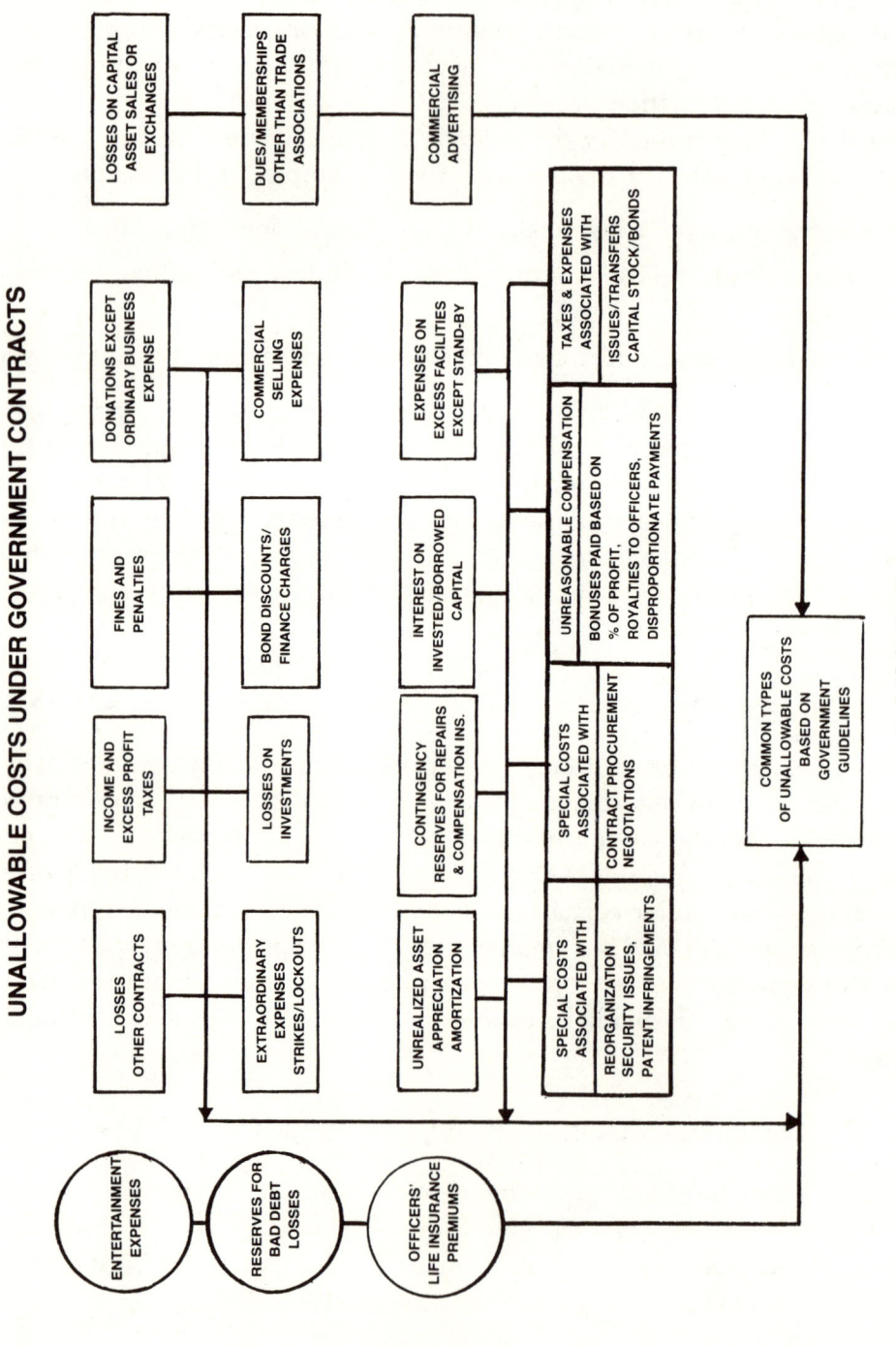

- LOSSES ON CAPITAL ASSET SALES OR EXCHANGES
- DUES/MEMBERSHIPS OTHER THAN TRADE ASSOCIATIONS
- COMMERCIAL ADVERTISING
- DONATIONS EXCEPT ORDINARY BUSINESS EXPENSE
- COMMERCIAL SELLING EXPENSES
- EXPENSES ON EXCESS FACILITIES EXCEPT STAND-BY
- TAXES & EXPENSES ASSOCIATED WITH ISSUES/TRANSFERS CAPITAL STOCK/BONDS
- FINES AND PENALTIES
- BOND DISCOUNTS/ FINANCE CHARGES
- INTEREST ON INVESTED/BORROWED CAPITAL
- UNREASONABLE COMPENSATION BONUSES PAID BASED ON % OF PROFIT, ROYALTIES TO OFFICERS, DISPROPORTIONATE PAYMENTS
- INCOME AND EXCESS PROFIT TAXES
- LOSSES ON INVESTMENTS
- CONTINGENCY RESERVES FOR REPAIRS & COMPENSATION INS.
- SPECIAL COSTS ASSOCIATED WITH CONTRACT PROCUREMENT NEGOTIATIONS
- LOSSES OTHER CONTRACTS
- EXTRAORDINARY EXPENSES STRIKES/LOCKOUTS
- UNREALIZED ASSET APPRECIATION AMORTIZATION
- SPECIAL COSTS ASSOCIATED WITH REORGANIZATION SECURITY ISSUES, PATENT INFRINGEMENTS
- ENTERTAINMENT EXPENSES
- RESERVES FOR BAD DEBT LOSSES
- OFFICERS' LIFE INSURANCE PREMIUMS
- COMMON TYPES OF UNALLOWABLE COSTS BASED ON GOVERNMENT GUIDELINES

Exhibit 9-C

expenses, the same basic principles are followed as in ordinary cost procedures. The guidelines follow.

- Organization of the plant structure into production and service departments and, if logical, cost centers.
- Account classifications follow departmental lines.
- Distribution of direct charges to departments.
- Redistribution of service department charges.

The degree of refinement in departmental analyses is governed by the size, complexity, and sophistication of its operations. Smaller, uncomplicated organizations pose far fewer problems in analysis.

Departmental Burden Rates

The burden rate represents the total departmental charges consisting of direct and redistributed expenses. It is derived by using the direct labor costs as the base factor. Rates can also be calculated on the basis of dollars per direct hour, dollars per machine hour, or expense cost per unit of measure (product unit, weight, quantity, length, or cubic content).

If labor is the primary cost and the pay rates are generally uniform, a percentage of direct labor cost is a simple method of expense distribution. If labor is a minor part of the cost and other expenses are relatively larger, the expenses are more equitably applied on the basis of machine hours. When pay rates *are not* substantially uniform, the more logical distribution of expenses is through a *dollar rate per direct hour*. If none of the above methods is valid and practicable, it may be that a common unit of measurement representing production volume can be used as the tool for expense distribution.

Selling and Administrative Expenses

Bidding, servicing and other selling expenses that can be directly identified to specific contracts should be considered as direct charges to the contracts. Allowable indirect selling and administrative costs are apportioned to the government and commercial type businesses on the basis of *percentage of sales volume*. The percentage used is the ratio of the contract price to the period total sales value of all work completed. Another method is *percentage of cost value*. The percentage is obtained by dividing specific contract costs by the total of all such work for the business as a whole.

DEVELOPING STANDARD OVERHEAD ESTIMATES

The numerator in the formula used to compute standard overhead rates is calculated by means of a careful analysis and revision of the budget estimates of overhead for the period. If the organization is departmentalized into service and production departments, the budget items must be classified and apportioned by departments, with the service organization estimates being re-allocated among the production departments.

When the standard for each item of cost has been agreed upon by the concerned estimating development participants, the standard values of cost are shown for each department on a standard overhead cost sheet. This sheet is used for comparing standard and actual costs as the monthly periods progress.

Computing Standard Rates

Instead of having a single standard overhead application rate for each production department or for the organization as a whole (if departmentalization does not exist), it may be more appropriate to have two standard rates for each department. One rate would be used for allocating fixed costs and the other for distributing variable costs to production. Examples of the formulas are:

- Standard fixed overhead for a given department by budget period divided by the department's standard direct labor hours (or dollars) by period represents the *standard rate for fixed costs.*
- Standard variable overhead by budget period divided by standard direct hours (or dollars) equals the *standard rate for variable costs.*

The fixed plus variable standard rates by period represent the total standard overhead rate which is then used in calculating standard unit costs and also in absorbing overhead as a manufacturing cost. Each month the actual variable overhead costs are compared with the standard variable costs and the differences analyzed for possible corrective action.

MACHINE HOUR RATE FOR OVERHEAD

The overhead rate by machine hour is calculated by dividing the overhead expenses for a specific machine by machine hours. Overhead is then charged to a job or process by multiplying this rate by the number of machine hours involved in a specific task. The computation is generally based on estimated actual or normal expense for the ensuing period.

The rate may be computed for a single machine or a group of machines if they are identical in cost and operation. Under these circumstances, the machine hour rate represents a *predetermined estimate* of the actual cost per hour for overhead. Differences between absorbed actual and estimate are generally the result of inaccuracies in estimating the indirect expenses and/or the number of machine time hours.

Requirements for Computing the Rate

In computing machine hour rates, consideration should be given to the following requirements:

- The department's *estimated overhead expenses* are determined by period for the projected year. If the budget is predicated on normal production, normal rates result.
- Expenses are regrouped into the following categories:
    1. Specific charges to each machine such as depreciation and maintenance.
    2. Allocated building costs which include utilities.
    3. All other general and service costs such as indirect labor, supplies, and supervision.
- Direct and prorated machine costs are combined to obtain the total overhead expenses to operate each machine during the projected year.
- The expenses are divided by the number of hours of machine hours to obtain the *machine rate*.
- The estimated hours may include setup time, depending on organization practices, or separate rates may be established for setup and running time.

The use of estimated machine hour rates may result in over- or underabsorbed overhead for the period due to actual expenses and hours of operation being different from the estimates. The difference may be disposed of by recosting the job through the use of a supplementary rate or by closing the amount into the cost of sales or the profit and loss account.

MANUFACTURING EXPENSE BUDGETS

Projected overhead expense budgets and rates for varying production volumes *cannot* be effectively established without a thorough analysis of historical data to determine the behavior of expenses during fluctuations of production activity. This evaluation study must consider the three basic principles involved in the flexible budgeting process. The requirements consist of adequate structuring of organizational units, appropriate classification of expense accounts, and the designation of the most relevant unit of measure to reflect changes in production and associated expenses.

Organizational units. Departments or cost centers in large operating entities should be based on lines of responsibility which are vital to budgetary control. In smaller, uncomplicated organizations, one aggregate rate segregated into variable and fixed may be adequate. Larger organizations require departmental segregation so that the concerned supervision can be held accountable for the expenses incurred that vary from the planned budget.

Classification of expense accounts. Appropriate classification and their identification to the responsible department is of vital importance if the expenses are to be controlled at their source. Expense categories should reflect the needs of both the service and production departments. Each service department should be charged for those expenses over which the supervision exercises control. For cost accounting purposes, however, these costs are either allocated or prorated to the department serviced.

Unit of measure. The unit used in measuring production activity is very important since flexible budgets are predicated on the concept that variable costs fluctuate with production volume. In a production department, the unit of measure can be direct labor hours or dollars, machine or standard hours, product units, tonnage, etc.

Separate budgets are prepared for each service department to provide a tool for controlling costs at their source. Under some circumstances, applicable units of measure can be developed, but, generally, the activities of these organizations are measured in terms of the combined activity of the producing departments.

Establishing the Flexible Budget

After the above evaluation has been thoroughly performed, and the basics of organization unit structuring, expense classifications, and unit of measure resolved, the next step is to develop the flexible budget criteria and allowances. This is a joint undertaking between the concerned shop supervisors and experienced budget and estimating planners. Historical data is assessed and expense accounts are reviewed in depth as to variability and correlation as changes occur in production volume. Two methods are commonly used in this evaluation which are described as follows:

High and low activity rates. This method involves the computation of the rate and degree of expense variability by comparing the historical cost results at two different rates of activity. Further, the specific relationship must be determined between the increase in activity as versus the movement in expense. The data selected should represent both the high and the low levels of activity by period. If past actual figures are not deemed representative, then realistic estimates should be used. An example of the calculations follows.

Assume:	Activity Rate	Direct Labor Hours	Expense Dollars
	High	6,000	$ 960
	Low	3,000	600
	Difference	3,000	$ 360

Variable Expense = 360 divided by 3,000 hours = $.12 per hour
Fixed Expense is calculated as follows:

	Direct Labor Hours	Variable Rate	Variable Cost	Total Cost	Fixed Cost
High rate	6,000	.12	$ 720	$ 960	$ 240
Low rate	3,000	.12	360	600	240

Based on the above computations, the allowed costs for a given rate of activity is derived by multiplying the hours by $.12 and adding the fixed cost of $240.

The *major disadvantage* of this method would be that it is based on two expense levels that may not be truly representative of what the costs *should be* at the two levels selected. To overcome this situation, departmental *expense items* are established at varying volumes of production and identified specifically as to their fixed or variable characteristics. Production activity is segregated into its representative or relative percent of plant capacity. The flexible budget would reflect individual or certain combined expense costs by department under each capacity level as follows:

	% Capacity			
	50	80	100	110
Direct Labor Hours	3,000	4,800	6,000	6,600
Total Expense Dollars	600	816	960	1,032

The budget would display individual major expenses and possibly combine certain minor expenses which have little impact on the aggregate total. The above expenses were computed on the basis of $.12 per direct hour for the variable expense and $240 for fixed. In the actual environment using individual expenses, the overhead totals could be somewhat different and probably more realistic at the various percent capacity levels.

Use of correlations. The second procedure for setting expense allowances overcomes the deficiencies of the first method above. Computations are based on the historical experience of a number of periods (12-24 months). The more variable the monthly production volume is during the year, the better the data is for establishing appropriate relationships. The correlation concept is presented in greater detail in Chapter 2.

Significant individual expenses are plotted on arithmetic graph paper. The appropriate independent variable (direct hours or dollars, headcount, machine hours, sales volume) are represented on the horizontal plane, whereas the dependent variable (indirect labor, operating supplies, utilities) are reflected on the vertical axis. A point is plotted on the chart indicating the intersection location of the expense(s) versus the unit of measure base. After all of the observation (past experience) points have been plotted, a representative line is drawn through the various points. This line is equitably fitted through the use of a calculated least squares formula or by visual judgement.

An extension of the line to the left vertical axis will provide, at the intersection, that portion of the expense that is considered to be fixed. The difference between the total expense and the fixed provides the variable expense value. This amount divided by total volume indicates the variable rate factor.

A single equation can be developed from the slope of the trend line which will represent the average trend of expenses in relation to volume changes.

ESTIMATING POINTERS

In order to estimate manufacturing overhead, the planning estimator should have a thorough knowledge of the basics involved in the accumulation, distribution, and application processes of manufacturing expenses. Expense characteristics must be understood in terms of their variability under certain operating conditions (changes in volume, processing, equipment). The estimator should be familiar with the formulas that are used in applying overhead equitably and further the disposition of the inevitable variances. In government contract oriented businesses, the estimator should be cognizant of the allowable and unallowable costs which can have a significant impact on profitability. Computing standard overhead estimates and manufacturing budgets provide the basis for realistic planning and estimating activities. The above overhead background, needed by the professional estimators, is provided in this chapter.

10

Progress Curve Utilization Techniques in Cost Estimating

A progress or learning curve represents a series of values which decrease on a geometric progression in direct proportion to the slope of the curve. When the data is plotted on logarithmic graph paper, the curve will appear as a straight line. The progress curve concept assumes that every time an employee repeats a task or an operation, he will improve in efficiency and speed and will perform the job more rapidly than the previous time. This increase in employee efficiency results in a reduction of labor time and cost required per product unit production.

The progress curve approach is an important projection tool in that it alerts the production organization as to the planned worker output and indicates to management the performance probability of production objectives. The learning curve plays an important role in establishing direct labor standards and wage incentives and in providing a cost estimate basis for product pricing.

COST ESTIMATE PROJECTIONS

Most organizations engaged in business activities are involved in some form of endeavor in projecting costs which are the basis for decision-making in developing and establishing profit plan objectives. Historically, a number of traditional techniques are used in developing cost projections. In some cases, the methods or combinations thereof listed below are most effective, but in other instances they may be lacking in the degree of sophistication desired or required.

- *Same or similar part projections.* Historical cost data provides the basis for projections on the *same* part to be produced, but the values must be adjusted for known or anticipated changes, such as wage increases, acquisition of advanced equipment, and material cost fluctuations. On costs for a *similar* type of item, historical costs for the old part are adjusted to reflect any contemplated changes that will have to be made to meet the new requirements of a similar type of product.

- *Engineering standards.* Where there is insufficient or no comparable data available on the same or similar part, the cost projections can be ascertained by a detailed analysis of the task(s) involved and an application of tested standards to the requirements. This method is most commonly used in job shop operations.
- *Historical and/or current experience.* In this situation, mass production organizations have generally developed experience-tested techniques for determining operational costs. A thorough analysis of the costs, plus an adjustment for anticipated future changes, should result in reliable, realistic cost projections in producing the same part.

Learning or Improving Concept

A new dimension has been added to the above techniques for further sophistication of cost projection; it is identified as the *learning* process. Throughout history, it has been documented that production efficiency results from the learning process of the employee. Repetitive performance of a given task can lead to improved effectiveness in accomplishing job requirements. There are many examples in industrial history of improved production efficiencies that resulted from the learning process which can be attributed to various factors such as:

- *Employee performance.* As an employee performs his or her daily routines, he gains skills and experience in doing his job. He learns how to reduce physical motions and improve on his time performance. In time, he may observe and initiate a more effective way of doing his task merely through a change in operating procedures.
- *Changes in procedures.* When new products are being produced, the initial work may not reflect the ultimate procedures of efficient job performance. As the effort continues, needed refinements can be observed by the employee, supervisors, or time and motion study engineers to overcome deficiencies in performance. Changes in operating procedures can lead to more effective performance and increased production. Observation and job learning therefore provide the basis for operating task improvement.
- *Rate of production.* In the initial stage of production, there may be many *unknowns* as to the effectiveness of operating performance. As production is increased, stabilized, and formally scheduled, usually a significant increase in learning occurs that affects operating efficiency.
- *Improved equipment and machinery.* After a product has been in production, an employee may observe that a change to the equipment or machinery could reduce employee effort and increase production.

The factors above are only a few of the forces that result from the continuous learning process that lead to production efficiencies and reduced costs.

PROGRESS CURVE FUNDAMENTALS

The progress or learning curve philosophy indicates that if the cumulative number of units produced is doubled, the last unit manufactured will cost a certain percentage less than the prior unit before the doubling effect. Costs are in terms of time, direct hours, or dollars. Assuming that the reduction would be 20%, the *second unit* would require 80% of the time required for

EFFECT OF AN 80% LEARNING CURVE

UNIT QUANTITY (SEQUENTIALLY DOUBLED)	MANHOURS REQUIRED (UNIT HOURS × 80%)
1	100
2	80
4	64
8	51.2
16	40.9
32	32.7
64	26.2
128	20.9
256	16.8
512	13.5
1,024	10.7

**80% LEARNING CURVE
ARITHMETICAL GRAPH PAPER**

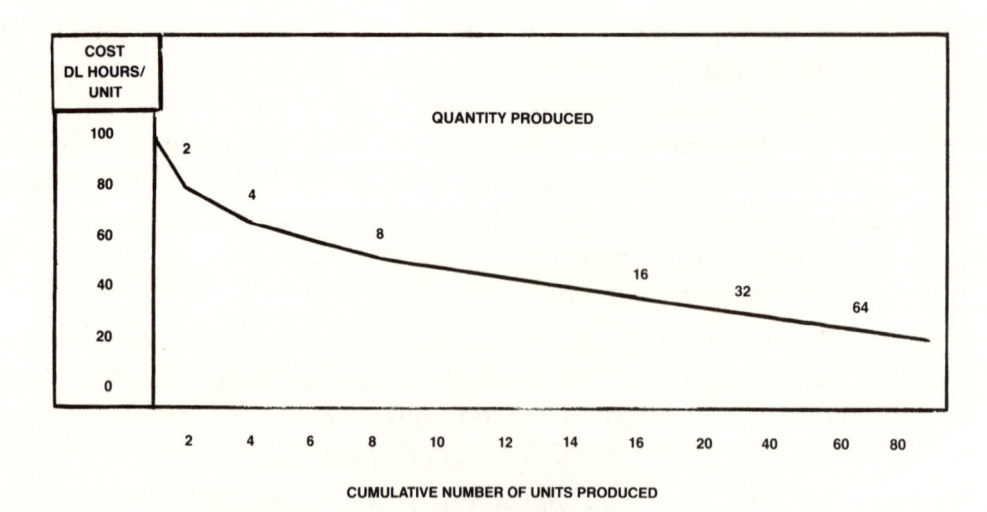

Exhibit 10-A

Progress Curve Utilization Techniques 283

the *first unit*, the *fourth unit* would be 80% of the *second* and so on. In other words, each time you double the unit quantity, the unit hours will be reduced by a fixed percentage. The hours will decrease rapidly at first until a point is reached when the reduction becomes relatively very slow as the number of units increase.

Using the above method, a chart (Exhibit 10-A) shows the effect of an 80% learning curve. The initial assumption is that 100 direct hours will be required to produce the first unit. As shown on this display, the direct manhours of effort are on a declining basis as the units of production are doubled.

Shape of Arithmetic Curve

When the above data is plotted on normal graph paper as shown in Exhibit 10-B, the values indicate the characteristic shape of a progress learning curve. The line drops sharply at first then slopes less sharply as the constant percentage (80%) of improvement becomes spread over longer periods of time between doubled quantities. The scale on arithmetic graph paper shows equal distance between coordinate lines. Equal quantities have equal distances. An arithmetic progression will plot as a straight line since there are constant differences between successive values in this series.

LEARNING CURVE TIME ALLOWANCE

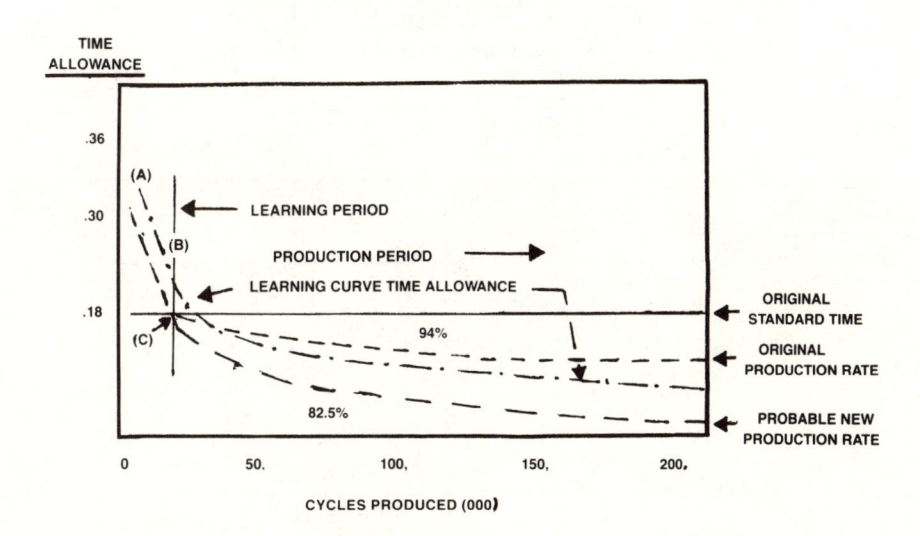

NOTE: (A) ALLOWABLE TIME ABOVE REQUIRED LEARNING TIME
(B) LEARNING PAY RATE SHOULD BE LOWERED AS PROFICIENCY INCREASES
(C) CROSSOVER — LEARNING PERIOD ENDS

Exhibit 10-B

Logarithm Curves

When progress curves are plotted on ordinary graph paper, wherein both the ordinate and abscissa follow an arithmetic scale, it is very difficult to observe any significant constancy in the improvement phenomenon. For this reason, progress curves are generally plotted on logarithmetic graph paper as shown in Exhibit 10-C. The progress curve then becomes a straight line because as the unit number *increases* in geometric progression (1,2,4,8,etc.), the variable time *decreases* in geometric progression (100,80,64,51.2,etc.). Therefore, the progress curve on log-log paper is more readily recognized and analyzed. The progress curve can be used in determining the manhours required

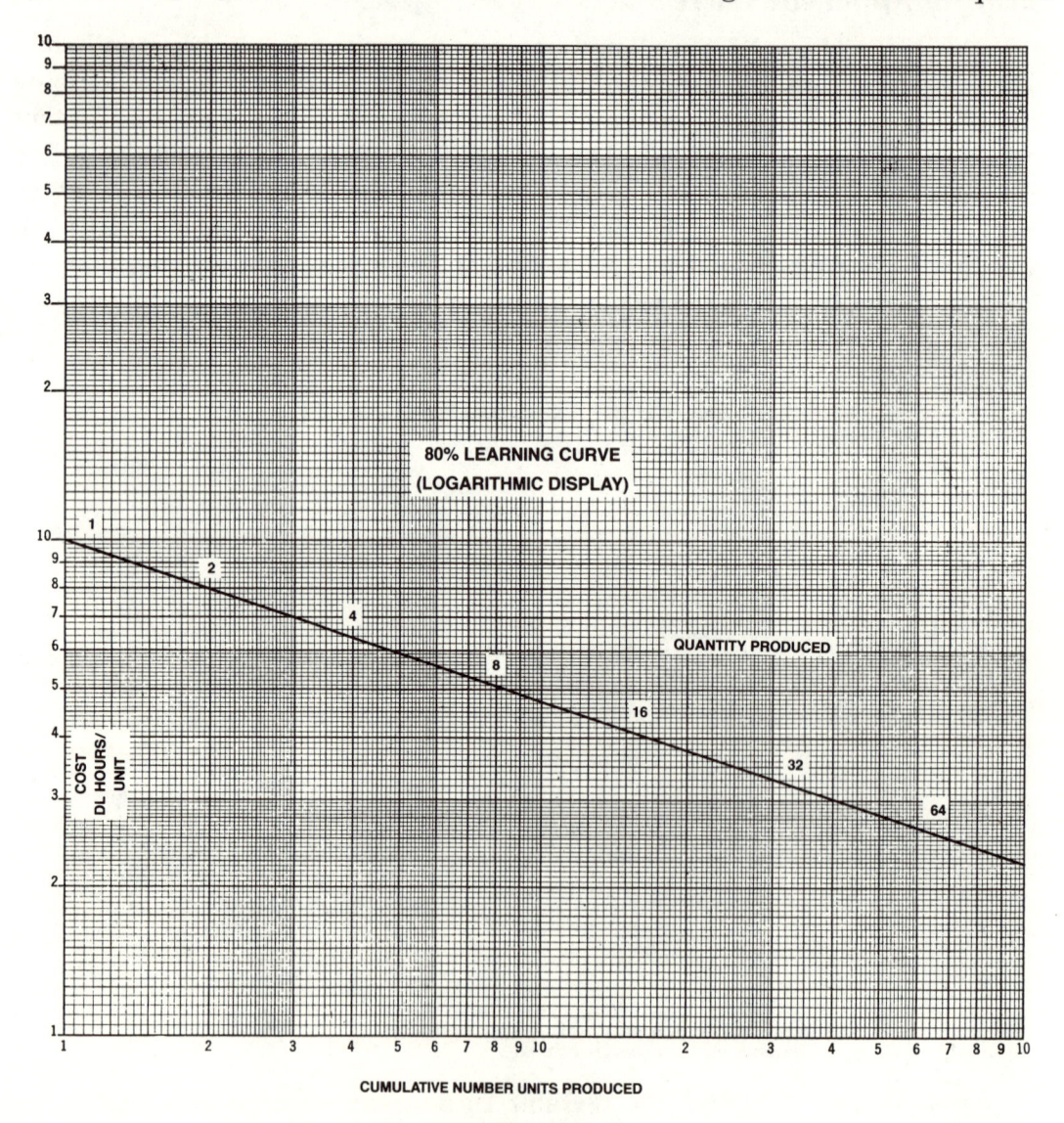

Exhibit 10-C

Progress Curve Utilization Techniques

for any given unit, extended very simply to accommodate larger quantities; the slope establishes its rate. All 80% progress curves plotted on log-log paper have the same slope.

In summary, the use of logarithm graph paper has two advantages:

- It permits rapid determination of the progress rate when actual data are plotted and compares proportional rates of change.

- It provides a graphical means of observing the relationship between two or more series which may differ widely in amount; for example, actual progress rate versus the projected rate. This display would then verify the accuracy of the projection.

LOGARITHM GRAPH PLOTTING

The logarithm chart shows a constant percentage of change between two sets of values, and the difference between the logarithms of the figures will be equal. To support this contention, the following examples are given.

Numbers	Logarithms	Numbers	Logarithms
2	0.30103	5	0.69897
4	0.60206	10	1.00000
Differences	0.30103		0.30103

Therefore, if the logarithms of the values rather than the original data sets are plotted, constant differences (increases or decreases) will equal constant percentage changes.

Characteristics of Logarithm Charts

- No zero or base line.

- When data is plotted on logarithm paper, a geometric expression forms a straight line. The logarithms of a geometric progression forms an arithmetic progression.

- Equal value increases or decreases reflect equal percentage changes.

- Logarithmic charts are ruled logarithmically on both scales whereas semilogarithmic charts have an arithmetic scale on the horizontal axis.

- Equal slopes on a logarithmetic chart indicate equal rates of change.

PROGRESS CURVE FORMULA

As previously indicated, the progress curve concept emphasizes that each time you double the productive quantity, the unit hours will decrease by a fixed percentage. Each time a task is performed, it is accomplished more effectively. A simplified formula can be used to plot the data on both arithmetic and logarithm charts. The formula is expressed as follows.

$$Y = KX^{-N}$$

Y = unit hours
K = hours for the initial unit
X = unit numbers
−N = expression of learning

Logarithm tables indicate all of the values for "X" and "N" that are required. The mathematical proof is rapidly ascertained as shown below.

1. Basic formula: $Y = KX^{-N}$

2. Use logarithm values for both sides of equation: Log Y = Log K−N Log X

3. Formula for a straight line: Y = MX + B

4. The equations in Steps 2 and 3 above are of the same form; therefore, the logic indicates that the formula in Step 1 above will be a straight line when plotted on logarithm paper that represents a progress curve.

After the learning curve has been constructed for a particular program, management has for reference a graphic tool that provides the normal advantages from routine cost projections. By reference to the charts, answers can easily be obtained to such questions as: what are the unit hours at Unit X and Y; what will the cumulative average hours per unit be at Unit X, and at what unit will the program break even?

ASPECTS OF THE PROGRESS CURVE THEORY

Human Nature Influence

During the initial phase of meeting progress curve standards, an employee would probably work very diligently to meet the imposed standards criteria. After reaching the required goal accomplishment, it is not unusual for an operator to *slack off* on his work efforts since he has achieved the incentive bonus pay status for performing an operation(s) in less than standard time. Generally, beyond this point, there is less incentive for him to improve on his efficiency. Further, the employee feels he must exercise caution in not accomplishing the task too rapidly for fear that a time-study engineer will reduce the time standard; this will make it more difficult for him and his co-workers to meet new revised standards. The concerned worker is also aware of the risk that his co-workers would criticize him for non-conformance to *shop views* relative to how quickly an operation should be performed in order to maximize take-home pay in the long run for all workers on similar tasks.

The Case for Variable Time Allowances

The above situation indicates that the ordinary fixed time standards do not adequately fulfill the requirements of either the worker or management due to the following related reasons:

- Experienced or new operators must go through a learning period at their base rate before they begin to earn any bonus pay.

- The employee works much more diligently during his initial learning period in order to achieve standards, but he earns less relative remuneration for his efforts.

- In the above circumstances, the work force tends to become inflexible —operators want to avoid new tasks that are more difficult for less pay. Employees can become frustrated and unhappy because they can lose take-home pay irrespective of whether a job change is their choice or that of the organization.

- Little if any recognition or pay is given to encourage optimum learning curve performance throughout the life-cycle of a job. Further, the operators must hold back production to preclude criticism from less efficient operators.

- Under the original concept of the learning curve, all operators are treated as completely average. It emphasizes optimum return for average performance.

- No incentive is provided to demonstrate versatility, increased productivity, or learning ability beyond the norm that would result in additional take-home pay as a reward from management.

- No status symbol of achievement is established for optimum performance.

- Operators run the risk that if they perform the task too efficiently, then they will be classified as *rate busters* and spoil the job for others. Therefore, the fixed time standard that is commonly used is a negative incentive in the long run.

- The above situation adversely results in increased costs for the organization and the worker because the latter is paid for lost and hidden idle time in spite of the fact that experience and performance capability has increased.

- Higher costs result when workers are not compensated in proportion to their actual accomplishment. Many experienced workers find themselves *locked* into the so-called *gravy train* wherein they do not need to produce to the limit of their capabilities or desires. The worker thus experiences frustration which promotes unfavorable employee reaction toward the organization.

The above environmental conditions provide the workers with little or no incentive to improve or to change jobs; this creates a negative incentive. On the other hand, *learners* are working diligently to learn new tasks but receive only their base pay.

To rectify the basic problems of the learning curve concept and provide an equitable foundation upon which the learning curve wage incentive plans can be established, consideration should be given to incorporating variable time allowances in the learning curve.

PROGRESS CURVE TIME ALLOWANCES

In developing a variable time allowance progress curve to meet human needs and performance which will overcome the deficiencies of fixed time standards, it is necessary that the job be divided into a series of steps for each change in job condition.

It is only fair that some sort of bonus be paid to operators while they are performing the more difficult learning phase of an operation. This is particularly appropriate if the operators are experienced and have been earning well on other tasks, but, because of changes in product requirements, they had to be assigned to new jobs. When such changes occur, management should provide an allowable time that is somewhat above the required learning time.

It is also reasonable to expect that this new *learning pay rate* should not be constant or fixed but should reflect a downward trend on the plotted graph as the experience becomes greater and proficiency increases. If this is not done, then there is no incentive for the operator to learn rapidly; therefore, the trend line must be lowered as learning proceeds.

Based on past experience relative to similar tasks and with similar operators, an organization should be able to determine the approximate amount of time required for an "average" operator to learn to perform within the framework of the original fixed standard time. It then should be fairly easy to establish the crossover point where the learning period ends.

Reality of Operator Performance

Experience has shown that as soon as the operator determines, under the old fixed time incentive systems, that he has achieved the standard time, he no longer sees any benefit in trying to become more proficient.

The operator is generally aware of the standard time value before he starts his learning process. The operator is also cognizant of the fact that as soon as he meets the standard he will begin to earn bonus pay. At the point of *standard* occurrence, he will be inclined to slack off his learning rate so that he will not *spoil* the job. This is the opposite of what management would prefer to happen.

For the above basic *human nature* reasons, management should eliminate the fixed standard time philosophy and reconcile itself to pay the worker proportionately for his learning progress from the beginning so that there will be no interval gap to disturb his learning pattern. This means that the variable allowable time line should reflect a downward trend on a plotted chart to maintain the average earnings of the average operator.

Operator Incentives

By carefully selecting the proper slope for learning curve time allowance, management may motivate the operator to continue his learning and produce, let us say, at an 85% rate. Under these circumstances, from beginning to end, management could allow him to earn satisfactory incentive bonus pay throughout the entire life of the job. The worker will continue to improve at his own personal learning rate from the beginning of training to the end of the job in return for an improved production rate.

With such logic in mind, it should be possible to establish a variable time allowance curve that is similar to an 85% learning curve from start to finish. This curve will permit the proper *bonus* to be earned and can be used more effectively than the old fixed time standard to establish the criterion for incentive pay for any operator on this task. Each operator would establish his own individual learning rate and be accordingly compensated in proportion to his production capability without being in any way in competition with other operators. An operator who learns slowly would have his base pay factored proportionately and those learning more rapidly on a sustained production output would receive a greater base rate. The operator's rate would be increased or decreased at certain intervals to reflect his future performance variables. His motivation would be to learn rapidly and produce accordingly.

Significance of the Change

Through the use of the variable learning curve time allowance, and the resultant learning curve wage incentive systems, it is possible that the past and current need for precise time studies and the calculation of fixed time standards could be eliminated except possibly as a check and balance system. There would still exist a method analysis to determine the most efficient procedure for performing a task, but whether this process would justify extensive quantitative analysis would have to be resolved on an individual organizational basis.

Use of *computerization* in the application of the variable time standard is a timely, inexpensive tool for developing learning curve wage incentive plans that will more appropriately reflect the human improvement phenomenon. Other objectives of the wage plan include increased productive performance, adequate compensation for the worker, and achievement of cost reduction goals.

PRACTICAL APPLICATION OF THE PROGRESS CURVE

As indicated previously, a progress or learning curve reflects a series of values that decrease on a geometric progression in direct proportion to the slope of the curve. When plotted on logarithmic graph paper, the curve is represented by a straight line which may be used to express either unit values or cumulative average values, depending on which application best fits the problem. The learning concept has proven to be a very useful tool in solving various problems associated with the development and production of sophisticated and ever-changing products such as aircraft, missiles, and automobiles.

Problems Associated with Production Costs

A number of problems concerned with the production process result either from the conditions under which the product is manufactured or from engineering requirements. The problems can affect either the value of the first unit on the curve and the slope of the curve or can alter the curve subsequent to the first unit—depending on when the condition first appears.

Manufacturing conditions that affect production costs are rework and replacement, skill of the labor force, extent and type of tooling, production processes, adequacy of facilities, schedule status, and management decisions such as *schedule recovery at any cost*.

Engineering requirements that affect production costs are as follows:

- Designs that are unusually complex, unproven in tests, advanced beyond the *state of the art*, or that require exceptionally close tolerances.
- Revisions in design that create additions, deletions or changes in specifications, processes or hardware.

In order to realistically project production costs for the purpose of developing quotations and shop budgets, it is essential that the above factors be carefully evaluated.

CURVE USE IN MANPOWER REQUIREMENTS

After a specific production budget progress curve has been resolved by management, it is necessary to determine the manpower required to maintain the projected manufacturing schedules. To make the necessary manpower evaluation, reference must be made to (1) the projected learning curve, (2) detailed releasing policy for parts, sub-assemblies, and assemblies, and (3) the delivery schedule for end item shipment. The procedure to be used in projecting manpower is described as follows:

- It is assumed that an 80% assembly budget curve is projected with Unit 1 at 40,000 hours and a fabrication curve with Unit 1 at 8,000 hours. The total sales order is 55 units.

Progress Curve Utilization Techniques

- *Step 1.* Determine from the fabrication releasing procedure the number of releases to be made and their scheduled start and completion dates. This data is summarized as follows:

Releases and Their Scheduled Dates

Release Number	Unit Quantity	Start Date	Completion Date
1	5	4/x1	8/x1
2	10	5/x1	10/x1
3	15	6/x1	11/x1
4	25	7/x1	12/x1

- *Step 2.* Determine from the fabrication budget curve the total projected hours for each release. These hours can be calculated rapidly if learning curve tables are available, but if not, then the midpoint theory can be used to approximate the average unit hours for each release. Applying this principle to the budget curve, it was ascertained that the allocated hours were as follows:

Average Unit Hours per Release

Release Number	Midpoint (Cum. Units)	Unit Hours (at midpoint)	Total Release Hours
1	2.5	5900 x5	29,500
2	10.0	3775 x10	37,750
3	22.5	2900 x15	43,500
4	42.5	2350 x25	58,750

- *Step 3.* Allocation of above hours by month for each release period must be determined. A common method used is the "S" curve. This identity results from the shape of a curve formed by plotting cumulative direct labor hour input to a contract by week or month. The number of periods over which this curve is formed depends on the delivery schedule for the given contract and the amount of lead time required to support the schedule. Any "S" curve can be expressed in terms of a cumulative percent of hours charged monthly to the total contract hours. An example follows.

Direct Hour Distribution

Production Month	Actual DL Hours Charged	Monthly Hours % of Total Hours	Cumulative % to Total
April	2,360	9.0	9.0
May	5,900	22.5	31.5
June	9,145	34.8	66.3
July	8,850	33.7	100.0
	26,255	100.0	

When the cumulative percents are plotted on graph paper, the result will be an "S" curve. Many organizations analyze their direct labor experience in this manner and compile tables of percentage breakdowns for various periods. The greater the number of periods, the more gradual the direct labor hour acceleration required in order to maintain the production schedules.

- *Step 4.* After the hours for each release have been distributed by month according to period of manufacture, the total fabrication hours per month can be converted to manpower required on a forty week basis. This is done by dividing the total hours by an average workday calendar month of 172 hours. The result represents equivalent employees required per month. Manpower can be further broken down for each fabricating department as shown below.

INPUT by Month on "S" Curve

Month	Rel. #1	Rel. #2	Rel. #3	Rel. #4	Fabrication Hrs Per Month	Conversion to Manpower Requirements
April	2,360	—	—	—	2,360	14
May	5,900	2,454	—	—	8,354	49
June	9,145	4,908	2,827	—	16,880	98
July	8,850	7,739	5,655	2,938	25,182	146
	26,255	15,101	8,482	2,938	52,776	

- *Step 5.* In order to determine assembly hour input by month, it is necessary to estimate the time from the start of the smallest sub-assembly for any given unit up to final shipment. In the example below, the time was established to be three months. The total assembly hours for each month's shipments are obtained by using midpoints on the assembly curve similarly to the procedure used for fabrication. The hours for each month are then distributed over the three month period using the "S" curve distribution.

Assembly Hours Input by Month

Scheduled Month	Sept.	Oct.	Nov.	Total Assembly Hours	Converted to Manpower
July	21,000	—	—	21,000 ÷ 172	122
August	54,600	23,500	—	78,100	454
September	29,400	61,100	25,900	116,400	677
Total	105,000	84,600	25,900	215,500	

Total Hours & Manpower Requirements

Month	Fabrication Hours	Assembly Hours	Total Hours	Fabrication MP Requirements	Assembly MP Requirements	Total MP Required
April	2,360	—	2,360	14	—	14
May	8,354	—	8,354	49	—	49
June	16,880	—	16,880	98	—	98
July	25,182	21,000	46,182	146	122	268
	52,776	21,000	73,776			

The above analysis provides management with a monthly forecast of direct labor hours for the entire contract and a manpower requirement for each month of manufacture in order to maintain proposed production schedules. The above procedure is simplified but, in actual practice, provision should be made for spare parts, multi-shift operations, absenteeism, re-work, and any major design changes that would require substantial work in addition to the basic task.

An inportant by-product of manpower requirements analysis is the evaluation of inventory in process in order to provide adequate financing to carry the contract to completion without an adverse effect on the financial resources.

CURVE USE IN INVENTORY EVALUATION

Realistic projection of inventory in process can be considerably enhanced through the use of the learning curve technique. A primary consideration in bidding on a contract is involved with the decision as to whether the organization can provide the necessary financing to meet the proposed delivery schedules. In recent years, the availability of progress (or partial) payments on military contracts, particularly fund-assisted, required many organizations to carry inventories for contracts that might otherwise be imprudent to accept.

Under the progress payment agreement, partial billings provide for monthly reimbursement based on a *percentage of the total cost input* for any given month. Generally, there is a limitation on the aggregate progress payment amount that is calculated on a percentage of the total contract price. Even though progress payments may be available for a given contract, a portion of the inventory must still be financed by the contractor. Therefore, in many organizations, inventory evaluation is of utmost importance in financing decisions whether the contract is militarily or commercially oriented.

Evaluation of Inventory in Process

The initial step in the evaluation of the inventory in process is to obtain the direct labor hour projections by month for each contract. This information is generally available from the manpower requirements forecast. Using the direct hours developed for the manpower forecast, the following price proposal detail is used as a basis for calculating the monthly inventory.

PRICE PROPOSAL DETAIL

	Per Unit	Contract Total (in 000s $ - 80 Units)
Direct Labor Hours		
Fabrication	2,750	220.5
Assembly	14,290	1,143.0
Total	17,040	1,363.5
Direct Labor Dollars ($6.00/hour)	102,240	8,181.0
Plant Burden ($7.00/hour)	119,280	9,544.5
Direct Material and Other Direct Costs	55,380	4,430.4
* Plant Cost	276,900	22,155.9
Selling & Administrative Costs	8,520	681.6
Total Cost	285,420	22,837.5
Profit Margin (12% on costs)	34,250	2,740.0
Selling Price	319,670	25,577.5

* Plant operational cost is $13.00 per hour (excluding direct material)

Calculation of Inventory in Process

MFG Month	Hours/ Month	Plant Cost × $13.00/Hr.	Material & ODC	Total Plant Cost/Month	Less C of S	Monthly Inventory In Process	Accumulated Inventory In Process
Apr.	2,360	30,680	7,670	38,350	—	38,350	38,350
May	8,354	108,602	27,150	135,752	—	135,752	174,102
June	16,880	219,440	54,860	274,300	—	274,300	448,402
July	46,181	600,353	150,088	750,441	67,260	683,181	1,131,583
Aug.	108,218	1,406,834	351,708	1,758,542	226,317	1,532,225	2,663,808
	181,993	2,365,909	591,476	2,957,385	293,577	2,663,808	

The first column reflects the direct labor hours by period. The hours are then extended by the plant cost per hour to obtain the plant cost (direct labor and overhead) by period. Material and other direct cost in the third column are allocated by month on the same basis as for fabrication. Column 4 represents the total charges to production work in process for each month. The inventory in process balance is obtained by subtracting cost of sales when available from the total costs incurred. The cost of sales in column 5 is determined for each month by multiplying the *unit* factory cost by the number of scheduled shipments for the month. The difference between column 4 and 5 represents the monthly inventory in process as shown in column 6, and inventory accumulation is shown in column 7.

Advantage of Inventory Evaluation

The inventory in process computation can be used to great advantage in the financing of a contract. In the above example, an inventory buildup prior to shipment of the first unit is $448,402 or about 15% of the total cost to be incurred on this contract. On a commercial contract, all of this money would have to be financed by the contractor. Even if this contract were subject to progress payments, the contractor would still have to provide a substantial amount with a partial billing allowance of 70%. Generally, the maximum inventory to be provided occurs when approximately 20% of the contract has been shipped. The value of this type of analysis is dependent on the accuracy of the basic learning curve. If the projection is too optimistic, the inventories will be overstated, and the opposite is true if the projections are on the conservative side.

The above discussion represents only a general approach to the evaluation of inventory for a proposed contract, and it can be refined substantially to meet the requirements of each product line and individual contractor.

CURVE USE FOR SALES PRICES AND PRODUCTION COST GOALS

When management commits itself to produce a product for a given sales price, the contract must be translated into a compatible measure of task accomplishment which is represented by allowable direct labor hours per unit. The progress curve is a very useful technique that can provide a discerning insight into establishing and measuring operational performance. When a part of a contract is completed, a break-even analysis is required to evaluate profit results. The analysis provides management with data relative to how the shop must be budgeted to achieve overall profit goals. The labor budget is basically presented to the production organization in the form of a learning curve which, in essence, reflects a distribution of manpower requirements by organization that will achieve the budget curve objectives.

Procedure for Curve Application

The average unit direct labor hours reflected in a unit selling price are generally based on a learning curve which is plotted on logarithm graph paper. Estimated standard hours are used but factored for the realization aspect. This is done at Unit 1 or some subsequent unit on the curve depending on the situation and/or planning decision. Realization represents the standard hour ratio to the anticipated actual production hours at a particular unit expressed as a percentage. The unit number at which this realization is targeted results from management's evaluation based on historical experience relative to what type of performance can be anticipated from the production organization to achieve the task requirements.

Realization Factor

For purposes of illustration, let us assume that the achievement goal was established at 60% realization based on 40 standard hours per unit, by Unit 100. A learning curve of 80% was to be used to determine the projected hours for the first unit. Using the learning curve, the average quotation hours for 40 units amounted to 148 hours per unit. The computations involved are detailed as follows.

- Projected hours at Unit 100 = $\dfrac{40 \text{ (standard hours)}}{.60 \text{ (realization)}}$ = 66.7 (production hours)

- Unit hours at Unit 1 = $\dfrac{66.7 \text{ (unit hours at Unit 100)}}{.226 \text{ (unit value at 100 for an 80\% curve)}}$ = 295

- Average hours per unit for 40 units = $\dfrac{\text{Unit hours @ 1} \times \text{Cumulative factor for 50 units on 80\% curve}}{40}$

- Average unit hours = $\dfrac{295 \times 20.12}{40}$ = 148 hours per unit

At this point, management may establish a goal of 119 hour unit average as the production budget or they may elect to set a more optimistic budget for incentive purposes—adjustment would therefore be required to the hours. After the budget hours have been resolved, the learning curve would be used to calculate budget hours by unit which would be communicated to the appropriate production personnel. It is noted that the budget is allocated by division or department based on manpower requirements which are discussed in this chapter.

Quote Curve Re-evaluation

As one or more units of the contract have been completed, it is necessary to re-evaluate the quote curve relative to slope and position on the graph. The actual hours may indicate that the task standard hours were underestimated or that the shop may not be able to achieve the required performance. Under these circumstances reflecting actual experience, it may be more appropriate to use a 70% curve in order to realistically reflect shop performance when plotted on a graph.

Although the shop may require more hours than anticipated to produce the first units, the indications are that the rate of improvement will effect a better realization by the end of the contract than the original quote curve. If

Progress Curve Utilization Techniques

the higher rate of improvement is insufficient to offset the excessive hours for the first units on an overall contract basis, then it may be necessary to re-establish the budget curve hours to the adjusted established trend in order to make the shop absorb all of the excessive hours by the end of the contract. The main objective is that actual trend experience is appropriately reflected in a revised budget curve.

Financial Implications of Increased Productive Hours

After the budget curve is re-established, management is provided with important information relative to the financial outcome of the contract. For illustrative purposes, let us refer to the data contained in the *Price Proposal Detail* under inventory evaluation process discussed on page 294.

- If the revised budget cumulative average unit curve intersects Unit 80 at 17,240 hours per unit, then the excess over the quote hours would be 200 hours (17,240 − 17,040).

- On the basis of an operational cost of $13.00 an hour, the loss of profit would be $2,600 per unit and $128,000 ($2,600 × 80 units) on the contract.

- The intersection on a plotted graph of the average unit quote hour line with the projected unit curve line would indicate the *first unit* to make the quoted profit of $34,250 per unit.

- The intersection of the budget cumulative average unit curve line with the average unit quote hour line would indicate the total order quantity that would be required in order to make the quotation profit on a contract basis.

- To determine the breakeven hour, the procedure would be as follows.

Unit selling price	$319,670
Less Material & ODC	55,380
Available dollars for labor, overhead, expenses and profit	$264,290

    Unit hours to breakeven at the *gross line* would be
    $264,290 ÷ $13.00 (factory rate per hour) = 20,330

- To determine the breakeven hours at the *net line*, the dollars available above of $264,290 would be divided by the total cost rate per hour.

It is often desirable to make breakeven analyses with learning curves on the basis of sales versus cost dollars. This can be accomplished graphically by indicating material and ODC as fixed expense and multiplying the unit hours at various points on the learning curve by the factory cost or total cost rate per hour. The slope of the curve decreases in the conversion from hours to dollars because of the addition of material and ODC as a constant.

The above discussion on the use of the learning curve techniques to achieve more profitable contracts can provide management with an effective tool to establish production cost goals and sales prices. The visual display of the data on logarithm graph charts provides an immediate insight into what happens to their operating plans when changes occur in their learning process, realization, projected hours, and costs. This information will materially assist in the decision-making process to increase contract profitability.

CURVE APPLICATIONS RELATIVE TO COSTS

All progress curve applications are initiated after the best estimate has been made or after actual hours have been accumulated. In the first instance, the estimated manhour value of a particular unit on the curve (generally the first) and the slope of the curve are established and used as a basis for projecting the anticipated value of subsequent units. In the second situation above, one or more units have been produced, and the actual costs are analyzed to determine the theoretical value of the first unit and the slope of the curve.

Before exploring the various aspects of progress curve application relative to cost estimating and budgeting, it is necessary to become familiar with the algebraic characters used in one organization for expressing progress curve formulas. The following discussion will be concerned with the algebraic symbols and what they represent.

- T — Unit manhour values on the curve prior to the first significant design change or addition in work content.
- T_b — Changed values of the units on a curve affected by a change.
- T_a — Unchanged values of the units on a curve affected by design change or deletion in work content.
- T_c — Unit manhour values on the curve affected by significant design change or addition in work content.
- x — Any unit on the curve.
- X — Percent of increased value of the first unit affected by any major design change or added work content.
- y — Percent of work affected by any major design change.
- W — Standard hour content.
- N — Cumulative units on the curve.
- n — First unit prior to any change.
- Σ — Cumulative values on the curve.
- $\dfrac{\Sigma}{N}$ — Cumulative average values on the curve.
- S — Slope of the curve.

The letter "T" is used only to signify the use of calculated manhours. When actual manhours, progress curve factors (from tables), calculated performance factors, or actual performance factors are used, "T" will be substituted as follows:

Progress Curve Utilization Techniques

    t — actual manhours
    F — progress curve factors (from table)
    P — calculated performance factors
    p — actual performance factors.

An 80% progress curve slope and a series of hypothetical problems have been selected for the examples used in the following discussion.

BASIC PROGRESS CURVE

An example of the basic progress curve is shown in Exhibit 10-D which utilizes an 80% slope for the first 80 units as displayed on the progress curve

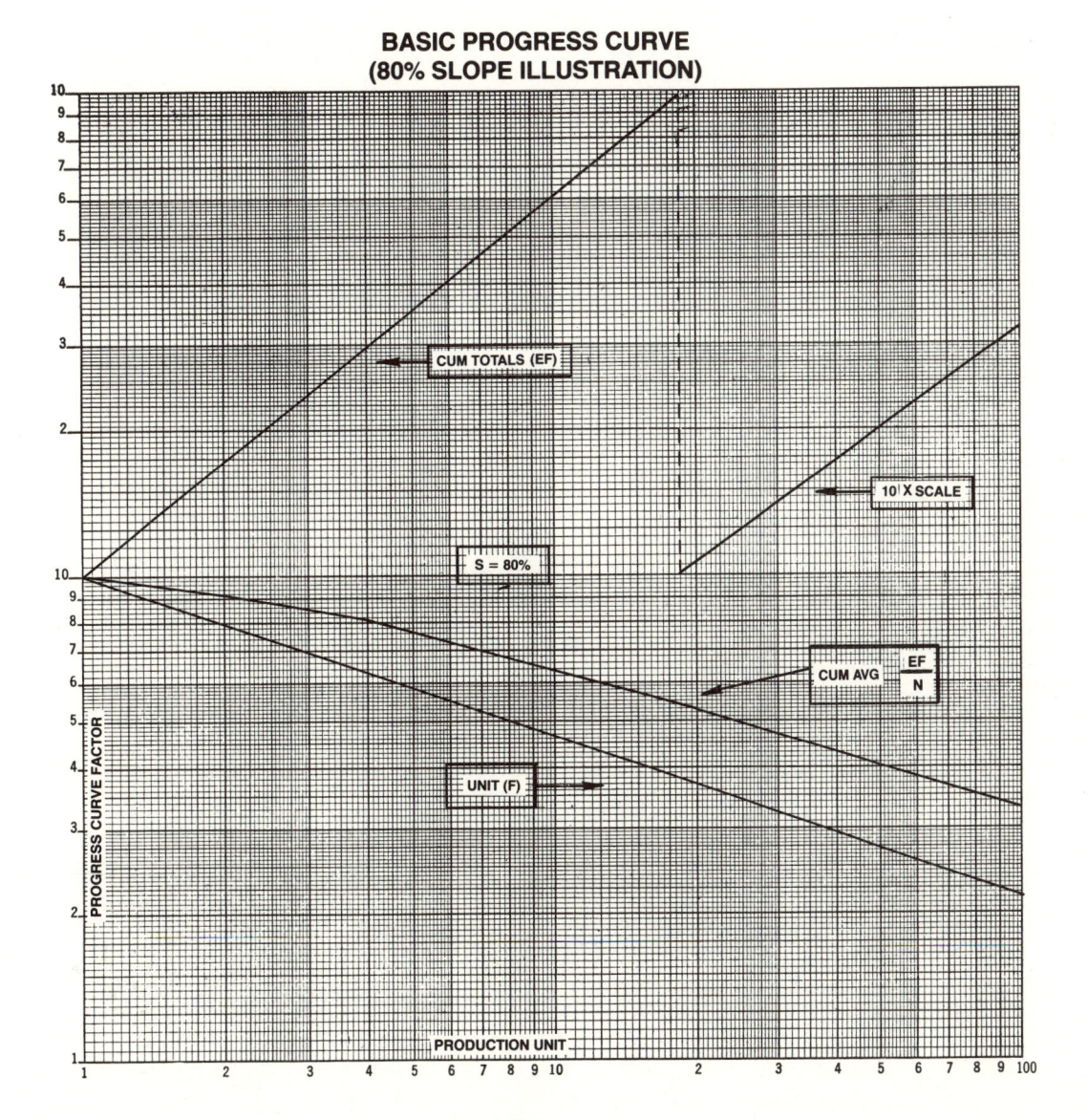

Exhibit 10-D

PROGRESS CURVE TABLE * 80% SLOPE

PROGRESS CURVE FACTORS

Unit No. (X or N)	Unit (F)	Cum Avg $\left(\frac{\Sigma F}{N}\right)$	Cum Tot (ΣF)	Unit No. (X or N)	Unit (F)	Cum Avg $\left(\frac{\Sigma F}{N}\right)$	Cum Tot (ΣF)
1	1.00000	1.00000	1.00000	41	.30255	.42673	17.49602
2	.80000	.90000	1.80000	2	.30021	.42372	17.79623
3	.70210	.83403	2.50210	3	.29795	.42079	18.09418
4	.64000	.78553	3.14210	4	.29575	.41795	18.38993
5 →	.59564	.74755	3.73774	45	.29362	.41519	18.68355
6	.56168	.71657	4.29942	6	.29155	.41250	18.97510
7	.53450	.69056	4.83392	7	.28954	.40989	19.26464
8	.51200	.66824	5.34592	8	.28758	.40734	19.55222
9 →	.49295	.64876	5.83887	9	.28568	.40486	19.83790
10	.47651	.63154	6.31538	50	.28383	.40243	20.12172
1	.46211	.61614	6.77750	1	.28202	.40007	20.40375
2	.44935	.60224	7.22684	2	.28027	.39777	20.68401
3	.43792	.58960	7.66476	3	.27855	.39552	20.96257
4	.42759	.57803	8.09235	4	.27688	.39332	21.23945
15	.41820	.56737	8.51055 ←	55	.27525	.39118	21.51470
6	.40960	.55751	8.92015	6	.27366	.38908	21.78836
7	.40168	.54834	9.32183	7	.27210	.38703	22.06046
8	.39436	.53979	9.71619	8	.27059	.38502	22.33105
9	.38756	.53178	10.10375	9	.26910	.38305	22.60015
20	.38121	.52425	10.48495 ←	60	.26765	.38113	22.86779
1 →	.37527	.51715	10.86022	1	.26623	.37925	23.13402
2	.36969	.51045	11.22991	2	.26484	.37740	23.39886
3	.36444	.50410	11.59435	3	.26348	.37559	23.66233
4	.35948	.49808	11.95382	4	.26214	.37382	23.92448
25	.35478	.49234	12.30861	65	.26084	.37208	24.18532
6	.35033	.48688	12.65894	6	.25956	.37038	24.44488
7	.34610	.48167	13.00504	7	.25831	.36870	24.70318
8	.34207	.47668	13.34711	8	.25708	.36706	24.96026
9	.33823	.47191	13.68535	9	.25587	.36545	25.21613
30	.33456	.46733	14.01990 ←	70	.25469	.36387	25.47082
1	.33105	.46293	14.35095	1	.25353	.36231	25.72435
2	.32768	.45871	14.67863	2	.25239	.36079	25.97674
3	.32445	.45464	15.00308	3	.25127	.35929	26.22801
4	.32135	.45072	15.32443	4	.25017	.35781	26.47819
35	.31836	.44694	15.64279	75	.24910	.35636	26.72728
6	.31549	.44329	15.95828	6	.24804	.35494	26.97532
7	.31272	.43976	16.27099	7	.24699	.35354	27.22231
8	.31004	.43634	16.58104	8	.24597	.35216	27.46828
9	.30746	.43304	16.88850	9	.24496	.35080	27.71324
40	.30497	.42984	17.19347 ←	80	.24397	.34947	27.95722

→ **DATA USED IN EQUATIONS UNDER FIRST UNIT ESTIMATE** ←

Exhibit 10-E

table (Exhibit 10-E). The value of the second unit on the curve is exactly 80% of the value of the first unit. These factors have the following relationship:

Cumulative total values — $F_1 + F_2 + F_3 + \ldots\ldots\ldots\ldots F_N = \Sigma F_N$

Cumulative average values — $\dfrac{\Sigma F_N}{N}$

Value of the first unit — $F_1 = \dfrac{\Sigma F_N}{\Sigma F_N}$ OR $\dfrac{\frac{\Sigma F_N}{N}}{\frac{\Sigma F_N}{N}} = F_1$

Progress Curve Utilization Techniques

$$\text{Slope of the curve} - \frac{F_x}{F_{\frac{x}{2}}} = S \qquad \begin{array}{l} \text{if "x"} = 2 \\ \dfrac{F_2}{F_{\frac{2}{2}}} = \dfrac{F_2}{F_1} \end{array}$$

CURVE BASED ON FIRST UNIT ESTIMATE

Exhibit 10-F assumes the first unit estimate to be 200 manhours which has been projected on an 80% slope. The manhour value of any unit on this curve is equal to T_1 times F_x.

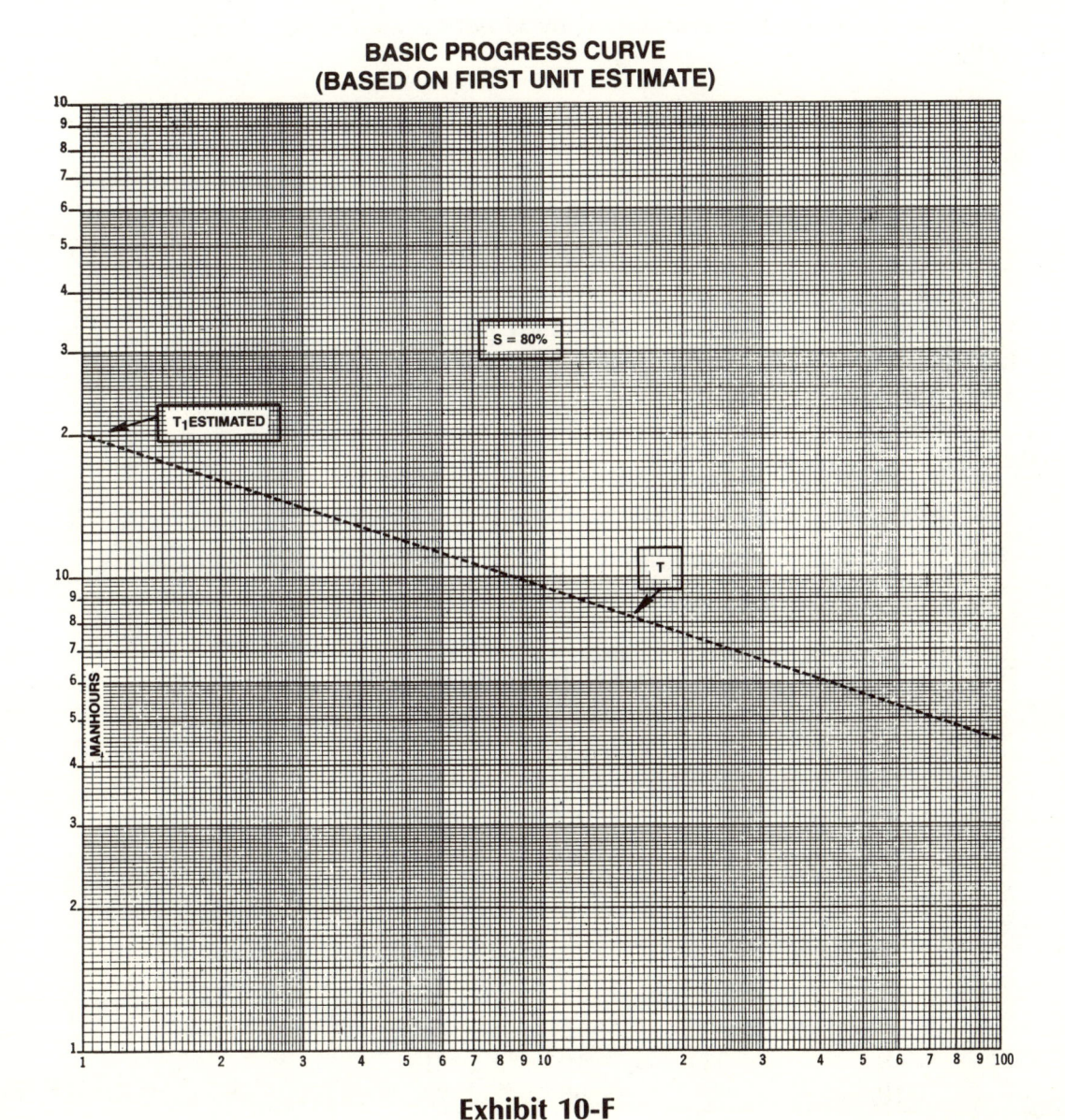

**BASIC PROGRESS CURVE
(BASED ON FIRST UNIT ESTIMATE)**

Exhibit 10-F

Example 1. $T_x = T_1(F_x)$; if $x = 10$ and $S = 80\%$

Solution. $T_{10} = 200 (.47651$—Exhibit E Table); $T_{10} = \underline{95.3}$ $(.47651 \times 200)$

Example 2. $T_N = T_1(\Sigma F_N)$; if $N = 20$ and $S = 80\%$

Solution. $T_{20} = 200 (10.48495)$; $T_{20} = \underline{2097}$ (10.48495×200)

In the above second example, the cumulative total manhours for any group of units on this curve are equal to T_1 times ΣF_N

Analysis of Unit Actual Hours

The slope of a line established by visual inspection may be determined as follows:

Example. $S = \dfrac{T_x}{T_{\frac{x}{2}}}$; assume $x = 4$ and "T" is obtained from a graphic plot

Solution. $S = \dfrac{T_4}{T_{\frac{4}{2}}} = \dfrac{T_4}{T_2} = \dfrac{128}{160} = \dfrac{80\%}{160}$

To rapidly determine the value of T_1, draw a line on the chart that parallels the trend of the actual points and establish the value of "S" using the above formula.

$T_1 = \Sigma t_N$ divided by ΣF_N.

Example. $T_1 = \dfrac{\Sigma t_N}{\Sigma F_N}$; $\Sigma t = 2097$; $N = 20$; $S = 80\%$

Solution. $T_1 = \dfrac{2097}{10.48495}$; $T_1 = 200$ manhours

The following t_x values can be obtained from the display exhibit.

x	t	x	t
1	230	11	86
2	140	12	79
3	160	13	82
4	130	14	88
5	110	15	83
6	120	16	77
7	94	17	84
8	110	18	75
9	95	19	81
10	97	20	76
Totals	1286	+	811	= 2097 (above)

Progress Curve Utilization Techniques 303

CURVE EFFECT FROM EFFORT DELETIONS

In many cases, deletions in effort will occur during the production of a series of units. When this effort is estimated as displayed on Exhibit 10-G, the line "T" is reduced by the percent (y) of decrease. The results produce a new line "T_a". "T_a" is equal to "T" times (1) minus (y) percent.

Example. $Ta_x = Tx (1 - y)$; assume $x = 21$; $y = .40$ and $Tx = 75.05$

Solution. $Ta_{21} = 75.05 (1 - .4)$; $Ta_{21} = \underline{45}$

**PROGRESS CURVE
(EFFECT OF DELETED EFFORT)**

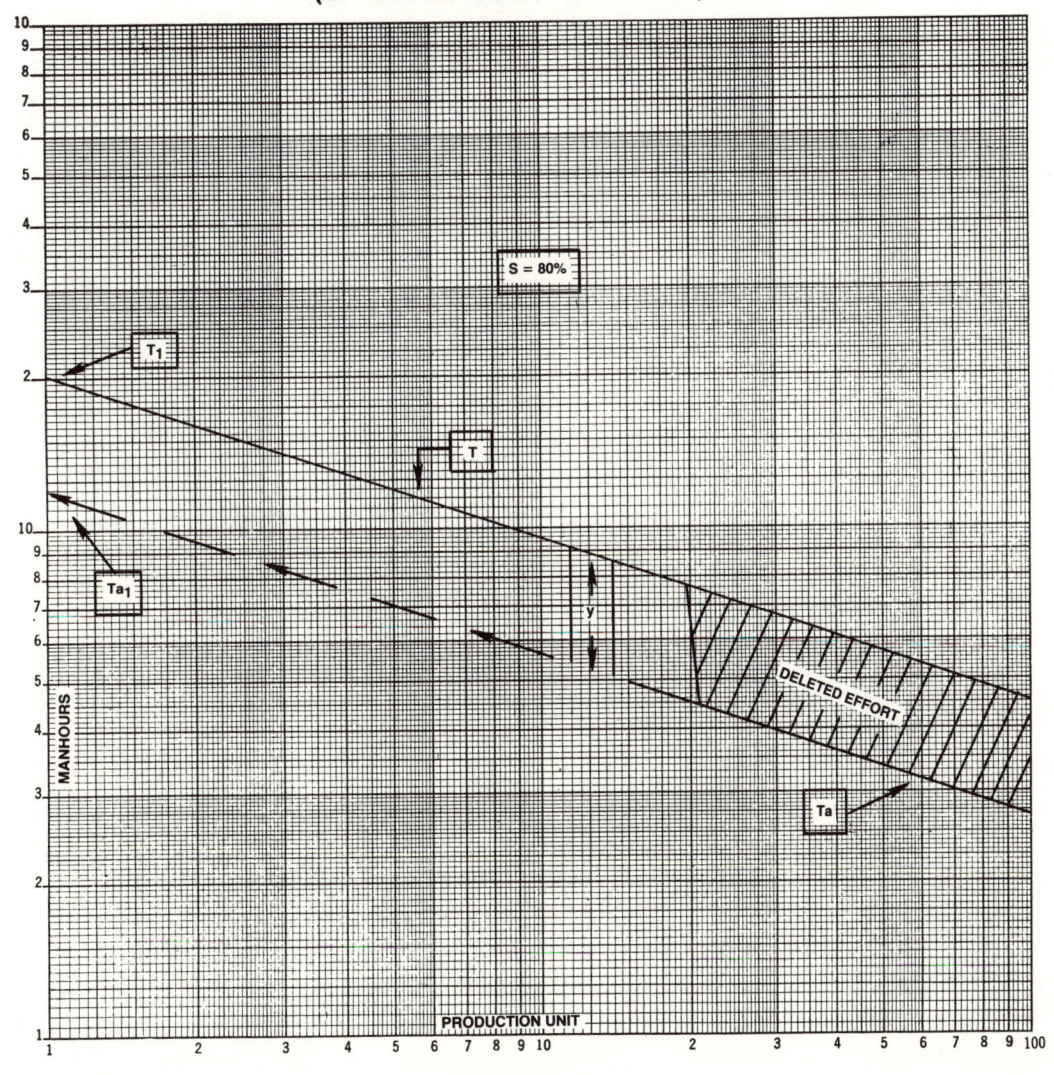

Exhibit 10-G

To calculate the Ta units beyond Ta_x without using the line "T" as a base, it is necessary to find the value of Ta_1. This is accomplished in the following manner:

Example. $Ta_1 = \dfrac{Ta_x}{F_x}$; assume x = 21

Solution. $Ta_1 = \dfrac{45 \text{ (above calculation)}}{.37527 \text{ (table above)}}$; $Ta_1 = \underline{119.9}$

The effect on actual hour deletions in work content can have a significant influence on the value of the curve. If the deletion does not change the slope of the curve, an analysis can be accomplished with minor effort. If it appears, however, that the slope has changed, then the percent of error should be calculated.

CURVE EFFECT FROM ADDED EFFORT

In situations where the basic work content of a product is increased by additional requirements of hardware which is already included in the product at a lesser quantity, the values of the affected units should be established using the progress curve factors which correspond with the sequence of the affected units. The total value of the curve, including the added effort, is identified as "Tc" which is equal to "T" plus the added effort. If the added effort is based on estimates shown in Exhibit 10-H, the following formulas will be applicable.

Example 1. $Tc_x = Tx(X + 1)$; assume x = 21; X = .50; Tx = 75.05

Solution. $Tc_{21} = 75.05(.50 + 1)$; $Tc_{21} = \underline{112.58}$

Example 2. $Tc_1 = \dfrac{Tc_x}{Fx}$; assume x = 21; Tc_x = 112.58 and S = 80%

Solution. $Tc_1 = \dfrac{112.58}{.37527}$; $Tc_1 = \underline{300}$

Example 3. $X = \dfrac{Tc_x}{Tx} - 1$; assume x = 21; Tx = 75.05 and Tc_x = 112.58

Solution. $X = \dfrac{112.58}{75.05} - 1$; X = .50

CURVE EFFECT FROM "NEW" ADDED EFFORT

When new effort is added to an existing product, the progress curve value of this effort is selected starting with the first value on the curve. This approach is relevant providing the "new" work has not already been included in the product such as an added component or an operation or process that is completely new in the production activity.

Progress Curve Utilization Techniques

**PROGRESS CURVE
(EFFECT OF ADDED EFFORT)***

Exhibit 10-H

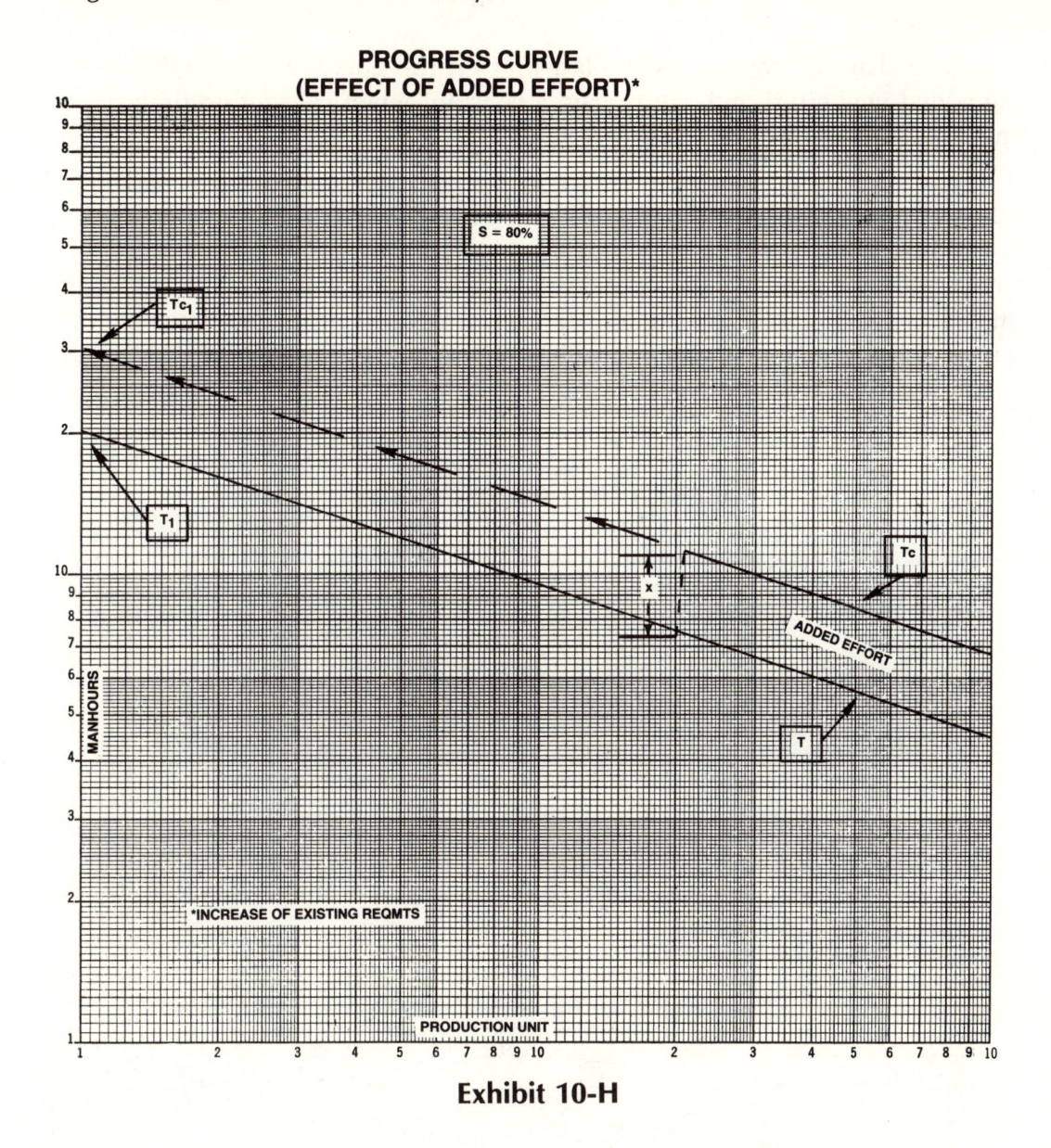

The sum of the existing effort plus the total of the new effort produces a new line—"Tc." If the change occurs at unit ten (10), unit Tc_{10} will be equal to T_{10} plus Tb_1, unit Tc_{11} will be equal to T_{11} plus Tb_2 and so on. The formula for calculating the value of Tc_x is as follows.

Example. Tc_x represents any unit manhours on the curve
$Tc_x = T_x + Tb_{x-n}$; assume x = 21; n = 20; Tb_{x-n} = 80;
$T_x = 75.05$

Solution. $Tc_{21} = T_{21} + Tb_{21-20}$; $Tc_{21} = T_{21} + Tb_1$; $Tc_{21} = 80 + 75.05$
$Tc_{21} = \underline{155.05}$

Note that "n" represents the last unit on the curve that is unaffected by the added new effort and will remain a constant when calculating the value of any "Tc_x" unit.

CURVE EFFECT FROM CHANGED EFFORT

When changes occur in design or processing which affect a portion of a component of a product, the revisions will result in increased manhours to produce the component even though the basic work content has remained the same—providing the change is new to production. Exhibit 10-I illustrates such

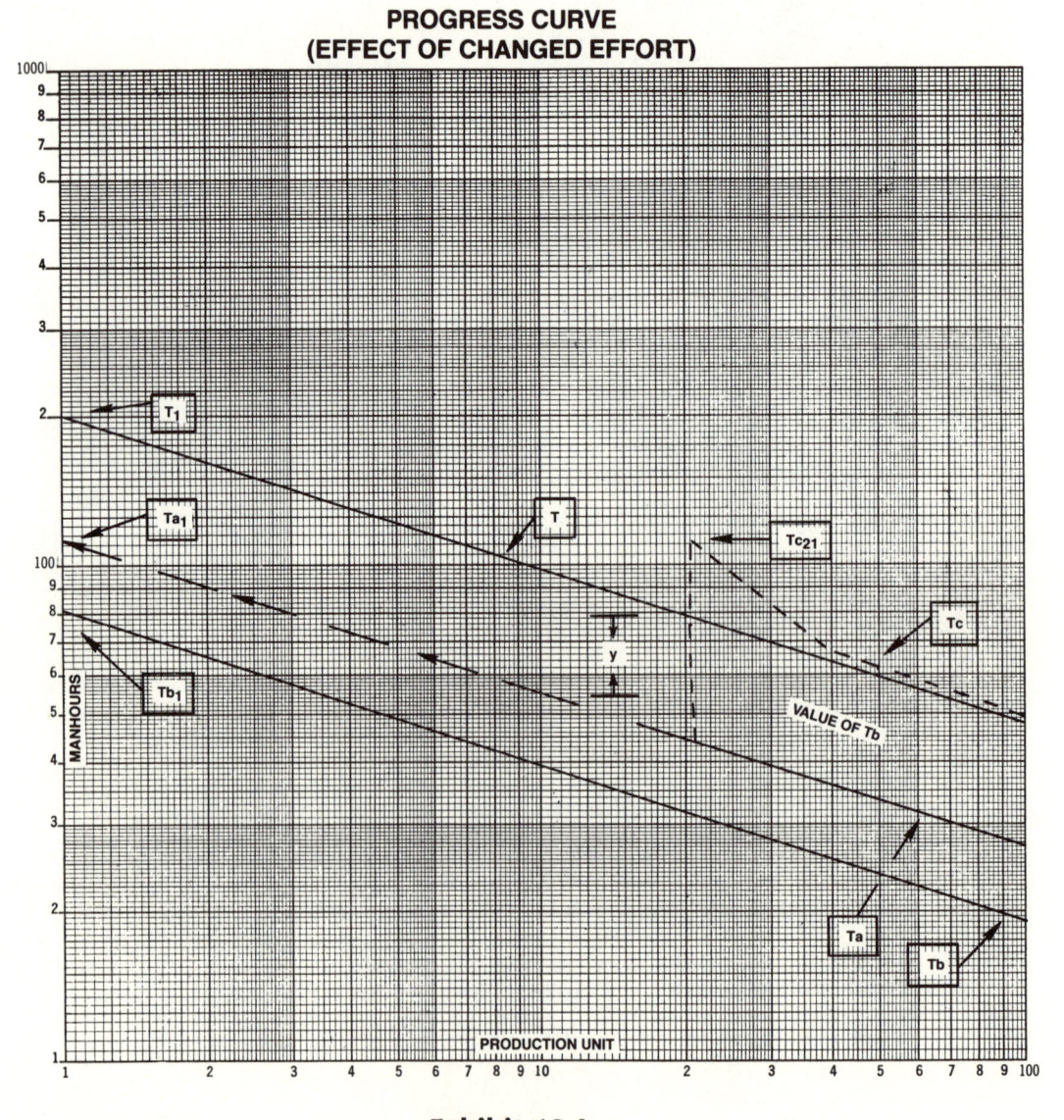

Exhibit 10-I

Progress Curve Utilization Techniques

a condition and is used when the estimated value of the changed work is known.

For the first change occurring in the product, the line "Ta" represents the value of effort unaffected by changes and "Tb" the value of the changed effort. The sum of "Ta" plus "Tb" equals "Tc" which is the total value of the product including the added costs to produce the change. The value of "Tb" may be found by multiplying the percent of change times the value of "T."

First Change

The formulas for calculating the values of Ta, Tb and Tc follow.

Example 1. $Tb_1 = T_1 (y)$; assume $T_1 = 200$; $y = .40$
Solution $Tb_1 = 200 (.40)$; $Tb_1 = \underline{80}$ (changed unit values)

Example 2. $Ta_1 = T_1 (1 - y)$; assume $T_1 = 200$; $y = .40$
Solution. $Ta_1 = 200 (1 - .40)$; $Ta_1 = \underline{120}$ (unchanged unit values)

OR

$$Ta_1 = \frac{T_x (1 - y)}{F_x}; \text{ assume } x = 21; T_x = 75.05; y = .40; S = .80$$

$$Ta_1 = \frac{75.05 (1 - .40)}{.37527}; Ta_1 = \underline{120}$$

Second Change

When a second or subsequent change occurs, the same general formulas are used as in the first change condition with the exception of the following substitutions:

1st Change		2nd Change
T	=	Ta1
Ta1	=	Ta2
Tb1	=	Tb2
Tc1	=	Tc2
y1	=	y2

Example 1. $Tb2_1 = Ta1_1 (y2)$; assume 1st $Ta1_1 = 120$; $y2 = .30$
Solution. $Tb2_1 = 120 (.30)$; $Tb2_2 = \underline{36}$

Example 2. $Tb2_1 = Ta1_1 (1 - y2)$; assume $Ta1_1 = 120$; $y2 = .30$
Solution. $Ta2_1 = 120 (1 - .30)$; $Ta2_1 = \underline{84}$

CURVE APPLICATION USING STANDARD HOURS

When standard hours are used in lieu of estimated manhours, the manhour value of any unit on the curve becomes a function of a performance factor. This factor represents the value by which the standards must be extended to obtain the projected actual manhours. Similarly to manhour estimates, the performance factor value and slope are "developed" using historical data.

The performance factors are the result of dividing the actual and calculated manhours by the standard hours. Since the standard hour content of a product may vary slightly from unit to unit due to minor design changes, lot size variances, or changes in production processing, a more accurate progress curve can be developed by analyzing the actual performance factor rather than actual manhours. This is accomplished by substituting the same formulas as used with manhours in the above discussion. First, however, the manhour data must be converted to the performance factor data.

PROGRESS CURVE COMPUTERIZATION

Practical application of the progress curve can be translated into a computerized program that will perform the various calculations discussed above. The progress curve table with varying learning slopes are entered into the file records for reference as the need occurs. The algebraic formulas are selected from the files based on need and program instructions. The various logarithmic charts are plotted and outputted from the computer. This type of mechanical program literally saves countless hours in the learning curve application process. Further, the computer provides the flexibility for testing alternate learning curve slopes for assessment and selection of the ideal curve for product costing and performance measurement. As conditions change in the operating environment, revisions can be incorporated into the program and the results ascertained.

PROGRESS CURVE HIGHLIGHTS

The progress curve techniques discussed in this chapter have proven to be an invaluable tool for establishing direct labor standards and wage incentives; effecting changes when workloads are added, deleted, or changed; and projecting manpower distribution requirements. Many algebraic formulas are provided to assist the planning estimator in projecting cost, production, and sales goals. Fundamentals, characteristics, and problems associated with the utilization of progress curves are discussed. A number of graphic displays demonstrate the construction and use of progress curves. Computerization of the various curve applications will significantly reduce manual effort and provide extreme flexibility in enlarging the scope of usage.

11

Computerized Cost and Schedule Surveillance for Performance Evaluation and Control

Most organizations involved in government contract activities have some form of a computerized capability to assist them in meeting specific requirements set forth by government directives. The mechanical systems range from ultra-sophisticated to *manually-propped systems*. In reviewing a number of organizations, the author noted some common deficiencies as follows:

PAST AND PREVAILING SYSTEM DEFICIENCIES

- Some mechanized systems did not provide *appropriate audit trails* and interface among task authorizations, schedules and budgets.

- In some instances, data were *not spread by month* or were unusually late (for example, 15–20 days after month end close) due to effort time constraints, in spite of the fact that it was a common customer requirement to receive the data much earlier.

- Since information was required at the *detailed breakdown structure level*, the manual operation, for all intents and purposes, was generally prohibitive for effective, timely reporting.

- Many of the mechanical systems were *not modularized nor online*; therefore, to obtain selective data, the complete system had to be run, resulting in high volume paper output and costly processing.

- System and program capabilities represented various degrees of sophistication, but the majority required *considerable manual and costly support effort*.

- Some of the aggregate systems were comprised of a series of *"add-on" costly operating programs* that, in most instances, provided inefficient data processing.

- There were existing *problems of integrating cost, schedule, and technical performance* so that the status of each could be directly associated.

SYSTEM DEVELOPMENT OBJECTIVES

To be effective, a well-planned and/or re-designed system will resolve the deficiencies noted above. Some major considerations are as follows:

- *Integrated* program controls.
- A comprehensive and integrated *work breakdown structure* that will fulfill multi-level reporting requirements.
- A *modular constructed program* capability that can be *run on a stand-alone basis* for selective reporting and also in a sequential mode.
- An *online operation* capability for rapid data retrievals, making changes, and playing the "what-if" game.
- *Timely visibility* of program data as work progresses in the production phase.
- The system should be *cost-substantiated* and effective in significant terms of decreased manual effort.
- An *advance planning* capability to monitor cost and schedule performance.
- A means to *test alternative* program direction decisions.
- Intensive *budgetary control* from program start date to completion.
- Timely *tracking of actuals* and feed-back of data to enhance future estimating and planning capabilities.

COST COLLECTION SYSTEM

One of the basic considerations to an effective cost, schedule, and performance tracking system is a sound cost collection system. The primary objective of the cost accumulation system is to appropriately identify, organize, and collect costs and to provide appropriate fields in the computerized file records to meet various reporting requirements. To accomplish this objective, specific identifiers must be established.

Data Collection and Reporting Control

Exhibit 11-A displays an overview of the cost collection process wherein costs are accumulated by cost element, are summarized to the various hierarchial levels, and culminate at the program types as indicated by the directional arrows on the exhibit. Time periods must be associated with each cost accumulation level. This overview cycle represents a systematic approach to data collection, summation, and reporting.

Basic Considerations in Cost Collection

Some basic requirements in cost collection are as follows:

- Each major program is assigned an abbreviated identifier for data collection reference. A number of smaller programs (task and dollar-wise) can be classified into one miscellaneous category for ease in data management. Effective *identifier structuring* is of paramount importance.

HIERARCHIAL DATA COLLECTION & REPORTING CONTROL CYCLE

Exhibit 11-A

- There must be approved *authorizing documentation* to support effort and cost expenditures that indicate task assignment and responsibility.
- Elements of cost must be identified to *source of charge* and its appropriate cost classification, such as direct versus indirect.
- Cost distribution must be *monitored and verified.*
- There must be *consistency* in data identification and structure in order to meet the needs of financial reporting, bids and proposals, budget comparisons, and customer requirements in terms of cost/schedule performance control.

WBS Cost Identifiers

The work breakdown structure (WBS) is a term used to identify a product-oriented family division of hardware, software, services, and other work tasks which organizes, defines, and graphically displays the product to be produced as well as the work to be accomplished to achieve the specified product.

Exhibit 11-B is a more detailed approach to a cost collection structure used by one organization that is engaged in effort on government contracts. A brief description of the requirements is as follows:

- A *program* is the first level of cost collection in the work breakdown. It may include one or more contracts depending on the tasks, size, and complexity.

Computerized Cost and Schedule Surveillance

COST COLLECTION STRUCTURE

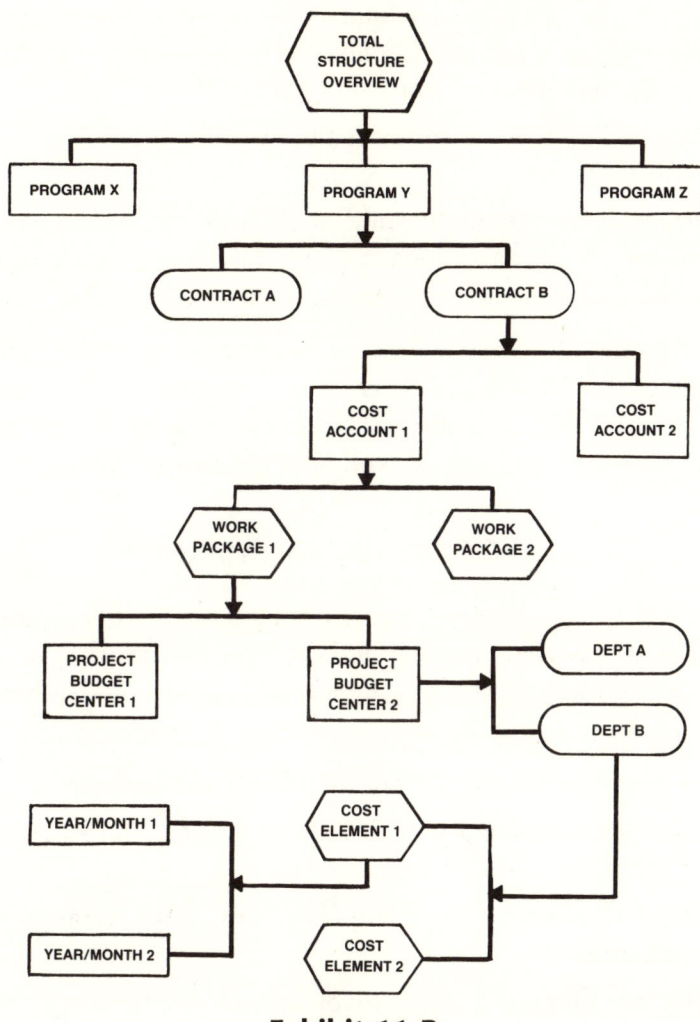

Exhibit 11-B

- A *contract* could have more than one cost account that represents collection points for accumulating actual costs. The actuals are compared to budgeted cost for work scheduled and performed to measure performance progress. The cost account may consist of one or more work packages.

- The *WBS table* contained in the computerized system file is used for the report extract and also to structure programs to provide data identification at all levels of reporting for each contract. Each level and its related work orders are identified by descriptive titles. Changes to this table are via manual input forms or online keyboarding, if that capability exists.

- *Project budget centers* (PBCs, i.e. manufacturing) represent functional groupings of organizations for accomplishing tasks, accumulating costs, budgeting, assigning task responsibilities, and monitoring and controlling operations. A sub-level collection point within the PBC is a department or group of smaller units—departments are shown on Exhibit 11-B.
- *Cost element* identifiers indicate the specific type of direct cost, such as labor and material.
- The *time element* is concerned with task effort and accomplishment. Depending on organizational policy, data collection can be in time increments of weeks and/or months, year, and cumulative-to-date.

The identifying WBS titles, work orders, and structure charts are provided by the budget and/or industrial accounting organizations depending on assigned responsibility. Cost tracking is accomplished in accordance with WBS and will include all current costs as well as estimates to complete.

WORK PACKAGE SYSTEM

A *work package* is identified with detailed short-time span tasks or purchased material items that are defined by the contractor for accomplishing work required to complete the contract terms. Some of the basic characteristics of a work package are as follows:

- It is *clearly distinguished* from all other work packages.
- The budget or assigned values are *expressed in terms of manhours*, dollars, or other measurable units.
- *Scheduled start and completion dates* are representative of physical accomplishment.
- It *represents units of work* at levels where the tasks will be performed.

The work package represents the tasks to be accomplished in engineering, manufacturing, logistics support, or any other involved organization. Operational tasks are related to end items of the WBS. Individual manhours and material budgets are assigned to each work package. These budgets and work packages appear at various levels of the WBS. Standard work packages are used to represent all of the effort.

In summary, the work package is the *fundamental unit* for planning, scheduling, budgeting, and tracking work effort. It can be *event-oriented* or *level of effort/apportioned*. An event-oriented work package contains definable points of accomplishment which are scheduled for specific time periods. A level of effort/apportioned work package is a time-phased allocated budget.

Work Package Baseline

Cost account requirements are converted into work package requirements which are assigned to the concerned supervision responsible for the work. Based on this data, a work schedule is developed as well as an expenditure budget.

The work package system is used to develop the dollarized work package and the baseline budget. This data is inputted into the mechanical cost/schedule system for performance measurement and reporting.

WORK AUTHORIZATION AND BUDGET CONTROL

The letter contract or change notice provides the basis for preparing a document identified as the *contract budget notice*; the nomenclature may vary among organizations.

Generally, the budget notice contains the following cost element detail:

- *Direct labor* hours and dollars by functional organization.
- *Overhead dollars* by prime expense account as well as the G & A expenses.
- *Direct material* dollars, bill of material for the end product, and engineering/tooling material requirements.
- *Subcontract dollars* by vendor.
- *Other direct cost* dollars for direct travel, computer usage, and so on.
- *Allocated prime costs* are included in direct cost elements indicated above.

Each category of cost above is allocated a definitive budget which is then converted into operating budgets by planning analysts and the program manager. The dollar values are allocated to the responsible organizations.

Work Order/Authority Structure

Many organizations use a ten-digit account number, usually alphanumeric for flexibility, in their cost collection system. The first *two digits* identify the type (fixed price, cost plus, commercial) of contract and work (subcontract, rework, outside production).

The *next four digits* identify "work orders" which, in addition to specifying the contract, further designate the major divisions of work such as a work statement paragraph or a major WBS item (classified as cost accounts in government contracts).

The *last four digits* identify the specific segments of work. In some organizations, these digits are classified as work authority, work plan assignment, or a work package in the PERT environment.

The number of digits can be reduced or increased depending on organizational needs for greater or lesser data segregations for reporting purposes.

PROCESS DATA OVERVIEW

Exhibit 11-C displays a generalized overview of a cost/schedule control system in terms of interfaces and data needs to achieve the type of reporting required by the various concerned system users. An abbreviated description of the data flow and interfaces follows.

1. After the proposal estimates are finalized, they are converted by the project budget function into direct task operating budgets and entered into the cost/schedule control system. The program manager reviews the budgets and, if necessary, makes adjustments which are entered into the system process. Involved organizations are also provided their portion of the operating budget for review and possible adjustment.

2. It is the responsibility of the program manager or director to develop detailed plans for the accomplishment of the program or contract that would include defining tasks, identifying performing organizations, scheduling work, and allocating appropriate budget for task performance.

3. Projected cost data is provided by the direct budget planning function, program manager, and affected operational performing organizations. This is done through a meeting of the participants involved.

4. The actual incurred costs are collected and accumulated in the cost ledger and the data fed to the cost/schedule system in order to provide the necessary information for performance evaluation relative to budget status and projected cost-to-complete.

5. Various detail and summary reports are produced for different levels of management who are responsible for task accomplishment, program, and task control. As shown in Exhibit 11-C, the type of reports required and distributed to concerned recipients are noted below.

General Management—Manpower and program cost actuals and projections.
Program Manager—Cost data and program status aligned to WBS and operating organizations.
Functional Staff and Concerned Departments—Manpower, labor hours and cost element status by project budget center and department.
Direct Budget Function—Pertinent operating statement data which are primarily program cost oriented.

6. At the lower supervisory levels, control is accomplished by monitoring labor hours and equivalent heads (derived from manhours worked) in terms of

Computerized Cost and Schedule Surveillance

**COST/SCHEDULE & CONTROL SYSTEM
PROCESS DATA OVERVIEW**

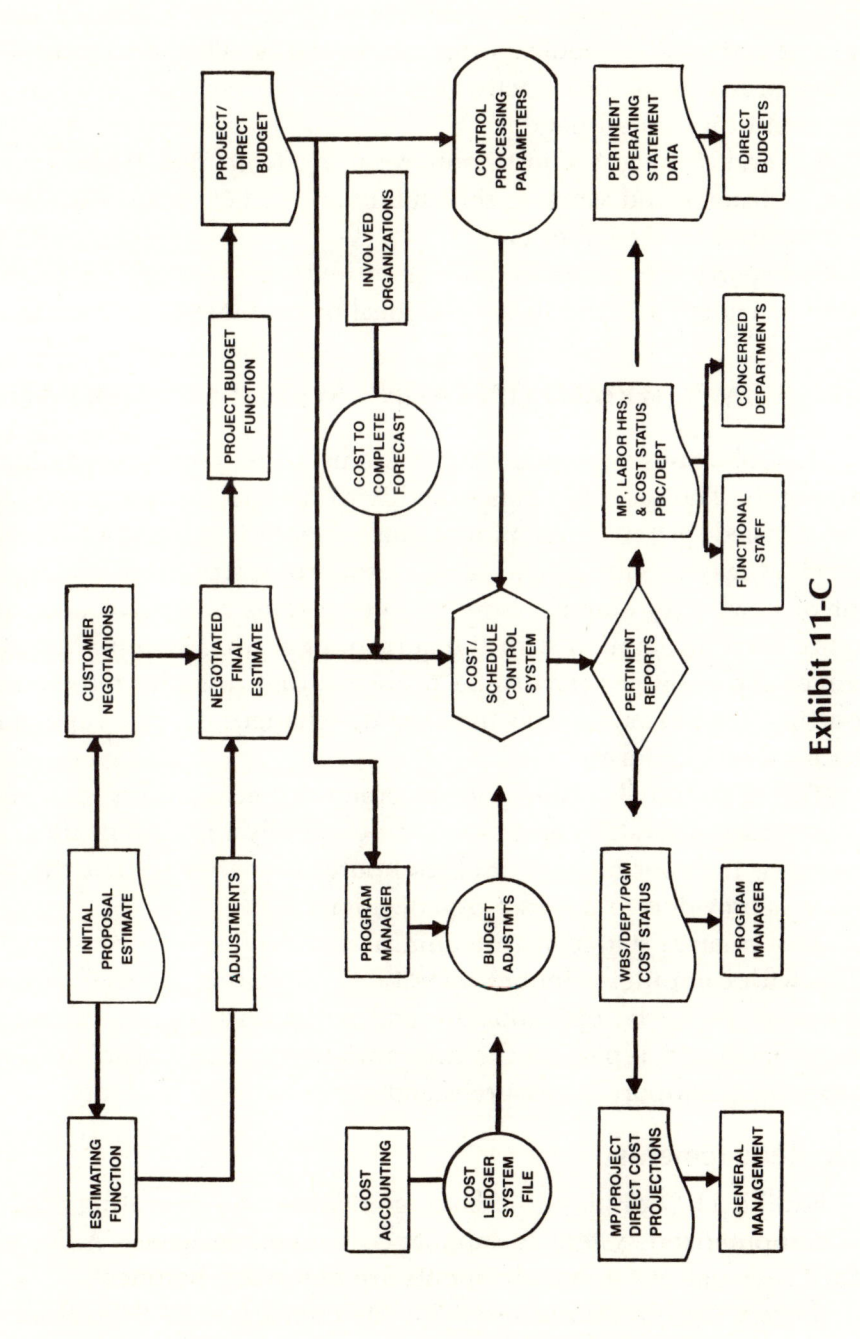

Exhibit 11-C

manpower scheduling and utilization in program task performance. Direct labor hours are converted to labor dollars to which other direct and indirect costs are added to obtain the cost of task performance.

7. Budgets are time-phased in order to provide a shorter time frame for assessing cost and schedule performance status. The shorter time span in reporting provides an immediate opportunity to correct problem areas before they get further out-of-hand.

8. Various budget adjustments resulting from task transfers, management reserve changes and work re-scheduling are direct inputs into the system and are processed on a current basis.

9. Reports are generally on a monthly basis but can be produced weekly (if data is available in the files) on critical or problem-associated tasks.

COMPUTERIZED OPERATING SYSTEM CONSIDERATIONS

Basically, most computerized systems have similar operating control requirements. The tasks are concerned with design improvements/additions and their detailed system development/implementation. Program support and control tables may require updating. Cost reporting structures change with the advent of new requirements. New related systems may have been initiated that require their integration with the current operating system. Making processing changes and additions may cause problems that must be resolved. Revisions to reporting requirements may necessitate changes to the reporting structure, identifications, or format.

The operational system control organization monitors and interfaces with all concerned operating units, who are generally the system users. Their major function is the coordination of all computer activities so that the most efficient service is provided to the user organizations.

The group is staffed with technical and professional personnel who are familiar with computer-oriented operations as well as the user environment and requirements. To be operationally and authoritatively effective in their tasks, the group should report to the appropriate executive who can ensure proper management support in resources and organizational backing.

Basic Requirements

Exhibit 11-D displays the basic guidelines and operating controls required in a computerized system to support cost/schedule needs. A description of the record files and system involvements are described below.

System Control Parameters. This file contains data control information relative to data extract; cost element identities; organizational, WBS, and work package titles; and report selection parameters.

Cost Collection Criteria. This file contains actual incurred cost data transactions by period and year-to-date. It is interfaced with the cost/schedule system for reporting purposes. It reflects data by expense, cost, and general ledger accounts.

Compatible System Interfaces. This is a system data integration file wherein the following programs are interfaced with the data base system, work package, estimating, earned value management summary, and program management.

Cost Reporting Structure. This is a reporting module file wherein the various type report formats are identified and stored.

Data Processing Programs. The various computer operating programs are stored in this file. The program routines permit data additions, deletions, and changes. Error detection and exception reporting programs are contained in this file, as well other mechanical data manipulation procedures.

Program Support Tables. Various support tables are contained in this file relative to: curve spread routine, cost/schedule structure/control, manmonth conversion, cost rates, and WBS.

Functional Responsibilities

As shown in Exhibit 11-D, the operating system control function participates with the user organizations in system upgrading, usefulness evaluation, and re-design needs. Problem areas are determined, assessed, and resolved.

Operating system control provides computer operations with audited input data, schedule report output, and table/report changes as shown in Exhibit 11-D.

The segregation of system activities and responsibilities among the above functional groups varies in different organizations based on their organizational structure, but similar tasks must be accomplished. Efforts are coordinated to effect the necessary system requirements to meet changing reporting needs.

COST TRACKING AND PERFORMANCE SYSTEM

Exhibit 11-E reflects an integrated cost tracking system that is composed of several subsystems or modules that provide information and support for the overall program. A description of this system follows.

User Inputs

- New additions or changes to the budget or latest revised estimates are inputted manually.
- The selected task curve spread provides designations for the budget and latest revised estimate. The type curve selected governs the time period spread of the designated tasks.

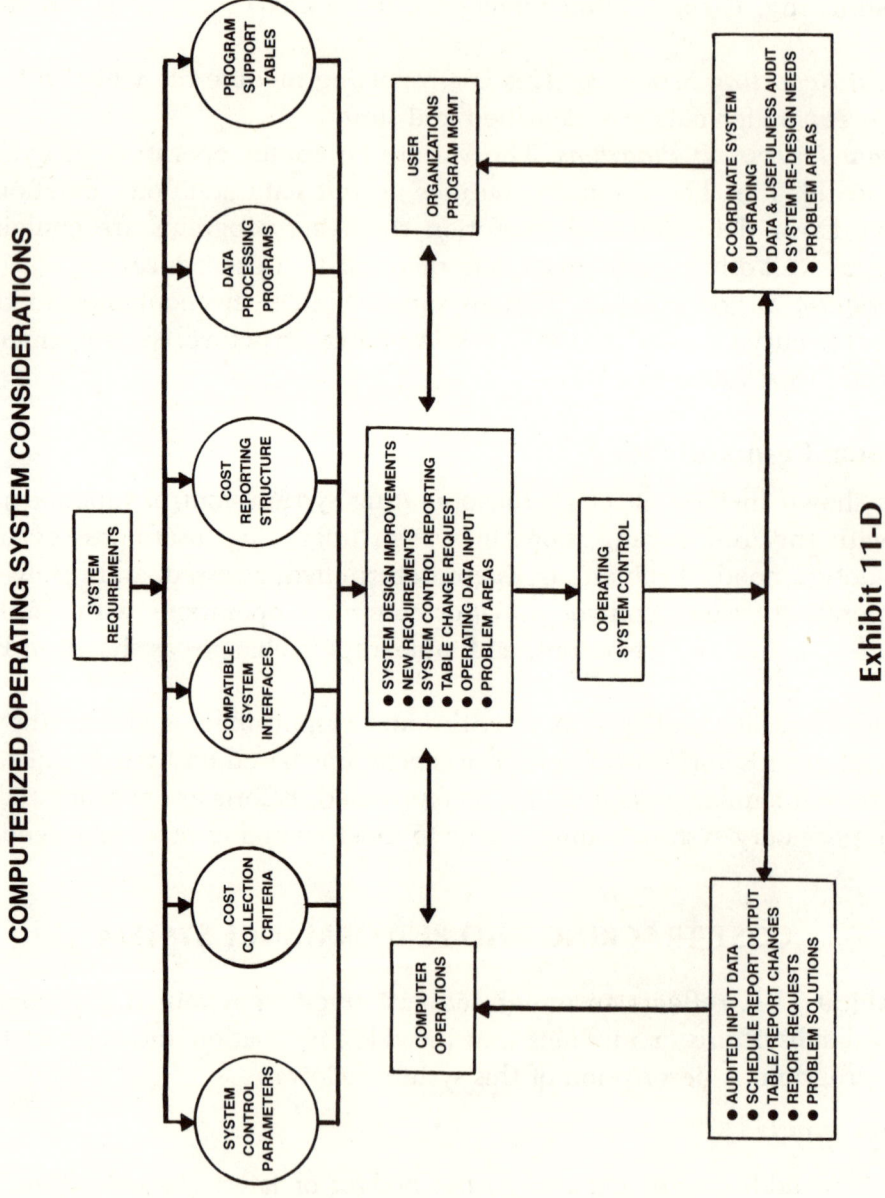

COMPUTERIZED OPERATING SYSTEM CONSIDERATIONS

Exhibit 11-D

Computerized Cost and Schedule Surveillance

**REQUISITES OF COST TRACKING & PERFORMANCE SYSTEM
COMPUTERIZED MODEL**

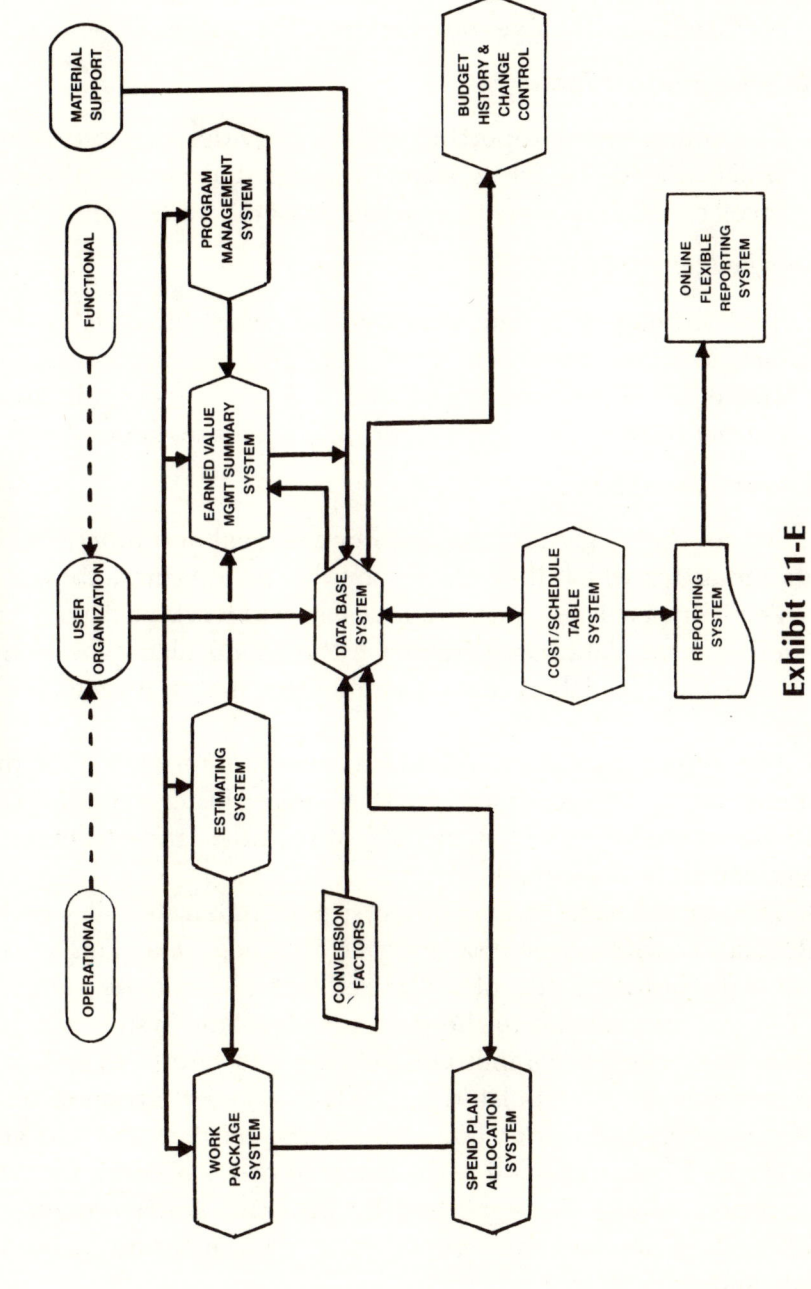

Exhibit 11-E

- Manually inputted are planned costs, planned value work schedule and value accomplished, cumulative cost actuals, total hours to date, and future latest revised estimates.
- Any changes required to the cost/schedule reports are made on the report itself and then keyboarded into the system.

Material Support Input

- The commitment reporting system provides committed material costs which are identified as subcontracted dollars, interdivisional material invoices, cost transfers, and actual material costs committed.

Cost Ledger Input

- This mechanical system provides the actual direct labor hours and dollars, overtime premium, overhead, progress payments, material costs, and other direct costs. The cost ledger includes file records such as journal transactions, and ledger data (expense, general and cost).

System Description

1. System user organizations, both operational and functional, provide varied data inputs for which they are responsible as indicated above.

2. The work package system establishes the work package baseline budget that is fed into the data base system via the spend plan allocation system. The type of data includes labor hours, manmonths, material costs and other direct costs.

3. The estimating system provides the basic information for the budget requirements which are generated by the budget history system. Upon contract award, the information would include WBS titles and structure, labor hours and manmonths, and elements of cost.

4. The earned value management system integrates all schedule and budget information with actual cost and performance data. This system maintains an up-to-date historical file of dollarized actuals, budgets, and other projections. The system provides to the data base tracking system the planned value work schedule, work accomplished, actuals, and latest revised estimates. This data is mechanically manipulated to produce (1) comparison of scheduled work value to accomplished work value at the work package and cost account levels, (2) summarized cost status, (3) and reports of cost variances that exceed predetermined percentages as established by program management. Also, this system is used to monitor and report any data inconsistencies between the schedule and tracking systems.

5. The program management system (could be PERT Time) provides the basic performance information to the data base. It develops work scheduling based on data provided by network planners and others directly associated

with the program tasks. The results from this system are provided to the earned value system, as shown in Exhibit 11-E, in the form of task performance schedule and anticipated, latest, and actual completion dates for every activity in the network.

6. For each of the three primary systems (budget history, spend plan allocation, and earned value) concerned with building and maintaining the data base, there is a two-way communication channel as shown in Exhibit 11-E. This interchange of data flow permits the transmission of all changes necessary to the data base and provides a feed-back to each involved system of the status of the data base items.

7. The data base system is designed to perform a formatting and calculating function based on the user's request and prior approved cost/schedule report structure. Computer processing produces the required information in prescribed formats. The data base records are composed of information that has been collected and stored as it occurs, and the data is transferred to the reporting system where the requested reports are produced in the formats required.

8. The cost/schedule table system is the controlling function of the performance tracking system. The tables prescribe the report formats, the cost elements required in each segment of the WBS or indenture reporting structure, specific contract identifications, rate tables, organization and WBS titles, extract control, and manmonth/hours coversion rate. Further, the tables control the file structure for data content and relationship.

COST/SCHEDULE REPORTING REQUIREMENTS

A number of basic reports are required from this system to provide the information required by management, program manager, and others concerned in tracking and analyzing cost/schedule performance. Some of the reports are described and/or illustrated in the following discussion.

Direct Manpower. The format of this report is shown at the top of Exhibit 11-F. This report reflects the projected direct head-count in equivalent heads over a twelve month period and the annual average by program code and descriptive identification. The head-count is initially segregated as to firm or potential contract business and then summarized to reflect the data to be outputted in Exhibit 11-F report format.

The projected head-count is compared at the end of the monthly period to the actuals, and the variances are calculated for analysis and investigation if significant.

A similar reporting format for projections and comparison to actuals is used for major functional organizations in order that they can monitor their specific performance and reconcile any variances.

PERFORMANCE SYSTEM REPORTING

DIRECT MANPOWER (EQUIVALENT HEADS)

PROGRAM		CURRENT YEAR PROJECTIONS											
CODE	IDENTIFICATION	JAN	FEB	MAR	APR	MAY	JUN	JUL	AUG	SEP	OCT	NOV	DEC	AVERAGE

DIRECT HOUR SUMMARY ANALYSIS

PROGRAM			PLANNED BALANCE	NEXT YEAR FORECAST	SUBSEQUENT YEAR PROJECTION	FUTURE YEARS	TOTAL TO COMPLETION	TOTAL INDICATED COST	BUDGET	OVER/(UNDER) VARIANCE
CODE	IDENTIFICATION	MONTH	YTD	CURRENT YEAR						

FINANCIAL VARIANCE ASSESSMENT

PROGRAM		CURRENT YEAR FORECAST							TOTAL CONTRACT FORECAST					
CODE	IDENTIFICATION	YTD PRIOR MONTH		YTD CURRENT MONTH		VARIANCE		CTD PRIOR MONTH		CTD CURRENT MONTH		VARIANCE	
		SALES	INCOME	SALES	INCOME	SALES	INCOME	SALES	INCOME	SALES	INCOME	SALES	INCOME

Exhibit 11-F

Direct Hour Summary Analysis. Illustrated in Exhibit 11-F is one approach for reporting pertinent detail relative to direct labor hours. It identifies work effort to the specific program. The report contains the actual hours as expended for the *month* and *year-to-date*. The planned hours to be expended for the balance of the year are reported, as well as a projection for two subsequent and future years. The sum of these periods provides an overall projection of total hours to be used for the completion of a specific program.

Projected manpower is generally the basis of conversion to obtain direct hours. Some organizations, however, project the task to be required in order to calculate direct manpower in equivalent heads. It is recommended that both approaches be used as a check against each other for more realistic planning. This type of dual projection process provides the opportunity to reconcile data differences and resolve which data appears to be most appropriate for the projection plan.

The direct hours are next converted to direct labor dollars using projected average wage rate projections by pertinent periods (it can be anticipated that the rates increase annually). The resultant cost values are compared to the formalized budget plan to obtain the anticipated over/under variance. It is suggested that the current year's projections (probably common practice in most organizations) be compared to the budget in order to determine a near-term evaluation of direct labor hours and dollars anticipated. This information can provide a basis for initiating immediate corrective action if required.

Financial Variance Assessment. Exhibit 11-F also displays the reporting format for program sales and operating income assessment. As shown on the exhibit, year-to-date prior month is compared to current month for sales and operating income to obtain the variance for that time frame. A similar comparison is made for the cumulative-to-date period to obtain the aggregate variances. Although the format indicates program level reporting, this data is also provided to management, as well as summary totals for all programs. This report provides an excellent overview of the most important financial data resulting from operations.

Monthly Cost Status by Contract. Exhibit 11-G displays one type of format that can be used to report cost status by individual contract and further summarized to an organizational total. The report shows the individual cost elements for the prior and current periods in terms of current month and cumulative dollars for actuals, budget, and revised estimate. Subsequent months' data are provided relative to the budget and the revised estimate.

For the end of the year, the total remaining budget is calculated by reducing the beginning of the year's remaining budget by the allocated budget for the current year. The revised estimate to complete is the sum of the revised estimates as shown on the report. The estimate at completion is a predetermined planned value—its difference from the revised estimate to complete will result in an over/underrun.

COST & PERFORMANCE SURVEILLANCE REPORT
(COST STATUS BY CONTRACT)

PROGRAM IDENTIFICATION _____   DATE _____

TIME PERIODS	LABOR HOURS	LABOR DOLLARS	PREMIUM LABOR $	OVERHEAD	MATERIAL USAGE	MATERIAL SUBCONTRACT	COMPUTER	TRAVEL	OTHER	TOTAL DIRECT	G&A/ ALLOC.	TOTAL COSTS
CTD PRIOR MONTH												
BUDGET												
ACTUAL												
REVISED ESTIMATE												
CURRENT MONTH												
BUDGET												
ACTUAL												
REVISED ESTIMATE												
ESTIMATED VARIANCE												
CTD CURRENT MONTH												
BUDGET												
ACTUALS												
VARIANCE												
SUBSEQUENT MONTH												
BUDGET												
REVISED ESTIMATE												
END OF YEAR												
BUDGET BALANCE												
REV. EST. TO COMPLETE												
EST. @ COMPLETION												
EST. OVER/UNDERRUN												

- REPORTS ACTUAL COSTS BY PROGRAM VS BUDGET BY MONTH & %.
- SUMMARIZES TOTAL ESTIMATED COST AT COMPLETION IN RELATION TO BUDGETS.
- SIMILAR REPORTING FORMAT IS USED FOR WORK BREAKDOWN STRUCTURE (WBS), PROJECT BUDGET CENT (PBC) AND DEPARTMENT.

Exhibit 11-G

The summary of the individual programs or contracts provides organization totals for management assessment of its operational cost status. Similar reports can be produced by WBS, project budget center, and department. Due to the extent of the detail and summations involved, it is a verifying indicator that mechanization is imperative if a successful and timely reporting system is to be achieved.

Work Breakdown Structure (WBS). An approach to WBS reporting which reflects the cost/schedule system is displayed in Exhibit 11-H. There are other variations of this report that can be used to fulfill the general reporting requirements of DOD 7000.2.

In the computerized environment, the data required are collected from other system modules and stored on tape or disk files until needed. Utilizing online operations, it would take only a few minutes to selectively extract any or all of the report data that was available at a particular point in time. A description of the report content follows.

1. As shown in Exhibit 11-H, the upper portion of the report indicates the results of customer negotiations such as product and quantity, negotiated cost, share ratio, etc. Other information is developed by organization or management edict, such as target profit fee percent, estimated price, ceiling price, and target price.

2. Current period and CTD budgeted costs in terms of work scheduled and to be performed are usually the initial data input maintained on file by period. Actual costs are extracted from the cost collection system module.

3. The difference between the budgeted work schedule and actual work performed represents a schedule variance. The difference between budgeted cost of work to be performed and actual cost of work performed is the cost variance.

4. The difference between budgeted cost at completion and the latest revised estimate represents the latest outlook on the expected cost variance.

5. Detailed items of the WBS are summarized to the hierarchial levels and contract totals by element of cost. Management reserve andundistributed budget are initial inputs into the file records—generally, a management decision for anticipated contingencies.

6. A similar formatted report would be outputted from this system by operating organization and functional staff groupings (engineering, for example).

WBS reporting provides an immediate overview to management as to program performance status for the current period and cumulative to date. The planned completion data and cost are also provided.

The detail required for this type of reporting is extensive from the standpoint of both processing and reporting. Since organizations usually have a

WORK BREAKDOWN STRUCTURE REPORTING

CONTRACT TYPE	NUMBER ID	PROGRAM TITLE	NUMBER	REPORTING PERIOD

UNIT QUANTITY	NEGOTIATED COST	EST. COST AUTH. UNPRICED WORK	TARGET PROFIT/FEE %	TARGET PRICE	ESTIMATED PRICE	SHARE RATIO	CONTRACT CEILING	ESTIMATED CEILING

	CURRENT PERIOD			CUMULATIVE TO DATE				AT COMPLETION		
ITEM WORK BREAKDOWN STRUCTURE	BUDGETED COST		ACTUAL COST WORK PERFORMED	VARIANCE		BUDGETED COST		ACTUAL COST WORK PERFORMED	VARIANCE		BUDGETED	LATEST REVISED ESTIMATE	VARIANCE
	WORK SCHEDULED	WORK PERFORMED		SCHEDULE	COST	WORK SCHEDULED	WORK PERFORMED		SCHEDULE	COST			

WBS SUMMARY

CONTRACT SUMMARY
LABOR
OVERHEAD
MATERIAL
MGMT RESERVE
UNDIST. BUDGET
TOTAL

SIMILAR REPORT WOULD BE PREPARED BY ORGANIZATION & FUNCTIONAL STAFF GROUPING

Exhibit 11-H

number of programs to track, it is logical to computerize this system in order to effect timely and detailed reporting and thus significantly reduce the manual effort involved.

In addition to the reports described above, there are a number of others that are generally included in this type of system, such as PERT Time and Costs, Expected Unit Production Costs, Summary Cost Status, Work Package Cost Variance, Cost Account Variances, and Exception Reports.

PROGRAM EVALUATION AND REVIEW TECHNIQUE (PERT)

PERT Time and Cost is a sub-system used by many organizations as a management control, planning, and evaluation tool. It has been used for many years in defense procurement. All of the primary reference goals are translated into product design parameters that are monitored as part of PERT-Tech. The matrix represents the relationship between each of the technical performance goals and design parameters. Equations are developed and computer programmed to calculate the values of performance given the tracked values of the design parameters.

System Overview

Functional coordinators provide the following information to the computerized system.

- PERT TIME—Schedule, plans and status in terms of time.
- PERT TECH—Performance plans and status.
- PERT COST—Cost plans and status.

The above data are inputted into the system and a program planning and control series of reports are prepared for management and concerned operating supervision, program director (program planning and control responsibility), and the customer.

To meet program objectives on time, PERT provides enhanced communication among operating organizations, "what if" simulation of the effects of alternate decisions so that their effect could be evaluated on program deadlines before implementation, an effective program planning and scheduling tool, and continuous program progress reports that permit the identification of problem areas that require corrective action.

PERT Modules

The network module, as the term infers, performs the required task composition, structuring, critical path analysis, and network calculations. A network model shows the sequence of work planned to accomplish the target and tracks major performance milestones and activities that connect them.

The report module permits the composition of reports from data developed in other system modules and inputs. A considerable degree of flexibility is available to the users for report generation at varying reporting levels.

The costing module provides labor costing rates, material usage, and other costs.

Milestone or Event

The *event* represents a specific task accomplishment in a program plan. It signifies the start or end of a task and an identifiable point in time which does not consume resources or time.

An *activity* represents the expenditure of work or other resources to move the project from one event to the next.

Network Characteristics

The general characteristics of a PERT network are as follows:

- A network consists of one or more sub-networks or subnets. Networks are always independent of each other. Subnets can either belong to a network or be permanent "stand-alone" subnets. Network levels are organized in accordance with the WBS.

- The operational task and the time required to move from one event to another is represented by an activity.

- The events must occur in logical sequence or order.

- No event can be completed until the preceding event has occurred.

- A designated milestone event is a major or control event within a network and provides a base for reporting schedule information to multilevel supervision.

- Summary events are those events that are shown on the summary network. These condensed-version events are supported by detailed events which are compatible with the WBS.

- Work package identifiers are generally reflected on the detailed networks.

- Technical achievement events are identified on the schedule and monitored through the evaluation of status reports.

- A critical path is identified to a specific network path wherein the events and activities contain the *worst slack* or time schedule problems.

- Every end event has an optional schedule date from which late dates and slack are calculated.

Time Estimates

The PERT planner develops the time estimate for all activities on the activity data input sheet based on resources available for the work package detail. The data may require rearrangement or summation before they are entered on the input form for entry into the mechanical system.

Unacceptable or problem deviations from the critical path are reported on a problem analysis report for corrective action.

Event Numbering

An identifying numbering system must be developed for entering and processing information in the computerized system. For this purpose, one typical organization uses a nine-character alphanumeric identifier which is described as follows:

- *First character*—an alpha to designate network (organization) source and responsibility code.
- *Next 2 digits*—numeric to identify network number.
- *Next 4 digits*—numeric to identify each event.
- *Next character*—alphanumeric to identify special events. A zero would be used if no special event were planned.

The above event numbering system provides for flexibility in processing and identifying events in the PERT mechanical system. It further provides a sound basis for achieving report requirements.

VARIANCE ANALYSIS AND REPORTING

A variance is identified as that value by which any schedule or cost performance varies from a specific outlined plan. Significant variances are those differences between planned and actual performance that require further analysis and action. Generally, in the mechanical environment particularly, appropriate "threshold limits" are established for variance analysis and computer output in order to preclude high volume reporting.

The evaluation of variances and their reporting is required to provide responsible management with appropriate data and a means to assess program cost and schedule performance. Further, it satisfies contractual requirements for management reporting and cost/schedule visibility.

Variance analysis and reporting plays an important role in the cost/schedule tracking system and is accomplished within the following guidelines:

- Must be accomplished on a monthly period schedule.
- The analysis is at the cost account and contract levels.

- Appropriate supervision prepares variance reports for cost accounts that exceed established variance *thresholds*.
- Contractually required variance analysis and reporting are at the work package level.

INITIATING INTERNAL COST CONTROLS

The necessity for maintaining constant surveillance and tight control over the cost/schedule performance cycle has been emphasized to ensure acceptable contracts and to be able to defend them. The final phase of the cycle demands that the work be performed within the cost limits that were calculated into the selling price in order that the anticipated profit will be realized.

The basis for establishing direct cost controls can be found in the data that is developed in the development of direct cost estimates. The estimates and the changes during various review actions become the direct cost budgets for measuring performance in the operating departments and for monitoring costs through control reports.

Direct labor operating costs must be developed in sufficient detail to permit comparison of actuals with the budget at timely intervals. One type of reporting is to show a comparison of actual versus budget direct hours by labor classification on a monthly cumulative basis. The report includes the percents of physical completion, expended, and overrun based on cumulative performance to date. Variances are analyzed and if problems, such as overruns, are encountered, corrective action is necessary to improve efficiency and/or obtain contract change orders.

If the project entails the continuous production of identical units, the learning curve can be effectively used as a control tool since estimated cost at any point in the contract is plotted. The surveillance and monitoring require primarily the plotting of cumulative actual unit costs as a comparison with the estimated costs.

The control of *direct material* costs is slightly different in that it is monitored at the procurement point rather than when the cost is paid or the material used. This monitoring can be accomplished by establishing detailed material budgets from the data used in the original material cost estimates. The actual cost, as incurred at the time of procurement, can then be compared with the detailed budget cost for control purposes.

Overhead costs must be controlled so that the total amount incurred in any period is recovered through the amount of overhead included in the selling prices of all contracts. This is accomplished by accurate forecasting and developing projected overhead rates which are applied uniformly to all work being contracted for during that period. The task of control then narrows itself down to a constant monitoring of actual overhead rates as compared to projected rates. In each case, the reporting of variances for corrective action, immediately upon detection, provides the control needed.

INCENTIVE PROFIT

Incentive profit should be addressed since it represents one of the major objectives of an effective cost/schedule tracking system. Incentive profit is equal to *target profit plus sharing ratio* and this *value is multiplied by target productivity times the inverse variance* in cost effectiveness.

The above equation and schedule incentives are used to relate cost, schedule, and performance results to determine the total incentive profit.

COMPUTERIZED SYSTEM CAPABILITIES

1. The computerized system provides integrated technical performance, time, and cost data that permit appropriate progress measurement and provide a more accurate basis for management decisions.

2. The system provides capability for projecting the expected unit production cost throughout the development phase. The type of product design generally governs the cost of producing it; thus, by placing production cost goals on engineering, then monitoring the progress toward meeting the cost goals, the costs can be more rigidly controlled.

3. The cost/schedule performance system includes multi-level budget performance reporting based on the requirements of each management level to control program cost. All changes to lower level reports are automatically indicated in summary status reporting.

4. The incentive contract is utilized to show how profit is influenced by the decisions that are made. The incentive contract is structured to provide the customer with the maximum cost effectiveness and associated compensable profit to the contractor.

5. Actual costs are processed automatically into the cost/schedule system from the cost ledger system, and the current status of each program is maintained in relation to the budget and projected cost-to-complete.

6. The system significantly improves management's cost/schedule visibility and anticipated results.

7. The system is interfaced with the estimating system, and it converts the proposal estimate into the project budget and subsequent direct operational task budget.

COST AND SCHEDULE TRACKING HIGHLIGHTS

Undoubtedly, a number of organizations either have a computerized cost/schedule performance system or are developing or enhancing one. This chapter discusses some of the more common problems in cost/scheduling tracking and the steps that can be taken to overcome them. System considerations, requirements, and desirable capabilities are outlined. There are descriptions of various desirable system interfaces and the reasons for their need in the integrated and reporting mechanical model.

The work breakdown structure and work package structure are defined and their uses presented, not only in the cost collection process but also in establishing cost and schedule goals for work to be monitored and performed.

Input, processing, and reporting formats are outlined and display exhibits are provided to supplement the text for a more comprehensive insight into system operation. The use of the PERT technique is described as to its role in the computerized cost/schedule system. Some basic internal cost controls are discussed as an aid in assessing costs more effectively.

The detail discussed in this chapter should save the reader countless hours of effort in researching, developing, or upgrading a cost/schedule tracking system that is not only effective in operation but also meets the customer and management requirements in terms of advanced planning, surveillance, cost control, and reporting.

12

The Computerized Estimating System in Action

The business environment is becoming more complex due to more product sophistication and varied new developments, such as space shuttle aircraft and its requirements, motor vehicle re-design for energy conservation and adverse foreign competition, nuclear submarine emphasis, and national defense needs in terms of advance weaponry. It is evident that increased intensity must be placed on timely, realistic, and detailed cost estimating and product pricing. Ever-changing products, due to the continual state-of-the-art advancements relative to the need for miniaturization further complicate the cost estimating endeavors. More frequent revisions are required to the prevailing and "on-going" cost estimating process. There becomes a more urgent need for mass data manipulation, processing, flexibility, reliability and more rapid data generation and response to changing cost circumstances with intense competition being only one of the significant factors involved. Additionally, cost estimating and expenditures entail cost tracking, surveillance, control and performance measurement.

AN APPROACH TO PREVAILING PROBLEMS

To resolve the requirements and problems indicated above, an organization can install complete computerization of the estimating and pricing processes. A number of organizations have already undertaken this task and implemented a mechanized system, whereas others are either in the development or feasibility justification phase.

This chapter will discuss the requirements and mechanics involved in the development of a successful computerized model that will sophisticate the cost estimating process and fulfill the needs of manual effort cost savings, effective data processing, turn-around time constraints, data reliability, and pricing decisions.

SYSTEM OBJECTIVES

Cost estimating and pricing involve the detailed development of product cost projections based primarily on historical intelligence and the translation of

The Computerized Estimating System in Action 337

these results into cost and price proposals for management's consideration in the decision-making process. The objectives of a computerized system include:

- A time-saving mechanical approach to (1) developing cost estimates for new business proposals and for initial and follow-on contracts and (2) effecting contract change requirements.
- A systematic approach and procedural guidelines to all involved in the mechanical preparation of the cost estimate.
- Control tables and basic audit routines to protect the integrity of data input, processing, and reporting.
- Detailed estimate processing in terms of spreading and re-spreading man effort over selected time periods, factoring costs and rate applications.
- Capability to reflect the progress curve concept and learning calculations in the cost estimate and thus to preclude the use of countless hours of manual effort and inaccuracies.
- Identification maintenance of basic estimating tasks and their requirements.
- Mass change and updating capability to accelerate cost estimate and pricing revisions.
- A means to transfer the developed negotiated values to the budgeting process.
- "What-if" gaming capability to test alternate courses of action.
- An output of a multitude of varied, selected reports to meet the needs of management, concerned operating personnel, financial personnel, and the customer (if required).

PRICE PROPOSAL AND COST COLLECTION INTERFACE

Exhibit 12-A displays the sequence of documentation and the interaction among organizations in cost proposal development. The sequence of events provides a firm, logical basis in establishing a price proposal as a negotiating baseline. An abbreviated description of Exhibit 12-A follows.

1. The request for a proposal is initiated by the customer to the contract administration organization (or a facsimile group) or to management directly in some organizations which, in turn, provide copies to the concerned organizations: Budget and Cost Control, Estimating, Engineering, R and D, and Manufacturing.

2. Working as a team, the designated representatives of the above organizations develop the detailed requirements in terms of work statement,

338 The Computerized Estimating System in Action

PRICE PROPOSAL & COST COLLECTION INTERFACE

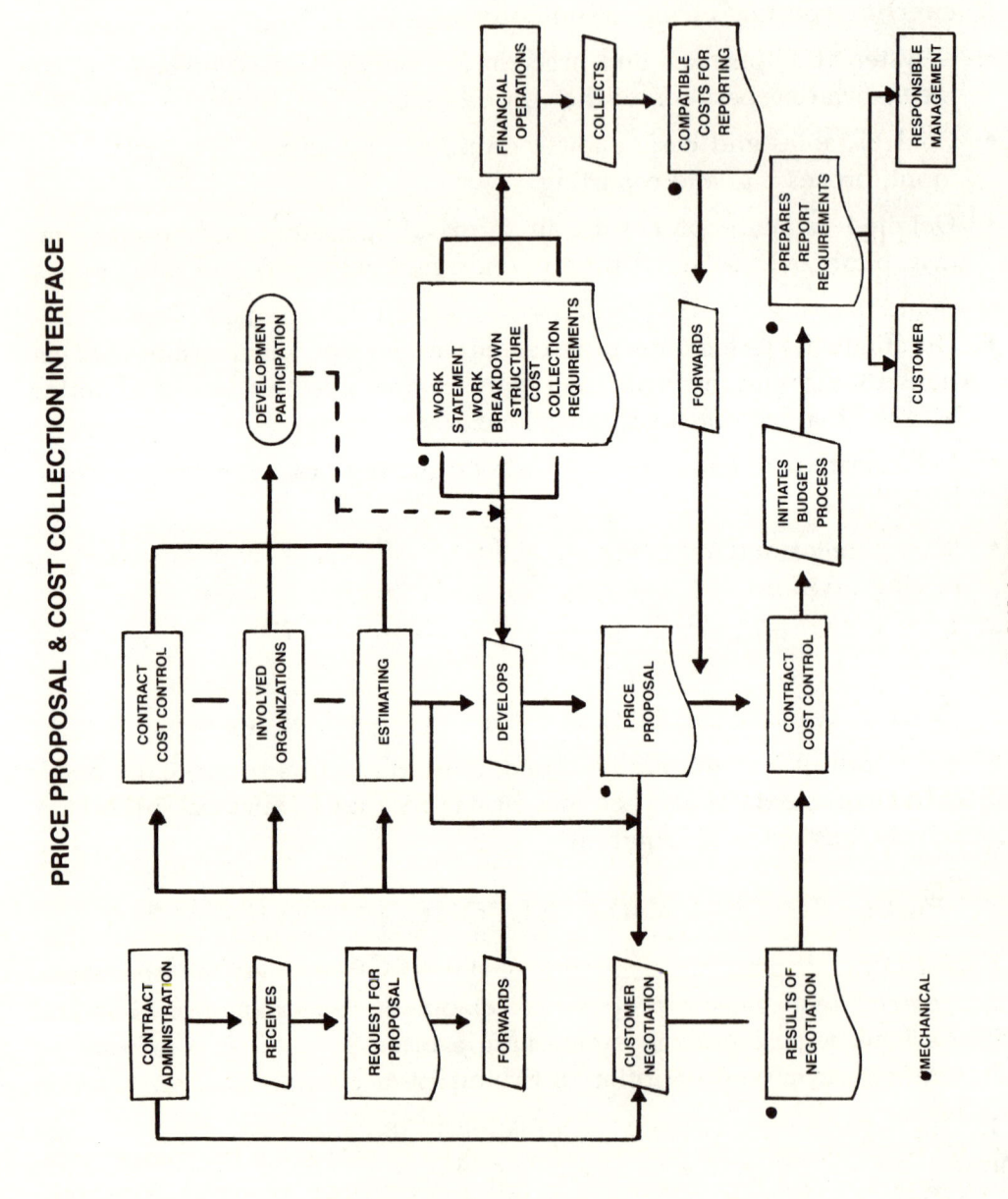

Exhibit 12-A

specific tasks, work breakdown structure, and cost collection criteria. The Program Manager is directly concerned and involved.

3. Based on the information developed and mutually resolved, effort on the cost estimate commences and a price proposal is prepared. Upon approval (or changes incorporated) by the responsible management, negotiations are initiated with the customer. Negotiations may take the form of formal presentations and/or group discussions to review the detailed price proposal.

4. Upon completion of the proposal negotiations, if approved (generally concessions on both sides), the negotiated proposal is forwarded to the above concerned organizations, which commence their individual detailed planning to accomplish the terms of the contract. Estimating function may have to revise some of the cost figures to conform to the outcome of the negotiations; engineering and manufacturing functions may have to revise the plans and tasks. If that should happen, the financial group would alter the budget projections.

5. The Financial Operations organization establishes the guidelines for collecting actual costs in a manner that is compatible to the negotiated terms. Project and work orders are assigned their identifying numbers for cost collection and task description.

6. Relevant reports measuring cost performance (actual costs versus contract negotiated) are prepared and issued periodically to the concerned recipients.

The above procedure may vary to some extent among contractors but, in the main, it represents a generalized approach to price proposal negotiation process and its interface with establishing cost collection procedural compatibility to meet reporting requirements.

ESTIMATING SYSTEM INTERFACE WITH BUDGET DEVELOPMENT

Exhibit 12-B reflects the interfaces that exist among the estimating, budget, and financial functions and also their relevant activities. In a sense, this exhibit complements Exhibit 12-A. Estimating provides the basic contract data that is used in developing the operating budget. This budget depicts the operational aspects of an organization in terms of cost elements including tasks and effort associated with contract/programs/projects.

In the course of preparing the price proposal, the estimating function must estimate or develop detailed cost data relative to each task involved. The budgeting function uses this information material in preparing the budget relative to manpower and time necessary in task performance, material usage, other direct cost, and indirect support.

The individual program managers review the budgets concerned with their own programs and make their experienced judgments as to the validity and realism of the formal operation budget development. In the interim, new

ESTIMATING SYSTEM INTERFACE WITH BUDGET DEVELOPMENT

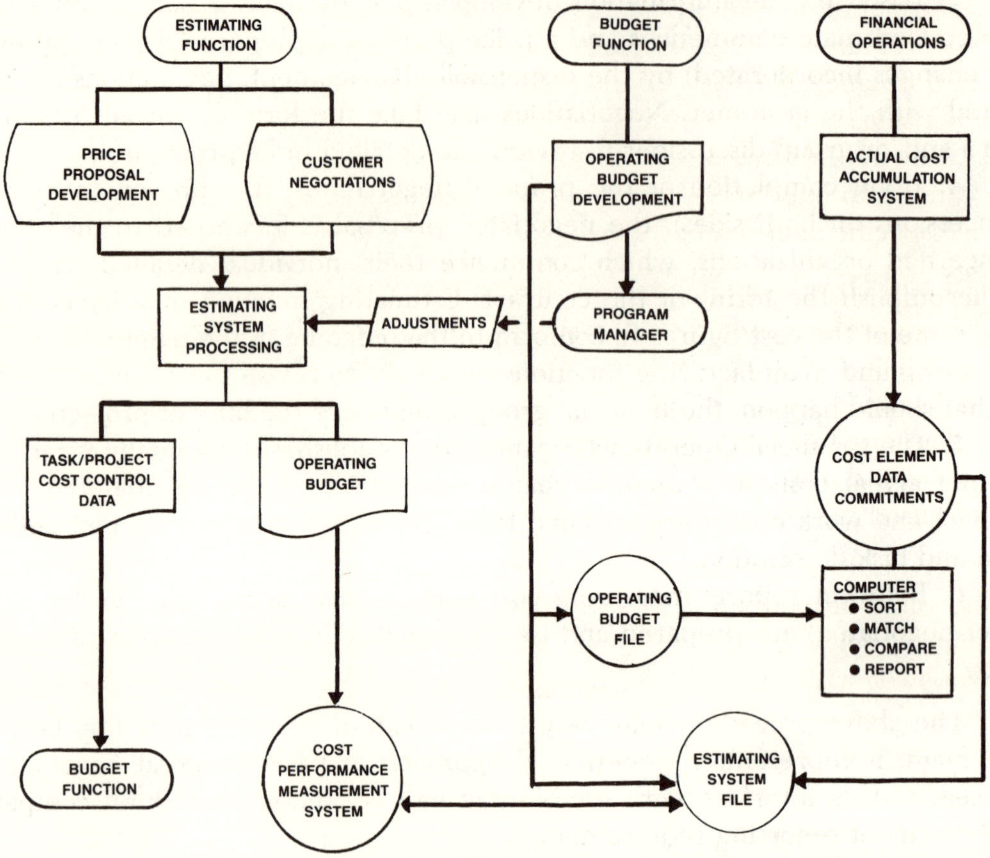

Exhibit 12-B

developments may have occurred or may be anticipated that could change the budget data. When this situation occurs, adjustments are inputted to the cost estimate computer file to revise the proposal records for subsequent performance reporting.

Financial Operations provides the vehicle for accumulating actual costs which are identified to the program tasks for comparative purposes and reporting. As shown in Exhibit 12-B, the cost element data are sorted, matched, compared, and reported. The cost estimating file is maintained as a reference to cost performance evaluation and also as a basis for future estimating judgments.

Any computerized system basically entails a series of events or considerations in design, development, and implementation. It must be constructed in a manner that will make the program process feasible and compatible for interfacing with other systems in order to provide or accept pertinent data for processing. For example, cost estimating values are often used as basic input into project budget development and, on the other hand, actual cost expenditure information is transferred from the cost accumulation system to the estimating program files for comparing costs, deriving variances, and measuring cost performance. Further, actual costs provide a prime source of data for estimate revisions and/or future cost estimating.

An overall system model should consist of a series of modules. Although integrated into one integral system, the modules can be run independently to achieve specific data requirements.

Design and Development of a Computerized Process

There are common procedural steps in developing a computerized process which would apply to a mechanical cost estimating and pricing system. The tasks can be accomplished sequentially and in tandem as shown below, or more than one task can be undertaken simultaneously. Some of the stated tasks can be deleted or others added depending on the needs and state of sophistication required or desired by the concerned organization.

1. Overall management goals and objectives relative to *computerized estimating* must be communicated to all concerned (estimating and operational function participants). This is a *must* in order that the proper support in terms of manpower with technical skills, equipment, and funding will be provided as required. Further, management's direction and support signifies their interest, involvement, and intent to monitor the progress of the project.

2. Concerned functional personnel are assigned to the project to develop detailed system requirements.

3. The estimating function provides the detailed estimating task requirements relative to the inputs, data manipulation, and reporting formats in terms of hard-copy and/or online operations. Upon compiling the documented needs, they are discussed in depth among estimators, concerned operational personnel, planning, financial personnel, and contract/marketing administrators. This is to ensure that the proposed mechanical cost estimating results will meet their individual requirements. The objective of the system is to meet, from one integral system, the varied needs of all concerned. This is necessary in order to preclude future costly add-on systems to meet *unique* individual requirements that should have been included in the initial specification.

4. The resolved detailed requirements are next presented to computer personnel who will have assigned specialists in financial programs such as designers, analysts, programmers. The representative computer personnel review and discuss with the system user(s) the specifications for complete understanding of the requirements. Then a feasibility study is undertaken which includes design, development, and implementation phases with their scheduled milestone and completion dates and associated projected costs.

5. EDP research and design tasks include determining (a) available routines that can be used (progress curve calculations, rate factoring, spreading and re-spreading formulas, etc.); (b) programming language to be used; and (c) detailed system design including operating procedures and the coordination of their efforts and plans with the designated using organization (estimating). Consideration is given to related program requirements such as edit, audit, table control, update, sorting, manipulating and reporting routines.

6. After the model has been designed and developed, it is necessary to discuss the results with the user organization to verify that the computer program processing will adequately meet the data needs and reporting specified by the users. At this point of progress, the detailed program instructions will have been written and compiled.

7. Upon resolution between the user and computer personnel (or changes incorporated) that the system is compatible with the needs, then the debugging process is initiated. Test problems are generated to verify the operation of the individual and collective modules in the system and, if the results are satisfactory, data reliability testing commences.

8. The estimating function provides historical data to test the operation of the program and the results therefrom. If the results indicate compatability with the known past experience, it is assumed that the computerized system satisfies the intended requirements.

9. Detailed system documentation is prepared to describe the system procedures such as input requirements, mechanical processing, mode of reporting, and associated formats to be used.

10. Attendant capabilities would be defined such as online operations, progress curve usage, manpower effort spreading, exception reporting, procedure for adding, deleting and changing data, etc.

11. The estimating system would be declared "operational" after all of the requirements discussed above have been accomplished to the satisfaction of all concerned.

COST ESTIMATING PROCESS

Cost estimates are generally developed in various activity phases. The planning estimator is involved in the effort well in advance of computer requirements. He defines the program and associated tasks, determines processing and reporting requirements, and provides proposal control inputs. The estimator's primary task is to project reliable cost element values that are based on (1) appropriate historical information, if applicable, (2) discussions with involved and concerned operating and financial personnel, and (3) his past experience and judgment.

Before the cost estimate processing can occur, there are basic and initial inputs that must be determined. The input needs are identified as follows:

The Computerized Estimating System in Action

System Inputs

- The work elements associated with the proposal must be identified and classified alphanumerically for computer processing.

- The system control input must be prepared, which consists of establishing a unique proposal and task time span. The planning estimator must provide report titles and define the specific system capabilities that will be required to develop that pertinent cost proposal.

- Cost element values with applicable task identifiers must be determined and inputted.

The input is thoroughly reviewed and audited before it is released to computer operations in order to preclude that old adage associated with computer input—"garbage in—garbage out." Upon completion of the input audit, the data is released to computer operations for processing and generating the required reports.

Mass Change Capability

After the cost element estimated values are received, they are reviewed in depth for any errors or misinformation. During the analysis phase, it may be necessary to revise the estimate because of new information or intelligence and/or management edict. It is possible that in the interim the customer has decided to redirect the program and its requirements. The redirection and/or changes could have a drastic effect on proposal accuracy and completion within the designated time frame. Therefore, a capability must exist to rapidly respond to the revision requirements. Although the problem cannot be totally eliminated due to the nature of the business environment, it is necessary that a "mass change" capability be available to aid in accomplishing these types of changes.

The "mass change" capability in the computerized estimating system permits the manipulation of any part of the estimate value in the data base by inputting an *action requirement* to accomplish the changes. The program additions make possible the following mechanical performance.

- Re-identifying or re-aligning any portion of an existing data record in the files.

- Making positive and negative revisions to any cost estimated values in the data base.

- Moving all or any part of the cost data forward or backward in time sequence.

- Creating new transactions from existing records but maintaining the original data intact.

- Rapidly re-processing all records on file to accommodate major revisions.

The above capability will significantly reduce much of the manual effort, time, and cost previously associated with making major cost estimate revisions.

COMPUTERIZED ESTIMATING FUNDAMENTALS

Exhibit 12-C displays some of the fundamentals of a computerized estimating system. Under the initial *planning phase*, the customer initiates a request for a proposal covering a product or service (study, research, technical support). The contractor translates this proposal into the tasks required to perform the request specification and identifies the responsible and doing organizations which will be involved. The cost estimate input requirements are defined, selected, and inputted into the computer program via a terminal input device. The data is sorted and the appropriate estimate control structure (program, value, and cost element structure) is generated which monitors processing identifications and procedures. As shown in Exhibit 12-C, the ouput includes the control structure tape file record, the report listing of the control structure criteria, and the basic input designated requirements.

Computer Generated Basic Input

On the computer-generated *basic input form*, (note Exhibit 12-D), the mechanical process enters the following RFP identifying information: type of input, program code and run identity, transaction code (add, delete) page and line numbers, keypunch card or keyboard entry number, type of program task, and cost element description.

The output, as shown in Exhibit 12-C, consists of the actual basic input form, a listing of the control structure (WBS), and a control structure tape file.

Development and Edit Phase

The lower portion of Exhibit 12-C displays the input requirements for the cost development and edit phase. A description of the actual input content is noted below.

Basic (Secondary) Input

The planning estimator provides the following information. (See Exhibit 12-D).

- *Organization element*—responsible and doing organizational units identity for performing the task(s).

- *Value*—indicates operational time periods involved in the estimate and the value element; identifies the cost element (labor, material) and its associated dollars.

The Computerized Estimating System in Action

COMPUTERIZED ESTIMATING FUNDAMENTALS

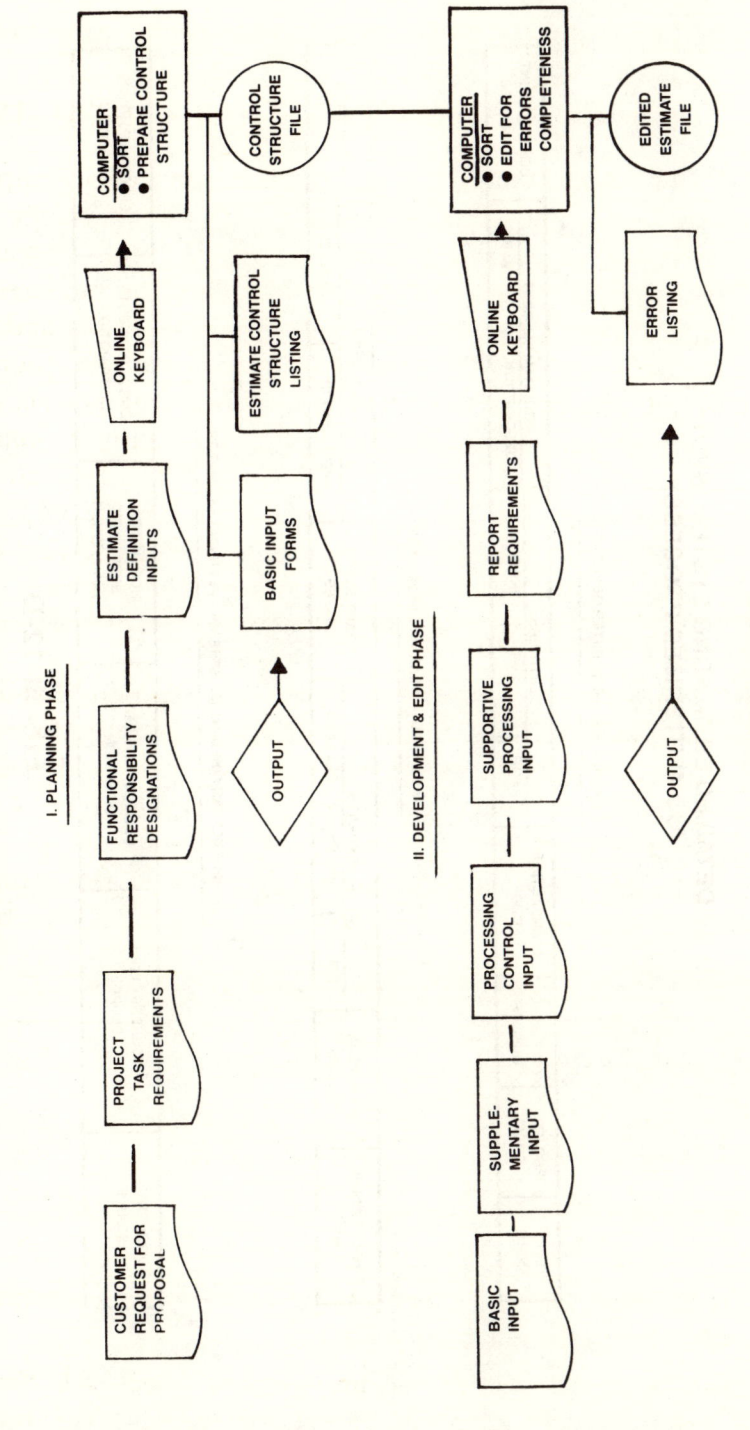

I. PLANNING PHASE

CUSTOMER REQUEST FOR PROPOSAL → PROJECT TASK REQUIREMENTS → FUNCTIONAL RESPONSIBILITY DESIGNATIONS → ESTIMATE DEFINITION INPUTS → ONLINE KEYBOARD → COMPUTER: SORT, PREPARE CONTROL STRUCTURE → CONTROL STRUCTURE FILE

Outputs: ESTIMATE CONTROL STRUCTURE LISTING, BASIC INPUT FORMS → OUTPUT

II. DEVELOPMENT & EDIT PHASE

BASIC INPUT → SUPPLEMENTARY INPUT → PROCESSING CONTROL INPUT → SUPPORTIVE PROCESSING INPUT → REPORT REQUIREMENTS → ONLINE KEYBOARD → COMPUTER: SORT, EDIT FOR ERRORS COMPLETENESS → EDITED ESTIMATE FILE

ERROR LISTING → OUTPUT

Exhibit 12-C

346 The Computerized Estimating System in Action

DETAILED ESTIMATING SYSTEM INPUT
(COMPUTERIZED PROCESS)

BASIC INPUT—COMPUTER GENERATED

TYPE INPUT	PROJECT CODE	RUN NUMBER	TRANSACTION CODE	IDENTIFIERS			PROGRAM ELEMENT		COST ELEMENT IDENTIFIER
				PAGE	LINE	INPUT REF.	DESCRIPTION	ID NO.	

BASIC INPUT—PLANNING ESTIMATOR

ORGANIZATION UNIT	NUMERICAL VALUES	VALUE ELEMENTS		START-STOP DATES	DATA SPREAD		DIRECTION
		MM	HOURS	DOLLARS		INCREMENT ID	BASIS ID	

SUPPLEMENTARY INPUT (TIME SPREAD)—PLANNING ESTIMATOR

DELIVERY SCHEDULE	PROGRESS CURVE SLOPE	BULK SUM SPREAD DIRECTION	INCREMENTAL SPREAD BY TASK PERIOD	CURVE PERCENT DISTRIBUTION	EFFECTIVE HOURS BY PERIOD

Exhibit 12-D

- *Start-stop dates*—provides the manmonths of effort to be expended between two periods of time.
- *Spread increment*—indicates the time periods to be used in estimating the effort in terms of week, month, quarter, and year.
- *Spread basis*—identifies the type of curve (linear, smooth, irregular) that will be used to describe the time, effort, and cost involved in performing the task and it indicates the direction of the curve—left to right or vice versa.

Supplementary Input

- *Delivery schedule*—provides the dates for load, complete, and percent of product unit completion; this data is associated to a program element identity.
- *Progress curve*—indicates the anticipated improvement percent over the task time interval. Generally, the common value used is 80%.
- *Lump or bulk sum*—reflects primarily the program element identifier value and value element, start-stop dates, and spread directions. The lump sum input is spread by the computer in accordance with spread instructions.
- *Incremental time spread input*—includes the task identifiers associated to the specific spread of values by task period.
- *Curve percent distribution*—indicates the cumulative percent distribution of task values (hours) over time periods.
- *Effective hours*—provides effective hours by time period (could reflect workdays in a calendar month or 4, 4, 5 week periods in a quarter).

Processing Control Input

As shown at the top of Exhibit 12-E, the input is described as follows:

- *Program structure*—identifies the work breakdown structure with its associated tasks and end items.
- *Cost element*—reflects the cost category, resource function, and operator skill.
- *Update/deletions*—reflects the type of processing to be involved.
- *General processing logic*—identifies program processing logic to be used.
- *Specific application*—indicates the specific type of processing to be used.
- *Time periods*—designates the time intervals involved in the estimate program processing.

Supportive Input

Exhibit 12-E displays the type of input required in the program processing which involves factors, relationships, and rates. A description of the input follows.

- *Factors*—program performance instructions are entered into the system to generate, change, or replace data in the cost estimate process.
- *Cost element time spread*—provides the basis for time-spreading cost elements at a predetermined rate or on a base rate spread plus curve factors.
- *Commitment factors*—reflects anticipated cost expenditures at specific current or future periods.
- *Pricing factors*—consists of direct charges (direct travel, subcontract) and the profit rate.

**CONTROL, SUPPORTIVE & REPORTING INPUT
(COMPUTERIZED ESTIMATING)**

PROCESSING CONTROL INPUT

PROGRAM STUCTURE	COST ELEMENT	ORGANIZATION UNIT	UPDATE DELETIONS	GENERAL LOGIC PROCESSING	SPECIFIC APPLICATION	TIME PERIODS

DEVELOPED SUPPORTIVE INPUT

FACTORS TO			COST ELEMENT TIME SPREAD RATE	COST ELEMENT BASE RATE & CURVE FACTORS	COMMITMENT FACTORS	PRICING FACTORS	
GENERATE	CHANGE	REPLACE				DIRECT CHARGES	PROFIT

REPORT DEFINITION INPUT

REQUIREMENT TYPE REQUEST	LAYOUT FORMAT MATRIX	REPORT FORMAT CONTENT	"EYEBALL" ESTIMATE STRUCTURE

REPORT OUTPUT EXAMPLES

INPUT LISTINGS	MANPOWER/ MANHOUR LOADING	COST BREAKDOWN SUMMARY	PROJECT COST REPORT	END ITEM SALES PRICE SUMMARY	PROGRAM COST PERFORMANCE

Exhibit 12-E

Report Definition

As outlined on Exhibit 12-E, this input designates a pre-determined report format, its content, the output sequence, and the relative degree of detail. Any number of varied reports are possible based on the needs of the organization. Some of the common types are identified on the exhibit, such as input listings for proof reading and audit trails, program error listings, manpower/manhour loading requirements, work breakdown structure summary, and project cost reports. The detail reflected in these reports are based on organizational and, if appropriate, customer needs.

The "eyeball" estimate refers to rapid summary type cost estimating wherein little detail is available on an estimate, or management requests a "rough order" of magnitude cost and price to assist them in preliminary decision-making as to whether or not to undertake or even bid on a project. Data are based on historical factors and rates, learning curve, performance assumptions, and profit goal objectives. These estimates are generally "one-shot" efforts that require immediate "turn-around" time. Also, this type of estimating can be effectively used to play the "what if" game wherein alternative decisions can be tested and results evaluated.

PROGRAM CONTROL REQUIREMENTS

Cost estimates are predicated on known and unknown factors which have to be, at times, based on the planning estimator's judgment and experience. The *known* elements are obtained from various sources in the organization who have the responsibility for their development, maintenance, and/or record keeping.

Known Cost Estimating Requirements

Under this category are included such elements as follows:

Organizational alignments and their identifying numbers. A look-up table is established in the computer file to indicate a number for the specific organization's name.

Cost Centers must be defined (identity and number) so that estimates can be associated with task groups or centers. Further, actual costs are generally collected at the cost center level for comparison to cost estimates or budgets. Reporting is often done at this level in order to monitor and effect cost control objectives.

Burden centers must be designated since, in most organizations, all indirect expenses are identified to and collected in several basic expense pools or centers. The burden centers have their own identifying number designation and are further associated to department organizations. This relationship provides a control in the mechanical process input in that if the wrong department number is entered with a valid burden center, or vice versa, the input is rejected. Further, if the cost estimate is to reflect actual cost collection data for comparative purposes, it is necessary that the expense distribution be at the burden center level.

Rates, factors and cost designations must be reflected in the estimating files so that their input will conform to accounting practices and identities. The chart of accounts designate cost collection identities and specific numbering. Various rates and factors are common accounting terminology, nomenclature, and usage.

Historical cost and performance records must be maintained on file for reference purposes in preparing future estimates, data comparisons, and reporting. Past experience provides management with a tool to evaluate future anticipations and a gauge to measure current cost performance.

Current actual data must be maintained on file which is obtained from the accounting's mechanical cost accumulation and collection system. This information is used to evaluate the authenticity of the projected cost estimate and to determine variances. It also provides the basis for future estimating endeavors.

Report requirements are designated by the users and the format structures are included and maintained in the estimating program files for periodic output as the situation requires. Reports are provided to management, to functional/operational organizations, and to the customer if required.

Having the above data available for use in the computerized system permits the planning estimator to devote his full time toward resolving the unknowns and problem elements in the estimating process. This effort involves evaluating and defining the tasks to be performed on a product or project, ascertaining the work responsibilities, and estimating the hours and dollar values of cost elements required for task performance and accomplishment.

COST ESTIMATE PROCESSING EVENTS

Exhibit 12-F reflects the cost estimate processing events that occur in the computerized system. The edited cost estimate file was developed as shown in Exhibit 12-C. An overview description of the computerized system is discussed below.

The *control structure file* of program, task, and organization identifiers is used to monitor the validity of the transactions and the applicable identifications in the mechanical system. This file represents the control criteria reference relative to inputs, processing, and reporting.

Product delivery and/or service performance schedule are provided to the system by the planning estimator. The manhour effort and cost expenditure patterns are inputted to provide a basis for spreading operating data over time interval periods.

The Computerized Estimating System in Action

COMPUTERIZED ESTIMATE PROCESSING EVENTS

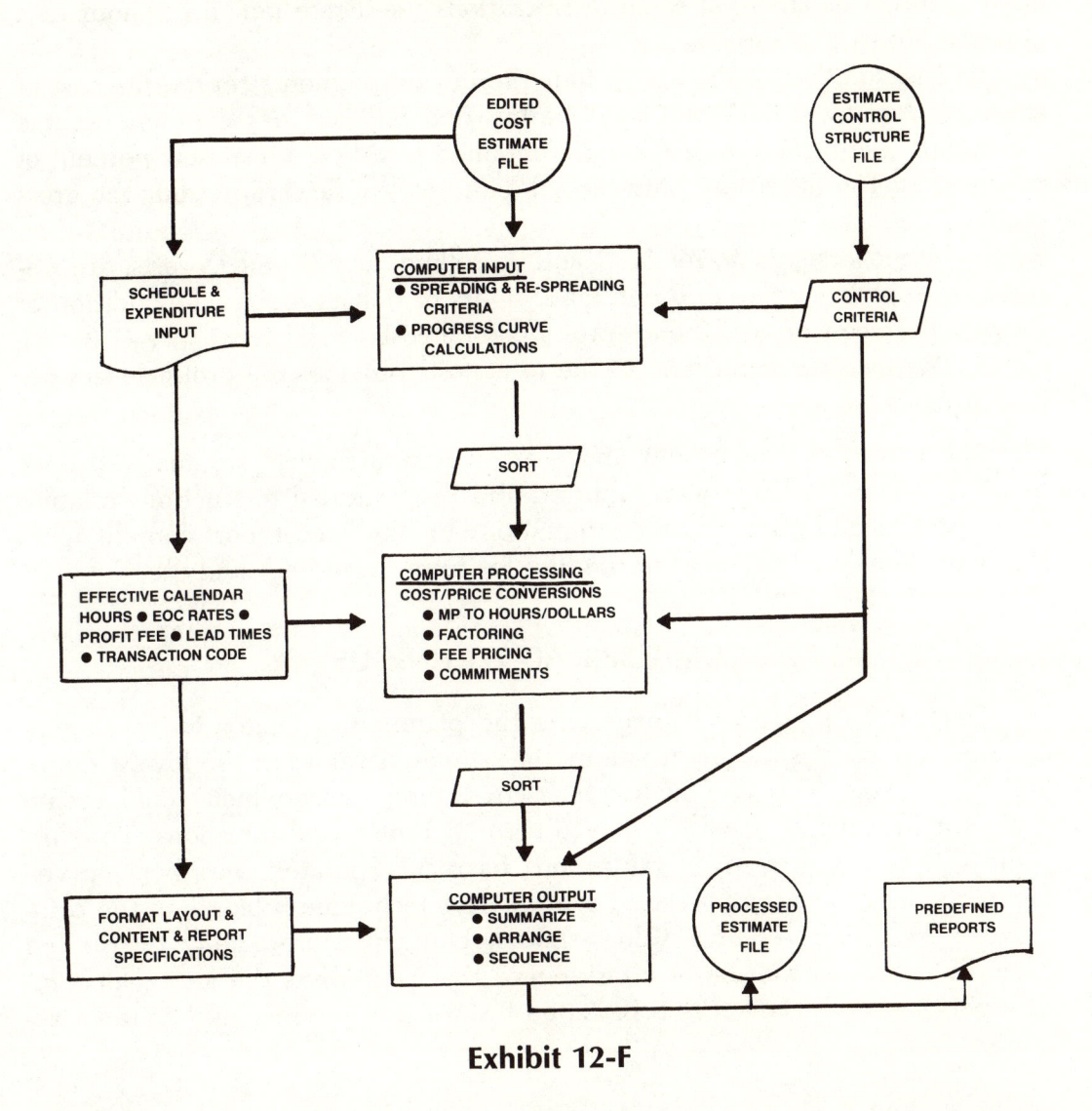

Exhibit 12-F

Progress or improvement curve factors are required to reflect the learning aspect of task performance.

Other basic input include effective hours, cost element rates or dollars, profit guidelines, and transaction codes.

Computer processing events include the following mechanical activities:

1. Conversion of manpower into hours (or vice versa) and application of applicable labor rates to obtain labor dollars.

2. Application of overhead rates to labor hours or dollars to derive overhead dollars by organizational unit, product, program, and (possibly) task.

3. Material dollars may be direct input values, an application rate to direct hours, or a percent of labor dollars and overhead.

4. Other direct costs (computer usage, direct travel, subcontract) are generally a direct dollar input some organizations use a rate per direct hour or a percent of direct material dollars.

5. The addition of the above four direct cost elements represents cost of sales. In the "overview" costing, wherein detailed cost development is at a minimum, cost of sales in total can be obtained based on a historical percent of sales values. The difference between sales and cost of sales represents the gross profit.

6. Period costs, in terms of G and A, selling, and R and D costs, are derived by applying a rate to direct labor hours or dollars input. The addition of these costs to cost of sales then represents total costs.

7. The fee rate application to the total costs provides the profit dollars before taxes.

The processed data results above are sorted, arranged, summarized, and sequenced in accordance with inputted and programmed instructions relative to preestablished layout formats, summation "breaks," and report content specifications. The data are stored in the files for future reference and use.

CURVE SPREAD TECHNIQUE

One of the major problems facing the planning estimator in developing detailed estimates is the input volume of estimated values at the lowest definable task levels. This is a highly time-consuming effort which could create problems in estimate accuracy due to error potential and omissions. To overcome this situation, many organizations have incorporated the "beta curve" technique into their computerized system. This technique is based on the principle of *bulk* task resource values (hours) being proportionately distributed over time through the use of a task curve that represents the anticipated future performance. The curve is based on historical experience and contract requirements.

Mathematical Table Factors

The curve spreads are usually represented by mathematical table factors for calculating labor values that are mechanically converted to manpower requirements for accomplishing the task or project. A graphic display of specific curves are displayed on Exhibit 12-G. It is noted that there are both unit or incremental and cumulative curves which can reflect effort versus approximate percentage of time (horizontal axis) and percentage of effort (vertical axis) versus percentage of time. Two examples (Table II, C and D) of the predetermined and inputted common curve factors to match the display on the exhibit are below.

The Computerized Estimating System in Action

CURVE SPREAD ALTERNATIVES

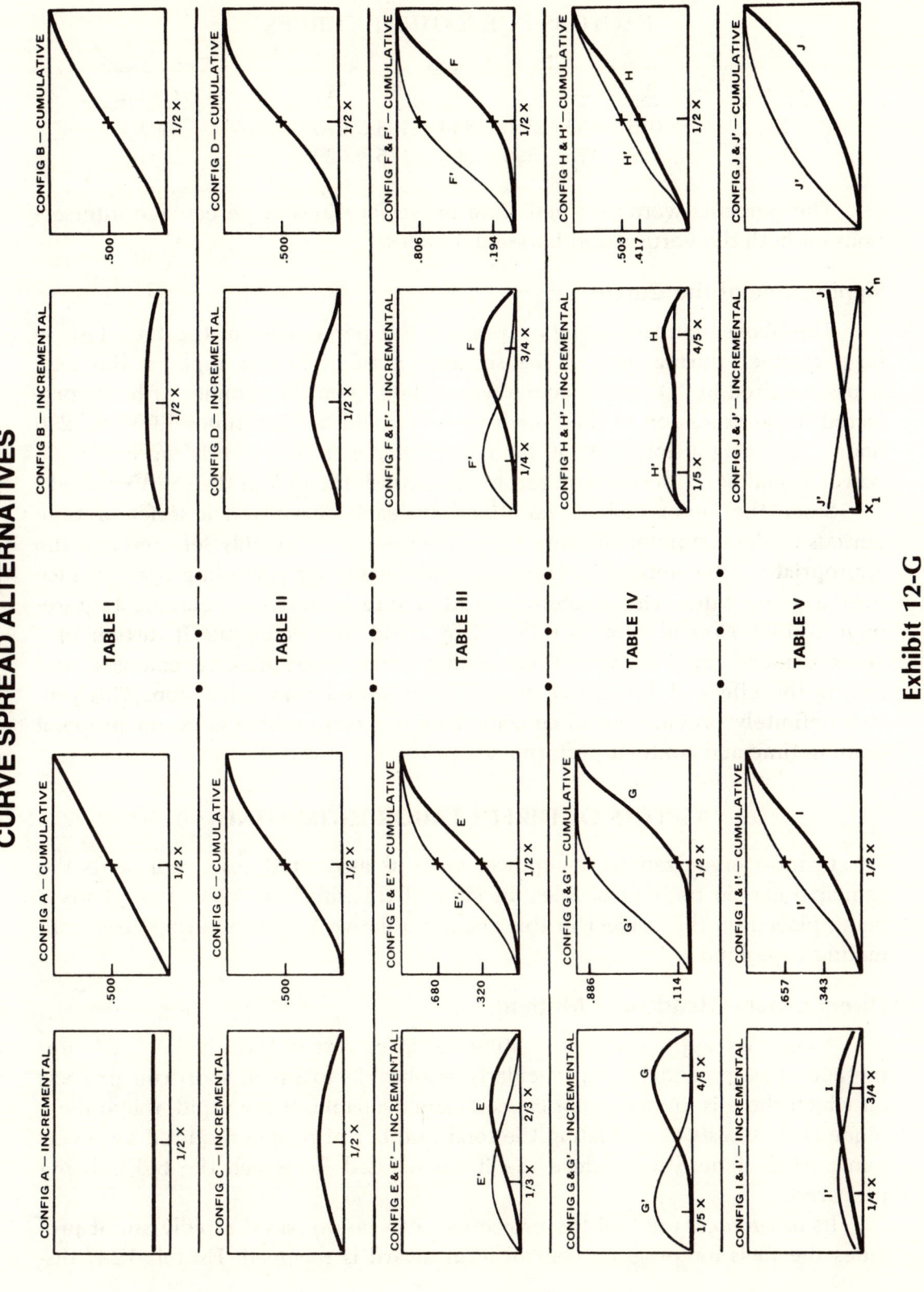

TABLE I

TABLE II

TABLE III

TABLE IV

TABLE V

Exhibit 12-G

FACTORS FOR EXHIBIT CURVES

Curve	_____ Time Periods _____						Total Task Percentage
	1	2	3	4	5	6	
C	.075	.185	.240	.240	.185	.075	100.0
D	.029	.175	.296	.296	.175	.029	100.0

The percents were obtained from curve locations at percentage intersections on both the vertical and horizontal scales.

Significance of the Curves

The above standard factors represent the percentage of the total task to be performed during each of the six time periods. For example, if the total hours required in "D" curve above were 1,000, then the number of hours projected to be expended in the fourth period would be .296 times 1,000, or 296 hours. Assuming a simplified 40 hour week per man, the translating into manpower would be 7.4 heads required to accomplish the task in the fourth period.

Since the factor table is identified by each curve and a series of time periods in the computer file, any type of curve can be readily selected and the appropriate factor applied to the total effort value for spreading performance over a given time. This is then translated into manpower resource requirements. Much clerical effort is reduced by using this technique. It further provides a more rapid means of visualizing projections, making changes, and testing the effect of alternative results from varied curve selection. This process definitely provides an organization with a competitive edge on proposal bidding time and contract performance price.

ASPECTS OF DIRECT LABOR ESTIMATING

In most organizations, manpower with its associated costs represents the principal cost in the cost of sales. In view of this situation, special emphasis is being placed on this subject in this chapter relative to computerized cost estimating technique.

Direct Labor—Headcount Method

A common approach to estimating the labor cost factor(s) is the *headcount* method. This procedure is particularly applicable to small, short-run projects on which there is limited historical cost data available. It is a rapid, rough technique that consists of estimating the total number of people required for a certain period of time to produce the items needed for which the bid is being prepared.

Its *advantages* are that the projections can be prepared rapidly and it provides the tools for program control if an award is received. Exhibit 12-H dis-

The Computerized Estimating System in Action 355

HEADCOUNT METHOD FOR ESTIMATING LABOR

PRODUCT _____ DESCRIPTION _____ QUANTITY _____					DATE _____ PREPARED BY _____ APPROVED BY _____		
	REQUIREMENTS BY MONTH						
	1		2		3		
	DIRECT		DIRECT		DIRECT		TOTAL
LABOR CLASSIFICATION	EMPLOYEES	*HOURS	EMPLOYEES	HOURS	EMPLOYEES	HOURS	DIRECT HOURS
ASSEMBLY							
ELECTRONIC	30	5,190	24	4,152	21	3,633	12,975
PRECISION	20	3,460	16	2,768	14	2,422	8,650
MECHANICAL	10	1,730	8	1,384	7	1,211	4,325
LINE INSPECTION	10	1,730	8	1,384	7	1,211	4,325
TEST	5	865	4	692	3	519	2,076
LINE SUPPLY	5	865	4	692	3	519	2,076
MACHINE SHOP	20	3,460	16	2,768	14	2,422	8,650
SUPERVISION	10	1,730	8	1,384	6	1,038	4,152
TOTAL	110	19,030	88	15,224	75	12,975	47,229
UNITS TO BE PRODUCED		100		100		100	300
AVERAGE HOURS PER UNIT		190.3		152.2		129.8	157.4

*TO DETERMINE HOURS—EMPLOYEES MULTIPLIED BY 173 HOURS/MONTH.

Exhibit 12-H

plays an estimate of manhours necessary to produce the units for a potential contract based on either estimated or standard production employee requirements by classification to perform the tasks involved. The number of employees for each labor classification determines the number of hours required.

The *disadvantages* of using the headcount method is that the organization's non-technical personnel would find it difficult to evaluate the number of employees projection at the time of an internal review of direct costs. Further, the estimate is difficult to support and substantiate in price negotiations with the customer, since many of the government's pricing people see non-technical information as the basis for negotiating prices.

The headcount method is used widely, however, in the development of cost estimates for engineering labor. In projects requiring the production of large quantities of a product that has been previously produced, engineering labor is relatively insignificant; however, with the advent of the aerospace age, the dollar volume of this type of project has declined in favor of those entailing considerable research and development effort that is followed by a short production run.

When using the headcount approach for estimating engineering hours, the estimator should subdivide the project into the tasks and sub-tasks that are to be performed and estimate the manhours required for each effort by labor classification. The tasks and subtasks include design, prototype, preparation of drawings, environmental test, design of production test equipment, reproduction, and preparation of handbooks. A detailed breakdown makes internal evaluation much more effective and provides a sound basis at the time of contract negotiation for supporting the cost estimate for engineering labor, since standards are unavailable. The detailed estimates thus prepared will also become the basis for establishing budgetary control over engineering labor when the project is awarded.

Direct Labor—Historical Cost Method

Another technique that is often used in estimating direct labor is the historical cost method. It is actually preferred by government negotiators and is more accurate for estimating production labor, providing historical cost data is available.

This method is most appropriate when the product being estimated has been produced under prior contracts; however the estimator must exercise caution in considering all factors that may tend to modify historical costs on future production runs. Included in this assessment are such factors as personnel turnover, wage rate increases, advanced equipment acquisition, and changes in processing technology.

The major advantage of this method is that it makes negotiations less difficult, since the customer's negotiator feels at ease and the arguments generally narrow down to a discussion of the anticipated factors that may influence historical cost data.

Direct Labor—Learning Curve

Another approach to labor estimating that has been employed extensively by aerospace vehicular production organizations, particularly, is the use of the learning curve. This procedure involves the use of historical or standard data that reflects costs for a given product quantity and plotting (log paper display) the changes in cost that will occur with quantity changes because of the learning that results from the performance of a repetitive task.

Learning curve applications are based on the premise that, as any repetitive job is performed, the efficiency and speed of the worker will increase. Generally, there is no limit to the improvement, although the rate of improvement constantly decreases after a point in time. A detailed discussion of this subject is presented in Chapter 10.

DIRECT MATERIAL COSTING

Many techniques have been used by defense contractors to estimate direct material costs. In the past, a number of aircraft organizations have used the dollar per pound approach. In the electronic industries, however, material estimates are determined by knowing the number of tubes in an electronic box and multiplying this number by a historical dollar factor. The advancement of the space age increasing competition have made these approaches no longer appropriate or acceptable.

It is the consensus of opinion and judgment that the only logical approach to material estimating is to actually price a bill of material or parts list. The bill of materials is generally developed from design drawings, an engineering specification parts list, or a model of the equipment. This list of material is then priced by obtaining firm quotes from vendors or by using historical costs or the procurement organization's best estimate. In many instances, a firm bill of material may be unavailable, particularly if the project entails design or development effort prior to fabrication. Under these circumstances, a gross material list may be developed by the technical specialists who outline the material items by major functions in the equipment to be used. Material costs may thus be estimated on the basis of historical costs for similar functions.

In either approach, sufficient data must be developed to allow management an opportunity to review the estimate and determine the extent of any possible variance in costs if the contract award is received. The adequacy of the data will generally influence the attitude of management in its final pricing action.

The above method should also provide data that can be used to support the organization's cost position at the time of negotiation. The state of final design will determine this requirement to a great extent. On completely designed products, the government negotiators will require more detailed data for material estimates, such as copies of vendors' invoices covering the cost estimate on individual parts. The same data used to support a negotiation will be used to provide budgets for internal control, during performance, to assure a reasonable profit.

MISCELLANEOUS DIRECT COSTS

Due to the peculiar nature of defense contracting particularly, several items of cost, which are normally charged on an indirect basis, are reflected as direct costs to projects. These costs include computer usage, direct travel, consulting services, special tools, test equipment, outside testing, subcontracting, and other items that can be identified with a special project. These elements of cost must be identified in as much detail as possible and supported in a manner that can be substantiated in negotiation.

INTERNAL EVALUATION OF DIRECT COSTS

After the direct cost estimates have been developed, they should be subjected to a thorough analysis and review by some designated authority outside of the operating departments where they originated. This review ensures that the cost estimating techniques used have resulted in estimates as accurate and realistic as is possible and that they are reasonable. This outside review should also verify that sufficient detailed data is available to support each estimate in negotiation and to provide a basis for budgeting if, and when, an award is made to the organization.

The extent of the review and the negotiating requirements will be determined by the type of contract to be awarded. For example, more latitude will be allowed the direct cost estimators in the preparation of a bid on a cost-type contract than on one that is being developed for a fixed price award. The use of well-defined techniques which result in detailed estimates that are adequately supported by some logical method will always benefit the contractor.

The reviewing authority is generally located organizationally in one of several departments, such as controller's office, operations planning, contract administration, or a specific staff group reporting directly to management. In any case, the review should always come under the scrutiny of the controller. His or her involvement in the pricing cycle solidifies the statistical data that will provide the basis for the organization's selling price, the ability to support that price in negotiation, and the development of realistic budgets for assuring a profit after the award.

The reviewing group should never be located within marketing or one of the operating departments. It is axiomatic that a salesman should never be permitted to set his own selling price and an operations individual should never establish, without review, his own standards for performance.

OVERHEAD APPLICATION

After the direct costs have been properly estimated and thoroughly reviewed, it is necessary to apply overhead costs in order to determine the total estimated cost. Some organizations use one overhead rate which is applied as a ratio to direct labor (hours or dollars) and others go to the extreme of using individual overhead rates for each cost center. For pricing control, any selected method of applying overhead may be adequate, providing it results in an equitable distribution of costs that can be consistently followed. Consistency of application in all pricing actions is a *must* if all overhead costs are to be recovered. This does not mean, however, that management may not take an alternative approach to establishing overhead in the final selling price.

There are several approaches that can be used in determining overhead rates for bidding purposes. Many small, uncomplicated organizations use historical rates based on the prior year's rates which are rounded off to an even percentage. An allied method is to use current actual rates which may be updated as often as every three months. The principal advantages of these two methods are that they are easy to compute and readily negotiated. Their primary weakness is that little, if any, consideration is accorded to changes in the economics of the organization from the current period to the performance period.

To overcome the above deficiency, many organizations use projected overhead rates for bidding purposes. These rates may be derived from historical rates modified to reflect changes in overhead costs, factory loading, and other economic conditions. They may be an "off-the-cuff" rate developed by forecasting the production load and overhead expenses for a given period or developed as a by-product of the organization's financial forecast. This latter method provides overhead rates that are an integral part of, and controlled by, the annual financial plan. This process should go a long way toward ensuring the adequacy of the rate for the complete recovery of all overhead costs.

PLANNED RESULTS FROM COMPUTERIZATION

Computerized estimating provides a number of advantages and capabilities that more than offset the costs of developing and implementing a reliable system to fulfill the estimating/pricing requirements of an organization. Some of the accomplishments to be achieved are delineated as follows:

- *Reduction in operating costs* through minimal manual effort for performing calculations, spreading and re-spreading values (curve techniques), factoring, and reporting.

- Increased *cost visibility* for analysis and decision-making policies by functional and executive management and the customer. The output is oriented to the needs of the project management.

- *Accelerated response* to "last minute" baseline revisions.

- *Computerized output* is tailored for immediate inclusion in the cost proposal with minimum effort.

- Improved and *more effective utilization* of assigned estimating personnel.

- *Curve charting* capability facilitates manpower loading and scheduling requirements.

- *Rapid* data processing *turnaround* permits more detailed study and response to program alternatives.

- *Online operations* permit selective data retrievals without requirements for hard-copy printouts.

- Estimating *results* are *significantly improved* through increased accuracy, reliability, change flexibility, and processing reaction time.

- Selective rate and factor applications as well as date time-phasing are readily made possible through input form requests.

MECHANICAL ESTIMATING HIGHLIGHTS

The estimating function involves the development of basic judgments and strategies that can be effectively utilized in the development of realistic cost/price proposals. In organizations in which considerable effort is directed toward this activity, computerization can be a very useful tool in the cost estimating.

This chapter provides the prerequisites involved in designing and implementing a computerized system. Consideration is given to the estimating fundamentals, various inputs required, and system processing and reporting.

Computerized estimating capabilities are discussed relative to the actual production of the estimate, mass changes, program control tables, data distribution curve, employee learning curves, and processing control. Interfaces are indicated between price proposals and cost collection needs and the estimating/budget development systems. Relevant discussions are concerned with approaches to specifically estimating direct labor, material, and miscellaneous direct costs. The internal evaluation of direct costs is described as well as the method of overhead application.

The planned results from computerized estimating are highlighted. Various exhibits are provided to supplement the written discussions. Computerization seems to be the only logical approach to enhancing the estimating process and producing significant cost savings.

Index

A

Absorption costing in pricing, 179
Accounting, cost:
   alternate methods, 120
   continuous process, 112–115
   job order, 115
   material costs, direct, 231
   production department, 117
Accounting, cost, procedural steps, 108–136
   accumulation system, 125–128
   collection reporting, 129–131
   control requirements, 133, 135
   determination criteria, 110
   direct product costing, 121–125
   direct versus indirect costs, 131
   estimate accounting process, 110–111
   estimate system, cost:
      overview, 108
      versus standard cost, 110
   job order versus process costs, 117, 119
   master audit file, 132
   systems, procedural accounting, 112–117
Accumulation, manufacturing expense, 252
Actual cost systems, problems with, 92
Adjustments, cost estimate, 29
Advantages, estimating system, 42
Allocation and proration expenses, 261
Alternatives, curve spread, 353
Analysis, breakeven point, 58–59
Applications:
   overhead methods, 266–268
   progress curve, 290
Arithmetic curve, shape of, 283
Art or science—pricing, 170–171
Attainable standards, engineered, 89
Average standard hours, 152
Award rationale, contract, 155

B

Background, estimator, 36–37
Baseline, work package, 315
   standards, 79
Basis for contract awards, 146
Benefits, formula computerization, 54
Bid proposal:
   computerized development, 153
   overview, 146–147
   presentation expense, 154
Bill of material projection, 237
Breakeven point analysis, 58–59

Budget:
   flexible, 276
   interface with estimating, 339
   manufacturing expense, 275
   notice, contract, 315
Budgeted costs versus standard, 93
Burden rates, department, 175, 273

C

Capital, return on, 172
Centralization versus decentralization, 32–35
Change orders, contract:
   constructive, 191
   formal, 191
   pricing, 192
Checklist, procedural, estimating, 19–21
Commercial products, flexible pricing, 193
Competitive pricing, cost aspects, 180–181
Computerization:
   bid development, 153
   cost accumulation, 128
   cost tracking and performance, 319
   estimating system, 336–360
   labor hour/manpower model, 206
   operating system, 318–319
   product pricing process, 185–188
   progress curve, 308
   records, cost estimate, 28
   standard costing, 104
   statistical formula estimating, 52–54
   system in action, 336–360
Continuous process accounting, 112
Contracts, Government (*see* Government contracts)
Control:
   cost, internal, 332
   cost, requirements, 133–135
   estimating function, 35
   program, 349
Correlations:
   expense allowances, 277
   gross income, 57–58
   linear, 55–56
   supervision versus direct hours, 26
Cost:
   accounting procedural steps, 108–136 (*see also*
      Accounting, cost, procedural steps)
   accumulation system, 125–128
   analysis, material, 234
   behavior, 47
   classifications, 25
   collection reporting, 129–131

361

Cost: (*cont.*)
   control requirements, 133–135
   data ledger, 129
   determination considerations, 24–25
   estimate system overview, 108–109
   estimating process, 342
   fundamentals for pricing, 174–176
   impact on pricing, 176
   internal controls, 332
   proposal development, 148
   records:
      historical, 23
      standard, 90–91
   reduction, aspect of, 93–94
   system problems, actual, 92
Cost absorption, 179–180
Cost and schedule surveillance, 310–334
   collection system, 311
   computerized:
      operating system considerations, 318
      system capabilities, 333
   incentive profit, 333
   internal cost controls, 332
   past and prevailing deficiencies, 310
   process data overview, 316
   program evaluation and review, 329–331
   schedule tracking and performance, 319–323
   system development objectives, 310
   variance analysis and reporting, 331
   work authorization and budget control, 315
   work breakdown structure, 327–328
   work package system, 314
Cost collection, 311–315
   expense records, 255
Cost estimate (*see* Estimating process)
Costing, standard (*see* Standard costing)
Cost proposal, manufacturing, 138–168
   basis for contract awards, 154–155
   bid:
      computerized development, 153
      presentation expense, 154
   decision criteria, 138, 140
   development, 148–154
   make or buy considerations, 157–164 (*see also* Make or buy)
   new proposal requirements, 144–146
   organization, 142
   overview, bid proposal, 146–147
   proposal status reporting, 164–167
   request for quotation, 138
   responsibility, estimating group, 141
   types:
      government contracts, 155–156
      RFQs, 140–141
   work scheduling, 157
Current versus measurement standards, 79–80
Curve, progress (*see also* Progress curve utilization)
   basic, 299

Curve, progress (*cont.*)
   computerization, 308
   cost applications, 298
   factors, mathematical, 352
   fundamentals, 282
   sales price and production, 295
   significance, 354
   spread technique, 352–355
   use in manpower requirements, 290

D

Day-to-day pricing, 178
Decentralized environment, 34–35
Defense contracts (*see* Government contracts)
Demand elasticity, 173
Department, production, 117–118
Design drawings/specifications, 238
Determinant factors, 23
Development, cost proposal, 148–152
Direct costing (*see also* Material and other direct costs)
   defense of, 177
   evaluation, 357
   pricing decisions, 177
   product:
      labor, 121
      manufacturing expense, 123
      material, 122
Direct labor (*see* Manpower and labor cost planning):
Disadvantages, estimating cost system, 42
Dividends, 183
Division manpower plan, 205

E

Effort (*see also* Progress curve utilization):
   added, 304
   changed, 306
   deleted, 303
   expended versus program completion, 73
Engineering standards, 281
Equipment, test, estimating, 69
Errors in estimating:
   controllable, 40
   uncontrollable, 39
   use of index numbers, 62
Estimating cost system:
   accounting process, 110
   cost determination, 110
   overview, 108–109
   versus standard costs, 110
Estimating process, 18–43
   adjustment to estimates, 29
   advantages/disadvantages, 42–43
   centralization versus decentralization, 32–35
   characteristics, general, 19
   computerized records, 27–28

Estimating process, (cont.)
   cost:
      classifications, 25
      correlation to direct labor hours, 26
      determination considerations, 24–25
      records, historical, 23
   determinants, product evaluation, 27
   disposition of variances, 29
   errors, avoidance of, 39–41
   establishing standards, 23
   estimating pointers, 43
   estimating versus standard costs, 38
   functional control, 35
   management decisions, 37–38
   new product estimate, 29–31
   objectives, 18
   organizational role, 32
   preparation factors, 21
   previous estimates, use of, 22
   procedural checklist, 19–21
   processing events, 350–352
   scope of estimate, 24
   shortcuts in development, 41–42
   standards, estimating, 23
Estimating system, computerized, 28, 336–360
   approach to prevailing problem, 336
   curve spread techniques, 352–354
   estimating process, 342
   fundamentals, 344–349
   interface with budget, 339–342
   labor, direct, estimating, 354–357
   material costing, 356
   miscellaneous direct costs, 357
   overhead application, 358
   price proposal interface, 337
   processing events, cost, 350
   program control requirements, 349
   results from computerization, 359
   significance of curves, 354
   system objectives, 336
Estimator, background of, 36–37
Event numbering, PERT, 331
Expense, overhead (*see also* Overhead accumulation, distribution and application)
   bid and proposal, 270
   bid presentation, 154
   classifications, 252–254
   engineering, 270
   general and administrative, 175
   material and supplies, 269
   miscellaneous factory, 270
   predetermination, 258–259

F

Factors, sales price, 181–184
FIFO pricing, 233
Financial variance assessment, 325

Fixed and variable costs, 194
Fixed charges, expense, 253
Fixed price contracts, 156
Flexible:
   budget, overhead, 276
   pricing, commercial products, 193
Formulas:
   multiple cost, 195
   overhead applications, 267
   overhead variances, 125
   pricing development, 193
   progress curve, 285
   statistical estimating, 50–54
   weight ratio theorem, 62–64
Fundamentals, computerized estimating, 344–349

G

General and administrative expense, 175
Government contracts:
   basis for awards 154–155
   cost considerations, 271, 273
   distribution costs, 270
   factory overhead, 269
   price considerations, 197
   types of:
      cost plus incentive fee, 156
      cost reimbursement without fee, 156
      cost sharing, 156
      definite delivery, 157
      fixed price incentive, 156
      fixed price escalation clause, 156
      time and material, 156
   unallowable costs, 271–272
Graph plotting:
   arithmetic curve, 283
   logarithm curve, 284–285

H

Headcount method, direct labor, 354–355
Historical costs:
   direct labor, 356
   records, 23
Hour rate, machine, 65–67

I

Ideal price standards, 243
Ideal work standards, 88–89
Incentive profit, 333
Index numbers for price correction, 61–62
Input, cost tracking system:
   cost ledger, 322
   material support, 322
   user, 319
Input, estimating:
   basic, 344
   processing control, 347

Input, estimating: (cont.)
   supplementary, 347
   supportive, 348
Interdivisional transfers, pricing, 192
Interfaces:
   estimating versus budget, 339
   estimating versus standards, 93
   price proposals and collections, 337
   standards versus budget, 93
Internal cost controls, 332
Inventory:
   expense accounts, 257
   evaluation:
      advantages, 295
      curve use, 293
   in process calculations, 294
   maximum/minimum limits, 249
Inverse proportion, 60–61

J

Job order:
   cost accounting, 115–116
   versus process cost, 117, 119–120

L

Labor cost segregation problems, 132
Labor, direct (*see also* Manpower and labor cost planning)
   cost development, 226
   cost estimates, 215
   estimating, 354–356
   hour estimates, 150
   quality standards, 214
   rate standards, 214
Labor, indirect, 211
Learning curve:
   concept, 281
   direct labor, 354–356
   significance, 94
   time allowance, 283
Letter of intent, 140
LIFO pricing, 233
Linear correlation, 55–56
Line of regression, 56
Logarithm:
   curve, 284
   graph plotting, 285

M

Machine hour rate, 64–68
Magnitude, rough order of, 141
Maintenance and repair orders, 257
Margin contribution in pricing, 176
Make or buy (MOB):
   assessment, 244
   basis for RFQs, 161–162
   considerations, 157–158
   data flow, 158–159
   evaluation worksheet, 163
   factors other than costs, 162
   plan, 158
   responsibility, 160
   source of data, 162
Management decisions, cost estimate, 37–38
Manning tables development, 216–217
Manpower and labor cost planning, 202–227
   approach to planning, 202
   computerized labor hour model, 206–207
   cost estimate, 215
   development, 226
   direct labor:
      dollar projections, 208
      time standards, 212–214
   indirect labor manning, 211
   manpower:
      and labor cost, 226
      forecast based on hours, 208–210
      loading for RFQs, 215
      operating department, 217–219
      planning procedure, 203–205
      project forecast, 219–221
      special tooling, 221
   production planning process, 224–226
Manufacturing cost proposal (*see* Cost proposal, manufacturing)
Margin contributions, product, 176
Mass change capability, 343
Master audit file, 132–133
Material and other direct costs, 230–250 (*See also* Direct costing)
   accounting for costs, 231–232
   bill of material projections, 237
   budget, 248–249
   cost analysis, 234
   estimating costs, 239
   make or buy assessment, 244
   other direct costs, 230
   price:
      selection method, 234
      standards, 242–243
      trends, 48, 240
      variances, 236
   projection problems, 244
   purchases, 231
   R and D material forecast, 238
   requisition pricing, 232–234
   shrinkage, scrap, and waste, 241
   usage ratio, 240
Material standards, direct, 85–87
Material variance, direct 101–102

Index

Mechanical cost estimating, 46–75, 336–360 (*see also* Computerization)
Misconceptions relative to standards, 80–81
Modules, PERT, 329

N

Network characteristics (PERT), 330
New added effort, curve effect, 304
New product estimate, 29–32
New proposal requirements, 144

O

Operating department manpower, 217–219
Operating labor time, estimating, 212
Operator:
    incentives, 289
    performance reality, 288
Organization:
    manufacturing cost proposal, 138–168
    role of estimating, 32
    small, standard costs, 95–99
Other direct costs:
    defined, 230
    projections, 238
Over- and under-absorbed overhead, 268
Overhead accumulation, distribution and application, 252–281 (*see also* Expense overhead)
    accumulation 252
    actual versus predetermined rates, 257
    allocation and proration, 261
    application methods, 266–267
    correlations, use of, 277
    distribution philosophies, 259
    expense:
        budgets, 275
        characteristics, 253
    formulas, 267
    government contracts, 269–271
    machine hour rate, 274
    primary distribution, 260
    purchase orders, 256
    reciprocal dilemma, 265
    secondary distribution, 262
    service expense, 263
    selling and administrative rates, 269
    setup and operating rates, 269
    standard overhead estimates, 273
    transaction records, 255
    unallowable costs, 272
    variances, 124–125

P

Payroll expense budget, 204
Performance evaluation and control technique, (*see* Cost and schedule surveillance)
Petty cash vouchers, 257
Planning:
    estimator background, 36–37
    manpower and labor costs, 202–227
    material projections, 230–250
    production, 224
Previous estimates, use of, 22–23
Price:
    estimating trends, 47–49
    lists, customer, 185
    standards, 243
    trends, material, 240
    variance, material price, 236–237
Pricing, periodic cost average, 232
Pricing team, involvement of, 170–171
Pricing techniques, product, 170–200
    computerized process, 185–188
    contract change orders, 190–192
    cost absorption approach, 179–180
    cost aspects, competitive pricing, 181
    cost fundamentals, pricing basis, 174–176
    defense contracts, 198–199
    direct costing in pricing decisions, 177
    economics for achieving profitability, 173
    effect of competition, 174
    flexible pricing, 193
    impact of costs, 176
    interdivisional transfers, 192
    pricing approach, 172
    pricing, art or science, 170
    profit criteria, selling price, 188–190
    sales price determination factors, 181–184
Product:
    estimate, new, 29–31
    evaluation determinants, 27
    pricing techniques, 170–200
Production:
    cost problems, 290
    department accounting, 117–118
    department forecast, 204
    material requirements, 238
    planning process, 224
Profitability, economics for achieving, 173
Profitgraph, 58–59
Profit incentive, 333
Program:
    control requirements, 349
    definition, 312
    evaluation and review technique, 329–331
Progress curve utilization, 280–308
    application:
        costs, relative to, 298
        practical, 290
        standard hours, 307
    basic curve, 299
    computerization, 308
    cost projection techniques, 280

Progress curve utilization, (cont.)
  formula, curve, 285-286
  fundamentals, 282-284
  effects from changing work effort, 303-306
  first unit estimate, 301
  inventory evaluation, 293
  learning concept, 281
  logarithm graph plotting, 285
  manpower requirements, 290-292
  sales price/production costs, 295-297
  table, 80% curve, 300
  time allowances, 288
Project:
  budget center (PBC), 314
  evaluation, 46-47
  manpower forecast, 219-220
  support equipment, 69-71
  tools, estimating, 69
Projections:
  bill of materials, 237
  manpower and labor costs, 202-227
  material, problems with, 244
  operating manpower, 217-219
  production, 224
  R & D material, 238
  techniques in estimating, 46-75
Proportions, use in estimating, 59-61
Proposal, cost (see Cost proposal, manufacturing)
Proration, joint manufacturing expense, 262
Purchase:
  dollar estimate, 248
  material, 231
  orders, 256

Q

Quality, material, 246
Quantities, material, abnormal, 246
Quotation, request for:
  make or buy as basis, 167
  manpower loading, 215-217
  types, 140

R

R & D material forecast, 238
Rate capability, special tooling, 71-72
Rate, machine hour, 274
Rate standards, direct labor, 214
Ratio, material usage, 240
Ratios and proportions, 59-61
Ratio theorem, weight, 62-64
Realistic price standards, 243
Realization factor, 296
Regression, line of, 56
Replacement costs, tooling, 182

Reporting:
  cost collection, 129-131
  cost/schedule status, 323-325
  estimating system output, 348
  proposal status, 164-167
  standard cost, 88
  variances, 331
Request for quotation (RFQ), 138-140
Requisitions, pricing material, 232-233
Responsibilities, estimating group, 141
Rough order of magnitude, 141

S

Sales price, determination factors, 181-183
Scattergraph concept, 55-56
Schedule and cost surveillance (see Cost and schedule surveillance)
Scrap costing guidelines, 247
Seasonal costs, 47
Selling price, profit criteria in, 188-190
Service expense distribution, 263
Setup and operating rates, 49, 269
Shortcuts in cost estimate development, 41-42
Shrinkage, scrap and waste, 241
Small business, 95-99
Special tooling:
  and services, 68
  manpower, 221
  rate capability, 71-72
Standard costing, 78-105
  adoption for small organizations, 95-99
  advanced concepts, 103
  basic, 79
  characteristics, 81-82
  computerization, 104-105
  considerations in setting standards, 82-87
  definition, 78
  effectiveness in setting standards, 88-89
  estimating versus standards, 93
  future outlook, 104
  highlights, 105
  labor variance development, 99-101
  material variances, 101-102
  misconceptions, 80
  problems with actual cost systems, 92
  records, 90-91
  responsibility for setting standards, 87-88
  revision of standards, 89-90
  standard versus budget costs, 93
  types, 78-79
  use in accounting, 90
  utilization advantages, 91-92
Standard error of estimate, 56
Standards:
  engineering, 281
  estimating, 23

Standards: (cont.)
   labor, 212–214
   procedure for changing, 90
   responsibility for setting, 87–88
Statistical formula estimating, 50–55
   computer:
      benefits, 54–55
      input, 52
      output, 54
      overview, 52–54
   development, 50–52
   formula definition, 50
Statistical techniques (see, Techniques, statistical estimating)
Structure, cost collection, 313
Supervision costs versus direct hours, 26

T

Table factors, progress curve, 300
Techniques, statistical estimating, 46–75
   breakeven point analysis, 58
   computerization benefits, 54–55
   cost behavior, 47
   cost estimating summary, 49–50
   effort expended versus program completion, 73–74
   formulas, statistical, 50–55
   index numbers, 61–62
   linear correlation, 55–56
   machine hour rate, 64–68
   profitgraph, use of, 58–59
   project evaluation, 46–47
   project tool calculations, 71–72
   price estimating trends, 47–49
   ratios and proportions, 59–61
   scattergraph concept, 55–56
   setup and operating rates, 49
   special tooling and services, 68
   special tooling rate capability, 71–73
   test equipment, 69–71
Time allowances, progress curve, 288
Time and motion analysis, 213
Time standards, 151
Tooling:
   replacement costs, 182
   special, 68–69

Trends, price estimating, 47–49
Trial balance, WIP, 129–131

U

Unallowable costs, 271
Unavoidable material loss, 242
Uncontrollable errors in estimating, 39
Unit of measure in production, 276
Usage, material:
   ratio, 240
   variance, 235
Utilizing standard costs, advantages of, 91–92

V

Variable:
   costs, 47
   expenses, 255
   time allowance, 287
Variances:
   analysis and reporting, 331
   computing material price, 236
   direct labor, 96, 99–101
   direct material, 101–103
   financial, assessment, 325
   material usage, 235
   overhead, 125
   reporting, standard cost, 88
Vouchers, petty cash, 257

W

Wage payment plan, 84
Waste and scrap usage, 242
Weighted average pricing, 232
Weight ratio theorem, 62–64
Work:
   authorization and budget control, 315
   breakdown structure, 327
   cost collection structure, 313
   ideal standards, 88–89
   package system, 314
Work in process:
   breakdown, 127
   computerized process, 127–129
   trial balance, 129, 131
Worksheet, make or buy evaluation, 163